A Glimpse of Olympus

A GLIMPSE
OF OLYMPUS

Diana Menuhin

Methuen

The author expresses her thanks to Curtis Brown on behalf of the Estate of Lawrence Durrell for permission to reproduced the letter on page 375. Copyright © Lawrence Durrell, 1962. She also wishes to thank Faber and Faber Ltd for their kind permission to reproduce 'Delos' and 'Marcotis' from *Collected Poems* by Lawrence Durrell.

First published in Great Britain 1996
by Methuen
an imprint of Reed International Books Ltd
Michelin House, 81 Fulham Road, London SW3 6RB
and Auckland, Melbourne, Singapore and Toronto

Reprinted 1996

A CIP catalogue record for this book
is available from the British Library

ISBN 0 413 69820 3

Typeset by Deltatype Ltd, Ellesmere Port, Cheshire

Printed and bound in Great Britain
by Clays Ltd, St Ives plc

To all my younger colleagues of the stage, actors and dancers alike, who incorporate the ephemeral and upon whom reality so often wreaks its revenge

Diana Menuhin

Contents

A Note from Lord Menuhin   ix

Prologue   1
1 Stock and Substance   3
2 *Per Ardua ad Astra*   18
3 Enter the Black Fairy   37
4 *Changez à Miromesnil, descendez Liège*   57
5 Les Ballets 1933   69
6 Redeemed from Bondage   88
7 A Plunge In and Out of the Jungle   105
8 Nijinska   125
9 Fluctuations and Follies   137
10 Finally Facing the Truth   164
11 Struggling Against Odds and Other Oddments   188
12 Consoling Work Amid Continuous War   207
13 Uneasy Paradise   220
14 War *à l'Italienne*   234
15 Back at Last in Paris   257
16 The Magic Mountain   268
17 Reluctant Reckoning   286
18 The Core Had Remained Constant   307
Epilogue   332

Letter from Lawrence Durrell dated 24
    September, 1962   375
Poems: 'Delos' by Lawrence Durrell   376
       'Mareotis' by Lawrence Durrell   378
       'The white country' by Robin Fedden   379
Index   381

A Note from Lord Menuhin

Diana's early glimpses of Olympus, vouchsafed by a fate which had accurately assessed her ardent, richly gifted nature, her eager mind and body, kindled a dream, the compelling vision of a promised land.

She has always had dedication to beauty and perfection, an iron sense of duty and purpose and a nature too self-abnegating to pursue triumph at the expense of broader, more generous commitments to human beings.

From unhelpful family, bereft of father, to a cruel and brutal teacher, even to rewarding companionship of colleagues and friends of her stature, and finally to the fulfilment and the demands of husband and children, she turned all her great talents to serving and giving rather than to her own direct expression, independent of extraneous means – her dancing, acting, mime, her writing, and exquisite literary gifts, her own body and mind, always fashioning beauty, enlightenment and communication directly from within to without – *sans intermédiaire, sans instruments*. Nor can I ever forget her play of fantasy as she would spin and weave an endless tale to the wide-eyed listening of the children before their goodnight kiss, already dreaming of the sequel.

I have been the chief beneficiary, although she has never spared herself with regard to four children (my previous two plus our own two), nor with regard to all those who cross her path, those who work for and with her, her friends, in terms of her sacred obligations in letters and deeds. But despite the fact that I am at the very centre of her universe – for she gave and gives her every thought, counsel, courageous moral and physical support, indeed her unreserved love to my life – I feel that in relation to *her* innermost personal life, I am a trifle off-centre. With much persuasion and encouragement she has written two beautiful books, she has composed her own poems for the Carnival of the Animals, acted and recited them on the BBC and on tour, and she has given a number of successful television appearances and poetry readings. It is true that we have shared so much.

Yet I always have the feeling that surrounding me with her love and beauty, creating most liveable and wonderous homes for us and for our children – from California to Greece via London and Gstaad – she has still denied herself and cheated the world at large of those radiant and in their turn creative fruits which were meant for a far larger stage and a wider public.

It would be preposterous for me to pretend that I could be to her that early Promised Land, for that was a land of her own exclusive creation, a Garden of Eden, somewhere between Heaven and Earth, full of her own lovely fashionings. She had to come down to Earth to suffer an often cruel mortality. If I have had 'Glimpses of Olympus' it is that she has drawn me up from Earth to Heaven.

In daily life she remains unfailingly betwitching to all, her brilliant conversation, her regal presence, her wonderfully expressive face; she is always for me the beloved life-companion for all seasons.

Yehudi Menuhin

Prologue

We have moved from the golden cage which was the Highgate house down into central London, to Belgravia where I was born. Standing on the balcony of this tall mid-nineteenth-century house overlooking the tree-filled square with its frame of white stucco houses, I watch fearfully as my mother's Bechstein piano, dangling perilously on its ropes, is being slowly hoisted up the four storeys to Yehudi's studio beneath the roof.

'Welcome home,' I say, unhooking my thoughts from the present and letting them roll back like a hall carpet to the far-off day when the piano, accompanied by two others, was squeezed into my parents' first house, No. 37 Lowndes Street, a few roads away.

By the time my parents had three children, the pianos proved too much for the comparatively small house and for the father I was never to know – or so I am told. Fastidious and stylish, he must have found the cacophony of three tiny children and three pianos less than harmonious. It was then that, searching, he came upon Mulberry House in Chelsea, and there that we were all moved. The pianos lived there, to be much played upon, for nearly a quarter century.

I think about the ghosts of pianists, great and gone, young and promising, who had enjoyed them; of their various journeys following my mother during the war and finally of this one, settling down in

Yehudi's and my first London home as it must have done in Daddy and Mummy's first home.

I

Stock and Substance

How much closer to truth is autobiography than biography? Can one really tell the whole truth about oneself, or is one so inextricably bound within unconscious motives that the breach between thought and action is somehow distorted? Can one really know oneself or can one be better known by another? What is truth? It is more than accuracy, but ever at the mercy of those who construe it. It can be as many-faceted as a prism and yet be manifest. Looking back upon the landscape of a fairly long life, at the contours, the hills and valleys, the exaltations and depressions, one realises that what once appeared as huge mountains are by now but tiny hillocks in the larger perspective of the added years – a modification engendered by forces beyond one's control and consequently beyond one's choice. Memory must have to reckon with the weather of the emotions, which as surely alters the mood of past experience as do the storms, the rain, ice, snow and sun shape the geographical landscape. How often have I stubbed my toes on the crazy paving stones we have been warned are on the way to hell? How bitter to discover that my well-meant concern can be, to the recipient, mere interference.

So, to return to the argument, am I, born Diana Rosamond Constance Grace Irene Gould, on 12 November 1912 in 37 Lowndes Street, Belgravia SW1, equipped to tell the truth, the whole truth and nothing but the truth about myself, or will it be grossly distorted

3

through my mind's unreliable eye – the 'I' through the eye, as it were? Are my reminiscences immutably tainted with the colours of my own emotions, not necessarily recollected in tranquillity? Or are they more than justified by the very fact that I am me, ineradicably intertwined with my own emotions and thereby more genuinely true to myself than could be any outsider, who has the material without either the light or the heat – neither the illumination of my nature nor the temperament of my own heart?

For what it is worth, then, here is a totally subjective tale. I have come to the conclusion that the subject – me – must ultimately be sovereign.

My mother was born in India, where her father, William Henry Hodson Suart, was a young subaltern in the Horse Artillery. Archetypically handsome, he had a passion for polo. She was brought back to Europe by her ailing young mother, Katherine, highly intelligent and devoted to her one child. This child, christened Daisy Evelyn (only cows are called Daisy, she remonstrated not much later), was five years old when she and her mother left the subcontinent. My maternal grandmother, abandoning her handsome young husband to the company of his polo ponies, settled in Brussels, quite alone except for this child. She duly put her in a school run by a Mademoiselle Rossignon – a divine school I imagine, for when the otherwise bright little girl proved ungifted at maths, they decided she could drop it as a subject, with the result that to the day of her death my mother could add and subtract but neither multiply nor divide. How I would envy her when I, equally inadequate, struggled to make sense of the abstractions of algebra and trigonometry.

So she was allowed to save her intelligence and energy for her music, in which she early showed real promise. My grandmother took her to the great violinist Eugène Ysaÿe for advice. He suggested she should study both the violin and the piano with one of his accompanists (Monsieur Storck or Monsieur Pugno), and after a year return to show him her progress. I asked Mama, when I was about ten, what happened

4

at that audition. It appeared that she and Irene Wieniawska (daughter of the famous Polish violinist and composer) had offered a rendering of the first movement of the Bach Double Violin Concerto. 'What was it like?' I asked eagerly. 'Cats on the roof,' answered Mama drily. After which it seems she played the piano, whereupon Ysaÿe announced '*Mon enfant, fais une omelette de ton violon, tu seras pianiste!*' Succinct, if nothing else. And so she did, with such results that her mother took her to the most renowned teacher of the day: the great Theodor Leschetizky in Vienna who, while deploring the French manner of holding her hands, none the less immediately accepted her as a pupil to join his current students Artur Schnabel and Mark Hambourg, the great Ignacy Paderewski having left him to start his legendary career.

Katherine Suart, herself a daughter of the Army, proved a wonderful mother. Holed up with practically no money in a couple of rooms through the wall-paper of which the lice would spring like pop-corn ('Nothing to be done,' said the landlady. 'The house was built on an ancient site and the bugs are in the foundations. I must send for the *Wanzenjäger* – bug-hunter – again'), she supervised poor young Evelyn's eight hours of daily practice as she painstakingly changed her whole technique. It must have been a marvellous epoch in that pre-First World War Vienna, the undisputed music capital of Europe and the mecca of all musicians, aspiring as well as established. Mama, ploughing away through the heat of the summer, all windows tightly closed by municipal edict (understandably when one realises that every apartment had at least its cottage upright if not its grand piano), soon reached the dreaded position where she had to perform at the weekly sessions before an invited audience of *cognoscenti*. My childhood was filled with colourful anecdotes of these evenings. Finally her studies came to an end and she was launched on a career as successful as it was short, including her early débuts with the two leading conductors, Artur Nikisch and Hans Richter in Vienna and Berlin, and continuing as the young pioneer of Debussy's piano works.

In mid-career and by now settled in London, she met my father, Gerard Gould, of an Irish family who had fled from Cork to Paris, via

Oporto where they had restored the family fortunes when their house had been destroyed during the endemic 'Troubles' of the late eighteenth century. It would seem that he loved music and even, though amateurishly, played the violin. He enquired of some mutual friends if they knew of a young lady suitable to accompany him. Thus Evelyn Suart, the brilliant pianist, was suggested. (One imagines in those socially rigid days she fitted the bill not so much for her success as for being the daughter of a cavalry officer . . .) He fell in love with this charming, witty young woman and she with the handsome, blond, cosmopolitan young man. I once asked Mama how he played: 'Oh *not* very good, darling,' was all she said. My father had had to learn English to enable him to go to school in England and that selfsame governess taught us small children French. Dear Miss Allsop, one of the few sources of warmth and affection I knew in my childhood.

Daddy died of typhoid fever carrying dispatches between England and France for the Foreign Office. Mama was left with three children under five (Gerard my elder brother and Griselda my younger sister), a big house, eight servants and £800 per annum after death duties. Barely three years old, I can remember a vague blond shadow that must have been Daddy. Mother, in the shock of her bereavement, rarely referred to him.

Eventually Anna, the wonderful Strasbourgeoise cook and her kitchen-maid Fernande had to be sent back to France, possibly to the relief of Webb the butler ('Aow! How I long for a pline, biled pertater'). Anna had been caught one day when my mother came into the third-floor nursery, her upper half invisible outside the window, her stout black-and-white striped cotton legs held by Fernande while she attempted to catch one of the pigeons squatting in the gutter below the roof. 'Anna!' shrieked Mama in horror and dismay, ordering her to be hauled in like so much wet sail. It appears that Anna, flushed and dirty, deprived of her prey, rebuked her in her Alsatian French: '*Mais Madom – zhe foudrais fous faire un pon coq-au-fin.*' One sad day, when my mother could no longer afford them, she and Fernande left in floods of tears, in which even 'Monsieur Vebb' joined.

Dear Webb stayed on for a bit to 'see Mama through' but the footman went, and somehow in the manner of those times she was able to keep a diminished but devoted staff and her lovely Mulberry House, with all its elegant furniture (mostly found by Daddy and Webb, dressed in old mackintoshes, in the Caledonian Road Market). During these sorties Webb learnt so much that when he left us he set himself up in his own antique shop just over Battersea Bridge. About thirty years later, Yehudi and I were staying with friends on the Chelsea Embankment. On an impulse I took him over the bridge, on the off-chance, looking for an antique shop. To my surprise I found one – to mounting excitement it bore the name 'Henry Webb' and to enormous joy there emerged a bald old man who immediately cried out: 'Miss Diana, well I never!'

Webb as a catalyst flicks my mind back to the misty image of Mulberry House. He cleaned huge quantities of silver in his pantry and pushed us on a toy motor round the garden, the gnarled and ancient mulberry tree, that tree whose fruit we always missed during our Normandy summers and only found splashed, blood-purple and rotting, in a pre-Raphaelite riot on the crazy paving on our return. Mulberry House, with all its music and the vibrant quality my mother brought to it: the dinner parties when, once the grown-ups were ensconced in the dining-room, we children would slip down to crouch on the last flight of stairs and beg titbits from the maids as they carried the dishes out. Memories of food smuggled from meals, hidden under pillows and extracted, once Nanny was safely asleep, in a repulsive clump which Gerard and I would clutch, creeping up the stairs to the attic box-room where, perched dangerously on the gurgling cistern among the romantic, rocky landscape of steamer trunks, hat boxes and suitcases under the naked bulb, we would devour the sticky messes as though they were not odds and ends of fruit jelly clamped to mashed potato and cream cheese but, as with all forbidden fruit, ambrosia, the food of the gods. How particularly innocent were our small battles against authority and how subtly clever the discipline imposed from the early years. And yet how grateful I am for just that ground bass, that rhythm that served me like an inner structure through a life that was to be as full of hazards as of challenges – rail against it though I did as a passionate child.

Life, with Mulberry House as a background, went on at that incredibly slow pace that is the reaction of impatient childhood longing to emerge from the strictures, the drill, the chastisements (for which I seemed to be a magnet) and the everlasting striving towards those goals that would please my mother. The dreaded end-of-term reports in which I had slipped from grace as first in class to an eternal second, due to those miserable abstractions, algebra, geometry and trigonometry, inimical to my nature and consequently to a brain that became addled before them in a kind of spontaneous combustion. As Mama read out the results, Griselda, calm before her scrutiny and perpetually top of the class, I would squirm wretchedly not daring to accuse Mama of masking her own similar failure. It mattered not that I was top in most other subjects – the aggregate marks were not sufficient to gain me the prime position Griselda held right through school.

I suppose it was then that I started losing my cheerfulness, developed an inner tension and began to know fear as the governing factor in myself – that dismal moment when a child no longer looks spontaneously and light-heartedly ahead, but anxiously to each side, its values now relative, forever anchored to others' achievements. But I still held on to one or two immutable joys – properties was what I felt them to be – the earliest, coming even before my aspiration to dance, was that of words. In fact, searching for those earliest memories, I realise that all my life I have been in love with words. Suddenly, at four years old, the shape of letters on the paper was transformed into sound; soon after that came poetry, the nearest I could approach to the music rising to the nursery floor from my mother's three Bechsteins below, the excitement of deciphering words on billboards, on buses, on the fascia of shops, muttering them to myself, feeling them on my tongue, hardly daring to say them out loud for fear of being scorned for mispronouncement. Soon I discovered French words, as we learnt to speak what had been our father's first language, and I began to hoard the two, both so beautiful in their disparate ways. I would walk along the pavements on those dreary pre-school days, gazing up at the writing in shop windows, dragging on Nanny's impatient hand as I slowly translated the large print and muttered to myself tentatively: 'FRESH FISH', 'SOLE TODAY'. My special treat was going to the Belgian *pâtisserie* in the nearby Fulham Road whose name, having taken agonies of time to decipher, proved the greatest deception when, on presenting it proudly to my mother in my best French accent, she abruptly corrected me in Flemish with a fine side-swipe.

I collected words in both languages and squirrelled them away as other children would collect cigarette cards or boiled sweets. As reading became easy, I treasured the miniature books of Tennyson (white vellum) and Keats (plain) that a dear old gentleman my grandfather used to call upon in Tunbridge Wells would give me. They fitted beautifully into my small pockets and became my own private possessions, so important to children trapped in that cage of nursery authority where the only unassailed refuge was the lavatory – the only peaceful place safe from the taunting of brother and sister. Their brains were quicker and nimbler than mine and their natural companionship gave them all the advantages of a forcing-house in which their ideas and opinions could take root and flourish. Clogged with the heavier soil of an incurably romantic and passionate disposition and attacked by the cold draughts of their combined sarcasm, my efforts at controlling my visions and my runaway imagination went unaided, while my intellectual self-confidence withered even before its first shoots emerged.

So I learned to keep my head down, when I could remember to control my irredeemable spontaneity, otherwise I had to train myself to duck the satirical coconuts shied at that conveniently stupid head from all sides of the nursery. My mother, charming, spoiled and gifted with the heartless wit of a well-developed ego, would join in the baiting on occasion. Thatched with a thick mop of curly dark hair, I would dip my head, physically as well as mentally, when the darts flew: 'Look,' Mummy would say in her offhand way, 'there goes Diana retreating into her *wood* again.' Cue for dutiful laughter, in which I would try to join to show I didn't mind. But how much I minded and with what intensity no one realised, nor did I wish them to. It became my own defended secret, a twisted strength, a negative value for want of a more positive one. To counter-balance my volcanic nature I slowly developed a resignation appropriate to the awe in which I held that cool and clever pair of siblings with their bright-blond curls, blue-grey eyes and closeness. Here was I, sandwiched between the two, dark and alien, a changeling who seemed, permanently and inescapably, to be in trouble, an Unfortunate Child. Indeed, a Maggie Tulliver, as I recognised ruefully, reading George Eliot's *Mill on the Floss* years later. Instinctively I felt that to crave sympathy would most likely evoke at best incomprehension, at worst the snub of dismissal, my mother herself, the brilliant pianist with a successful if brief career behind her, would give me short shrift.

I lied frantically in a clumsy attempt to avoid punishment for breaking my porridge plate in typical haste or ripping my dress by tearing around the edge of my cot like a demented hornet. However, I was far too artless to become a successful liar, so at seven I quietly gave it up, cut my losses and took a somewhat sour delight in getting the rap for even those misdemeanours I had not committed. But I was not for a diet of gall and wormwood. I was, in those far-off days, still of a sanguine disposition, refurbishing my drooping spirits with storms of tears which cleansed the situation as efficiently as a pair of wipers on a besmirched windshield.

There came a time when even those releasing showers were brought under control. One day, racing along the King's Road SW3 well ahead of Nanny and the more circumspect Griselda, I tripped and fell, scalping my knees for the umpteenth time in my eight years. As I bawled in my usual full-throated way into the shrubs of Carlyle Square, I heard a voice saying: 'What a very noisy little girl you are!' Opening my eyes, tight-screwed with pain and fury, I saw an elderly gentleman with that pale violet face that goes with the status of the retired military looking at me with total disapproval and no sympathy. I stopped as abruptly as would have any of the frightened troopers on his far-gone parade ground, sniffed, swallowed, tried not to look at my bloodied knees and limped off, never to forget his disapprobation. I suppose it was my first lesson in Stiff-Upper-Lip-Die-With-Your-Boots-On which from then on was either imposed upon me or which I masochistically embraced. Self-discipline was actually inimical to my volatile nature, but proved useful in saving me from a few of the tumbles into hot water always so alarmingly near at hand.

A hapless child, God wot.

When the first governess arrived (Miss Smith, of that kind of deliberate plainness that seems to have gone out of genetic fashion today) she tried to train me by making me sit at the table for a full minute, hands in lap, staring straight ahead; only after this Draconian sixty seconds was I allowed to start. I concentrated, during this agonising hiatus, upon seeing whether I could hold back the brimming tears and became quite adept at it. For I was nothing if not dramatic, even as a child, swinging like a monkey on a vine from ecstasy to gloom and managing to collide with persons, places or things on my emotional trajectory. By and large I was cheerful, bouncing back elastically after each concussion, possibly bloody but definitely unbowed.

At seven my mother had put me to the piano to see whether I had inherited her gift. It did not take long to prove my inadequacy, nor to ignite the short fuse of her impatience. The post-breakfast lessons became a nightmare for, born and brought up in a house filled with music, the hideous hash my disobedient fingers made of the melodies singing in my seven-year-old head created a dichotomy painful to bear. If only I hadn't known how the tune should sound, I mightn't have suffered so acutely. Griselda, however, took to the piano as her natural element. I would have to alternate with her for half a dreadful hour before we were trotted off to school by lumbering Nanny, racing through the neighbouring streets, always short of time, a consequence of my mother's total inability to measure it in terms other than those governed by her own designs.

The failure at the piano must have knocked quite a lump off my cheerfulness which imperceptibly broke out less and less. However, the gradual discovery that I did possess a musical instrument I could probably manage, that of my own entire body and not merely my recalcitrant fingers, led to my starting at the weekly dancing classes at Mr Gibbs's, at my brother Gerard's day school where sisters were invited to learn ballroom dancing with the young gentlemen. The teacher was a kind and perceptive woman who began training me in solo dances. At the end of the second term she put on a display in the Mews hall behind Sloane Street where I danced 'The Irish Jig' (I can hum the tune to this day although I remember few of the steps) – it would seem to great acclaim. I was about eight and Nanny had made me some sort of costume. I can recall my excitement, that early thrill of communication; of coming out into the damp alley afterwards with the first feeling of a sense of direction, even though I didn't recognise it as such, merely a sort of tingling. I didn't seem any bigger, but my world did . . .

I no longer felt quite so contained within the pincers of the clever brother and sister. I even had a couple of proposals of marriage from two of Gerard's ten-year-old school friends: 'I say, Gould, I'd like to marry your sister.' Some five decades later one of the two recalled his spontaneous offer when we met again, he as a Lord Lieutenant, I as Yehudi's wife. Nice of him, I thought, for the second time.

On the first occasion such was my elation, waiting on the pavement with Nanny and Griselda to take my brother home, that I coyly leant against the metal gate leading to the area steps and promptly fell backwards down the lot, rolling to a halt against the dustbins. I remember a frieze of horrified faces staring through the palings and cries of consternation. Struggling up, sore but unhurt, comforted by boys, nurses and parents who ran down to haul me to my feet, I was too terrified of Nanny's unavoidable crossness to feel sorry for my bruises.

There were more to follow my début in 'The Irish Jig' than two proposals and a painful tumble, however. The teacher confided in my mother that I should be properly trained as a dancer.

I must have been about eight when, at the suggestion of the lady dancing teacher whose name I have sadly forgotten, my mother (too preoccupied to take me herself) sent me along the King's Road to The Pheasantry, there to consider a class of the retired Diaghilev ballerina, Serafina Astafieva. I went with my nurse – an eight-year-old girl and a very dour woman from Inverness, whose only artistic attribute, as far as I recall, was that of a pretty fair rendering of 'The Campbells are Coming' by means of putting a stout finger up one nostril in imitation of the bagpipes. This ill-assorted pair climbed the staircase of the lovely old house and entered the first-floor classroom. Someone was banging away at a piano and the air was full of flying legs. We were gestured to a bench by what I can only describe as one of the most beautiful Ruins I have ever seen – before or since.

Attired in an ancient chiffon evening dress hitched up with something or other, grey-white tights and frayed satin evening shoes, her hair (of various colours) escaped from a kind of voile bandage that, owing to the elegance of her head, assumed the look of a turban. Her skin was very white, her bones very fine, her eyes riveting and the whole physiognomy fudged by a mixture of what seemed to a small girl to be flour and charcoal, but which I suppose comprised the cosmetics of those days, applied with an enthusiastic but myopic Russian eye and hand. I remember a cigarette, a long holder and a great deal of gesticulation, backed by some incomprehensible orders rapped out to the flying limbs.

In the front row was a sprite, made of the thinnest wire, black and white as a pencil drawing and with the same unerring line – probably just in her early teens. Beside her, slim-limbed and slender with feet like swans' necks and a long, narrow, well-bred face, was a youth with a sense of rhythm and directness that also remained in my child's memory. Judging by a fine outcropping of acne, he must have been about sixteen or seventeen. They were Alicia Markova and Frederick Ashton.

Class finished, Madame Astafieva beckoned Nanny and me into her sanctum sanctorum, a kind of Tamburlaine tent stretched across the entry to the room, acrid with smoke. A huge table occupied most of it, covered with a thick carpet, a dozen ashtrays piled with pyramids of red-stained stubs and a welter of books, papers, periodicals, an odd point shoe and some more of those gauzy scarves. She poked around the compost for a time and finally extracted what I suppose was a prospectus, stared at the speechless small child, glared at Nanny and dismissed us with a wave of her freshly lighted cigarette.

'Och! Horrible,' snorted Nanny in her best Inverness, and so reported, no doubt, to my mother on return – alas and alas.

One night, it must have been at the return of Diaghilev to England in the Twenties, my mother flew ecstatically into the night nursery, tore me out of bed and bade a protesting Nanny to dress me at once, as she was going straight back to the Coliseum, where she had just spent the afternoon, to take me to see his ballet company. I can remember little now except an atmosphere of pure fairy-tale; that heavenly other-worldness with which most of us are born and which gradually fades from the awakening mind before the rationalisation of growing up, as will colour before too crude and naked a light. . . . Everyone and everything was beautiful and it belonged to the world of Once Upon a Time . . . Only the Venusberg music, that brassy stand-by the Coliseum band regularly thumped out during the interval, strove to explode the magic, coming as it did between the two ballets, but such was the power and beauty that not all the puffings and snortings of the Teutonic gods combined succeeded in dispelling the heavenly illusion.

I never forgot that dream of sound and colour and smell. Surely you have noticed that a ballet has its own peculiar aroma, of tarlatan and sweat and rosin and benzine; of size and seccotine and of dust, layer upon layer of dust from countless stages stirred and blown about by the legs and arms of a thousand dancers, and by the draughts of a hundred flies, stamped into cloth and canvas, ironed in, painted over, sealed, forever imprisoned in costume and décor, and so carrying with it the misty history of each and every one. Once I could have told in the pitch dark the *Carnival* from the *Schéhérazade* backdrop merely from the smell alone. From that first awakening to the Byzantine world of the dance, 'The Irish Jig' must have faded in the child's mind and, together with a stirring – undefinable but of far deeper significance – a passionate desire to translate my love of music into movement was born.

The lady dancing teacher at Mr Gibbs's fortunately returned to the attack and this time my mother roused herself sufficiently to take me personally on the number nineteen bus to Cambridge Circus, there to enter, on Shaftesbury Avenue, one of those dread Victorian buildings that would make a prison look like a jolly brothel in comparison. Again, we found ourselves in a large studio, one wall a sheet of glass, the *barres* on each side and no sign of a soul. No sign, maybe, but *sound* enough: emanating from a neighbouring room was the yell of an elderly voice declaring in a mixture of Italian, Russian and English '*I raz, i dwa, i tri, i tichiri – ma oojus! – una porceria! ischuraz! cara, again*' and more of the same as I sat in frozen terror waiting for some fiend to emerge. After about ten minutes and more of the tri-lingual abuse, a darling old man emerged, in a black alpaca jacket, with a round head powdered with what looked like rock salt, merry black eyes and that kind of all-embracing smile that only Italians can bestow. My mother said something apposite, I suppose, as to my wanting to dance and he ordered me to take off my coat and shoes and get going. I daren't think what idiotic gyrations I offered in an attempt to convince him, but Enrico Cecchetti, the Diaghilev Ballet's great teacher, after turning me this way and that and pinching my legs and feet for all the world like a farmer judging a heifer at a country fair, pronounced me excellent material and told my mother that I was to come to his class every morning.

Again, alas and alas! She told him that as it would be a good six years or more before I could prove his trust, she did not intend being landed with an illiterate nitwit of a daughter and I was to start day school next week. Cecchetti, sensing my disappointment, gave me a hug and told my mother that he had an excellent disciple who had started a school at Notting Hill Gate and, as she held afternoon classes, I could go to her.

When, later, I was to drag my own recalcitrant nine-year-old limbs through Enrico Cecchetti's method (surely devised to deter all but the stoutest souls from pursuing the dance?) it was still Diaghilev and his dream-like Tamara Karsavina (than whom there never had been anyone more beautiful) who were my idols, and oh! the wonder of such stars to which to hitch one's wagon!

And so I went to Madame Marie Rambert at nine years old, shooting through class like a rocket, squeezing in school, interminable journeys on that number thirty-one bus to Notting Hill Gate, journeys which were to be burnt into my body as ruthlessly and painfully as the brand A of the Massachusetts Puritans, except that A in my case stood for 'Ardour' or 'Aspiration' rather than 'Adultery'. On those journeys I chewed sandwiches which laid the foundation of every ulcer I have since harboured. For ten long, harsh years I underwent teaching which – totally committed and informed with an almost fanatical fire as it was – was so abrasive as to flay the skin off any self-confidence that I had once possessed.

The important fact remains, however, that it was by far the best ballet school in England, and from it came Frederick Ashton, Walter Gore, Anthony Tudor, Andrée Howard – among a host of others to become great choreographers, and if I did cry into my pillow most nights and cringe through a hailstorm of criticism every day, was it not worth being Freddie's first partner at fourteen and creating his first ballet *Leda and the Swan*, and the same with Anthony Tudor for whom I danced the title in his *Lysistrata* some years later? One day I plucked up the courage (not yet totally doused by then) to ask 'Madame' who could have been the victim of the trilingual exhortations I had heard two or three years earlier through the wall in Cecchetti's studio. 'Oh,' said she, 'that would have been Anna Pavlova having a private class.' I shuddered.

Admittedly, those of us born in what might horridly be named the 'teens' of this century, born, as we felt, for the dance alone – with little thought of such collision-mats against the harshness of the career as films, public relations or any other such comforting and cosy material gains as now come the dancer's way – were fated to become a lost generation in the annals of the ballet. And had it not been for Rambert, her energy and vision, those of us who did belong to her school would never have been carried on to our later careers in what was to become a rapidly expanding profession.

It was the trough of the wave into which we were thrown and in which we struggled; its crest had been the great Diaghilev seasons behind and still before us, and we were destined only to maintain the motion against the next crest, the one that was to carry the ballet to its present popularity. Diaghilev was still alive and was a god – indeed the God of my childhood prayers was always inextricably mixed up with the magician of the *Petrushka* curtain, reposing with a faintly canny benevolence in a beautiful blue bathrobe upon a fluffy cloud, and therefore he was also somehow Sergei Pavlovich Diaghilev.

Thus we bore patiently the cold, damp studios, the constant and vituperative correction, the long, exhausting hours spent steaming in the depressing penumbra of the inadequate electric light. We were taught that everything must come second to the Dance. We were not to skate, to ride, to ski; never were we to smoke or drink; and was not the great Karsavina the very embodiment of Stanislavsky's dictum: 'You must love Art in yourself and not yourself in Art.'

2

Per Ardua ad Astra

And so we grew up, slogging our way through *cabriole* and *entrechat*, battling with *batteries* and all the hideous muscular agonies which lay between us and our elusive goal, and with every year the Diaghilev Ballet arrived to refresh our faith, to lift us from physical despair to airy regions, to a phantasmagoria wherein the stubborn flesh was magically subdued and where the limbs of the dancers made poetry out of problems. And we were blessed, for were we not growing up in a world in which the fairy-tale need never desert us, where it would be forever tangible, a thing of magic and yet of flesh and blood, transcendental though actual, at once a legend and a fact? Small wander I put my clothes on mostly back to front and didn't know Chelsea from Fulham. . . .

Gradually we came to know the great names: Leon Woizikovsky, Léonide Massine, Lydia Sokolova, Lubov Tchernicheva, Alice Nikitina and Vera Nemtchinova, Alexandra Danilova, Anton Dolin, George Balanchine, Felia Doubrovska, Bronislava Nijinska, and a score of others, and if my style suddenly resembles a telephone directory, then you must just bear with me, for those names were magic – an incantation to us – and were the very essence of our lives.

There was that unforgettable season at Covent Garden when Olga Spessivtseva danced *Swan Lake* and I, not yet in my teens and a very self-conscious little English girl, cried all the way through, moved to anguish by I knew not what unfathomable beauty and unearthliness of movement.

But oh! the agony of pushing one's own inadequate legs through the masochistic manoeuvres of the Cecchetti method the following day. What a bitter contrast, and yet what promise, what bright and lovely promise the great dancers held out to us in our pedestrian struggles. . . . There was, *then*, always a light for us, however obscure the way, however dim and fraught with difficulty. Olympus existed: of this we had certain proof at least once a year, and what more could one ask?

And so, just as in these days schoolgirls and boys follow their favourite film star, or pop idol, pinning their images on the wall, so we would cull, from those few magazines which published them, pictures of Danilova in *Bal*, of Nemtchinova in *Les Biches*, or Lopokova in *Les Femmes de Bonne Humeur*. And how much more satisfactory were our pin-ups, what sound and movement they evoked; how inspiring it was to enjoy a world outside the one of bus tickets and banana skins, to grow up knowing that there really are Elysian fields to dance in, that one need never entirely abandon those illusions which are so swiftly shattered by the ink bottle and the blackboard; our exquisite dream, then, was of escaping to a planet hung with heaven's embroidered cloths, where the people trod so softly that they never harmed our dreams. This was the fabric of our lives, the background against which we worked, the inspiration which drove us to emulate that which we knew to be unattainable.

Reflecting upon that first decade of struggle, it seems miraculous that one's vision held at all; that it was not ineluctably dimmed by the sweat and effort, the daily round and common tasks of school and class, of ink bottle, exercise book, bus journey and ballet classes, joyless with the apprehension of constant criticism; of days ending with a pile of homework and nights of crying into pillows. Humiliation at home added to humiliation in class would be too much to bear. So I chose to keep my anguish to myself, thus isolating myself even more from my siblings. Somehow, perhaps because it seemed to be my own and only personal treasure, I battled on, the ingot of my longing to dance enshrined secretly in an attempt to keep it separate and untarnished.

Nevertheless, slowly and inexorably, the glow of that early rapture would be extinguished, as surely as my early self-confidence was to dwindle away. The more I toiled, the greater the efforts I made to please, the thicker fell the showers of sarcasm: 'Diana!' (to the wretched eleven-year-old) 'Come out here and show how *not* to dance that *enchaînement*.' Second lesson of 'stiff-upper-lip' and suchlike maxims. I fought on doggedly, hiding my wounds, dry-eyed until I could reach my pillow and douse it with hopeless tears.

No one must know. Why ever not? I never analysed it (a habit I was to develop to a fine technique all through my life) when to analyse threatened to destabilise a dangerous situation. At home I assumed the rôle of odd man out, an impetuous, overly energetic creature, ironically dubbed: 'Battling Gould, the Wild Half-Caste' (after the manner of the posters advertising all-in wrestling) by witty Gerard, so beloved by Nanny that on the day he left for prep school she threw her apron over her head, leant against the wall above my small bed and wept like a Gaelic Niobe. As for the pretty puss Griselda, nicknamed 'Grumps', she ruled the nursery with a mixture of charm and stubbornness, so what hope lay there for comfort, and at what risk of loss of pride? Little of the first, a lot of the latter.

I battled on through those early years, so infinitely long in the slow time of childhood, accepting the psychological pain even as I was beginning to learn to acquiesce in the physical pain of a malfunctioning digestion. I suffered bouts of agony from my eighth year, unattended because of my mother's refusal on religious grounds to permit doctors. Oscillating between two kinds of combat, I grew up in one way a Stoic, yet unable to quell the incurable inborn Romantic, tortured with silly, inextinguishable hopes, accesses of inexplicable joy and an unbidden radiance that would possess me in that single moment when I knew I had danced well and before Rambert could intervene to blow out that flame. That stupid, obdurate flame so easily extinguished – how many times was I to try to rekindle it, as the years went on, with ever-dwindling energy?

Rushing with all the impetuosity of a ten-year-old to greet my mother, I, luckless child, managed to tug on to her gold watch-chain as I flung myself upon her: 'Oh, for heaven's sake, Diana, you've broken my chain – you are the most clumsy child!' Stung to tears, I drew back, never to hug her again. She, gloriously indifferent to anyone's feelings but her own, christened me, from that moment, 'Clumsina'.

Not that my mother was a monster. She was merely cast in the wrong rôle, like an actress struggling determinedly with a part for which she was definitely miscast. This did not detract from her talent for life and for living. Greatly gifted musically and full of a kind of innocent charm, I would say she was an arrested prodigy of about fourteen years; childlike and childish, full of vitality, totally egotistic and as incapable of objective reaction as is a detached retina of assisting sight. 'When the ballerina moves the house shakes,' she said, as I managed to collide with a chair, tearing out of the room at my usual hectic pace. 'Darling, your hair *stares*,' she would declare, gazing abstractedly at my mass of dark, frizzy wool. What was painful was that she was right. One can cavil at an unjust judgment, it is the dart in the bull's-eye that hurts. But it never hurt as much as Rambert's 'All this negroid hair!' accompanied by a savage tug at a recalcitrant tuft. I arrived earlier than most other children at an awareness of my appearance, owing to a performance Rambert put on at the Scala Theatre in Soho where at nine and a half I was a rose petal (managing with typical skill to impale one small bare heel on a nail sticking up from the edge of the stage floor, leaping around with gusto and a liberal trail of blood). By eleven I was convinced I was irredeemably ugly: 'Eyebrows like George Robey' (a famous comedian whose logo was handlebar brows) she remarked, going out of her way to compliment other girls for their 'golden curls' and well-defined features.

The difference between the two women who dominated those early years lay in the fact that my mother was blithely and unconsciously unkind for the most part, whereas for some unfathomable reason

Rambert's behaviour towards me seemed deliberate. After a class during which I had been showered with poisoned darts and had gone to change into my day clothes, Griselda, waiting in the deserted studio, overheard two women who'd sat through the whole two hours asking 'Mim' (short for Miriam, her real first name) why she was so very hard on that highly-talented child. 'Oh,' came the swift reply, 'she's so gifted that I am afraid she will become conceited, so I keep her down.' Oh! Uncle Sigmund, what would you have interpreted from that piece of casual hypocrisy?

So it happened that, except for the reunions of the summer holidays, I grew up increasingly separate from my brother and sister. Gerard was at boarding-school in the usual English way and Griselda was swinging through day-school, immovably first in class till the day she left. Gerard and she, close companions, were the self-appointed intellectuals, reading voraciously. I, with slower mind and bogged down with exhausting travel, would have to use any spare time in the nursery or on the bus trying to memorise my school work from isosceles triangles to Shakespeare sonnets, racing along ahead of Nanny to get home, flinging myself through tea and on to my homework. Griselda, calmly rid of hers, would devote herself to Smollett and Fielding and Richardson, lying on the floor, or, later, on the sofa and digesting books at an enviable rate.

Our maternal grandparents we had nicknamed 'Gannerwanner' and 'Goggo'. They had bought a lovely little Tudor house on the outskirts of Rusthall Village on his retirement. Gannerwanner created a ravishing garden in a couple of acres belonging to Rusthall Cottage and together with his two gardeners, Kemp and West, grew every kind of flower, fruit and vegetable, to the delight of us children who spent our early summer holidays in digs in the village while Mummy stayed with them.

Those were halcyon days. Kent was unspoilt. Gerard and I early learnt to ride bicycles and, to our mother's understandable anguish, sped off most mornings to explore the countryside at its most fruitful. Nanny would be taken round the vegetable gardens by my grandfather, choosing fresh peas, scarlet runners, cabbage, cauliflower, potatoes to be cooked by our landlady, while we children would pick whatever fruit was in season: gooseberries, raspberries, strawberries, cherries (allowed to eat one for every dozen or so) while Gannerwanner plucked nectarines and peaches from the espaliers on the red brick wall. I was allowed to accompany him with his huge, evil-smelling smoking tin tub to the chicken yard where he emptied the contents into long tin trays and to fetch the still-warm eggs all plastered with dung and tiny feathers. A long and magnificent herbaceous border edging the croquet lawn was his pride and delight. No children could have invented a more lovable and splendid grandfather. When he would upbraid Gerard with a mild: 'Confound you, Sir, where have you put my bicycle pump?', 'Sir', aged eight or nine, would look suitably contrite and retrieve it from the yew hedge where it had unaccountably lain since our last venture to pick bluebells near Ashdown forest.

The original Tudor house had been enlarged with a drawing-room and two bedrooms and smelt of beeswax and camphor, or roses floating in big Chinese bowls, and was furnished with that special style which comes of having little money and much taste. Despite having a cook, my grandmother always made her own jam at the close of summer, stirring it by the hall fire in what I recollect to be a huge cauldron from which arose smells that would waft through the whole house, dominating both beeswax and roses. We children, furnished with saucers, would have delicious gobs of strawberry or raspberry or cherry or quince or blackcurrant scum dumped on them, bubbling hot, red or pink or purple, and scoop them up with tin spoons – our faces bearded and moustachioed, as we licked at the last glorious drops of the jam-to-be.

I knew (and still remember to this day) the position of every fruit tree, bush and espalier in the garden, lavishing on them all the devotion to the spirit of place which lay in my romantic child's heart, agonising at night upon the awful day when Rusthall might be no more. Croquet lessons, picnics among the foxgloves; the wasp-nests of Speldhurst woods, wild rolls down the sloping field on the way there; Nanny,

23

furious as we crashed through cow-pats, bicycling madly through hordes of importuning gypsies and 'pearlies' (costermongers down from London at the end of August to pick the strange-smelling hops from those galleried green fields we rode past); scuffed knees from countless falls off my bike. The nearest I was ever to come to companionship with my so-superior brother.

It was from there that poor patient Cecil Harcourt finally kidnapped my mother, put her in the sidecar of his motor bike and drove her up to the little church on the Common amid the blackberry bushes. The first attempt to pressure her into marrying him failed, apparently, and she sat stubborn at the back of the church inhibited by what combination of superstition, loyalty to my dead father, waywardness and sheer cussedness I can only imagine. However, on the second attempt he broke down her resistance and she became Mrs Cecil Harcourt (albeit she defiantly referred to him as 'my sailor' and never 'my husband' when mentioning him to a third party). Younger than she, he spent most of our childhood at sea pursuing his career of naval officer. He proved a good and kindly stepfather, though his total adoration of my mother was such that I was never certain that he would not have boiled us all and chopped us for fodder had she been short of food. Mama, of course, ran rings round him, threw toy rages and tiny temperaments which brought helpless tears to his eyes. I, fonder of him than either Griselda or Gerard to whom he seemed hopelessly 'square' and uncultured, would long to comfort him; at such moments of deliberately raised temperatures he would nervously rattle the loose change in his trouser pockets and gaze mistily out of the music room, ready and longing to be allowed to re-enter the haven from which he had so summarily been dismissed. I was far too young and simple-minded to realise that this was part of the success of a marriage that was to last till my mother's death in 1950, that this worship which her tantrums and exigencies kept so fresh inspired Cecil to climb upwards through Naval Secretary to the Admiralty, to Second Sea Lord, to Governor of Hong Kong and his knighthood, and finally Commander-in-Chief Nore.

Oh! enviable woman, having her cake and eating it, fearless in her pursuit of transmuting her professional career into her Sunday musical salons at Mulberry House, all of us grist to the mill of her artless and obvious self-absorption. She charmed the birds off the trees, feigned inscrutable malaises when convenient, emerging (with added admiration for her stamina and fortitude) when she had tired of artificial wilting. She had a lovable and absolute lack of snobbishness. In all those harsh years when she brought us up on a shoestring, so as to hang on to Mulberry House, she never indulged herself either. When a rich friend asked her why she travelled third class on the train she answered swiftly and sweetly: 'Because there isn't a fourth.' Such things redeemed her to us, however unwillingly, and defused our anger and exasperation. She was indeed *sui generis* and the longing for a more maternal and warm-hearted mother in my early years faded, once I learned to abstract myself and admire her as a very gifted and attractive woman.

So much of my life was spent rattling between Notting Hill Gate and Roland Gardens (the address of Miss Robeson's school for young ladies) that I grew apart from the family physically, in a way not unknown in that period of English upper-middle-class life, where the father was away on duty or off at work most of the time. Mothers stuck their heads round the nursery door to bid good morning, or appeared exquisitely apparelled at night, a vision going out to dinner; the children had their own small world of day and night in nurseries at the top of the house. Later the boys would be off to prep and public schools, the girls to ever-longer hours at day-schools. Luckily my mother couldn't bear the idea of girls at boarding-schools any more than with her own Continental upbringing she would put us in a school where uniform was *de rigueur*. The unexpected result was the agony of being dressed by my Paris grandmother, Guggan, who would send over batches of elegant French dresses, thus singling us out horribly from our baggy-jumpered, shapeless-skirted colleagues. The crisis of this self-conscious anguish was reached when, Lord Carter having opened up Tutankhamun's tomb, poor Griselda and I dragged

ourselves to school in cotton dresses covered with Egyptian hiero-
glyphics and wearing huge hats made of orange reeds from Madagascar.
'What in the world have the little Gould girls got on now?' called one of
the older girls following our path to school. . . . Shame and scarlet
misery. Oh! the need to conform, to belong, to be the average child in
the England of that time. As Webb had longed for a plain boiled potato,
so I longed for a dreary navy-blue gym tunic, thick black cotton
stockings (our skirts and dresses were Parisian-short and we sported
long white knee socks) and those sandals that make one's feet look like
soap-dishes.

'Very well,' said Mummy, when I begged to be allowed to join
'Games' on Wednesday afternoons; for this way I would have to wear
my yearned-for gym tunic. 'I believe I have to stay for lunch after
morning school,' I added nervously. 'Very well,' said Mummy. She
couldn't have known the full meaning of that regulation any more than
I did. It was my first British-cooked meal: mutton boiled to a dark
brown consistency of boot leather, a mass of indeterminate green
oozing wetly, for all the world like the seaweed clinging to the bottom
of an old boat, a greyish poultice of mashed potato, the whole varnished
o'er with a thick, burnt-sienna sauce. It was that sauce, I reckon, that
was my undoing. Gulping horribly, with bulging eyes and my hand
clapped firmly over my mouth, I shot out of the dining-room, pelted
down the stone backstairs and brought the lot up in the junior loo.
Mortified and abject, I returned the gym tunic and Mummy got a
rebate on the 'Games'. I was never any good at them anyway.

And then came the dread moment I had long worried over, turning
my mind's eye away and shoving the apprehension into the back of that
closet full of half-hopes. Nanny for once had accompanied us to
Sunday School, 'Papa' and Mama had suddenly disappeared to
Tunbridge Wells; we were walking back from church when Nanny
announced that beloved Gannerwanner had died the previous night.
The blow stunned me. At nearly ten years old death is a shadow
inhabiting another, nasty world and its absoluteness strikes all the
dormant senses with a twang that brings them painfully alive. I felt

giddy with the shock, turning my head away from Nanny as we trotted on, seeing the shop windows at my side in a blur of tears, trying to swallow, sniffing, longing for the privacy to cry out all my sadness, my first real loss. Together with that handsome, stylish, affectionate man would go the beauty and friendliness of Rusthall, the only part of my young life that was warm and lovely and fun.

Goggo was stoic but very forlorn. I sensed in her grief a remorse I was too young to fathom clearly and which I suppose is inescapably part of the loss of someone one has lived with for most of one's life – recollections in tranquillity of unkindnesses in moments of discordance; small sins that rise to mock the aching heart into a feeling of grief that can no longer be assuaged. We took her away for the summer and I had to share a bedroom with her. All night she would moan 'Oh Will, oh Will', and cry softly while I pretended to sleep, putting my fingers in my ears to try to shut out the sound of her unbearable pain. For the rest of my life I have lived out those early lessons in the loss of a close companion, of what must seem like a severed limb causing one to move in circles until the balance is restored to some extent, the heart settled, resigned to the remains of an unravelled life, to be rewoven.

Goggo achieved just that. Alone, she sold Rusthall and most of her elegant furniture and one day rang my mother to invite her to visit her in her small flat in Stanhope Gardens, just three rooms and a bathroom with a little stove to cook her dinner. Mr and Mrs Balcomb, a pair of retired domestic servants who superintended the converted house, would give her lunch and generally look after her. She was cheerful and proud of her accomplishment. I thought of the jam making, the masses of flowers, fruit, vegetables all now to be bought and paid for, her own servants, the sweet country air, the space, but she never mentioned it, never looked back, managing to live on a general's wretched pension and always finding money to spare to take us on holiday to Italy, to pay for massage for my muscly limbs, to give us material for dressmakers. . . . And she was so gifted; drew like an angel; imitated like a devil; at every party the young men would flock around her, loving her for her coquettishness, that ready wit and the charm that died out with her generation. Dear Goggo was a refuge to me all my life and as different from my other grandmother, Guggan, as could be devised: Goggo, independent, creative, resourceful, the daughter of a general, ravishing, married at eighteen, always short of money, always managing to be stylish. Goggo, whose anecdotes were so fascinating that she was the best company I can recall; a little over-demanding emotionally perhaps, but so lovely and lively. Goggo, who devoted herself to her brilliantly gifted daughter all the way through her career into marriage. How admirable, how enviable compared with my mother, gloriously indifferent to all my adolescent worries, physical and psychological, never there to counsel, to succour, only to criticise in her detached, uninvolved way as though she herself had never known the shoals and rocks of a career. Maybe, indeed, her unconcern stemmed from the fact that Goggo had shouldered all her burdens for her and she was genuinely oblivious of the underside of the performing world.

Even to my childish eye the contrast with Guggan, born to a wealthy family and married out of the schoolroom to her first cousin, was abundantly clear. Guggan who had never handled money until she was married, had settled in Paris with her husband, my grandfather, Gérard Louis Eugène Gould (so called after his godfather, Louis Napoleon III). She had been one of three very beautiful sisters who had only known the padded cage of the rich Edwardian family. The Goulds all lived in total disharmony in their large, dark, South Street house, equidistant from Hyde Park and Farm Street Jesuit Church, shuttling between the two, when not quarrelling amongst themselves. I was never to know my grandfather Gould, whose passion for food – shared by my grandmother – led to his bursting in the Grand Hotel in Paris on return from a gastronomic tour in his early thirties, or so family history has it. My father, an only and lonely child, was taught English so that he could go to Eton. According to his great friend Harold Nicolson, he had lovely golden hair ('even more beautiful than yours, Yehudi,' Harold said when we drove him home from the Swiss Embassy in London after they'd celebrated Yehudi's fiftieth birthday), had been known as the best-dressed young man in London, was witty, clever and lazy, and I imagine looked upon my mother as an enchanting, gifted child. He dressed her at Paul Poiret, the Dior of that era, and I remember those exquisite clothes worn threadbare in the stringent years after his early and shocking death. 'Sexually,' said he, so it is told, 'my little wife is an umbrella, folded.' 'Oh dear!' he exclaimed, looking at a group of arty-crafty highbrow English gentry. 'They're the kind of people who go for long walks together and then rub themselves down with spirit under railway bridges!' It appears that I proved difficult to house-train so Daddy said of me at two: 'My eldest unmarried daughter finds such utensils new-fangled and affected.' Some eight weeks after his death, when my brother went to Eton, old Mr Brinton the house-master stayed on for a short while to welcome Gerard to the house where his father had been so much loved. . . . Idle, elegant and amusing, he would not have greatly enjoyed the world between the two wars nor really have fitted in, but I would so much have liked to have known him.

So, Rusthall was gone for ever. My mother, more or less cured of her aversion to all that reminded her of Daddy and of the painful associations with all they had shared in those short five or six years, decided that we should go back to France. Together with a close friend, also a war widow, and her two small boys, she decided to take the plunge. Gerard had just gone to Eton, I was eleven and Griselda nine. Again there seemed to be some light at the end of that ever-lengthening tunnel that the wrestle between school and ballet classes had engendered.

First, however, came the long discipline of the summer term with the apprehension of the coming exams added to my daily trips on the number thirty-one bus to Notting Hill Gate to run the gauntlet of Madame Rambert's scorching epithets. Small wonder that the England of my childhood and adolescence seemed grey and cold and arthritic with its twisted, knotty structure of rules and regulations, of inflexibility, of discomfort to be ignored and damp and cold to be battled with as endemic to life. The excitement of this first trip to the country whose language we spoke at home, whose culture belonged to both my parents, was well-nigh uncontrollable. Across the Channel the sun would surely shine, the summer beaches of Normandy beckoned as, school term at last over, Rambert's rasping receding to a distant echo, we finally crossed the waters to Cherbourg. We piled our bikes and luggage on to the ancient bus, enduring happily the smells of squawking chickens, unaired clothes, sweat and halitosis, and bumped and rattled our way down the peninsula to Carteret and the second-class hotel up the estuary a kilometre's walk from the vast beach. Tinged with the glamour of a foreign land, tinted with Latin hues, any shortcomings dissolved before our youthful and ecstatic eyes.

Bare floorboards, hard wooden beds and a noisome loo at the end of the corridor, were offset by marvellous food, fresh fish, fresh bread, fresh vegetables, all exquisitely cooked with that respect the French reserve only for what they eat or wear or create artistically, and not for humankind in general. Long, slow meals of five courses or more, accompanied by libations of the local cider, caused my brother to behave so unpleasantly after them that my mother appealed to the local priest, he of the greasy, green-black soutane who played football with the village boys on the beach and with whom in her spontaneous way she had struck up a close friendship. He answered: '*Chère Madame, votre fils est tout simplement ivre.*' Thus forbidden the potent cider, Gerard returned to a normal thirteen-year-old and Mama no longer had a drunken lout to parry. Sad; the cider must have been delicious.

All morning we spent on that wonderful sandy beach, getting acclimatised to the cold sea with its exciting waves, its tide receding nearly half a mile, allowing us to walk round the jutting headland where great boulders were scattered like giants' dice; huge rocks riddled with pools in which shrimps were stranded and lively red-brown sea anemones closing with an angry snap when we poked our child's fingers into them inquiringly; where lay great piles of bladder-wrack and other seaweed with poppable bladders and broad, slimy ribbons attached to long tails, which we would drag across the wet sands or wash clean in the lapping sea-edge.

It was a child's paradise, romantic, picturesque, offering a wide scope of adventure, of escape from less nimble nannies and parents; of whole days on the enormous beach, chasing the sea as the Channel tides drew it even further outwards, splashing in and out, swimming like small, strong amphibians under and over the stormy waves, of the reluctant retreat to lunch and the joyous return in the long August afternoons, trailing unwillingly back in the lessening light to our second-class hotel, mopping knees scuffed by sharp barnacles, hanging on to pails full of salt-and-fish-smelling trophies: shells, moribund shrimps, scraps of coloured glass, grumbling at having to leave behind the sour-green swags of seaweed whose lovely, slimy, yard-long frills would have decorated our dreary bedheads so evocatively, past feathery tamarisks, stealing figs hanging heavily over orchard walls or scavenging fallen cider apples. Nanny, with her evil-smelling thermos drained of its strong black tea, chivvied us along like a dour old sheepdog.

Poor Nanny, faced with *tripes à la mode de Caen* or *raie au beurre noire*, must have longed for Ardbroach smokies and mutton stew, nor, I suspect, were the delicious morning croissants and yards of crisp French bread any substitute for a nice stiff plate of porridge and four cups of strong, sweet tea.

Came the inevitable day when, all packed up to go to Paris at the end of the holidays, the battle to keep treasures of shells and dead, tiny fish and rank segments of seaweed lost in tears and sulks, we all, Nanny, Mummy and later our stepfather Cecil Harcourt on leave from the Navy, caught the train to Carentan where we would connect with the Paris express. Safely over the first lap, our raggedy collection of trunks, cases, spades and buckets assembled on the platform, we watched the huge train come to a stop with the usual menacing hiss common to all French engines. 'Poff' (our stepfather) was ordering the porters about in his best quarterdeck manner and his inimitable French. '*Prenny lar bagarge,*' he bellowed, unaware of the withering Gallic glance as the porter wheeled his trolley at his own sweet pace towards our allotted carriage. 'Get in, get in, children!' So we helped Mummy up those vertiginous steps, hopped in after her, found our seats, let down the windows and helped the porter heave in what could go in the compartment while Nanny stood like a cairn at a crossroads indicating nothing in particular. Poff jumped up the steps into the compartment the better to distribute various cases. Leaning over, arms outstretched in a gesture of willingness to receive, he unwittingly formed part of a flash–second's tableau, for at that moment the guard blew his whistle, the train glided out and the other half of the tableau was involuntarily represented by poor old Nanny standing abandoned on the platform amid the remainder of the luggage.

I remember being transfixed for a second as Nanny dwindled into the distance, Mummy wailing incoherently. Then I sprang up on to the seat and hauled at the communication cord. With an eldritch shriek the angry train ground to a halt, furious heads stuck out of every window, clamour abounded, an enraged official metamorphosed from nowhere shouting imprecations. I descended from the seat defiantly explaining that our nurse, with little money and less French, was stranded back at Carentan. Unimpressed, the train conductor continued his indictment to the accompaniment of the siren. Finally Mummy, playing her *charmeuse de serpent* rôle, persuaded him that the train was losing precious time and it was better to let our stepfather off to walk back along the line and join the abandoned Nanny.

The frustrated train, siren muted and heads withdrawn, renewed its glide. Mama got to work on the conductor, hinting that if he insisted upon the statutory fine she would regretfully have to resort to an appeal to our family friends, the Rothschilds who owned the line (which they did not). He capitulated entirely, Mummy was triumphant, we three children less so as the picnic basket remained on Carentan platform and we were extremely hungry. What was even more exasperating was the fact that our stepfather had stepped blithely off the train armed with all the money and our tickets.

However, Mummy was equal even to that. Arrived at the Gare du Nord our conductor (by now total putty in her hands) led us to the *Chef de Gare* to whom she explained our tragic tale, begging to be allowed to collect our luggage without the holy *bulletin* or check. Adamant, he refused. Equally adamant, she continued to argue, using all her wits backed by occasional sad interpolations from the three famished children. Finally he asked her how it was we all spoke French so fluently – were we really English? Mummy launched into a potted history of her past, ending by producing her passport to prove her nationality. He looked long and earnestly at it. '*C'est bien vous?*' he asked dubiously, pointing at the photograph. Mummy, bridling at the thought that he found the image did not do her justice, simpered and confirmed that, alas! it indeed was. '*Ah! mais beaucoup plus jeune!*' he exclaimed with a total lack of Gallic chivalry. Mummy, intent on winning, swallowed the insult and returned to the charge. The *Chef de Gare* after one more peer at the picture, snapped the passport shut, handed it brusquely back muttering '*Mais, quelle femme, voyons!*' and resignedly ordered the porter to collect our trunks and be gone.

And so we arrived for the first time at Guggan's pretty little house, 29 rue Henri-Heine in leafy Auteuil. To say that it was to become my second home, to which I was to return again and again to continue my ballet studies, would be leaping ahead; suffice it to say that the tiny garden at the back, where the flowers mingled with the delicate smell of French cooking emanating from the kitchen windows, immediately established it in our child's judgment as totally appropriate in every way. Nanny, Poff and the rest of the luggage arrived at midnight.

Ever apprehensive Mama, only really confident within the walls of Mulberry House, lost her anxiety and to a certain degree her vague dissonance towards Guggan; it was decided from then on, to my utter delight, that the Easter visit would become a part of the family pattern. Every April holiday we would travel directly from London to Paris, that magical Paris of my childhood and adolescence which I added to my secret and separate world where I hoarded all those emotions I knew would be considered fulsome and plebeian by my cooler siblings. The anticipation of the voyage would keep me awake for nights beforehand; together with the tracing of what should have been a thoroughly tiresome journey, especially as my function from the age of eleven was to organise my mother's travelling incoherence. At Victoria

'Oh dear, I've forgotten the tickets!' 'No, Mummy, they're in the other side of your handbag.' 'Oh dear, what should I give the porter, do you think?' So, on a series of 'Oh dears', Griselda and Gerard retreating in their joint companionship to the intellectual plane, Battling Diana was left to deal with our dithering mother on this hiccupping journey first to Dover, then on to the heaving boat, off again at Calais, and finally on to the train for the four-hour trip to Paris. An excellent sailor, neither the bouncing of the boat nor the sullen porridge sea held any horrors for me; having installed Mama and my two siblings on deck chairs, I would lean on the rail and wait for the never-failing thrill of that moment when Calais hove into view and with it that ghastly, huge, simpering baby lifting a coy shoulder to advertise *Savon Baby Cadum*, painted sixty times life-size on the side of a harbour building. With that long-awaited monstrosity I knew I had arrived in France.

Screaming, jostling porters grabbed at our bicycles; English children, splendid prey for a tip to be extracted from their parents. No such thing. We all three let fly a barrage of French epithets, I directed them to the luggage and, muttering, they dissolved into two sulky donkeys invisible under a pile of cases strapped on with a skill known only to the French porter. Off we tripped down the gangway and on to French soil and so to the snorting train. Mama's tip was met with classic expostulations expressed in a massive crescendo to match. 'Oh dear! Should I give more?' '*Non, allez-vous-en espèce d'escargots!*' we yelled and sheltering Mama hoisted her up those mountainous steps, found our second-class carriage and installed the flustered parent in a cosy corner, where she continued her litany of petty worries as the train drew out past flowering fruit trees and those lovely, large, hedgeless fields of Normandy till we reached my next registered Imperative View: the wooded ravine at Chantilly, no sooner arrived at than gone in one beautiful flash of massed fresh green, clothing the steep sides in leaves and spring flowers. In the autumn with blazing colours afire it was even more of an Imperative View, nor did I ever miss my twice-yearly greeting.

Paris, thus gradually reached, met one in all its special difference.

The milling crowds at the Gare du Nord, the grasping porters, the smoke, the very hiss of the engine, held a Latin *empressement*, an insistence at once challenging and rude. Gone were English reticence and kindly manners, here were immediate contact and sharp, impatient minds. I enjoyed the bitter invective of the taxi driver, inevitably anti-government no matter what the present political complexion might have been, all the way to Auteuil and to my grandmother's house. I suspect the marvellously anarchical tone must have been refreshing to a schoolgirl weighed down with obedience and conformity, adding a delightful touch of wickedness to the general feeling of escape Paris always offered me.

And so to Guggan. Alas! now there was little trace of her having been one of a trio of beautiful sisters in the very fat, small woman who gave one the impression of a tea-cosy moving on casters as she glided on tiny feet. Guggan thought (as had her husband) that the world was well lost for the delights of food. Therefrom came the growing *embonpoint* and the relish with which she rolled from luncheon to dinner, from which of course we profited hugely. To wake up early in the morning to the all-pervading smell of the local bakeries wafting through the open windows, to eat fresh croissants, six inches of crisp *baguette*, Normandy butter and home-made jam accompanied by chicory coffee meant Paris to me. That *réveille*, added to the smell of cooled air coming up from the pavement vents from the Métro, together with light filtering through the plane trees of the avenue Mozart, comprised the shrine I kept in my nostalgic heart till next we would visit France. My strongest senses were always primarily of smells and in those far-off days petrol had not entirely superseded all others. So Paris was still a city of cooking, of meals ritually and respectfully prepared, of bakeries baking four times a day, where the Parisians' 'Feev o'clock', their version of the despised English tea-time, would see them standing up in Colombia or any other *pâtisserie* ceremoniously gobbling *mille-feuilles* or *madeleines* and sipping the tea at small, waist-high circular tables. Mainly feminine, the gobblers were plastered with make-up and each smelt pungently of the

35

particular scent in which they seemed, to my childish nose, to be drenched.

It was the glorious possibility of sharing in this sophistication, I recollect, that was one of the charms of those bi-annual trips. Here, children were not antiseptically relegated to the nursery-cum-schoolroom, but were allowed to spill over into the adult world. True there were such dreary conventions as compulsory outings to the Théâtre Nationale de l'Odéon where, to improve our knowledge of classical French, we would be subjected to an interminable evening of their great, long-since superannuated actor, Sylvain, whistling through his uncertain teeth like a high wind on Dartmoor while he declaimed the Alexandrines of *Britannicus*, or a terrible evening spent in the Rothschild box at the Opéra where the smell of dust swept into the audience as the ancient curtain rose on a still more ancient Desdemona (the faithfulness and loyalty of the Parisian public is legendary and long after Sarah Bernhardt sported her wooden leg, or Eidé Norena croaked through Desdemona's arias they still accepted their one-time idols with, I suppose, a sliding scale of appreciation adapted to the occasion). We used to love, nasty children that we were, the story of Cecile Sorel – their great *tragédienne*'s visit to Egypt with the Comedie Française. The irreverent tale held that Sorel wandered out into the desert one night to commune with the Sphinx. As her voice died away into the cool air came the response: 'Maman.' Gerard, my brother, would retire into the back of the box where, not so very long before, had been a sign requesting '*les Messieurs sont pres de ne pas uriner dans les loges*', and tie and retie his black bow. We wretched girls would have to sit through the ancient, dog-eared repertory the Opéra still offered in those far-off days.

Otherwise Paris meant emancipation, glamour, elegance and Gallic style as we shuttled between the comfort of my grandmother's pleasant little house and the leafy streets, rowed on the sulphur-stinking Grand Lac in the nearby Bois de Boulogne and finally returned to the discipline and sobriety of England, heady with the inebriation of those Easter trips.

3

Enter the Black Fairy

Dover again. Grey April skies hanging like flophouse bedding over the white cliffs in a remonitory frown. Pull yourself together, Miss, they said, no more skylarking about, get ready for the number thirty-one bus and Miss Robeson's algebra. And yet those kindly open faces of the unurgent porters asking us if we'd had a good time in Gay Paree, the relaxed tempo, that odd organic quality so fundamental to our vegetable England did tug at my heart a little and much more later when, school forever over and the escape from Rambert absolute, I could better judge the balance between the two countries and appreciate with a maturer mind what each had to offer.

Mulberry House above all was beautiful; even though there was little money and endless calculations to be made and Nanny still sewed many of our clothes and to break a plate was a massive disaster. Families still lived for the major part in houses, from the grand mansions of Grosvenor Square to the Georgian workmen's Chelsea cottages, not yet huddled together in flats with little privacy and plenty of irritation.

Off to school, on to Rambert with an occasional performance for charity to give the growing school experience. Rambert, for all her shortcomings in terms of human kindliness, had a divine energy, an overwhelming ambition which served her developing dancers very well. Freddie Ashton was by now one of her dancers and beginning to create lovely small ballets. He had already composed *Leda and the Swan* for me and himself by the time I was thirteen and we'd performed it at a matinée to raise money for some respectable cause. All I remember is having to lie on my back on the stage for a few minutes and in my experienced way doing so with eyes wide open gazing into the batten of bright white lights hung way above my head. Came the moment to arise gracefully to dance the adagio with Freddie I found myself totally blind, groping my way towards him in a blur of phosphorescent cotton wool and cold fear, true to my destiny of Unfortunate Child. My untutored state was not confined to a lack of knowledge of stage lighting alone; more drastically, it extended to a complete ignorance of the libretto of *Leda and the Swan*. Fred, resplendent in a beautiful white feather toque from Messrs John Barker of Kensington High Street, sublimating rape in the subtle language of choreography, had given me no clue as to the relationship between himself and Leda. Quite extravagantly innocent of all idea of sex, prepubertal and coming from a house so asexually inclined that I used to say later on that my mother must have obtained us from one of those grocers with 'Families Supplied' painted on the shop front, I danced with my usual mixture of passion and ecstasy quite removed from sexual intention. I had not yet seen Michelangelo's explicit cartoon, therefore I must attribute the success of my interpretation to technical accomplishment and to artistic ardour rather than to any artful conveyance of the classical meaning of the legend.

And then one day, when I was at my most elated (for was not the Ballets Russes in London, and had not my mother already taken me *en matinée* to see *Aurora*, *Sylphides* and *Petrushka*?), Rambert rang early and asked my mother not to let me go to school that morning, but to pack me off to class and, above all, to see that I was furnished with a clean tunic. (I was evidently well on my way to earning the title bestowed on me some years later by Freddie Ashton – of the 'Safety-Pin Queen'; obviously my sartorial condition could not be left to chance.)

That was all: Class and a Clean Tunic.

Nor can I remember now, looking back with nostalgia upon that enviable sense of security and exaltation which is the happy prerogative of youth, whether I half guessed who was thus to be honoured with a Clean Tunic by me, albeit I do recall a feeling of extreme desire to do well, coupled with the simple pleasure of being given the opportunity to do so. Oh! the lovely untangled nerves of the young and dedicated, so soon to be become threadbare with the advent of anxiety and first misgivings. . . .

The bus drive to Notting Hill Gate, engraved upon my heart with a tattooing needle, seemed endless, lurching and swaying through the stucco jungle of Earls Court, past the great open bazaars of Messrs Pontings, Barkers and Derry & Toms, to attack with a grind of gears and in a protesting baritone the antique-encrusted slopes of Church Street, Kensington, and finally with a Freudian jerk to eject one upon the pavement wherefrom could already be discerned the Gothic fastness of Madame Rambert's Ballet School. And over a dozen times I looked into my little case to see whether my clean tunic was still there and as pristine as when I had set out.

At last, however, I reached the studio, ran up that narrow passage, bounded by the disapproving church on the one hand, and the Gentlemen's toilet on the other, and rushed to the dressing room . . . and was nearly catapulted from it, so thick was the atmosphere of terrified tension within. The girls, all of them older than myself by several years, looked for all the world as gay as pigs in a slaughterhouse. I changed quickly in a strange silence and we all trooped out to the *barre*. I, beastly child, as gay as a cricket. No name had been mentioned; the Exalted Visitor was but a Symbol of Terror, as yet unmaterialised. Maybe Madame had forbidden those who knew to reveal their dread knowledge? However it was, the *barre* began with leaden legs (which were in no way lightened by the grimly determined accompaniment of the piano where, in the tradition of the time, a long-suffering and half-frozen effigy thumped out scraps of dog-eared operas and the less happy efforts of those nineteenth-century composers whose music unfortunately had not decomposed as quickly as they). The *barre* over, we continued the routine torture in the centre.

And it was then that the door opened and Diaghilev stood framed in the entrance.

He looked as my God should look – imposing, aristocratic, omnipotent. He was indeed the Benevolent Despot in the blue bathrobe of Benois's *Petrushka* curtain, only now he was dressed in black, very elegant and discreet and, instead of the pointed beard and necromantic hat, there was the magnificent leonine head of dark hair with that single white animal streak through it.

I do not know what the others felt, nor did I ask them afterwards; all *I* remember was a feeling of electric shock, as though my whole body was galvanised. There must have remained a few tattered rags of the original high-flyer whose only thought was to command sufficient technique to be able to express her love of music by dancing, for I remember no fear, only a passionate desire to fulfil that purpose that swept all self-doubt away. I remember class continuing, the girls and boys (I among them) sweating like bulls; Harold Turner leaping wonderfully, and then Diaghilev calling me out to do a variation from *Aurora's Wedding*. I danced the Carnation Fairy on ancient shoes. Then he asked for more. I distinctly remember (with that perverse and triumphant self-disparagement that is one of my most salient attributes) doing an *enchaînement en diagnole* which included *tours en attitude*, and which I executed I thought with all the grace of a broken umbrella. . . . However, he was very kind about this and I was allowed to recover such laurels as I had gained by dancing the variation Freddie Ashton had written for me in that first full-length ballet *Leda and the Swan*.

Class had long since finished and I found myself alone as I made my *révérénce* and retired, somewhat blown, to the empty dressing-room, feeling a trifle flat, as though I had only half explained myself.

I was removing one of the antique wrappings which in those days I considered adequate point shoes, when there came a knock at the door. I hopped to it one shoe in hand, opened it, and there, smiling with devastating charm, was God! '*Alors, ma petite fille,*' he said, with a lovely Slav accent, '*tu vas venir a mon ballet.*' And I, anxious to reveal to my God that I was, however unbeknown to him, in no need of being proselytised, but already a devoted follower and disciple, answered, '*Mais oui, Monsieur Diaghilev, je viens avec maman, ce soir!*' To which he replied, laughing: '*Non, mon enfant, je voudrais dire que tu viendras danser chez moi, comme l'a fait la petite Markova avant toi!*' He tilted my silly chin and smiled; that I should think he was inviting me to attend a performance, when he intended that I should join the company, struck him as very droll and he laughed again and led me out to where Madame was waiting in the studio.

All this had happened in the half-open door of the dressing-room and when the full realisation of what he meant dawned on me, I had let out some sort of sound, an ecstatic gasp that I had hoped yet held the respect due to a god from his humblest vestal virgin. There followed a discussion between him and Rambert about next year and governesses, and that I would certainly be tall because of the length of my thighs (I was then, oh, happy days! not the Eiffel Tower I was destined to become), and that I wasn't to overwork and get too much muscle. (Rambert, stoutly: 'But Diana is an *eel*'). But I was drunk on honey-dew and took in little. And I was now to go at *night* to the performances of his ballet company (not just to matinées) as much as possible to absorb as many ballets as I could before the close of the season. They were at His Majesty's, I believe, and Madame took me and we sat in the stalls and I wore my best party dress, a disastrous affair of two 'shades' of taffetas joined together by some very unfortunate silver lace which made me look like an unsuccessful lampshade.

After each performance Diaghilev would take me backstage and introduce me to the Company as '*la seule jeune fille que j'aimerais epouser*', and to receive such a proposal of marriage, even couched in vague and general terms, completed the heaven in which I had so suddenly found myself; added to which I was to see my idols face to face; Danilova and Lifar, and from thence to the lovely Tchernicheva, whom he delegated to look after me when, the following year, I was to join Les Ballets Russes de Serge de Diaghilev.

Here was I, then, in my horrid pink-and-mauve frock, my feet splayed like Charlie Chaplin's in silver party shoes, treading the Elysian

Fields . . . not yet dancing in them, to be sure, but the grass was there quite definitively beneath my determinedly turned-out toes.

So it was that I saw the whole last week of *Chatte* with '*la petite Markova*' as perfect and delicate as silver wire; *Fils prodigue* with Lifar, decorative and disturbing, and the panther-like Doubrovska: *Sacre du printemps* magnificently danced by Sokolova; Dolin with his beautiful pure classic line; Woizikovsky, pagan and exciting. . . . There was *Apollon Musagète*; *Pas d'acier*; the haunting, melancholy *Las Meninas*; Danilova's eloquent legs in *Lac des cygnes*, partnered in such a clumsy way by Lifar that I myself was a witness afterwards to an acrid row between them in Russian and French in Danilova's dressing-room, while Rambert tried to soothe and I shrank into a corner, filled with terror at the thought of Things Undoubtedly to Come.

How I worked, once they were gone, and how I ate my heart out doubting that I should ever prove worthy of Olympus. . . .

The months passed, ten classes a week, and then the summer, spent hanging on to the ends of brass bedsteads in small hotels in Brittany and on the Côte d'Argent doing my *barre* – slipping on linoleum, the bed skidding away from my grim grip, now on splintering wood with hard knots to bruise the instep, but always slogging, pulling, twisting, sweating, hoping, despairing, and always before me, now so near, the vision of my gods and goddesses within focus, so that I would forget the weariness of the grind, the tempting sound of tennis balls on the courts outside, the noise of other children splashing in the sea.

At last it was August and one stifling morning I was working early, hanging on to the wash basin in a room in the annexe of a little hotel in Guéthary which smelt of yeast from the bakery below. The door to the adjoining room opened and Mummy came in, a newspaper dangling from her hand, saying the impossible: 'Darling, I am so sorry, Diaghilev is dead' and there was no cry: 'The King is dead: Long live the King!' For there was only the one Diaghilev and no one to follow.

Nothing that ever happened since quite lightened the heavens which for me the dark had suddenly invaded. It was then that I invented the character I called Black Fairy, who seemed to beat her wings throughout my dancing career.

Nevertheless, I was still very young, only just out of school, and, the double-edged sword that was the accolade of being the last dancer ever to be chosen by Diaghilev did bring a few benefits. During that waiting period to join the company I had given my first recital, aged fifteen, in the Maddermarket Theatre in Norwich, paid Harold Turner (as my mother told me) £5 to be my partner and danced a programme with all the radiant insouciance with which one is still endowed at that age and that would have made me a chattering nervous wreck four years later. After a week's intensive rehearsals (during which Harold dropped me inadvertently on my foot spraining my ankle) and the collecting of the odds and ends that would comprise my costumes, we travelled up to Norwich on the eve of the performance.

The performance was somewhat blighted by the fact that poor Rambert had one of her migraines which made it difficult to lose oneself in that ecstasy that propels a dancer while the sounds of violent retching bid fair to drown the piano, to say nothing of turning one's stomach. At least it kept her from hissing animadversions from the wings while one was in full flight, one of her least lovable habits. Anyway the little recital, despite a throbbing ankle and the off-stage accompaniment, was a success and one paper added: 'Diaghileff's got her and Diaghileff knows.' Alas! that within a year that heart-warming prognostication was to be nullified. . . .

And history or destiny was to repeat itself.

Still with Rambert about a year or more after that first shattering blow, the door opened in the middle of class and the most extraordinary figure stood framed in its Gothic arch; half bird and half Egyptian mummy, a small, erect, dead-white-faced woman with enormous obsidian eyes, black silk hair and wrapped, I realised, in clothes of very chic but very individualist style. She was greeted as the goddess she indubitably was, led to a chair in front of the big mirrors and proceeded to watch the class with a totally expressionless and quite terrifying face – it was as though a spiritual Effigy of the Dance had suddenly materialised in protoplasm and I, at least, felt both bewildered and bewitched. By this time I was the tall string bean Diaghilev had said I would become, therefore impracticable to the company already forming itself from the Rambert School and thoroughly wretched, demoted and unwanted. It seemed to me that when I was dancing on the right of the front line, Anna Pavlova was looking to the left and vice versa. Heavy-hearted, I made my curtsey with the rest and retired to the changing room. Imagine my ecstatic surprise when two weeks later my mother received a letter from Rambert reporting that Pavlova wished to engage Diana Gould as a soloist, that she could be partnered by Aubrey Hitchins, a tall dancer in her company, and that as Pavlova was returning from holiday to rejoin her company in Holland and from thence to London, would I please call on her at Ivy House to settle my joining the company? The black cloud was dispelled, my Olympus was in view once more and soon I would be on the slopes again. A small confidence fluttered in me once more and warmed my over-long limbs. I began to throw off the image of myself as some large unwelcome bird with ugly plumage and useless claws. I worked even harder (this time hanging on to German hotel beds on the Rhineland). The days passed. I was impatient to abandon the family holiday and return to London; however no such *lèse-majesté* would ever have been accepted by my mother, so I kept my growing impatience to myself, only went for ineffably dreary walks in the pinewoods with Griselda accompanied by Herr Professor Pfromm who resembled a calcified plum pudding and compensated in pomposity for what he lacked in the skills necessary to introduce us to the complex agonies of German grammar. I had anyway, with all the arrogance of sixteen years, decided that a language that held the sun to be feminine and the moon (my moon, Artemis) to be masculine was utterly unacceptable.

One late afternoon returning wearily from clambering up the same old member of the Siebengebirgen on which our hotel sat like a broody hen, I am again met by my mother in her rôle of Greek Messenger.

Pavlova had taken the train from the Midi, there had been an accident on the line ahead, all passengers had been made to vacate the train in a chilly dawn; on reaching Holland Pavlova had developed pneumonia followed by pleurisy and had died.

It would seem that heaven's embroidered cloths were never to be for me.

My sole comfort lay in the fact that I had at least seen her dance once when Freddie Ashton took me to see *Esmeralda* at Golders Green. It must have been soon after Pavlova had visited Rambert's class and before she engaged me. I was totally carried away into another world, away from the arduous gymnastics of the Cecchetti method, back into the realm of dancing, of which this extraordinary creature, half fairy, half goddess, wholly magic despite her age, was the embodiment.

Here was no trace of the structures of technique – she had sublimated them all, and emerged as free as a bird to fly, dancing. Schoolgirl though I still was, I recognised a passionate body wholly committed to movement. There was no separation of mind, heart or body; all was mysteriously integrated, driven by one motive: to serve the dance. Nor did she let the inevitable restrictions of age reduce the passion with which every movement was informed. She flung herself into one arabesque downstage, arms stretched out in ecstasy – for a moment our attention was caught by the other dancers – when suddenly I clutched Freddie's arm and whispered, 'Fred, she's *still there*!' She had held that ecstatic arabesque a full half minute *sur pointe*. 'Thank you, Fred,' was all I could say. Fred smiled saying, 'She said about you that you were the only English dancer she'd seen who had a soul.' I've kept that like an amulet in my heart.

More blackness followed, only relieved by flashes of light such as being taught Chiarina in *Carnaval* by that dearest and most unusually gifted of all Diaghilev's English dancers, Lydia Sokolova (Hilda Munnings), who was gentleness itself, chasing me round and round the classroom with, 'Diana, duck, more *ballong*. No, dear, your arms look like washing drying in a high wind!' whereupon she would demon-strate how it should be done with a joyful grace that was all her own. She also taught me the 'Seventh Prelude' of *Sylphides* written by Fokine for his wife and always given to the 'lamp-posts', the string beans in ballet companies, and she would regale us with horrifying stories of her time with Diaghilev: one such is burnt into my memory. Her health, though she was still young, was going through a very precarious stage, and one evening she dragged herself to the little Opera House in Monte Carlo, grateful that she only had the *Sylphides* 'Mazurka' to dance. To her horror she read on the billboard backstage that she was down to dance the highly demanding 'Blue Bird' variations with Stanislas Idzikowsky. Somehow, with the help of others, she got her make-up on, and in an agony of pain put on her *Sylphides* costume and tottered down to the stage, propping herself against one of the flats, knowing that it was Sergei Pavlovich's habit to come through the pass door from the front of the house just before curtain to check up and then go out front again for the performance. Standing there, giddy and grey in the dismal pilot light, her heart thudding with fear, she saw Diaghilev come through the door: 'Sergei Pavlovich,' she said, 'I can't dance "*Oiseau bleu*" tonight.' He looked at her through his icicle of a monocle and said: 'You may die, but you may not be ill in the dance.' Watching her fall to the floor in a dead faint he stepped with careful distaste over her prostrate body and disappeared to his office backstage. Ten minutes later the rest of the cast came down and found her lying there.

Gradually after changing studios over and over again Rambert and her playwright husband Ashley Dukes had bought the hall adjoining the church at Notting Hill Gate. With her unflagging energy and her increasingly successful pupils, they decided to build a small theatre adjoining the studio and there in 1930 to create the Ballet Club, the first of its kind which would provide a window for her choreographers and dancers alike, keeping them together as a group. It was a brilliant stroke, for both Diaghilev and Pavlova were dead by 1931 and there were no companies other than Sadler's Wells where de Valois had her own dancers.

With more ambition than wisdom, perhaps, the Ballet Club started as any other theatre with six evening performances and two matinées a week, for which it was soon abundantly and depressingly clear that the 200 or so people needed to fill it were not forthcoming. Those were the pioneering days of English ballet, the slough between the miracle seasons of Diaghilev or the general popularity of Pavlova's company and before the gradual building up of a really solid audience for both the home product and the visiting Russian companies-to-be. Only those who have experienced it know the chill of dancing your feet off to a handful of people scattered among rows of empty seats, like badly seeded corn. There is no half speed in dancing insofar as effort is concerned, no bottom gear to be engaged to make climbing a hill easier. We had to crowd into the two tiny dressing-rooms, one for the girls, one for the men, put on our make-up, our costumes, our wigs, crawl down the tiny staircase behind the 'backdrop', squeeze into the wings and get going on-stage with three ballets a performance whatever the dearth out front.

Poor Renée Dukes, Ashley's long-suffering sister, would dutifully spread herself trying to occupy two seats, while two splendid pianists, Charles Lynch and Angus Morrison, would offer us the only inspiration to draw on in those very dismal days. Soon it was decided that it was too much of an expense of spirit in a waste of shame (albeit it was hardly 'lust in action' but 'dust in action' as I said, incurring Rambert's wrath) and she cut her losses, deciding to give seasons of Sunday nights only. As time went on the little theatre filled to capacity with what the French would have called '*une assistance très élégante*' comprising many of the *aficionados* of the Diaghilev ballet, and moreover we young dancers were free to accept engagements during the weekdays in other theatres.

In time, Robert Helpmann and Alicia Markova joined us, lending their glamour and experience to the young company. One night one of the girls leading the *corps de ballet* in *Sylphides* was ill and I offered to fill in for her in between dancing my solo role of the '*Prélude*'. I duly took up my pose in the group, slipping back into the wings again so as to be able to make my entry when the time came for my solo. Tired, as one so often was in those days of class, rehearsal, helping to sew the costumes and general strain, I sat upon a pile of coat hangers stacked in a corner of the tiny wings. Bobbie chatted me up in a loud and comic whisper. Suddenly to my horror I realised I should be on-stage filling in my part as understudy. I shot on as gracefully as I could, assuming a rapt expression and a becoming pose, surprised to hear a distinct titter from the audience and a suppressed guffaw from Bobbie in the wings, and feeling something alien bobbing about on my backside. Looking over my shoulder with as dreamy an expression as I could muster, I saw a large coat hanger hooked on to the placket of my tutu and swinging about like the pendulum of a long-case clock very deliberately from side to side. . . . I sidled backwards sticking my behind in the wings and hissing desperately at Bobbie who took his wicked time in ridding me of the damn thing. Unfortunate girl again. Never out of trouble. Far from being thanked for my gallant attempt to come to the rescue in the dilemma of the absent coryphée, I was suitably strafed for my clumsiness while Bobbie teased me mercilessly for years after.

Nigel Playfair, owner and director of the Lyric Hammersmith, the most distinguished small theatre outside the West End, offered to give a season to the Rambert dancers. But we badly needed a star name to add to our potential at the box-office. The divine Tamara Karsavina, Diaghilev's great ballerina on whom Fokine had created most of his ballets, came out of retirement to lead the young company. Still wonderfully beautiful, she was a beacon to us all and especially loving and kindly to me.

She was my first great love and I would go without my between-show meal rather than miss the moment when she would return to the theatre from her tea at home to prepare for the evening performance. With the dressing-room door open I would await her turning the corner of the narrow little stairs, she would catch my eye as I watched her and, raising her own beautiful eyes, smile at me and say:

'Dianochka, come and help me put on some more rouge on my old shoes, you know, the Blushing Brides!' I would follow her like any acolyte, pick up the frayed old ballet slippers, grey with cleaning with benzine, and we would try and restore their pink satin youth by desperate applications of a hare's foot dipped in her rouge-pot until they looked like a pair of alcoholic noses, while she regaled me with talcs of the Maryinsky, of heat so terrible in Milan that 'every time put on make-up, darlink, would slide down face on to boozom, so not good, isn't it?' I will never be able to repay those flashes of warmth and advice and love she showed me in that time of increasing isolation. To us she became 'Madame Ta-Ta', loving and beloved.

Far from being envious of us young dancers, she would encourage us, give us invaluable advice and again and again protect me from Rambert's scathing utterances by praising my dancing to her. I found out that she was as mystified as myself at Rambert's persistent antagonism however hard I worked, nor did the success I had during that first exciting season seem to bring Rambert any satisfaction. My heart was so often heavy that without darling Madame Ta-Ta's sensitive help and affection it might have burst. As it was, the last dregs of that rapturous self-confidence I had once known finally ebbed away then, I imagine, and in its place a growing fear manifested itself, never to be conquered, always to be contested for the rest of my career.

The lingering shadow of Diaghilev hung over us. Woizikovsky, his splendid Polish character dancer, sometimes danced with us, and taught me the rôle of the Chief Nymph in *L'après-midi d'un faune*; Sokolova had already taught me the part of Chiarina in *Carnaval*; Alexander Benois, his great designer, came often to see the company and nicknamed me 'The Giorgione Venus', which helped shore up my constantly wobbling self-esteem (until that time I saw a postcard of the portrait and was much reduced in pride, for indeed the melancholy nude with the Easter-egg face and the woolly hair parted sedately in the centre and framing her pale cheeks was undeniably like me and therefore all the less flattering).

After a couple of sessions at the Lyric Hammersmith we were

successful enough to move to the New Theatre and from there to Manchester where I had my first taste of theatrical digs in the notorious Akers Street, dismal shelter of a whole generation of aspiring stage youth. Three of us in a room, a geyser spitting reluctant tepid grey water into a bath that looked as though it were regularly cleaned with sandpaper and a breakfast of strong black tea and charred toast to provide us with energy for a long morning's class and rehearsal. Apart from the fact that Rambert deliberately refused to announce that the rôle of the Chief Nymph in *L'après-midi d'un faune* was wrongly attributed in the programme, so that another dancer got the credit for being 'brilliant and beautiful' which should have been mine, it was an exciting week and a new and more varied kind of audience, which easily balanced the damp shared bedroom, lack of hot water and terrible food.

And so I shambled on, rudderless, hating my growing height which would rob me for ever of any of the standard classical rôles, trying not to feel unwanted as other dancers much better fitted to the tiny Ballet Club stage were chosen for the increasingly interesting repertoire, making the most of what I was given to dance.

These were muddy years when life seemed to have lost its tone, when doubts flowed in, carried by the current of fear; when I longed for help, consolation, for someone in whom I could confide. In a moment of desperation I had turned to my mother, but she was a stranger to despair; my dear Goggo was always so sweet and kind; but Griselda was wryly irritated by my too-constant tales of betrayal and intrigue and dubbed me 'The Tragic Fuse'.

More and more I was coming to realise that no career could be made without support. All around me the other girls were finding either choreographers who felt they were the perfect interpreter for their ideas, or rich men willing to invest in them, or dealing with amorous manager-directors or producers, the age-old challenge of the 'casting couch' which I too was soon to meet over and over again, drearily being chased round and round large office desks like an oversized rabbit escaping a hunting dog.

One day, however, a man I barely knew, Anthony Asquith (Puffin), the leading film director whose distinguished productions were changing the whole character of British films, asked Rambert to send any of her girls for a film test. I was only sent as an afterthought, went down to the studios, made the test with a very handsome actor, Carl Harbord, and was asked to come again the next day. At the end of the second day I could tell that Asquith was interested but nothing transpired and my disappointment faded away into the general fog of dashed hopes. However, one evening Asquith brought the most prestigious producer of the day, Charles B. Cochran, to the Ballet Club. I have no recollections of what rôles I danced that night, all I do remember is Cochran mounting the stage by the little steps at the end of the show, saying lovely things to me and deploring the fact that he had nothing to offer me for he was up to his ears in putting on the morality play *The Miracle*, with Max Reinhardt, the great German director. Lady Diana Cooper, the famous beauty, would be the Madonna, and Tilly Losch, the Viennese dancer who had starred in his last revue, would play the part of the Nun; there would be many other rôles and a chorus crowd of one hundred. Reinhardt had already produced it in New York some years before, but this would be an entirely new production. I leapt at it, begging him to let me play any little rôle and to understudy Diana Cooper. 'All right, my dear, I'll ring you up tomorrow,' he said.

I didn't sleep all night and when Whittle the parlour maid called me to the telephone (the only one, in the cloakroom off the hall) I tore down the flights of stairs from my third floor bedroom, ripping my right instep on a twisting mule, and threw myself gasping on the receiver (the tall standing one of those days).

'Yes, Mr Cochran?'

'Well, my dear, I feel you should understudy Tilly Losch as well, and there is a little band of novices which demands mime and Léonide Massine is doing the dances. He wants only five good dancers so you could be one of them too. Is that all right? Rehearsals start next week.'

Nursing my grazed foot I gazed out of the window unfocusing in a mist of bliss. Escape at last. The big theatre, Reinhardt. It mattered not if I only swept the stage, just to breathe a different and deeper air, to be in another and larger perspective, not perpetually to be measured against the same things and always found wanting. The challenge was a little frightening, but if I could remember that Cochran had said 'You are the most beautiful thing I've seen recently on the stage', and if Massine liked my work (oh please God) then I would have something to sustain me.

Massine, one of the gods of my Olympus, was standing on the stage at the Adelphi when rehearsals began. Small, slim, erect with a handsome head and those electrifying huge black eyes I'd seen in the Russian sketches, caricatures and photographs, he looked to me like an exclamation mark or a coiled spring. I performed a few tentative steps. He stopped me, nodding. I was in. We moved on to the big theatre, the Lyceum, where the whole fascinating production was to be staged. Cochran had proved a darling, his advances very gentle, my repulses duly accepted; we settled for a paternal kindliness that did much to build up my confidence. Every day he would come, sit by me if I weren't working and, obviously realising my total ignorance of things sexual, tease me while giving me advice of a general kind about the theatre, its horrors, its glories, its pitfalls. Among the others was Wendy Toye, as gifted a dancer as I have ever met and already at fifteen beginning the choreography which was to lead her to a great career in the musical theatre. At least three years younger than I, Wendy took me under her wing, appalled at my ignorance, fighting my battles while I, wilfully sticking my head in the sand, would try not to recognise plots, gossip and the inevitable spoils and stratagems endemic to the stage.

To be able to escape both the strictures of the tiny Ballet Club stage – which by then I could cover diagonally in one *grand jeté*, only just avoiding landing on the tail of the grand piano – and the stridence of Madame's discouragements was bliss unbounded, albeit she had so successfully broken my self-confidence that I recollect being crippled by sheer fright at those first rehearsals, convinced of my inadequacies. What would the great Massine think of me with my 'negroid hair' and 'George Robey' eyebrows? I looked into Massine's great black burning eyes and all but ran away. I suppose it was only by the time I had escaped worse-than-death in his dressing-room a few days later that, paradoxically, I began to emerge from the chrysalis in which I had been deliberately imprisoned and to feel my cramped wings at last take flight. Massine gave me a signed photograph: 'To my wonderfull [sic] Diana.' Little matter the price to pay: his 'wife', with whom I unfortunately shared a dressing-room, attacked me both verbally and with a wobbling revolver which our dear dresser, coming in as though on cue in a bad melodrama, bade her in outraged Cockney: 'Look 'ere, put that thing away!'

At least this was a great battlefield, far from the pettifogging bitchiness and incestuous favouritisms of the Ballet Club; here were giant figures like Max Reinhardt with his teapot nose and merry omniscient blue eyes; Massine whom I worshipped in an idiotic, tremulous haze; dear, beautiful Diana Cooper to exchange witticisms with in her dressing-room into which she always drew me after the hour-long first act; mischievous, lively Tilly and the whole wonder of being part of that unique production.

The Miracle was a morality play on a huge scale. Wordless, composed of mime, dance and song, it did not really belong in a theatre nor appeal to a general public – especially that of 1932; its blend of religion, fantasy and moral indictment was at once too eclectic and too elusive. Despite the innovative scenery, the beauty of movement, the ravishing costumes by Oliver Messel, the fact that for the first act Reinhardt had lifted an entire Catholic Mass and hardly tampered with it; despite the hundred-strong crowd that surged into the brilliantly feigned church to worship the incandescently lovely Madonna (Diana C. had to stand immobile for forty-five minutes), despite the dancing, the drama and the tragedy, this marvellous production failed, running only a few months.

No nice uncomplicated 'Anyone for tennis?' I suppose; no rattle of teacups; not a glimpse of a soubrette's tail attired in camiknickers caught in a deliberate doorway. Above all, no happy ending and no jolly jokes.

For myself it meant a sudden expansion – I felt like one of those Japanese paper flowers which put into a glass of water open up into full beauty. I was, despite the jealous intrigues, befriended for the first time: by Cochran whose avuncular kindnesses gradually restored a little confidence; by Massine driving me home every night (one hand on my knee, the other on the wheel, his mistress in the rôle of bodyguard on the far side); by Reinhardt who, having discovered me wickedly imitating poor Maud Allen as Mother Superior, would call out from his seat in the centre stalls: '*Diana, mach Maud Allen!*' and I, with all the evil satire of youth, would plunge into a dumbshow of flailing arms, bulging eyes and a whole diapason of hoots while he rolled with laughter and wiped his eyes; and not least the loyal friendship of Wendy Toye.

Another, and a different Wonderland, if you like, but it was inspirational to be watching and working for the greatest German theatre director of his era and one of the two last great choreographers of Diaghilev, when I was still only in my teens. I learned two unwritten mime rôles as well as the extra bits Wendy and I were given as the young novices; all this, added to the various dance sequences, entailed a seventeen-hour day.

Locked in the Lyceum all day working at one rôle or the other, occasionally filling in for Diana or Tilly, was frightening and arduous, but working for Leonid Feodorovich was ardour plus pure bliss. He was always prepared, rarely changed an *enchaînement*, and had a sense of the musical line that made memorising easy and moving lovely. I was of course totally mesmerised by him and spiritually ensnared by the savour of my beloved Russians which emanated from him like incense. I was dazzled by his coming to sit by me whenever I wasn't engaged in either frozen immobility as The Madonna (while the divine Diana was at lunch) or racing up and down the stage passionately (while the mischievous Tilly was more alluringly occupied). He it was who first gave me my nickname 'Diny' or, on very fond occasions, 'Dininka', and I loved him very deeply and very platonically (he less the latter).

Came the day when Cochran announced that there would be a whole final week of dress rehearsals starting at nine in the morning, ready in full make-up and costume. These would most often end at three the following morning with no transport to get home and a handful of hours' sleep before we set out again for the next day's work. After four days of this, the chorus-cum-crowd went on strike. Totally undisturbed, Massine told them to go (six p.m.) and turning to his six dancers announced: 'Dininka, you will be twenty peoples – Wendy you twenty' . . . and so on till he had absorbed the whole absent crowd within his six dancers.

In the middle of the stage there stood an intriguing piece of scenery designed by Oskar Strnad in the shape of a huge quadrilateral block, fifteen feet high and about twenty in width, whose four sides were turned according to the requisite scene. This structure could be mounted and descended by a precipitous staircase angled in such a way as to expose either the mounting upwards or the descent, depending on the whims of either Reinhardt or Massine. For hours on end we six dancers toiled up and down (it would never have occurred to any one of us to have refused) while Massine shouted orders from centre stage, holding in his mind's eye a crowd of over a hundred medieval peasants in the reality of six hobbling, weary, devoted young dancers. Meanwhile I stood in for Tilly or for Diana, or danced and mimed my own rôles and wallowed in it all, even when Reinhardt called out to us novices in our black gowns and white wimples that he would like to see real tears when the Nun's baby dies, and I cried effectively enough to wash my false eyelashes down on to my painted cheeks and felt very foolish.

Looking back all that way down the wrong end of a telescope, what tiny piece did that whole new experience comprise in the mosaic of a young dancer's career which in those days of few companies and fewer jobs was composed of hard-won and fiercely fought-for engagements? For myself it meant first and foremost a joyous release from a bondage that had all but arrested the circulation that fed my whole artistic system. In a bigger world I had been tried and not found wanting; I'd been desired, loved, even admired – I had at last reclaimed the value that Diaghilev had granted me and which, with his and Pavlova's combined deaths, I'd lost. Never again need I be dragged so low in my own esteem, however long and hard the way ahead would still prove.

4

Changez à Miromesnil, descendez Liège

When *The Miracle* closed and my final sitting to Diana Cooper's mother, the Duchess of Rutland, for a drawing in my novice's get-up also finished, Griselda and I went to a small place tucked at the foot of the French Alps called Montroc with Goggo as our nanny-chaperone. Griselda was bored stiff saying that she deplored a place where one had to strap one's handbag to one's back every time one went for a simple walk (because of the vertiginous slopes all round) and that she longed for a nice excursion in a tunnel as she was mortally sick of views. None the less I would climb a half-mountain or so, leaving her behind, for my romantic soul loved the solitude of the heights and I had a confusion in my mind to clarify, away from people, places and things.

Massine, amorously insistent, had invited me to join a new company of a vagueness and insecurity even the most nomadic of Russians would challenge; he had also suggested I get away from the somewhat gymnastic teachings of Rambert and go to Lyuba Egorova's class in Paris, in the city in which he and the rest of the old Diaghilev company were living. He would give me an introduction. At the same time I'd received a cable offering me a job in England. The decision had to be made immediately: should I risk the chance of continuing in the 'big' theatre in which, thanks to C. B. Cochran, I had got my first foothold, or should I take the chance to polish my technique in Paris at

Egorova's. She was one of the chief ballerinas from the old Maryinsky Theatre in St Petersburg, where she had settled since the Russian Revolution together with her great colleagues Mathilda Kschessinskaya, Olga Preobrajenska and Trefilova, all of whom had their ballet schools there. Apart from the faint hope of Massine's nebulous ballet company materialising, there was thus an opportunity to learn the Russian style direct, rather than handed down from Cecchetti via Rambert. I sat half-way up my mountain top enjoying the clean air, the pure light, the hot sun, pondering for a good hour. Griselda called to me and we climbed down, my mind made up. Paris and Egorova. I suppose the hour's meditation had been worthwhile, albeit the price I had to pay was sunstroke and an enormous serpent-like blister across the back of my silly neck. Dear Goggo kept me in bed till my temperature went down, I sent a cable of refusal to London and wrote to Guggan in Paris to ask if I could come and stay with her for the autumn.

It was with terror in my heart that I took the Métro (*changez à Miromesnil, descendez Liège*) to get to the rue de Clichy. Egorova's studio was a long room sunk in the basement of the usual *immeuble*. The tiny, improvised dressing-rooms, curtained off in a kind of antechamber, were one's introduction to the class and to Egorova herself. Met with alien and mainly hostile faces, I hesitated miserably, not knowing what my next move should be. Down a few steps I caught a glimpse of the studio where a class was in progress. I stood there helpless and wretched. At last the music stopped, Egorova dismissed the pupils and, catching sight of this tall, blank-faced young stranger, beckoned me. This was my second vision (the first had been Karsavina), of the indomitable carriage of the St Petersburg dancers. Ramrod straight, imperious head, relaxed shoulders, light of foot, perfect co-ordination defying age. Egorova's face was as narrow as an icon, pale, with dark eyes exquisitely placed in those deep-lidded sockets that give all Baltic Russians a beauty apart from other women, indeterminately coloured hair dragged smooth and shining back across her well-shaped head into a roll behind her small ears. Not a ravishing woman but a strikingly handsome one.

I explained (all that generation of Russians spoke fluent French) that I was Massine's English candidate for her training, and was given a very charming welcome underlying which I could detect sharp appraisal, and was told to change in readiness for the coming 'professional' class. Only those dancers who have been through the test of being the new foreigner, the trembling alien upon whose every movement sharp and critical eyes will be focused, can appreciate the ordeal. Dancing even in those far-off days was a highly competitive profession and strangely enough, once the Revolution had shut the door to the Maryinsky dancers, Diaghilev had found their replacement in England: *vide* Lydia Sokolova (Hilda Munnings), Anton Dolin (Patrick Healey-Kay), Alicia Markova (Alice Marks), all of whom had become stars in the last years of his company. Small wonder that to be an aspiring English girl meant two points down to the Russian dancers whose parents had fled in the aftermath of 1917, whose careers were crucial and whose only security was a Nansen passport. At least my determined hard work of the past years (the nearest to a pleasant remark Rambert ever made about me was that if everyone worked as hard as Diana there would have been three Pavlovas) paid off at the *barre*, but further on through adagio and worse still allegro I found myself floundering helplessly. The rigidly coded Cecchetti classes allowed of no licence and less improvisation, one simply ploughed through that day's diet of whatever steps the maestro had chosen for the *table d'hôte* – e.g. mutton and all its variants on Monday; tomatoes Tuesday; wild mushrooms and wagtails on Wednesday; right through to sausages on Saturday – so that one had developed an admirable digestion for all those immutable technical steps but was left with no ability whatsoever to assimilate the more complex and sophisticated cuisine that comprised the High Art of the Dance.

Ballet then having no script, nor staves on which to write, dancers had to develop a quick mind and steady memory capable of taking in the steps the teacher showed and, however long the *enchaînement*, immediately repeat them by heart. I found myself floundering like a beached whale, partly from unfamiliarity with her particular idiom, partly from tension, mostly from the copybook rigidity of my training. Wretchedly I returned to the back of the group, desperately trying to follow the others as they wheeled and jumped and turned in perfect repetition of the steps Egorova had set them; I was always a half-beat behind. Her improvisations were so lyrically lovely I longed to accelerate my sluggish mind and torpid memory and felt like fleeing the class to howl in the dressing-room. Now I fully understood why Massine had sent me here and with the realisation came the awful perception of what I had lost in the long years of dogged training – simply how to dance. I could jump as high as any of them, turn as fast, balance as steadily, but I'd lost all co-ordination, most of the fluidity of line and that impetus that must prompt every phrase. I also know that I had begun to be aware of this growing loss and was fighting to interpret my sense of line and rhythm in arguments with Rambert, explaining that a tall dancer like myself should draw out the beat imperceptibly, never anticipate it, as dancing lay surely in the transition from pose to pose, not in the poses themselves. Wouldn't she agree? 'Stupid, high-born fool!' she'd snapped and told me to get on with whatever it was I was dancing.

No such refusal to comprehend from Egorova. At the end of my trial by fire, she beckoned to me, sensing my bewilderment and discomfort, and said some very complimentary things to restore my leaking faith. Suddenly stretching out her arm until the palm of her hand unfurled like a fern, she tapped the centre just where the long outstretched fingers began, showing me the whole language and importance of the hands and their manipulation as the perfect elaboration of every moment. I hadn't known until then that she was famous for just this quality and for the finesse of her shoulders and arms. I was infinitely grateful to her for her gentleness, for treating me as a potential artist and not slanging me for technical errors. Despite my despondency at my dullness in not catching on to the *enchaînements* quickly, my journey back in the Métro to Guggan's house found me inexplicably joyful. Just one class and her treatment of me had transformed me from a forlorn, deflated creature for whom no amount of hard work seemed to bring back the exaltation and confidence she had once known to another level altogether, offering me an utterly new approach to what had always been the whole significance of my life: to dance and to dance well.

Egorova's classes were a revelation and a joy. Cecchetti's method did undeniably furnish a dancer with a very strong technique, but, without his inspiration, tended to knock all spontaneous dance out of one. Egorova's lyrical improvisations made every class a performance, cleared the gymnastics from one's movements and related arms, head, wrists, neck, hands and legs into one co-ordinated body that responded to music.

Not being of an analytical turn of mind in those days, it never occurred to me as I shot out of the Métro at Jasmin in the avenue Mozart and ran up the rue Henri-Heine to number twenty-nine with its three steps up to the front door and its prim little glass marquise, to have the door opened by Ramon, the tiny gnarled Spanish butler, that my grandmother (sitting stout and placid with that kind of matchless appearance due to her maid and manicurist from the thin white tendrils of her silken hair to her delicately lovely and useless hands), was to prove the perfect chaperone, and yet that was exactly what she became. A true Edwardian, once a spoilt beauty, long a widow, totally unawakened, furnished with the unshakeable power of utter stupidity against which I found there was simply no argument, settled in her pretty nest with her few very boring friends, Guggan gave me unconsciously a feeling of tranquillity and security. Her satisfaction with herself and her life, her enviable lack of imagination, of any desire other than that for a perfect meal and the continuation for ever of the devoted ministrations of poor Gabrielle, the lemon-faced slave from Tours, with the long, frighteningly insecure teeth, made her an ideal disciple of Voltaire, whose edict to cultivate one's own garden she carried out to the letter.

And did I profit from it? Of course and gratefully. I'd always loved

France. The dichotomy between me and my siblings thereby grew even wider than it had been during my separate life with the pilgrimage between Chelsea and Notting Hill Gate. Now, somehow, I had sloughed off the English schoolgirl, never a very well-adapted uniform despite that aborted longing for the gym tunic, and was able comfortably to slide into the passionate side of my nature carefully hidden from the cool and clever Gerard and Griselda. As my lessons progressed with Egorova I was able to discard my English conditioning without fear of scorn or sarcasm, to drop the inhibitions which encrusted me like barnacles on an unseaworthy boat and to start floating freely.

Egorova gave me the inspiration and gradually I learned her technical language and gained in confidence. The ex-Diaghilev stars arrived. Danilova, still young and lovely and full of fun, used to take me through my pirouettes at the end of class, whipping me through my *double tours* till she tripled and quadrupled them. Woizikovsky, who'd taught me the rôle of the chief nymph in *L'après-midi d'un faune* and the tall and elegant Doubrovska, the last of Diaghilev's ballerinas whose height recharged me with hope (Balanchine admired her length and had already created *Fils prodigue* for her in that last season). But would I ever reach that eminence?

Anyway, that was not important; I had to make the most of the present and these heaven-sent winter months. Class was harmonious, there was no shouting, no abuse, no tension. The prima ballerina of the Paris Opéra attended every day: Solange Schwarz, beautifully exact, faultlessly placed feet and legs, as cleansed of all technical misdemeanours as she was of either fire or flight. The rest were mainly Russian, their careers bright with hope or a little threadbare, but all alike fired with the same determination. Occasionally there would be a slight flurry ruffling the serenity. One of the more antiquated of the male dancers, the vapours of the Maryinsky still hanging round his long, corseted frame like undissipated fog, had been dispossessed of his usual place of honour at the *barre* and was registering rage in a low hiss of Russian expletives directed at the innocent pirate who'd committed the arch-solecism. Poised between hitting the miscreant or flouncing out in a perfect cloud of lavender powder, he was intercepted by Egorova with a deftness marvellous to watch, his place duly restored, his powder resettled on his face, and the signal for the opening chords from the upright piano given with an imperious nod of the head. Class began and with it the end of all nonsense.

One day Massine himself turned up. Egorova was indisposed and he would give the class. Moreover he gave the classic Cecchetti class and I, hardly emerged from my early confusions and preferring to remain at the back, found myself dragged to the front by Léonide Fedorovich, there to flit with ease through the technically taxing but otherwise good plain cooking of the Italo-Russian method which Rambert had taught me for nearly a decade. I have to admit a secret satisfaction in that the strength and endurance acquired by my long training came so easily to me that by the end of the class I had earned added respect. Thank you, Léonide Fedorovich. By this stroke of fortune my too quickly assumed inferiority in the previous month's struggle suddenly dissolved and I knew myself placed several rungs higher on that slippery ladder by my colleagues. While they panted with the sheer strain of finding enough breath to sustain the endlessly repeated series of basic steps, the high jumps, the *batteries*, the very slow adagios all unadorned by anything other than the plainest of *ports de bras*, lacking lyricism and therefore offering no escape from the naked mechanics of ballet technique, no means of clothing one's imperfections with grace of presentation or favour of subtle polish, I analysed for the first time the value of Cecchetti's method, while still deploring the naked application favoured by Rambert. Obviously Cecchetti had proved invaluable as a strengthener and a rectifier in an art form vulnerable to all kinds of debility, needing a constant vigilance to keep it trim as the sails on a yacht. However, in his case he had given a basic structure to dancers already trained in all the expressiveness and artistry of the Maryinsky ballet – dancers who had no need of being taught the art of dance itself, merely in want of a good taskmaster and a system to support and underpin the execution of their rôles, all the more stringent now that the door back to their original school was closed forever.

I myself, buried under the dead weight of the 'Method' – a fate I would surely have escaped had I gone at the outset to Cecchetti himself or, again, to Astafieva – found myself having to revive a rapture and a spontaneity so submerged I sometimes felt that the flame had been extinguished for ever. As well as growing unusually tall I had also added to that the over-production of muscle that unadulterated Cecchetti classes caused. I recalled how on the day that Diaghilev visited her class Rambert had been convinced he would shape up her leading man Harold Turner, a splendid dancer by all standards: '*Trop de muscles,*' he said tersely and turning to Rambert begged her not to let me develop that way. . . . Three years later and Diaghilev dead, my determination to justify his choice of me, backed by Rambert's insistence that I work ten classes a week, had certainly given me a strong and enduring technique but at the cost of a pair of legs like jodhpurs fashioned in cement. Now at least *chez* Egorova and during that one Massine class I felt a little less bitter about the loss of my once slender legs, at that time despairing of ever reducing my thighs to their virginal smooth lines.

One day, coming up the steps at the end of the class, I was accosted by a pale rather plump young woman with bright, frizzy hair. Looking me straight in the face with a terrifyingly accurate eye, which in later years must have driven many a dancer to dedicate themselves unequivocally to her, she said: 'You are the most beautiful thing I have ever seen.' Embarrassed and delighted, I stuttered something silly. Realising from her accent she was American, I asked her if she were intending joining the class. (This because obviously she was not a trained ballet dancer, nor young enough to start.) 'Sure,' she said, with the same admirable aplomb that I learned to enjoy and envy so much. 'My name,' she continued, 'is Agnes de Mille and I've been watching you. I know who you are and I'd like you to give me advice as to where to go to study in London.' I brought Aggie to Rambert. Aggie knew exactly how to handle Mim. The little Ballet Club being ideal for her purpose, she later gave there some of her first solo dance recitals in England.

Meanwhile, rumours abounded as to the revival of the Diaghilev Ballet. One of his older dancers, Tatiana Chamié (the clockwork doll in the first scene of *Petrushka*) had managed to find a money raiser. His name was Colonel (oddly ill-attuned to the world of Terpsichore, surely) de Basil (a self-conferred dignity).

Colonel de Basil was a large monument of a man, with a head so round and ill-fitting it gave the impression of a pedestal with a reject cannonball atop. Wearing the bottle-end spectacles of the very myopic, he successfully prevented all detection of what was going on behind them. Busy gathering together the shattered and dispersed remnants of the Diaghilev Company, he proved to be a wizard at finding money and, I might add, as great a magician at not handing it out to his dancers. Thanks to Grigoriev, Diaghilev's irreplaceable *régisseur* in whose remarkable memory reposed the scores and choreography of most of the ballets, de Basil drew together bit by bit many of the *ci-devant* Diaghilev dancers to whom, coming from the studios of Preobrajenska, Trefilova and Kschessinskaya, he added such magnificently equipped 'baby ballerinas' as Toumanova, Baronova and Riabouchinska and other promising ones for his *corps de ballet*.

Massine again begged me to join. Again I felt too inexperienced to risk so vague a scheme and declined. Difficult. In the face of those hypnotic black eyes, I felt feeble as well as worried that he might never ask me again and so continued my lessons with Egorova. The fact that some weeks later that tentative resurrection ended ignobly in a siding in the station at Basle, leaving the wretched dancers hiking penniless back to Paris, did relieve me a little of my paranoia.

Kyra Nijinska (Nijinsky's daughter whom I had known at the Ballet Club) joined the class. An extraordinary looking girl with a male Slav face, broad and flat with her father's slanting eyes, she had a beautiful head on a short body ending in her father's huge, solid legs. The young composer Igor Markevitch was courting her and we would go out to cheap cafés *à trois*, discussing with all the arrogant seriousness of advanced teenagers, Art and The World. Kyra was impulsive, jolly and straightforward, Igor shy and waspish and as conceited as might be a young man who as a boy prodigy had been commissioned by Diaghilev to write a ballet for his company. Alas, they finally married, and it was not much fun for poor Kyra.

Back at No. 49 Henri-Heine, Guggan was being really very forbearing, especially when, visited by a bouquet of her more dreary elderly friends, I would be presented as her granddaughter. After careful appraisal through the raised lorgnette, the inevitable question was posed: '*Eh, bien, Mademoiselle, vous faites vos études à la Sorbonne?*' Pause, '*Mais non, Madame, je suis mes classes de ballet chez Madame Egorova.*' Deadly hush, followed by a look of horror switched to my poor grandmother: '*Madame, vous permettez que votre petite-fille fasse une telle carrière?*' Guggan muttered something about my not being her responsibility and if my mother approved of ballet lessons for her daughter there was little she could do. I, together with the whole British race (*ces perfides Anglais*), was promptly relegated to that limbo shared by most of my nation in the French mentality.

In an effort at compromise with Guggan, now condemned by her *haut bourgeois* friends as dreadfully lax, I agreed to accompany her on a weekend to one of her more ancient but quite witty acquaintances, the Duchesse de la Motte Audrancourt who lived in a dismal *hôtel particulièr* skulking in one of those weirdly angled streets which abound in Paris – having unfortunately escaped Haussmann's clean sweep of the sixteenth *arrondissement*. The weekend was to be in her country *château* – De la Fayel near Compiègne. Off we went in the train, were duly met and driven to the really very elegant seventeenth-century *château* (pink and white brick is all I remember and shatteringly damp rooms). The duchess lived in one faintly heated corner.

The food was sublime, the conversation that of two old hens, the plumbing archaic and the night damp. We must have done something on the Sunday to fill the long, dank day, but what will stay in my mind for ever was my adamant demand to be shipped back to Paris on the Monday in time for the ten o'clock class. It would never have occurred to me to miss it, any more than I would have taken off my clothes and danced a fandango in the *petit salon* after dinner. The duchess was the perfect hostess. I would be given coffee and croissants at five a.m. and her chauffeur would drive me to the station, some distance away, to catch the early Paris train. Guggan apologised for her granddaughter who not only was pursuing the career of a courtesan of low stature but was ill-mannered enough to disturb the even tenor of her hostess's *ménage*. I said my farewells after dinner as apologetically as I could and retired before their united gaze, astonished and censorious in equal parts, to close my modest suitcase and prepare for another damp and short night.

The following morning my coffee was served by a sullen maid but worse was to come. The chauffeur, obviously furious at being roused, scowled at my bright '*Bonjour*' and grimly refused to reply to my gay chatter, freezing me into nervous silence after the first few miles. At last we arrived at the station. My one ambition was to get out of the car and escape being stifled by his halitosis of disapproval as quickly as possible. Opening the car door in advance, as the chauffeur stopped with a squeal of brakes and a jerk that threw me against the jamb, I stumbled out, tearing the right heel clean off my one good pair of Raoul shoes. The look of naked delight on his face as he handed me my case and the lost heel almost made me retract my tip, but I gave it with ill grace and hopped defeatedly up the steps and on to the platform. From my right shoe where the heel had been torn off a fang-like collection of long, sharp nails impeded any but the oddest form of progress. I managed a kind of hop, skip and jump technique and somehow reached a carriage, having now and again to dislodge the remains of the upper part when the nails impaled me savagely to the floor. Furious and resigned I finally took the whole shoe off and with a ragged dignity found a seat, shoe in hand. Desperately I tried to unite the two halves of my right best shoe; the nails had been bent irretrievably in the wrenching and nothing would persuade them to be annexed to the alien heel. Somehow on arrival I got through the crowds and up the stairs at the Gare du Nord to the café, where over a cup of filthy boiled chicory I contemplated the moral lesson of the morning. Obviously my blind obedience to my profession ranked low in the estimation of whatever gods judged my behaviour. Far worse had been the social error, the crime of bad manners and lack of regard for others' domestic arrangements. QED.

So much for gestures towards Guggan's social life, albeit I did go to a very elegant ball at Robert de Rothschild's lovely house in the avenue Montaigne and got suitably chased round the garden (but I was already versed in dodgem by then) and had a fascinating lunch with Solange de Mora (of Suez Canal fame) who'd known and loved my father when they were both very young and talked to me about him. Darling Solange, who on occasion would try her English out on Griselda and me: 'Dear children, where have you went?' Also I would get up extra early several mornings a week to take the Métro to somewhere near the Lion de Befort and there sit for my portrait by Alfred Jonnaiux, one of the leading Paris painters of those days, sessions I much enjoyed as he was a charming and intelligent man. It was there that I discovered what I proved on many another sitting with other artists to come, *vide* that I had two speeds only: zero (I could sit for hours without moving) or a hundred miles per hour. Yehudi has that portrait now, the head of an eighteen-year-old with rapt eyes and hair done in a ballet dancer's strict chignon. Every time I pass it on my way upstairs it recalls that wonderfully happy and satisfying winter when I found a tributary to the mainstream of my dancing life in which the current had been so often deflected by rocks and shallows and my progress so irregular.

5

Les Ballets 1933

Nineteen thirty-three saw me back at the Ballet Club with renewed self-confidence and slimmer thighs (thanks to Egorova's classes, together with the painful but productive ministrations of Mademoiselle Bati, the Comedie Française's masseuse whose anecdotes of the male and female stars of that eminent company relieved the agony of her pounding). Even Mim's ill-disposed announcement that Freddie Ashton no longer wanted to write anything for me, but might with financial encouragement be persuaded to do so, did not hit me in the solar plexus as it might have before Cochran and Egorova reinforced my confidence. I simply conveyed the sour news to my mother and supposedly she and Rambert came to terms. It was incidentally one of the very few times I had ever appealed to Mama and I'm happy to say that, whether this reported reluctance was genuine or not, the Ravel *Pavane pour une Infante défunte* that was the result proved one of the most beautiful and successful of all the works he created for the Ballet Club. I'd always loved working for Freddie, his instinctively musical ear, his taste, his lyrical style exactly suited my belief that dancing was the representation of music in visible form or it was nothing.

In my heedless way I'd put on the seventeenth-century Spanish costume – probably bought fifth hand from some theatrical costumiers – without bothering much about its fit or its allure, and equally carelessly shoved on the shaggy, huge chestnut wig of that period (standing away from each side of the face in stiff, vertical curls) with only a glance in the mirror, typically impatient to get on to the stage and interpret the wonderful sad monotony of Ravel's music. The dress, with its heavy farthingale, hung about me in loops like the sail of a becalmed ship, so when Freddie remonstrated I took three or four safety pins, tightening the bodice up the back – surely, I reckoned, as the whole court dance from beginning to end passed across the stage in one long glide, nobody could ever see my back? The wig, which resembled unravelled knitting and sat on my head like a dotty tea cosy, I secured in much the same unregarding way by means of large hairpins, gathering in the slack, as it were, presenting, I hoped, an acceptable appearance from the front. Freddie was very pleased with what I made of the dress, less so, I fear, with my incurable sartorial negligence, for it was then that he first dubbed me 'The Safety-Pin Queen'.

More pleasant things began to happen. Ninette de Valois asked me to dance the '*Prélude*' in *Sylphides* at Sadler's Wells, as well as the rôle of Lady Clara Vere de Vere which I had recently created when Freddie choreographed a ballet on Tennyson poems set to Mendelssohn music. It was the brainchild of the leading London music critic, Edwin Evans, and had been given by the Rambert dancers at a charity matinée some time before. Based on copiousness rather than a judicious selection of the poems, the ballet seemed endless. Markova had the leading part of Katie Willows, Anton Dolin the male lead, and Lady Clara was the second lead. We each had about six or more 'numbers' of our own to say nothing of the minor variations interspersed between a dozen other dancers. One vivid memory is of Alicia and myself desperately clocking up each number on a programme pinned to the wings during that terrifying ordeal at His Majesty's; the other is of Lydia Lopokova coming on stage at the end where we stood panting physically and aching mentally with the efforts involved. 'Freddie,' she cooed in her inimitable gleeful way, 'I absolutely *loved* the first five days!'

There followed isolated performances repeated at Sadler's Wells, the chief joy of which was dancing with Dolin. This was my first experience of working with a communicator, by which I mean a partner who shares in the creation and interpretation of the rôle, responding rather than merely serving as a support like an inanimate lamp-post. Despite this, and the unaccustomed tranquillity and fairness of de Valois's company, something unruly and passionate within me was too long rooted in the Russian jungle to allow me to feel at home.

Meanwhile, back at the Ballet Club, Anthony Tudor had started work on his new ballet: *Lysistrata*, to the music of Prokofiev. I was to have the title rôle; William Chappell designed the beautiful costumes and scenery. Working with Tudor was as different as could be from working with Ashton, whose background and conditioning had been quite otherwise. Tudor was a self-made man, an erstwhile manual worker, which made what he had become all the more remarkable. Obviously possessed of a good brain, a searching mind and a real creative gift, he had come to the ballet fairly late and would never make a real dancer of himself. By nature cool and withdrawn, I found him somehow sticky to work for. Where Freddie would engage one at once with his warmth, his passion and his ready fund of steps and poses, where he was able to demonstrate clearly as he was a graceful mover and had an ineffable sense of line, Anthony at that time lacked the essential equipment to convey his choreographic meaning. He would take one by the hand absent-mindedly and walk about the studio picking abstractedly at the tip of his long, rather elegant nose, gazing inwards until one wondered whether he remembered one was there. After some minutes of this concentrated wandering he would tentatively produce a series of steps, usually complex and rather awkward to perform having, unlike Freddie, never been a long-trained dancer and obviously not aware of the inherent difficulties they contained. After I had done my best he would most likely change the whole *enchaînement* and we would start our peregrinations again, I glad to have jettisoned a technical problem that had filled me with apprehension. Slowly this phase would pass and his whole and very intelligently musical conception take shape. Tudor's was an interesting intellectual approach to the dance, more modern perhaps, certainly more abstract. I always felt that his choreography was restrained within his own physical limits and that he was expressing his own serious ideas in a plastic form, using his dancers as prototypes rather than seeing in any particular one those qualities he wished to develop. The hope of every dancer is to become a choreographer's muse. That unique fusing of the two elements – the creator and the ideal interpreter – was not in those days his aim. Later on, in America, he met with great and deserved success in a country more abstract in its approach to the arts. I can only allow myself to speak of the Tudor of the London days. I thoroughly enjoyed my part as Lysistrata, plenty of drama and lots of *grands jetés*, barely contained by the tiny Ballet Club stage. The audience probably cowered as I leapt, but all that never occurred to me: once I was unleashed I lost all consideration of anything other than the music.

Tudor created another ballet, *Atlanta*, in which I recall being fearfully bored as a goddess, an emotion possibly reciprocated by the public, followed by a parody called *Boxing* in which I was the 'Vamp'. Anthony was by now developing a sense of humour, sly and witty. The last ballet of his I remember dancing was *The Planets* by Gustav Holst. He chose me for Mars. Long will the appalling difficulty of my first movements, from a tangled crouching position on the floor to a rapid leap and turn, stay in my mind. I, with my inconvenient height, was in no position to cavil at anything, added to which Rambert's attachment to dancers better suited to her small theatre was by now becoming painfully obvious. When later Ninette de Valois added *The Planets* to her repertory at the Wells I was assuaged by Peggy van Praagh, one of her most gifted soloists, ringing me up to remonstrate: 'Diana, it just isn't possible to begin like that in "Mars"'! 'Oh yes, alas,' I said, 'it is, but so *only just* that one is terrified at every performance.' Cold comfort.

At home Mummy's musical Sundays were gaining in substance and interest. Her old Vienna colleague Artur Schnabel and his wife, would lunch or dine and Griselda and I would be submitted to long and tedious lectures on 'Active Fatalism' in a strong Austrian accent. Nor did he want one to intercede. Turning a basilisk eye, he would pulverise his victims to cowed silence. I took a long and wearisome walk with him after lunch one day and felt I had plumbed the depths of didactic diatribe, however wonderful a pianist he might have been.

Feeling increasingly unloved, unheralded and certainly unsung, I thought it might be a good idea to take singing lessons to add another string to my bow. I enlisted with an Italian lady long-established in London. All I recall is my lack of a real voice and her odd smell. She was circa sixty, stout and parcelled rather than dressed, always in the same vaguely black outfit plus hat (indoors). The flat was dark, cluttered and unaired and she matched all three factors, enhancing them with her dark-yellow face, her beads and her gamey breath. Every time she moved to correct me or touch me the odd odour augmented as though stirred by some invisible spoon, striking me as something very ancient, very sinister and secret, like the hovering vapours of some unholy sacrament. After a few lessons, I fled for ever into Baker Street and there cannoned into the divine Tamara Karsavina – my beloved Madame Ta-Ta. All the woebegone efforts to expand my marketability were suddenly submerged in a wave of nostalgia at the sight of that most aristocratic angel of all great dancers.

As I greeted her in the street that day, probably near tears, she must at once have sensed my wretchedness. 'Darlink Diana,' she said, looking me straight in the eyes with her own great black ones, 'you cannot make career *alone*. You must know that.' And kissing me, she walked off. The buses rolled by. I would soon have to find one to take me away for ever from that foetid flat and my own wobbly warblings and reflect upon what she'd said. Such advice taken from anyone but Madame Ta-Ta could have been dismissed as loosely immoral, but by someone whose distinction was well established from early days in St Petersburg and the dignity with which she had conducted her own marriage and her whole life, it would not have been lightly said. I felt more than ever dislodged and unanchored. My mother's rigid code, the golden prison of Mulberry House, my own passionate nature, all combined to terrify me when it came to the inescapable demands of sex; cowardice complicated by ignorance constituted a contraceptive as effective as an iron chastity belt for many romantic girls in the Thirties and I was the archetype. I, who was as Madame Ta-Ta hinted in dire need of 'protection', had already panicked and refused three of the most powerful men in the theatre and I wasn't yet twenty. What hope lay there in the future for such a foolish virgin?

My failure to become England's most promising mezzo decently buried, I continued at the Ballet Club, was painted in *Sylphide* by a leading RA, and spent the whole of one day addressing envelopes from my mother's social list in the Ballet Club for Agnes de Mille's coming recital, her London début. At that time Ruth Draper, the famous *diseuse*, was giving one of her inimitable solo performances and came to dine at Mulberry House. She filled me with a mixture of delight and alarm. Together with her younger compatriot Aggie, they both shared seriousness of purpose allied to an enviable self-assurance. I felt sure that Ruth Draper had never entertained any doubts as to the soundness of what she created and presented, none of that debilitating diffidence that so often is the result of the endemic criticism and latent sarcasm inherent in all English education. Goodness knows, Ruth Draper's tremendous success later proved her self-faith. But Agnes, hardly launched in her career, revealed the same unshakeable confidence in what she was doing, was elated by the prospect of demonstrating her creative potential, with no thought of the limitations imposed by never having been properly trained in any field of the dance. Both she and Ruth Draper came from a country that encourages rather than carps and were creators as well as performers; theirs were both the root and the flower. Agnes de Mille's development into the greatest and most innovative of choreographers of the American musical – *Oklahoma*, *Carousel*, *Brigadoon* et al. – was testimony to the rightness of her unwavering faith in herself.

As I looked across the dinner table at Ruth Draper, bright, black eyes bird-like head, exuding warmth, talking with ease and volubility, I was reminded of Aggie preparing for the coming recital, tossing back her head, gazing down her fine aquiline nose, declaring 'Diana, do you know *what* music I'm taking for my eighteenth-century dance? The minuet from Mozart's *Jupiter* Symphony, no less!' followed by one of Aggie's honks of laughter, delighted with her acknowledged piracy and not the least abashed. Oh covetable quality! For I knew that had I the courage or the creative gift, this was one line I might consider taking. I was already becoming known for the variety of rôles I could cover; it might indeed be an evolution from my present impasse. But there was always that fear of the cold, derogatory voice that had so often sounded in my ears at home, at school, at class, till it rang like some tintinnabulation inside my head and inhibited me. A passionate loner, I lacked that extra inner impulse to explore fearlessly, nor did anyone else offer the incitement that might have emboldened me. The phantom of failure always lurked uncomfortably near and I knew I had no safety net. How right Karsavina had been – even a loner needs some sort of indefinable element in which to develop, rather as the salt in the sea provides a positive buoyancy for the swimmer, else the struggle will end in drowning.

So the year ticked on and I ticked over. I was asked to do some modelling for Fortnum & Mason which tickled me immensely but hardly cleared the foggy future. Then, one never to be forgotten day, Rambert disclosed that Balanchine was starting a company of his own in Paris, had engaged some of the Russian dancers still waiting for the resurrection of the Diaghilev ballets which so far had been only tentatively got together by de Basil. Balanchine would open first in Paris and then come to London. In order to do so he would have to please Equity by employing two English soloists and two members of the *corps de ballet*. To my joyful disbelief she suggested myself and Prudence Hyman (a close friend since childhood and a lovely dancer), together with two excellent pupils, Betty Cuff and Betty Schooling. The prospect of working with Balanchine himself, at a moment of such empty darkness, was as if the sun had blazed out from behind impenetrable clouds. However much I might have suffered from Rambert's ceaseless acerbity, it was thanks to her close association with Diaghilev that I had entered the ballet world through the Russian door and was to continue working my way through that perilous jungle all my chequered career; thanks to her that Diaghilev had engaged me at fourteen, thus giving me the chance to see one of Balanchine's great ballets *Apollon musagète*, to recognise so early the extraordinary clarity and purity of line perfectly translated by Lifar, Doubrovska, Nikitina and Danilova. There was not a movement that was extraneous, no fuss, no trappings to fudge the basic idea, simply his intention to interpret Stravinsky's music as faithfully as he could.

At that tender age I doubt I fully realised what a unique pairing of minds *Apollon* presented, but I do remember a sort of excitement, a recognition of choreography shorn of thirty-two *fouettés* and all the other ballet baggage that treated the ballerina as a kind of piano stool, small and round and eternally spinning. Of course Fokine, Diaghilev's first choreographer, had already liberated dancers from the statutory technical prowess endemic in what we called the 'oldy-poldy' horrors of the big set pieces of *Esmeralda* or the three-act *Swan Lake* school, and introduced his particular brand of romantic lyricism in *Sylphides*, *Carnaval*, *Spectre de la rose*, etc., so there did exist a bridge between those ancient crustaceans so disliked by Diaghilev and the spare and lovely bones of the young Balanchine's creations.

Working with Massine had been very rewarding, he was always well-prepared, extremely musical and easy to follow, changing little, using one in a very plastic way with a sure and practised hand. His choreography was basically romantic, large-scale, somewhat Brahms tinged with the Rockettes at its least worthy, wonderfully expressive and danceable at its best – totally other than Balanchine's work which was finer-tuned and more private. Massine, in his later works for the de Basil company, was using bigger and bigger canvases, symphonic music, exploiting the exciting techniques of the so-called 'baby ballerinas' Toumanova, Baronova and Riabouchinska. When one looks back across the years to this epoch of the Thirties and compares those last two Diaghilev choreographers, one sees that Massine's tradition lies in a direct descent from the *Esmeralda*s and the *Corsaire*s, whereas Balanchine marked the beginnings of a completely new vision of the dancer. He was the future, Massine was the final flower of the past.

That, I imagine, was what had caused Balanchine's breakaway from any plans of de Basil's. His great good fortune lay in the fact that Edward James was looking for a framework in which to show off his wife Tilly Losch – and perhaps inject a little life into their failing marriage – and was therefore the catalyst that brought about 'Les Ballets 1933'.

When the time came for Prudence Hyman and myself to travel to join the company in Paris, the start was ominous. Pru and I had no sooner arrived in Calais than we were summarily stopped by an official who, looking with distaste at the entry on our passports: 'dancer and actress', demanded to see our *permis de travail*. These being not forthcoming, for the simple reason that nobody had thought of furnishing us with them, he refused to let us go one foot further for fear of polluting France as illegal immigrants of indeterminate moral status. Furious, I asked for the telephone, rang Edward at the Prince de Galles in Paris and luckily found him, whereupon he apologised, saying he would send someone down by early morning next day. Pru and I had a marvellous dinner in the Hôtel Terminus famed for its *pommes de terre soufflées*, and thus assuaged, climbed into bed (very dingy and a bit suspect) and slept like logs. Next day, permits having arrived, we went on to Paris where we would be staying with Guggan. The following morning, together with Betty Cuff and Elizabeth Schooling, we presented ourselves with apprehension to Balanchine, holed up in a very small studio with a linoleum floor, no ventilation and the thermometer mounting towards ninety degrees Fahrenheit outside (inside 110). We were received coolly, George giving us all four a sharp look of appraisal with that ornithological head of his. Trim and neat, he was dressed like Massine in black alpaca trousers and a white shirt, but there the similarity ended. No banked fires, no blazing eyes – a very cool face, highly intelligent air, aquiline nose, so that the whole head resembled two profiles neatly stuck together.

He swept the whole company to the *barre* and proceeded to conduct from the upright piano on which he played wonderful improvisations of jazz, operatic tunes and snatches of whatever fitted the rhythms in a marvellous medley. It soon became cruelly obvious that he was all set to kill the newcomers, to grind them into the dust if need be. Not twelve *battements* on each side, but fifty, and the same number with every other technical exercise. We came to a slow and steady boil, agonisingly determined to keep the Union Jack flying. After that punishing *barre* followed complicated *enchaînements*, with George pounding away and we sweating from every pore. At last, after two hours, we were freed and could snatch a look at our colleagues. More of the same tug-o'-war ensued till, at the end of that nightmare week, Balanchine suddenly smiled and we knew we'd been accepted.

Balanchine had brought with him the lovely Tamara Toumanova, all of thirteen, or was it fifteen? Anyway I do remember celebrating her fifteenth birthday repeatedly over the years which makes it difficult to be more precise. What was not to be disputed was that she was very young, very beautiful and had that marvellous rock-hard technique that Preobrajenska gave her and Irina Baronova. Toumanova had a beautiful Georgian face atop a rather plump body. Poor Irina, her mother would wrap her in rubber under her practice clothes, which entailed having to stand her in an enamel basin when she stripped at the end of class, the sweat pouring off her in floods. She was sweet and warm-hearted, and we soon became friends. With Roman Jasinski as principal male dancer and a little padding from the vast pool of dancers to be found in the various Paris studios, Balanchine had by now a small but strong company which suited his needs. For me it was a total innovation to discover that he had no use for the old style *corps de ballet*; evidently to him it simply represented a dreary frieze serving to fill in blank spaces, or to dress the stage while permitting the soloists to catch their wind in the wings.

Its significance for Edward James, with all his taste, his means, his real vision for painting, was that it represented an ideal moment to try and form a company in the image of Diaghilev, full of fresh productions in which great composers and designers created each ballet as a composite whole. I had known him slightly when I understudied Tilly as the Nun in *The Miracle*, and Tilly of course I knew well. Naughty, mischievous Tilly, with her huge ice-blue eyes and her beautiful erotic arms and hands; Tilly who ran circles round the fresh-faced, eternally boyish Edward; Tilly who was the despair of Balanchine who found his inspiration totally blocked when it came to devising a ballet for her; Tilly who finally triumphed in *Anna-Anna* and *Errante*.

Came the day when we moved out of the Black Hole of Calcutta and were transferred to the rehearsal room above the stage at the Théâtre des Champs-Elysées and began to be allotted rôles. Tilly was there, looking a trifle out of place; we must have appeared if not formidable, certainly a little alien, for all of us were in our teens, all highly trained technically, whereas this was very probably the first time Tilly had had to compete with such a company. Trained only in the Central European school of dancing, she had carved herself her own special and very successful niche in Cochran revues. A beautiful mover, she had only her own brand of sensuality, together with particularly expressive hands, upon which to rely and so was not exactly equipped to face such a band of young and strong dancers.

In the end the Tilly problem was more than successfully solved in *Anna-Anna*, a typically Berlin Thirties production concocted by Kurt Weill and Bertold Brecht on the Seven Deadly Sins, which most of us loathed because any left-over dancers (like yesterday's cold meat) were garnered to pull on huge, hooded cloaks and rush on, distractedly brandishing poles, exuding either one of the sins or the punishment thereof. Tamara Sidorenko and I never did find out what we were doing. Pavel Tchelitchev and Balanchine solved yet another Tilly problem by means of hanging four kilometres of white silk as a backdrop combined with some very ingenious lighting, and putting Tilly into a marvellous dress of emerald-green satin with a ten-foot train. It was our task to gather it up in the wings and let it fly after her, as she ran on to the stage and up and down and round about looking suitably bewildered, to the music of the *Wanderer* Fantasy (Schubert–Liszt) in *Errante*.

Now we had at last got into the theatre, the very Théâtre des

Champs Elysées. The rehearsals were strangely spasmodic, sometimes in the afternoon, sometimes at night. As one was never sure what was going to be rehearsed, one simply turned up – and anyway to watch Balanchine at work was no time wasted. I remember one rehearsal in the upstairs room to which Josephine Baker came, almost unrecognisable with clothes on and no bananas.

Gradually the five ballets took shape: *Mozartiana*, *Songes*, *Les sept péches capitaux*, *Fastes*, *Errante*, to which George suddenly added a sixth: *The Waltzes of Beethoven*, for which a rich and not very gifted South American called Emilio Terry designed a dotty décor and hideous costumes representing the four elements: Earth, Air, Fire and Water. I was Earth, in a deplorable sort of chiton in Bovril-coloured chiffon (Old Mother Manure, I called myself). Standing dismally for hours while the magnificent Karinska, the great Russian dressmaker, adrip with amethysts, would drape and redrape, muttering the while, somewhat hampered by a mouthful of pins: '*Ach, Boje moi! Kak oojasnia.*' Which, meaning 'Oh my God, how awful', did nothing to cheer me on my way. On the opening night of *The Waltzes of Beethoven*, trembling with nerves, we were still awaiting the head-dresses backstage, the audience clapping with impatience, and panic all round. At last Karinska arrived in a flurry in a taxi. Distributing the head-dresses at top speed, she handed me a monstrous sort of cairn at least two foot high, evidently made of plaster and mud. I put it on my head, burst into tears and appealed to George. Mine was the opening solo and I was to be found as the curtain rose reclining on something or other (a plaster couch I think, extremely uncomfortable) from which I had to spring into the fourth position *en pointes*, flinging the top half of my body back as far as it would go (Balanchine had discovered that I had a double-jointed back). What was to happen to this monument on my head was anybody's guess and very obviously *my* funeral. Fortunately, George lifted the thing off, wiped my tears, gave me a kiss and a gentle push: 'Go on, go on, Dianochka' and I ran, knees knocking, to take up my lonely position on stage and try not to listen to the mounting anger or the derisive applause the other side of the curtain. Despite lovely solos for myself, for Prudence as Air, Sidorenko as Fire and Ouchkova as Water, the ballet – written mainly for Tilly (Daphne) and Jasinski (Apollo) – did not set the theatre alight and was fortunately dropped. No one really minded, for the difficulty of turning Daphne into a laurel bush proved insurmountable. I remember we four elements messing about with green branches made of paper leaves in a pathetic attempt to attach them to Tilly, fondly hoping that the metamorphosis from nymph to shrub had really taken place. Neither the look of wistful wonder nor much rolling of those ice-blue eyes by Tilly, served to convince the very chic audience that she did not look like a surburban hedge. The sorry affair died an unregrettable death after a couple more performances. Farewell Mother Manure! I had enjoyed my solo.

Now that we had finally left the squalid studio and got on to the stage and into our dressing-rooms at the Champs-Elysées, the real excitement had begun. At last we met the various collaborators that Boris Kochno (Diaghilev's renowned secretary), Balanchine and finally Edward James, had brought together: André Derain (one of the 'Fauves') with his enormous, cask-like belly and his jolly bulging eyes; Bébé Bérard the painter, all mince and wince (he was perpetually having toy rages and being offended): 'Pavlik' Tchelitchev with his beautiful, haggard, romantic face; 'Nika' Nabokov the composer, a marvellous Russian with a mane of dark-blond hair and witty blue eyes. These latter two would take me out all over Paris on various purposeless and very Russian outings to see friends who were usually absent, or to chatter with American expatriates and have tea. Tchelitchev would read my hand: 'Dianochka, you have palm of very old lady!' And there were the composers Henri Sauguet, always smiling and pleasant, and Darius Milhaud, a big lemon-coloured face and dreamy black eyes, all of them walking up and down the stalls or watching their ballets, discussing changes and adjustments with Balanchine. I was bewitched, astounded to find myself part of this illustrious gathering and to realise how privileged I was to belong to this moment of creation. Not one stale, taken-out-of-the-cupboard-and-dusted-over ballet. All fresh or rarely heard music, fresh designs and fresh ideas. It is an earnest of Kochno's grip, as well as Balanchine's genius, that any of it came to fruition. True, there were moments when one felt a certain lack of roots, of the security that the well-tried ballets gave one, a sensation of giddiness at the extent of Balanchine's vision. And the newness of it all – so many conceptions, so many precarious births, so much peril taken quite calmly. Nor can I recall one angry impatient word from George as he took us through the steps, the *enchaînements*, the solos, *pas de deux*, adjusting, readjusting here and there. One day, much later, walking together in London he said: 'You know, to my mind, ballets should be only topical – disposable – once they have lasted a season, they should be thrown away.' I expostulated, finding the idea a little troubling – a step too far.

After Paris, with its *assistance très élégante*, we arrived in London to perform at that stiff little theatre, the Savoy. By then I was dancing the *Demi-monde* in *Les Songes* and the blue *Saltateur* in *Fastes*, while Edward, fearful of the coming competition from the company de Basil and Massine had assembled to perform at the Alhambra, to say nothing of a projected appearance of Serge Lifar at the Aldwych, nobbled the latter to join us instead, giving a number of separate performances to be inserted on various nights. Suddenly London was awash with ballet companies. Lifar brought with him Nikitina, Doubrovska, Slavinsky and a few other leading members of the defunct Diaghilev company. On their first performance at the Savoy, Serge raised the fury of both audience and critics by performing *L'après-midi d'un faune* in solitary grandeur, dispensing with the lovely frieze of nymphs. Edward reproached him: they had a resounding row and came to blows in the foyer of the Savoy Hotel, after which pleasant exchange he, Serge, relented sufficiently to allow the Chief Nymph, a rôle which I had learnt from Woizikovsky, and accepted me. All afternoon I hung anxiously about the theatre hoping for a rehearsal, finally going to Lifar's dressing-room in frightened desperation. No rehearsals, no time, just do the part, entering the stage from the OP side *there*, jabbing at the score. Nasty fellow! So I went on, trembling. Unfortunately

Serge had not been to class since Diaghilev's death some four years before and had developed a fine wobble in the very difficult parallel stance on *demi-pointe* in which idiom the whole choreography is written. Facing him, nose to nostril, while he yawed from side to side, I was forced to fix my eyes on the arch of the proscenium to keep my own balance and not look at the malicious glare from those eyes moving from east to west like the hand on a metronome. I have never enjoyed a performance less. Nor did it improve during the two later ones. Sad to get such an opportunity and to be so disillusioned. Lifar had gone to seed and was evidently proud of it.

I have zigzagged from London to Paris to London and back, because seen down the wrong end of a telescope of more than fifty-five years, scattered memories weld the two seasons together as the flesh of immediate experience falls away and the bone structure remains. Paris had offered me a heady few weeks watching the evolution of so many recently conceived ideas as they took form and put on substance; being instructed in new rôles by Balanchine, seeing the coming together of composer, designer, librettist and choreographer all creating from scratch. *Mozartiana* alone used an old score (Mozart excerpts arranged by Tchaikovsky) and the music for *Les Valses de Beethoven* was odds and ends of Beethoven orchestrated by Nabokov, while even though Schubert was used for *Errante*, none the less it was again a pastiche including the *Wanderer* Fantasy put together by Koechlin.

The impression I carried away with me was one of a season of great distinction, more like an exhibition of motion than the run-of-the-mill ballet seasons with their draconian fifteen hours daily of work, class, rehearsal and eight performances a week. Here, we danced on specific nights only, the repertoire was slight. Again, Balanchine always worked with a loose hand, no shouting, no commands, simply showing the steps, correcting, with a precision and a musical perception that was the joy of any dancer who has suffered the struggle with intractable arrangements that cut across phrases and melodies, twisting one's instincts and one's mind in the process.

Here was a logical and utterly musical mind. After all, Balanchine had first studied music in Russia and it showed in everything he created. He used the human body as a musical instrument, preferring the female dancer to the male, and above all the tall dancer who interpreted his long lines. One has only to recall Doubrovska in *Fils prodigue* – where he pulled her lovely legs like so much soft toffee – to recognise the innovations that he, supported by Diaghilev, introduced and one only has to wonder in what iconoclastic form the great Diaghilev would have continued his unique company had he not died comparatively young, and creative ballet in the big companies of those days mark time. Echoes of his famous dictum '*Étonne-moi*' spring to mind. Which brings me to the final curtain of the London scene. Jasinski had injured his foot, so to my delight Balanchine himself danced with me in the *Demi-monde* sequence of *Les Songes*. It was there in the backstage dock that Derain, while I was waiting to go on, whipped out his fountain pen and on a blank page in his Savoy Theatre souvenir programme made a wild drawing of my head, the unruly ink running all down my cheeks, and signed it for me;

> *À Diana. A. Derain*
> *À mademoiselle Diana en toute amitié*
> *A. Derain. Souvenir*
> *13 Juillet 1933*

Another less than fond memory of the Savoy, where most of the dressing-rooms, being out of earshot of both stage and orchestra, left one isolated and insecure, occurred when I was happily slacking. Suddenly Balanchine burst in shouting, 'Diana, the *Saltateurs*.' He shovelled me into my tights while I smeared my face with blue; fastening my hip-belt, I tore out and down the stairs to hear to my horror what I thought was two bars left before my entrance from upstage OP corner. Panting, I dashed across behind the backcloth and erupted on-stage, only to find in my frantic haste I had come on about two bars early and all but collided with my opposite number, Tamara

Sidorenko as the other *Saltateur* (all-over peach). With a twist in mid-stage, we managed to avoid a head-on crash, but I shook with anguish until I could get off-stage and apologise both to George and Tamara. . . . One of the classical nightmares of all stage people is to miss an entrance and I had all but done so. I loathed the Savoy Theatre even more after that.

The final performance sadly over, we had a party in one of those modest Bloomsbury hotels where dancers always stayed, partly because they were inexpensive and cosy and partly because they turned a blind eye on those strange combinations and permutations that comprise the looser terms of 'marriage' according to the Russian code.

Balanchine took me for a walk round and round Russell Square afterwards in the warm July night. 'Dianochkha,' he said, 'today a man came to see me, an American man, and said he could offer me a school and company if I go to America – would you please come?' Longing to say yes, but young and frightened at such a great leap into what might be the dark, this idiotic English virgin again said no. Though we must have circled that square a dozen times, even though Balanchine pleaded and I was torn in two, my fear and my cowardice won and sadly we returned to the hotel and said a loving goodbye.

History knows the rest: the American was Lincoln Kirstein and Balanchine, deservedly, never looked back.

Edward James, who had been practically bankrupted, retired to West Dean to lick his wounds, twice inflicted – for Tilly was not going to be reconciled to their marriage and the ballet company he had backed to give her a show-case was dissolved, leaving him with sorry ghosts in the form of a few costumes and a little inert décor. Hoping, I suppose, that it might somehow be salvaged, requickened, and wanting to keep us away from Balanchine, he 'kidnapped' the two Sidorenkos, Tchinarova, Leslie, two mammas and I think Ismailova and Matlinsky, Prudence Hyman and myself, putting us all up at West Dean for a week of luxurious comfort. We put on those costumes he'd been able to salvage and posed ineffectually on the lawns.

Every morning Edward and I watched the total bafflement of the

Russians at the sight of the row of chafing dishes on the sideboard at breakfast. Prudence and I took to getting up early and going for a walk through the lovely estate before that orgy of an irresistible meal.

At lunch, Edward and I would compete with each other in producing the greatest amount of French past-tense subjunctives. Poor Edward – always butterflying towards a new idea and rarely getting to the heart of anything. Dear Edward – always to be betrayed, to be imposed upon. Had he not been so rich, might he not have got further in one or other of the specific arts he embraced? Would he perhaps have written his poetry more profoundly, been content running a picture gallery in London or Paris, had that been his only hope of eating a square meal? Or was it a combination of his wealth and his own lack of profound talent that led him from venture to venture – allied to a certain lightweight approach to life that made him the perfect prey of the charlatan?

I recall being rung up by his lawyers asking me (of all people) whether I could in any way help protect him from 'those Russians' – in this case Lifar's administrators – who were milking him dry, as 'the family' (so-called) were beginning to worry about it. As I was legally under age then, I said there was little I myself could do but warn Edward, who mightn't listen.

So the week passed and Edward having finally resigned all dreams, we left the sybaris of West Dean. Some dancers returned to de Basil, I went into a play. Edward was left with the dissolution of his marriage and the heel-taps of Les Ballets 1933, which would never have come to life without his money and his enthusiasm. I do hope he felt it was well spent.

For myself, the experience of those months with Balanchine was inestimable. It had been a real harvest, sustaining me in so many ways, increasing my voracious appetite for all that is necessary to the ballet: painting, design and music; expanding also my original vision of my profession, shrivelled during the harsh discipline of training. Despite the feeling of a tide withdrawing yet again, leaving me on an unmapped shore, I could store in my heart and mind such treasures as I would never forfeit, upon which I could always draw.

6

Redeemed from Bondage

*I*was young then, with enviable powers of recuperation. When Les Ballets 1933 folded I went off on holiday with my family, driving through Europe to Yugoslavia. Simply because Mama told Griselda and me that we wouldn't enter the beauty competition for the title of 'Miss Dubrovnik' out of typical English inhibition and cowardice, we did exactly that, I winning first prize and Griselda second. From there we went on to Venice.

Everyone who is seeing Venice for the first time should arrive by boat, as we did coming up the Illyrian coast. Venice: together with the Taj Mahal the visual cliché that one has seen since childhood decorating everything from boxes of noodles to lavatory walls. I was terrified of being disappointed, could not believe that the real, the tangible, could offer as much as Canaletto or Longhi depicted. Coming upon it from the sea both diminished and enhanced it. As we leant on the rail of the boat the long-familiar vision floated into view, at once evanescent and tangible, breath-stopping in its beauty. Distanced from it, you perceived the peerless whole in one wonderful shock; the impact was absolute and unforgettable.

And so back to London and the drill of daily classes without which no dancer can hope to keep up her technique, far less improve, in an art form whose struggle for perfection is elusive as the horizon. The de

Basil Company, whose success had contributed to the minor misfortunes of Balanchine's venture, was only now drawing to the close of its flourishing season at the Alhambra, and I was invited to their farewell supper, again held in another of those Bloomsbury hotels where vague discrepancies in conjugal habits were not censured. Sitting next to Léonide Massine would have been both a compliment and a pleasure had it not once more meant a challenge to my eternal cowardice. 'Dininka, now that company is big success, please join. Soon we go to America. I have part for you in new ballet I am doing now. Tchaikovsky Fifth Symphony. First movement will be you.' And those burning black eyes turned their full power on me as he grabbed my hand under the table. I tried to return his gaze, flustered, stuttered and with beating heart caught the murderous eye of his 'wife' on the other side (she who had once advanced on me with a waggling revolver in our dressing-room during *The Miracle*). Wretched creature that I was, I begged for time to consider the marvellous offer. As far as my untutored heart could feel through the cladding of my conventional upbringing I was falling in love with him. Bloomsbury, it would seem, was always to be my *champs de bataille*, only this time, some four months later, I was not taken round Russell Square in an attempt to persuade me; Massine, with hand deployed under the table and glowing eyes above, sought to seduce me. Maybe, had he been able to use his tactics without the malevolent searchlight of his 'wife's' eye on his other side, I might have succumbed to his proposition. However, the quantum leap from iron-clad virginity to a *ménage à trois* meant an acrobatic feat for which I still lacked nerve – so again I lost an opening, closing the door myself, craven ninny.

Back to the *barre* and the hazards of dodging Mim's still steadily aimed verbal coconuts. One day Sir Nigel Playfair, whom I had not seen since he gave the young dancers their début season three or more years before, visited the class. I gathered that he was putting on a play with music and dancing at the Saville Theatre, based on the character of Beau Brummel, the arbiter of fashion during the Regency at Brighton, and to set the dances had engaged Andrée Howard, one of Rambert's most gifted choreographers. He had just emerged from the little theatre (the Ballet Club) adjoining the dance studio, looking extremely glum. It appeared the girl he had chosen as young lead was proving at rehearsal in his theatre to be a very poor actress and it had just been proved that she was also thoroughly deficient as a dancer. Poor Andrée had been struggling with her under the misapprehension that she could act, Playfair suffering the same illusion imagining that she could dance. The dreadful denouement had just befallen. Suddenly he espied me and asked Rambert why she hadn't thought of suggesting me. Rambert looked slightly embarrassed, but said nothing. 'Diana,' said Nigel, 'run up to me from the far side of the room and ask me how I am.' I did so. 'Now approach me and tell me something – anything you like that's dramatic.' I obeyed. 'Good girl, you've got the part. I know how you dance anyway, so that's that. Come to the Saville Theatre this afternoon, you've only got ten days to learn the words and the dances.'

I worked non-stop for those ten days, shuttling from rehearsal room to studio, to theatre, losing a stone in weight and loving every minute of it. It was a pretty awful play, alas. Nigel Playfair's last production; looking back I cannot perceive that he had ever thought – he with his wit and humour and exquisite taste – this boring vehicle for an actor-singer could be anything other than dismally dowdy.

Beau Brummel – or 'Bow-legs Brummel' as I called it for the eponymous hero had the tenor's obnoxious habit of bending and flexing his knees before a high note as though he were facilitating some invisible acrobatic feat – ground to a rusty halt by the end of January of the new year, 1934. I had got nice reviews, more experience, a few weeks' pay and a short tour to try and recoup poor Playfair's financial losses, but it again led nowhere special and I returned from the gritty glamour of wintry Birmingham digs to the comfort of Mulberry House, very conscious of my good fortune in having such a home. The gap between myself and my siblings was growing ever more perceptibly, for in those far-off days I was as remote from being the self-analyst I was to become as the sun from the moon. It is only looking back through that distorting mirror of the memory that I realise how unaware of anything faintly practical or factual I even attempted to be; all part and parcel of the cowardice that underlay my romantic nature. The more the hazards and harshness of the way forward were daily and hourly presented to me the more obdurately I wrapped myself round with the tatters of my illusions, refusing to accept the rational or the quotidian, the necessity to plan, to succumb to darling Madame Ta-Ta's counsel whenever the opportunity presented itself, which of course it increasingly did.

I was asked to do a film test with Maurice Evans (later to become the greatest Shakespearian actor in the States), a test of such absurd banality that he and I, with the arrogance and insouciance of youth, made wicked fun of it from beginning to end. However, the very next day I put all my energy and burgeoning dramatic talent into the offer Ashley Dukes, Rambert's playwright husband, had made me, that of the rôle of Tonya in the Russian author Kataev's wicked parody of the newest Soviet social experiment *Squaring the Circle*, all about two couples registering to live together, the whole idiot scheme ending in total disaster.

By this time the Ballet Club had also become the Mercury Theatre under Ashley's auspices. A benevolent, highly intelligent and gifted man, he transformed that little building into a place of gladness, of zealous work, unrecognisable for me as that same stage upon which I mostly danced with heavy heart if not, I hope, with leaden feet. At the same time Anthony Tudor engaged me to dance the part of the 'Paramour' to his close friend Hugh Laing's rôle as my partner in the Oxford University Dramatic Society (OUDS) production of Marlowe's *Faustus*, so those whole months were busy and rich ones, going up to Oxford for one lot of rehearsals, coming down to London for rehearsals of *Squaring the Circle*, followed by Oxford performances. I enjoyed a positively Zuleika Dobson time there, escorted everywhere by a possé of most chivalrous and amusing undergraduates, ending with one entire night spent revelling with at least two breakfasts to usher in the dawn, helping perhaps to break down the grim ardour with which I then pursued my lonely career. Fortunately the rôle of the paramour was hardly exacting technically, simply requiring a good deal of undulation of the hips and eyes and such alluring gestures of the arms as I suppose had gained me my coterie of devoted young men. Never had I worked so little for so much delighted gain; never again, either, was I to feel the ugly duckling that both Rambert and my mother had induced me to believe I was.

Squaring the Circle opened and was an immediate success. For me it was miraculous not to come off-stage panting and with bloodied feet, to say nothing of the opportunity of playing comedy. Tall and classic of looks I was constantly cast as a goddess or some other equally humourless character and I had been aching to make people laugh the way Freddie and I had in the early days of the burgeoning Ballet Club cheering up the others with our parodies of a *pas de deux*: Fred as Madame P (Pavlova) in my point shoes and I as his male partner. Alicia Markova, having joined us by then, lent her exquisite dancing to enhance the Club in every way. Ninette de Valois had put on a very amusing ballet to the Manet picture of the *Bar aux Folies Bergère*, in which Markova was delightfully witty as the chief courtesan. I had begged de Valois to let me play one of the accompanying tarts and had had enormous fun improvising and 'feeding' Alicia in a duo which went down very well with the audience.

During the run of the ill-fated *Beau Brummel* I had been supping at the Savoy Grill with one of my young men when the head waiter told me that Alexander Korda, the Hungarian film producer who had been fixing me with a steady glare all evening, had suggested I get in touch with him. Airily, I had accepted the compliment and done nothing at all. However, once poor old 'Bow-legs' had died a whimpering death, the OUDS *Faustus* had run its course as well as *Squaring the Circle*, I conveniently remembered the message I had treated so cavalierly, duly got in touch and was told to go down to Elstree to meet the Great Cinema Mogul. He was busy on the set of some film or other, seemed very polite and pleased, drove me back to London and suggested I come down again to see him and seriously discuss certain projects. I already had a film test to do at some other studios at Teddington two days later, so he asked me to come towards late afternoon the day following that.

It proved a lovely May day and I put on my best silk tunic and skirt and my most becoming hat, and full of excited anticipation took the train to Elstree once more. My elation was somewhat daunted as I was told to wait in one of those dreadful cinematic No Man's Lands, the wings of some huge set rising Piranesi-like into the vast height of the studio, composed of gantries, ropes, galleries, all lost in an inspissate gloom. I sat there isolated, feeling increasingly like an old boot washed up by the tide, while from the far side of the great black wall emanated either unintelligible yells and cries or else a silence as in a country of deaf mutes. Obviously the whole artificial business of 'shooting' was in operation.

For two nerve-racking hours I sat there, every now and then receiving little apologies from the sanctum sanctorum in the manner of stale crumbs thrown to an importunate and bothersome bird, till at last – the day's work ended – Korda emerged explaining that it had been a 'difficult take' and led me up some stairs to a room where a group of secretaries sat. Dismissing them for the day, he opened the side door into his private office. I heard a click behind me as he locked it, turned and seized me with a clumsy haste that not only knocked my breath away, but also my best hat. Had I had more experience, had I not been a nineteenth-century heroine, I might have been able to laugh. As it was, all I could do was struggle like a hooked hake, nauseated with shock and disgust. When I extricated myself from his half-Nelson I found the breath to expostulate at his crudeness and lack of grace. 'My dear child,' he replied, 'I'm an old man; I haven't time to waste like you have. What did you expect?' Indeed what did this silly simpleton expect, given the circumstances? I picked up my hat angrily, he unlocked the door; clutching the torn neck of my best tunic, I bolted down the stairs and howled all the way to the station. Merle Oberon got the rôle: Anne Boleyn in *The Private Lives of Henry the Eighth* with Charles Laughton. QED.

Meanwhile the lovely Griselda, having left school and gone through a couple of years' theatrical training at the Central School of Speech and Drama and having appeared with acclaim in some Sunday night shows, was trying to decide whether she too would care to go on the stage professionally. In due course she had gone to be interviewed by one of the leading actor-managers, Leon M. Lion. When she came home and I asked her the outcome she looked dispiritedly at me. 'All he said when I gave him my name was "Are you any relation to Diana Gould?" When I told him I was your sister, he said "She's the funniest thing I've seen on the stage for years. I saw her dance in the *Bar aux Folies Bergère*; tell her to come and see me." ' This time I didn't let the invitation cool. Leon M. Lion was a very nice and kindly man. However, he confessed he had nothing suitable, was putting on a play by Arnold Ridley (of *The Ghost Train* fame) called *Headlines* and the only uncast role was that of the headmaster's young daughter, hardly my type. Boldly I grabbed at it, begging him to let me try. It was not a very good play, but he had assembled an excellent and distinguished cast. I learned my part of the 'young lead', we opened on tour in Birmingham followed by a few other provincial towns and I was terrible. Thank the Lord it folded at Wimbledon. R.I.P.

Autumn came and some time around the end of October 1934 my mother took me to hear Yehudi Menuhin at a matinée concert in the Albert Hall. We had been, Griselda, Mama and I, to his début recital when he was thirteen and his family had been given a letter of introduction to us by close mutual friends, but had never responded.

So, again, we were transported by his playing, but left without visiting the artists' room, a lacuna in my mother's musical life, to us inexplicable to this day, unless it be explained in terms of Yehudi's mother's ruling of the Menuhin family life, which I was much later to encounter. So destiny delayed Yehudi and me meeting each other by nearly fifteen years.

Soon after, Agnes de Mille gave her long-planned recital, to me a revelation of the triumph of a richly creative mind over the hindrance of an insufficient technique. She exploited every nuance of movement which was hers to command, enhanced every gesture, invested every facial expression with subtle meaning and all with a clarity and confidence enviable to one like myself who, equipped with a strong technique, dramatic gifts and a driving passion, was none the less harnessed by those inhibitions implanted by upbringing and conditioning in a perfect cat's cradle of doubt and apprehension.

Arnold Haskell, the first genuine ballet critic, who had been an ardent follower of the young Rambert dancers and written a small book on us, returned from following the de Basil Company to learn that I had lately been working in what is weirdly called the 'straight' theatre. Some time earlier he had put a full-page of me in the *Tatler* dressed as one of Oliver Messel's ravishing wood-nymphs for *The Miracle* under which he stated: 'Diana Gould, the most musical young dancer the English dance has produced' and thereupon took me to task, accusing me of betraying both his taste and his trust. Quickly realising how unhappy and hampered I was *chez* Rambert, he carried me off to Paris, there to introduce me to the great Mathilda Kschessinskaya, the erstwhile *prima ballerina assoluta* of the pre-Revolution Maryinsky Theatre, the one-time mistress of the young Tsar Nicholas II before his marriage and, until the Russian Revolution, the most powerful woman in St Petersburg.

I was again to stay with the hospitable Guggan, once more to live in my beloved Paris and this time, at least, to be protected and introduced by Arnold. None the less, it was with anguish that I attended that first morning's class. Equipped with two further years' hard work since my first Egorova class, I had gathered as well the further knowledge of the multiple hazards and jealousies, the plots and intrigues with which this highly competitive and over-populated profession abounded; ergo I was more or less back to square one as far as nerves were concerned. The studio was a delight, light and airy on the first floor of an *immeuble* in a street no distance from my grandmother's and presided over by a being whose legend became totally credible the moment you set eyes on her.

Tiny, sparkling with an almost incandescent quality, bubbling with life, full of charm that had nothing deliberate about it, imbued with gaiety, warmth and a kind of tough tenderness, Kschessinskaya was the embodiment of all I needed to give me back the dance as I'd first longed to serve it. It was a lovely lyrical class, full of improvisations to the accompaniment of the first real pianist I'd ever met in a classroom. Madame Wassmund had been a professional pianist before the Revolution had smashed her career and she brought to bear all her classical repertoire, her Chopin, Tchaikovsky, Mozart, Schubert et al., with a passionate intensity to which Kschessinskaya added her choreographic improvisations. I, of course, gloried in it. Here at last was the translation of music into movement in a classroom – not the ghastly ta-ra-ra-toom, ta-ra-ra-toom, ta-ra-ra-toom-te-toom, ta-ra-ra-toom of the average *tapeur de piano* to which one tried hard to dance and not produce physical jerks.

Wassund's gnarled old head, like some hedge animal topped by a crimpy red wig, bent over the keys of the cottage upright as she played her soul and heart away, adoring her precious Mathilda Felixovna, never tiring through the three or four long daily classes, watching Kschessinskaya's demonstrations of adagios or allegros and skilfully matching them to the correct rhythms and tempi of her large repertoire. It was sunlight come into the classroom.

At the end of class I must have passed the test all right, for the parents, who usually in such classes formed a small audience, came up to me and asked wherever I'd learned my strong technique. I gave full credit to Rambert and Cecchetti and walked on air to the restaurant where Arnold gave me lunch, the pair of us bathed in mutual satisfaction and gratitude.

One day at the end of class a tall, handsome elderly man came into the studio to fetch Kschessinskaya. By his long, narrow forehead and beautifully set eyes it was easy to detect him as a Romanov. She introduced him to me, the Grand Duke André, her one-time lover and now her devoted husband, the first cousin of the Tsar and a man so gentle and beloved of his peasants that he and she together had managed to escape from his estates, none the less taking all of two years to reach

the Black Sea and finally board a boat which took them to Venice. All
of this I learnt gradually during that wonderful winter and spring as
both of them adopted me, inviting me to the pretty villa in Auteuil
which the French government had given them and generally showing
me a loving kindness of which I had been mainly starved till then.
'Dianochka,' said Mathilda Felixovna one day after I'd been there
about a month, '*le pauvre Grand-duc est tout seul le mercredi après-midi
quand je dois donner la classe, sois gentile et va prendre le thé avec lui!*' So I
would take the tram to the Villa Molitor, open the gate into the little
private street, cross the tiny garden, be greeted by Monsieur Georges,
the Grand Duke's handsome and devoted ex-batman and valet and
ushered into the pretty drawing-room where my darling 'Lucy' (as I
nicknamed him after the feminine equivalent of his name-date André)
would be sitting waiting for our Russian tea served in tall glasses with
silver holders, cherry jam floating redly in the bottom, accompanied by
little biscuits baked by Madame Georges, the wonderful cook and
drunken wife of dear Monsieur Georges. And how we would chatter
and giggle, he in his fluent Nanny-taught English with its haunting
Russian diphthonged vowels, looking at me with those large, doggy
eyes that held such a touching sweetness and innocence that one
quickly realised he would never have survived without the basic
strength and iron will of his adored Mathilda – 'Mala'.

A more perfectly united couple I have never met. They had adjusted
themselves to the comparative narrowness of their lives as only
Russians of that extraordinary generation could. They seemed to be
made of some magic material that could expand or contract at will
without losing the intrinsic value of the basic elements of which they
were composed. They never complained at the restrictions of their
lives, never talked of the past unless to relate with gales of laughter some
scene they found intolerably comic. The past was not for tears, the
future not for fears, only the present to be lived and savoured to the hilt
and above all to be shared. 'Poussia!' cried Kschessinskaya one day at
luncheon (five courses minimum, all delicious, which I gradually learnt
to worry at as though I'd eaten the lot, hiding bits under the covering of

forks and knives and spoons), 'Poussia, let's tell Diana the story of that cigarette case.' The Grand Duke had just taken out what must have been one of his few remaining valuables, a lovely Fabergé *étui*, made of red and white gold and was putting a piece of tissue over it to let me see the shades of difference in the two metals. She proceeded in her chattering Slav French: 'After two years of making our way down to the Black Sea, sometimes swimming in the rivers – ' Here the Grand Duke interrupted, 'Dianochka, I shall always swear by Garris Tweed.' (Russians always replace the letter H by a G – thus 'Gamlet, Shakespeare tragedy, you know'.) 'I swim, it does not shrink in two years my English suit.' 'Well,' says his wife 'we finally reach Odessa, get on a boat and arrive in Venice where *le Grand-duc* and I had spent so many "honeymoons" in the Hotel Danieli. We are very hungry and together with the *Grand-duc* Gabriel and his wife, who had joined us in our escape, go straight to the restaurant. We wait. And wait. And no waiter comes near us. Suddenly I wake up and look at ourselves. I am dressed in a blue velvet dress covered with' (here an expressive gesture of her tiny hands down her body) 'large stains. The Princess Gabriel looked much the same fright and whatever the Grand Duke may say about his Garris tweed it had not been pressed for two years. "Poussia!" I said, "take out your Fabergé case." He did so, putting it on the table with a bang. The head waiter looks around at the sound, for the first time allows himself to take in this quartet of scarecrows he had been avoiding, gazes at the cigarette case, claps his hand to his head and says: "*Dio mio! Monseigneur*, forgive me, I did not recognise you at all." We roared with laughter it was so funny. And he was so kind and brought us lots of such good food and nobody asked us whether we could pay or not. That case was our talisman!'

'Did *you* manage to keep anything, Princess?' I dared to ask. 'Oh yes, for a time I did. I hid my pigeon-egg emerald necklace in a pot of flowers which I took everywhere with me, replacing the plant when it died.' Here she tailed off vaguely. The truth was that they had had enough money banked abroad to take a beautiful villa at Cap d'Ail after they left Venice, but with that typical Russian heedless prodigality had soon gambled all the money away, till the day came when there was nothing to do but to cut their losses yet again, move up to Paris, open up a ballet studio, settle in the little villa and for her to teach from nine in the morning until six in the evening, going there and back by Métro. This extraordinary woman, when I knew her, without a grey hair in her head and as sprightly as a dragonfly, must have been nearer seventy than sixty, and on returning home from nine hours of class would play poker till the small hours, sleep a bit, breakfast and take the Métro back to class. That mould is surely broken for ever. What a pity.

And so that happy year rolled on, full of hard work. We, the 'advanced' pupils, would drive Kschessinskaya mercilessly, begging for more and more allegros until the class would last over three marvellous hours. One day I limped up to her, slipped off a shoe showing the toes of my socks soaked with blood: '*Pauvre Diana!*' she said sweetly. '*Va faire encore douze fois!*' and I tied my shoe on again and indeed repeated the steps twelve more times as she had commanded.

I went out little. I didn't want to, except perhaps to an eccentric elderly American, Miss Fleming Jones, who knew just about everybody in the artistic life of Paris and who invited me to dinner one evening when Alexander Benois, Diaghilev's great designer, was there. He was an enchanting elderly man with the air of a benevolent *antiquaire*. I reminded him that he'd seen me dance a few years before, when the young Rambert dancers had made their début under the aegis of Karsavina, and flatteringly dubbed me 'The Giorgione Venus'.

One day a theatrical producer came to class, seized upon me, said he was putting on a hybrid kind of opera to be called *Messaline*, the title part required someone who both sang and danced, and would I care to take on the part? I confessed to having a totally untrained voice. He begged me to try. There followed an absurd few days when I threw myself upon the mercies of Guggan's next-door neighbour, the famous Spanish composer Joaquin Nin, and together we tried to find a few simple songs that lay within my small register, practising in gales of laughter. I went to see the producer again in a very elegant apartment on the *rive gauche*, sang my pathetic songs and suggested that the rôle might be tailored to *chant parlant*, a kind of declamatory style in which only the occasional word has actually to be sung. He agreed. We discussed it at great length. I hesitated, it all seemed a bit vague, the dream of a very rich man with large ideas. However, he seemed to have come some way in shaping and organising the musical and begged me to consider, as I would be his ideal for the part. As I got up to go I mentioned that I was barely of legal age and would need a *permit de travail*, a work permit, which takes an aeon to acquire. 'What?' said he, 'you're not French?' 'No, I'm English.' 'Oh *quel désastre*,' said he. 'I had no idea. You don't look or speak like a young English girl.' Nothing came of it in the end. It all dissolved like so much ectoplasm, as do so many of the projects of rich, artistically gifted amateurs. Disappointed, I applied myself harder than ever to my classwork.

Joaquin Nin asked me, grinning broadly, what had happened to my 'opera career'. I told him. He gave me an autographed photograph: '*À la chère jeune Diana Gould, lumière d'aujourd'hui, étoile de demain.*'

The year came to an end with a performance at the Ritz for the Union des Jeunes Russes and a fantastic Christmas Caucasian dinner for thirty-two people. Ten courses of semi-oriental dishes of an infinite variety of sublime tastes and combinations accompanied by rivers of Crimean wine. I came to the envious conclusion that Russians have elastic-sided stomachs made of cast iron, which was definitely not the case with English girls, and lived on boiled rice till New Year's Eve.

As the New Year progressed, I worked like one possessed: not content with the three-hour morning class, I would return for the late-afternoon one and work almost as long. It was as though my appetite for acquiring more and more technique in this never-ending pursuit of the elusive had for so long been frustrated by lack of encouragement and sympathy that I dared not waste an instant; I had for all those early years butted my head against a wall of resistance combined with evil luck. At last, carried with the current instead of against it, I could now relax and swim with it, but still felt compelled to apply the same dogged persistence. Instead, to change the metaphor, of coasting down the hill,

I was engaging the bottom gear and grinding away automatically and obtusely. I knew no other way and one day I collapsed completely, physically and nervously. Guggan put me to bed, the good Dr Crussaire tried to convince me of the limits of even a young and strong body and darling Kschessinskaya came to visit me, to bring me the loving counsel of all her great experience. She told me how she had had to transfer the purely physical attitude towards work to the mental one, to plan her strength and watch for stress. 'But then, *chérie*,' she said, 'I was protected both by the great Maryinsky Ballet Company itself and by [pause] friends.' There it was again, the need for the power of a friend in high places. Comforted by her maternal kindness I soon returned to class, trying hard to work more wisely.

During that time Great-aunt Minnie, Guggan's sister, died. Lifar put on a show for various dancers at the Salle Playel, *Soirée à la Mémoire de Pushkin*, one of his vaguely conceived titles that might just as well have been *Soirée à la Mémoire de Robespierre* or *de Tallyrand*, but more honestly should have carried the legend *Soirée pour la Gloire de Serge Lifar* at which he could appear in his former rôle as the High Priest of the late Sergei Diaghilev. I remember dancing a waltz arranged by Kschessinskaya.

Then Guggan, looking over the top of her spectacles, announced that it was already February, she would soon be off to finish the winter at Menton and I must go back home as she could not possibly permit me to remain in the house alone with Ramon, the butler. As Ramon was a wizened little Spaniard who looked as though he had been put through some weird process of soaking, twisting and drying under great heat, with gnarled and ropy hands and face, and as he was the dearest little man, far past any wild sexual fancies or the performance thereof, Guggan's edict seemed to me preposterous. But here her power of total stupidity came into play and I couldn't budge her.

Determined not to give up Kschessinskaya, I found through another pupil a house near the studio with rooms to let. I hired the only one that offered a *cabinet de toilette*, together with a lumpy bed, a wardrobe and rickety table. The bathroom (extra) was on the floor above. Addie Rothschild (Guggan's childhood friend, the *Barone* Edmond) sent the car for Guggan, driven by the statutory English driver, Carter, and I saw her off with poor old yellow Gabrielle and an enormous quantity of dark-brown luggage (Vuitton, I suppose) on 18 February 1935, collected my few belongings, bade farewell to the bemused Ramon and moved into my cheerless room. I had written to Mama asking for more money as I would now have to pay rent, but it was very slow in arriving and as I have always dreaded debt I closely budgeted my small allowance. The little band of Russians with whom I worked in class – all of them from the de Basil Company: Riabouchinska, Baronova and others – and I used to eat lunch in a Russian grocer's in the nearby rue Nicolo. There was a dark little room behind the shop where they served whatever was on the menu that day to about three small tables always occupied by fellow Russians. I was soon reduced to Russian salad, the only thing I could afford, and the proprietor, a darling man, realising my constricted purse, would heap my plate again and again and only charge me for one helping. I never ever touched Russian salad again after that.

The bath upstairs was a total fraud, spitting out tepid water in a desultory way as though despising anyone so foolish as to want to bathe their whole body. By the time it had filled to a depth of ten inches it was shiveringly luke-warm. And this was mid-February, bitingly cold as Paris can be in the late winter months. I trained myself to forgo the five francs' worth of what looked like flat beer (the bottom of the bath was gritty grey) and to wake punctually at three a.m. every morning when I'd discovered the water in my *cabinet de toilette* was really hot, sluice myself down and, wrapping my blanket round me, crawl back to bed. Thereby I laid the foundations of the insomnia I have suffered ever since.

Inez, the girl who introduced me to the villa, lived in the room under mine. Both of us were short of cash, also cold and mostly hungry after the late-evening class. She had a little smelly primus stove on which she cooked in a battered saucepan a *soupe au foin*, a kind of nourishing oat soup. This and a hunk of bread served as supper. I bought a bottle of rum, we shared the cost of lemons and, after the saucepan was cleansed of the soup, we boiled some water, filled up two glasses, added the juice of two lemons and a good shot of rum and carried our glasses to bed in our woollen gloves sipping our nightcap in the growing cold of the dark rooms in which the radiators had long since been turned down. Breakfast consisted of chicory coffee rapidly cooling in one large cup and a slice of toast so hard that I broke one of my back teeth on it. But I hung on, doing my two classes, living on that slice of toast, the Russian salad and the oat soup and bread.

Occasionally a beau would take me out and I would eat like a horse. Kschessinskaya was very strict with me. I kept on getting enormous bunches of lilac or lilies (how I longed to eat them) from one particular and very handsome, middle-aged Russian, but she refused to let me accept his invitations. '*Non, Diana, il n'est pas propre.*' So I bored myself stiff with a young provincial *comte* until even my hunger couldn't stand him any more and, finding it difficult to rid myself of him, I hit on a brilliant idea. We were dining in one of the big cafés on the Champs-Elysées. When I'd finished my meal, talking wildly about nothing to fill the vacuum of his own triteness, I fished out a toothpick from the container and covering my upper lip with my free hand stretched across in a kind of protective modesty, little finger daintily perked, proceeded to work away at my teeth underneath this manual umbrella with a concentration worthy of all those good French workmen I'd watched in the little cafés I often frequented. Poor Jean was appalled '*Diana! Mais voyons, qu'est-ce que tu fais?*' I, disgustingly smearing the edge of my plate with a mythical tit-bit I had supposedly extricated, turned wondering, innocent eyes upon him and continued to chatter while busily working away. Shocked to his tiny aristocratic core, he hastily called for the bill. I finished my search, re-applied my lipstick, beamed upon him, was terrible in the taxi and never saw him again.

Haskell was writing to me regularly, pleased that I was so happy with Kschessinskaya, delighted that she was so pleased with me. Occasionally he would come over for the weekend and I would plead with him to write a book on this unique woman. He would have made an excellent job of it – alas, he never did. Life in the hired bedroom was becoming well-nigh intolerable. All heating in controlled buildings in Paris is turned off at the beginning of April whatever the prevailing temperature. It started snowing the following week and even the hot grog didn't offer more than a couple of hours' sleep.

At last my grandmother returned on 15 April, the money had arrived from Mama and I could pay my dismal room's rent. Soon after, I went back to London, darling Mathilda Felixovna coming all the way to the Gare du Nord with a huge bunch of flowers to see me off.

Not unexpectedly, I collapsed with near pernicious anaemia on return, diagnosed by dear concerned Goggo who took one look at my ashen face, pinched my ear lobes and sent me to bed for a week's cosseting and feeding.

Three weeks later I returned to Paris and Kschessinskaya and a great welcome from the studio. De Basil visited the class and yet again I was invited to join the Company. '*Vous serez un article de luxe, Mademoiselle,*' said the old fox, '*parce que vous êtes si grande.*' I pointed out that he had another soloist as tall as I. '*C'est vrai,*' he admitted and accompanied by a lascivious look somewhat hampered by those beer-bottle-end spectacles, '*mais beaucoup meilleur faite.*' I swallowed the compliment of being better constructed physically and was delighted when he told me I would be dancing Zobéide in *Schéhérazade* and the rôle of Constanza in *The Good-Humoured Ladies*. I began to realise the extent of his guile when, on going to collect my contract and my ticket for the coming London season, neither was to be found in the office. The good Ramon rushed to the station and Guggan bought me a ticket. Again Kschessinskaya came to bid me Godspeed and dear 'Lucy' with her. 'Take care, darling,' he said, 'and come back soon.' So I travelled back with the whole de Basil Company to London for the Covent Garden Season.

7

A Plunge In and
Out of the Jungle

I am sorely tempted to draw a little black curtain across those
following weeks in that jungle of a company where intrigue and
plotting reigned in an atmosphere in comparison with which the
Court of Medici would appear like a nursery school. No sooner had I
arrived than Massine, happy to see me at last there, confessed sadly that
as extracting money from the Colonel was worse than pulling an
impacted wisdom tooth, he had finally insisted upon down payment
for his ballets, thereby losing all control over casting and by the same
token any right to insist I dance those rôles which he had intended for
me. Secondly, on hearing I was to dance Zobéide in *Schéhérazade* and
Constanza in *Good-Humoured Ladies*, both Lubov Tchernichcva and
her daughter-in-law (the strongest faction at court) presented de Basil
with an ultimatum. They would never share the rôles with me. Either
they go or I. Pleasant. Furthermore, Tchernicheva – in her fifties (and
doubly bitter thought, the one who had been designated by Diaghilev
to be my 'mother' six long years ago) – happened to give all the classes.
Taking her revenge, she peppered me with a veritable barrage of
criticism, hurling sarcasms and generally making my life wretched.

The morning started in the seamy, squalid rehearsal rooms of Poland
Street, deep in Soho; class followed by sundry rehearsals until we
moved to Covent Garden. The 'foreigners' (English and American of
whatever level in the sharp pecking order of the ballet), were all

shovelled into the basement dressing-rooms, where an occasional rat would keep us company. (In Paris, I thought grimly, the young coryphées were aptly called *les rats de ballet*.) I gradually learnt that de Basil's adroit dodge was to hold auditions in the major American cities, picking up some excellent dancers who, like myself, would be badly treated, have to fight for their salaries and generally suffer as so much steerage.

Unwilling to be accused of vanity or lack of co-operation, I patiently waited for destiny to sort out my invidious position, meanwhile trying to learn the rôles for which I'd been engaged. Early on, I had realised it was wiser not to risk asking any dancer to show me a rôle and now resignedly avoided the sneer, the shrug, the refusal. Early on, too, I had learnt the lessons of not being so foolish as to stand in the darkened wings watching the ballet in the hope of picking up the steps; all that was picked up was myself, sharply from behind, flung on to the huge divan pillows of the *Schéhérazade* décor and libidinously set upon with an ardour that summoned all my furious strength to escape, and the added insult of the payment for a torn costume. Sadly I watched the hideous in-fighting, the jostling for precious rôles, the dreary bedding with one power or another to gain them, the stark prostitution of all that should have been exciting and beautiful and inspiring. Worn out with overwork (fifteen hours a day), travel and constant adversarial conditions, the dancers had become brutalised, inverted, almost doltish. This suited de Basil admirably. He knew they had nowhere else to go, the more docile they were the less trouble. So they sloped into class in their hair-curlers, or missed it altogether, trapped into paying the fine which indebted them all the more to him. None the less some of the dancers were glorious still – the young and wonderful Toumanova, Baronova, Danilova, or the men, David Lichine, Shabelevsky, Woizikovsky and Massine. But all these were safely elevated from the jungle beneath and freed to give of their best with only the occasional battle or endemic *scandale* to roughen their way. These young ones had been my friends with whom I'd worked in the Paris studios and as for the men, whatever their behaviour towards me, it could hardly be called antagonistic. So I suffered that ghastly season, did nothing worthwhile and having been paid nothing took myself off sadly, bidding Massine goodbye. To compensate I had the good fortune when I needed it most to be asked to join a newly formed company headed by Alicia Markova and Anton Dolin beginning in the autumn.

My beloved Kschessinskaya and the Grand Duke visited London and I took them to lunch at my grandmother's, my own family being away. I spent a glorious summer with friends of my stepfather's in a Danish castle, coming back to England to start work for the Markova-Dolin Company with which I was to dance for the next two years.

Whatever the hazards, the Byzantine intrigues, the fierce and fearful competition, it was only within the Russian ballet's world that I felt completely at home. To a degree, this empathy seemed mutual. Wherever and whenever I had danced from childhood through adolescence it was always I who had been selected by the Russians, were it Diaghilev, Massine, Balanchine, even Lifar and later on Nijinska. Nicknamed 'Sparja' meaning 'asparagus' by my many Russian friends because I was tall and slim and green-pale, my colleagues in those friendly pre-Basil days would say, 'You know, Dianochka, you not English, you very Russian,' and I would answer that it probably came from my father's Irish family – both races being artistic, spontaneous, unreliable and passionate. It was in that very compost heap of the Russians that I felt rooted, nourished, growing. The trouble with the de Basil Company was that no one had turned that compost, which was by now slowly combusting. Both Markova and Dolin, although English, had been Russian trained, had danced in all the last Diaghilev seasons and were thoroughly Russianised, so I wasn't to feel alien and out of sorts in the new company, whose repertory contained the basic classical ballets: *Swan Lake, Carnaval, Sylphides, Casse-Noisette, Giselle* et al., to which were added many new works as the company continued to flourish.

For six solid weeks we rehearsed all day at the old Scala Theatre in Soho (the very one on whose stage I had left a trail of blood at nine years old). Pat Dolin had the pick of the field in choosing dancers in those days when only one company, Sadler's Wells, reigned and there was not, as in Paris, even a permanent opera ballet. He had a very strong team of female soloists, my old colleagues Wendy Toye and Prudence Hyman among them; as male soloists Freddie Franklin, Keith Lester among others, and a splendidly trained *corps de ballet* (the envy of de Basil, who told me the following season that he would like to throw his *corps* out lock, stock and barrel and engage our perfectly disciplined one). Finally, on a working day at the beginning of November 1935, we were all packed on to the train for Newcastle, there to rehearse for a further few days and open on the eleventh in the old theatre. Pru Hyman and I had got ourselves horrendous digs – a room at the top of a large, decayed house with two knobbly beds with matching pillows, the obstreperous geyser in the bathroom, and in the basement our landlord and landlady, a rough Geordie pair who very reluctantly permitted us to hang our washed tights and sundry other articles of underwear by their stove overnight, with the result that they all bore the insalubrious smell of their perpetual diet of fish and chips. Added to that was the desperate situation of facing a première each night of the week, for such is the ineluctable fate of a brand-new company presenting the usual quota of three ballets each performance for six nights and two matinées. One of my rôles was that of the '*Danse Arabe*' in *Casse-Noisette*. Old Sergeyev of the Maryinsky, discovering my rubber spine, busily rewrote the part adding endless back-bends and serpentine adulations. I might have enjoyed the rehearsals more had they not taken place in the Grill Room of the Turk's Head, the local hotel-pub, with the fire at full blaze and a nauseating stench of years of primaeval beef drippings emanating from the fittings.

However, worst of all was the orchestra. In those penurious days no company on tour could afford more than a token few 'front desks', the rest were picked up in each town. That in itself need not have been disastrous, had Dolin chosen a good conductor. Alas! this one was quite the most incompetent musician one's wildest nightmares could have created. On the first orchestral rehearsal he could be seen feebly waving his baton as though it were a fairy wand capable of bringing harmony and sweet sound from the very weird rabble in the pit. Nothing emerged but a cacophony reminiscent of the macaw house at the zoo. We wretched dancers would struggle, stop as Old Blowitz or whatever his name was, would give up (every forty-eight bars or so), wait exasperated while he tried to disentangle the score (which he most probably couldn't read), resignedly go back to the beginning of the ballet as he seemingly had intended himself (somewhat hampered by the fact that many of his players were gaily plodding on regardless) and finally be reduced, poor things, to counting loudly and getting through the steps oblivious of the anarchy below our feet. A growing consternation crept over our tired bodies. Dolin, who had a fine temper, finally lost it. Alice said, 'Well, I mean, I can't dance to this.' Old Blowitz and his bunch of merry men blew and scraped for all the world like a gathering of mental defectives being taken out on their annual beano and I wrote a 'Ballad to Blowitz', a resort to which Griselda and I always turned at moments of misery or drama (long since lost).

The stage had a terrible rake, sloping precipitously towards the orchestra pit, the dressing-rooms were cramped and only had cold water. Opening night loomed and however arduous and dedicated we might be, we were utterly defenceless in the face of this musical nincompoop. Sore of foot and heart, Pru and I limped back to our shoddy room, ate our sardines on toast and fell on to our unfriendly mattresses into a disturbed sleep. We were awoken by the comforting sight next morning of the little maid sweeping the crumbs of last night's banquet off the table with the same brush she had used to persuade the ashes back into the rusty grate. 'Top o' the morning,' I said to myself as we got ready for a whole day's rehearsals right up till the opening night, to say nothing of the grim prospect of having to resort to counting our way through *Sylphides*, *Casse-Noisette* and *Divertissement*.

The barren Blowitz had either sat up all night or got someone to help him decipher the score, for some faint semblance of the music was emerging from the general rattle; however he totally lacked that basic attribute in all ballet conductors, viz. the necessity to watch and follow the dancers, to study their tempi, accelerating or decelerating wherever imperative for the comfort of the performer. Actually he lacked any basic control whatsoever. One was left to the mercy of that bloody baton which in his hopeless hand seemed to have a quixotic will of its own. That whole first week was one vast challenge to us all and it speaks volumes for the *esprit de corps* already developed in the young company that we surmounted the appalling conditions. It also is an earnest of the fact that no ballet dancers are ever indulged, especially in those pioneering days. It was not a profession in any sense, it was a vocation and only those who were ready to surrender to that vision remained in it. The rest – wisely maybe – dropped by the wayside.

There followed five more weeks of tour, of icy-cold digs, iron cots, tepid water, poor food, a fifteen-hour day and long Sunday journeys in gritty trains, and at last we returned to London. Theatricals and fish travel on a Sunday, they say.

On 23 December 1935 the Markova-Dolin Company opened at the Duke of York's Theatre in St Martin's Lane. For Christmas, Pat, with whom I danced Chiarina to his Eusebius in *Carnaval* (choreography by Fokine, music by Schumann, one of the stock ballets of the Diaghilev Company), gave me a lovely blue velvet blotter adorned with a nineteenth-century lithograph of Taglioni, which I use to this day.

For the next year and a half I knew the haven of a well-run ballet company. Once the teething troubles of that first tour were over, and Blowitz and Incompetence dismissed, replaced by Leighton Lucas, a perfect ballet conductor, capable of choosing musicians whose playing inspired one to dance; the knots and snarls unwound in the myriad skeins that compose such a complex version of the theatre as is the ballet and the first London season successfully accomplished, we knew that we had created a place for ourselves in the English ballet scene. With Dolin, the great *danseur noble* of his time, and Markova, the first native-born English ballerina, we were set to develop as a serious company. Sadler's Wells was already well-established, but there was none the less a glut of dancers that one company could not ingest. For me, faced with returning to the Byzantine jungle of the de Basil or performing sporadically as a guest artist, the Markova-Dolin Company came as an enormous blessing, nor could I have borne the thought of shrinking back into the miniaturist Ballet Club, so long the cause of all that was wretched and miserable in my career, even had Rambert welcomed me.

As that first year developed there were the usual tours interspersed with London seasons, for no ballet company can survive unless it be eternally and ceaselessly working; new ballets were created and I found myself at last as a very useful member of a company, not just an over-sized *article de luxe* as described so restrictively by de Basil. By now I covered almost every style, from comedy through classic, romantic, dramatic and what is weirdly known as 'character' and which has less to do with one's moral nature than the ability to interpret a variety of national dances. Long since realising the drawback of my height (5 feet 8 inches when not *sur pointes*), I had decided I would have to make myself as adaptable a dancer as possible, especially as I had behaved in such a jejune way in eluding the advances of both Massine and Balanchine, thus ruining my chance of either of them creating rôles for me; I had thereby forfeited that most significant of all necessities in a dancer's life: a choreographer of your own whose music you might crystallise. As I have already mentioned, he had told me that both the first movement in *Les Présages*, Massine's ballet to the Tchaikovsky Fifth Symphony and the andante in *Choreartium*, his ballet to the Beethoven Seventh Symphony he had written with me in mind. Oh! most silly fool! And had I accepted Balanchine's pleas to go to New York in 1933, there would have opened up a wholly different career for me, for he loved long lines and would never have let me feel like some ill-fitting piece of furniture in an otherwise well-designed room – say a grandfather clock ticking away abashedly among a mass of occasional tables.

So I was at last able to slough off that clinging apparel that had cloaked me psychologically ever since the shock of Diaghilev's death and my increasing height. Dolin himself wrote me a lovely minuet to Mozart's *Eine Kleine Nachtmusik*, while in the same series of divertissements I might dance a ribald can-can and finish in a Tchaikovsky polonaise. 'Quick-change Queen of the divertissements' Pat nicknamed me, as I would tear off my can-can false fringe, purple tights and frilly skirts in two and a half minutes in the wings, shovel my head into a white powdered wig, while my dresser fixed my heavy farthingale round my waist and dropped my wide gold dress over my head, often fastening it from behind as I ran towards my entrance upstage centre swallowing hard to control my breathing and be ready for the curtains to part and reveal me as the image of a calm, self-possessed eighteenth-century court lady pining for a *billet-doux* from an invisible lover.

During that first heady season at the Duke of York's, King George V was slowly dying. I well remember the night when, sore-footed and longing for an excuse to avoid the performance, we hung by the radio listening for the latest bulletin. Should the King die before a certain hour the show would be automatically cancelled. But the news did not come and woefully I tried to look as ethereally romantic as possible on my bleeding toes in the seventh prelude of *Sylphides*, relieved to follow it bare-footed in the '*Danse Arabe*' of *Casse-Noisette* which only demanded a rubber spine and much suggestive waggling. We got the day off for the King's funeral.

That year, 1936, was a sadly eventful one, for dear old Guggan died in April and my beloved Goggo in November. Two of the rare props in my ill-supported life had gone for ever; two members of the family who had always shown me kindness and very practical help – I suspect it was partly because neither of them felt particularly warm towards my mother, who they knew showed me little of that kind of close concern so necessary to a young girl bent on a difficult career, and were thereby able to express both their reproof of her and their affection for a rather lonely and lost granddaughter.

My Paris nest was gone for ever: waking up to the smell of baking all over the town, of chicory coffee; running down the Métro steps breathing that strange cooked air peculiar to it, which remains in my nostrils to this day; emerging into the warmth and light of that wonderful city and the studios of Egorova and Kschessinskaya; above all regaining my love and devotion towards the dance. All this and more had been based on the general good fortune of my grandmother's house in Paris. I was no stranger, no visitor, I belonged there in that country whose language had been my father's main one and which we had spoken as a second tongue at home. Furthermore, that period in Paris signified a closer approach to the Russian origins of my profession – there lived most of the pre-Revolutionary Russians, vital, spontane-ous, colourful, warm, everything a young dancer shivering in the ice-cold studios of London could dream of. No more having to wait for her woollen practice tights to steam off their endemic dampness by the anthracite stove, no longer peeling off knotted cardigan after thick jersey like some frozen, many-layered vegetable; an end to driving herself desperately into circulation in a frenzied *barre*. There had lain the true heart of all a dancer strove for, made easier by a myriad factors physical, psychological, spiritual, material. Paris, my Franco-Russian second home, gone for ever.

Came a second tour of the English provinces, full of the excitement of recognising the growing audiences our pioneering company was sturdily creating with new ballets and a really large following. I had also collected quite a number of fans and some particularly special men friends who would unfailingly turn up in whatever city was theirs. One memorably delightful late supper I recall in the Pompadour restaurant of the Caledonian Hotel in Edinburgh. One of my two young men, a rugger blue who played for Scotland, Army, very handsome, over six foot and as large as his sport demanded; the other equally tall, Irish Guards, slender, good-looking and both with an exquisite sense of humour. They had decided to share me, so we sat at our table, ordered food and Christian, the Scot, asked me to dance. We had no sooner taken one turn round the tiny floor but the head waiter tapped Christian on the shoulder and in his best Knoxian manner told him I was not permitted to dance because I had a hat on and thereby was not in the correct 'evening dress'. Embarrassed, I looked about me; there were indeed one or two women dancing in the kind of dowdy chiffon dresses that made them look as though they had left the 'cello in the cloakroom or were using up that unfortunate bridesmaid's dress of four years ago, the only definite thing about whose appearance was its date. I had on a very smart black satin tunic and a small black satin matador hat – all very Parisian, as they genuinely were. Miserably, I made as if to sit down. 'Madame', said Christian, 'will certainly *not* take off her hat,' and followed me fuming to the table. 'My God, what a place we've brought you to, darling. I apologise.' I pointed out that I was staying there and that it was one of the few places open after theatre. Muttering imprecations, Christian subsided. All of a sudden the band struck up a tango. Without a word or even a signal, Michael, the Irishman, leapt to his feet, seized a rose from the vase and offered it with a low bow to Christian who, accepting it, coyly put it behind his ear, allowing himself to be drawn on to the floor and into the arms of Michael from which close hug they proceeded to perform a solemn and very passionate tango. . . .

The other couples stared with a mixture of incredulity and sneaking envy; the face of the head waiter was a lovely study in buttoned-down rage; his glare impotently followed the pair as they swooped and glided, stamped, gazing hotly into each other's eyes with true Hispanic lust. Finally with a concerted stamp and a loud '*Olé!*' they and the music ended. Christian bowed low to Michael, Michael returned the compliment and they rejoined me where I sat at the table tears pouring down my cheeks. Nothing was said. We chomped away at our food. The band struck up again, Christian whisked me round the room in a waltz, hat and all. The head waiter was nowhere to be seen.

That was one of the gayest companionships I have ever known. My Scottish-Irish pair dragged me to 'taxi-dances' where Christian fought with two men who wanted to dance with me and Michael and I had to hustle him down the steep stairs to keep him out of trouble. The week came to an end. Christian came to see me, his moustache shaved off. Why? 'Because I thought you didn't like it, darling.' I sent him sadly away with no hope. I don't think either of them came through the war.

Pru and I made an apple-pie bed for Pat complete with uncapped tube of toothpaste, sewn-up sheets and a buried alarm clock. He found it singularly unfunny and deprived me of one of my performances of *Carnaval* with him in revenge.

Oh, well. In Manchester, in the only late-night restaurant of the Midlands Hotel, dropping some sauce on my dress during the first-night supper, I said '*Merde alors*' within earshot of the handsome head waiter who darted over, seized my hand with a love-sick look, dabbed at the stain and let forth a flood of pent-up French. Paul became a wonderful friend, and from then on we ate like princesses, Pru and I, for the price of one. The only drawback was that he would give our room number to any of the men dining in the restaurant, so that inevitably on returning to our room the telephone would ring. Man: 'Is that Miss Gould?' Me: 'Why?' Man: 'I was at the show tonight.' Me: 'Why?' Man: 'Would you have supper with me tomorrow?' Me: 'Why?' And down with the receiver. One such, unsnubbable, followed me on to the next town, sticking like flypaper, forcing me to be hideously and unhappily rude and unpleasant to rid myself of him.

The tour wound on. Sundays on the long train journeys: Pat usually sleeping with his head on my lap, the rest of him extended across one side of our second-class carriage; Alice as chic and self-contained as ever, sipping from a thermos offered her by her sister Doris; I reading above Pat's head. 'Gould! Why in God's name do you have to travel with a huge trunk of clothes?' 'They're not clothes, Pat, they're books.' Pat and I in a constant spat for some reason or another. He was a glorious dancer with an impeccable technique, unfortunately his taste did not match his gifts and it seemed to me – young and therefore somewhat circumscribed in my view of what Diaghilev's last great dancer should be – that he constantly traduced the gifts and the inimitable training he'd been so fortunate to have had. A predilection for dreadful little numbers in which he would appear in a gold frock-coat, top hat and point-shoes and execute six or seven turns *sur pointe*, ogling the audience as he finished hat in hand on one knee; or vamping round and round the stage in Spanish trousers, naked torso and bolero, prancing like some stallion to that endlessly wearying piece of camp, Ravel's *Bolero*, disturbed my sense of propriety. He who could reduce one to tears the next night in *Giselle* or be the perfect prince in *Casse-Noisette*, elegant, courteous, adding beautiful, clean dancing to his natural sense of style. Upset, outraged, I would protest. Pat would snap back, tease me, insist that I join him for supper with Alice after the performance, be furious if I had another date. Alice's style was entirely other. She was the last of what I call the 'Ornithological Ballerinas', the pure, classical, disembodied, birdlike dancer. Fine-boned to the point of brittleness, she was incapable of a fussy movement, a muddy line, a grimace. She simply gave her beautifully trained body to the interpretation of the steps, her face inward-turned and serene. We were friends and fond of each other, even though her career had started before mine and she was the *ballerina assoluta* of the Company; but I never knew her as a person, nor, reflecting, did it occur to me to try. Alice was the embodiment of classical-lyrical dancing and was a joy to watch. I left it at that.

The tour finished and at last the summer break arrived with no more of those limp weeks at watering-places to spoil a whole month of holidays. My beloved Kschessinskaya and her Grand Duke had again come to London. She and Lydia Sokolova made an appearance at a Covent Garden gala to vast excitement and both Mathilda Felixovna and dear André lunched at Mulberry House.

Appointed by my mother, I went to Paris to settle Guggan's house and her affairs.

Poor old Gabrielle (sad and yellower than ever) helped me sort and firmly reject the boundless assemblage of those tiny glass-topped tables known as *tables d'occasion* filled with unattributable objects of glass and silver and porcelain over which I had tripped or into which I had cannoned since childhood; stuff the mammoth trunks with linen and silver and china, strip her *cabinet de toilette* of its mosaic of yellowing snapshots thumb-tacked up to the ceiling like so many wall-paper reminiscences of her whole life: here 'With the Marchesa Osso Bucco in Florence', there 'With the Harvard P. Waveslangers in Santa

Barbara'; 'Dear Connie, much love Egbert and Wilfred', showing two gentlemen of indeterminate sex shaded by a clump of faded umbrella pines. I slipped the lot reverently into a large envelope. Dear old kindly, obdurate Guggan. I owed her so much.

I settled Gabrielle's pension and then went to Cannes where, at the Hôtel du Cap at Antibes, I joined Dolin and Beatrice Lillie and her son Bobby, Belita a talented young skater to whom he was giving lessons, and with her mother (in the role of chaperone) spent two lovely, slightly crazy weeks. Bea was of course the begetter of all the fun, whether it was wickedly managing to lead *à la* Pied Piper the entire human contents of one night-club out into the street singing nonchalantly, to dump them into a nearby one several hundred yards down, returning to the emptied night-club grinning elegantly into the face of the furious proprietor, or whether it was tipsily crying *Banco* to the croupier at St Juan, until Pat and others persuaded her to leave while she could still pay her bill at the hotel; whether it was her early morning telephone calls to the bewildered switchboard: '*C'est Lady parle Peel*' (off-stage she was Lady Peel); wherever she was, whatever the setting, Bea was the illuminated centre and perpetually in a happy mood, devoted to her beloved Bobby, one of the nicest unspoiled young men imaginable. That was 1936. A handful of years later Bobby died when his ship went down in the Far East. They told Bea during a performance in Manchester. She insisted upon finishing the show.

The holiday also helped loosen me from the frigid conventionalities of the London social season in which, some years before, to please my mother, I'd consented to being presented at Court. Again one of my more Unfortunate Child performances.

Unlike the other debs, I'd already appeared on-stage and had none of the nerves from which they inevitably suffered before the prospect of the strict Court etiquette the ceremony demanded. As soon as the *Corps Diplomatique* had gone through their paces in the Throne Room of Buckingham Palace where we were sitting, Mama, whose third Court this was, suggested we get on with it. This entailed moving out of the main room and entering the corridor that ran alongside it, joining the queue of anxious mothers and shuddering daughters who would advance pair by pair to where finally their turn came to re-enter the Throne Room at the level of the Sovereign's throne, drop their curtsies before each one and then pass on into the antechamber. It happened to be the last Court of the very traditional old Queen Mary and King George V. One of the Court chamberlains, a friend of my mother's, warned me firstly not to mind that the King would look over my head as all that bobbing and ducking gave him nausea to such a degree that the pages behind his great chair had smelling-salt bottles at the ready if need be to slide under the royal nostrils, and secondly that I must on no account smile at the Queen; should she feel like looking with favour on the seventeen-year-old that would be her choice, not mine.

So Mama and I proceeded slowly up that corridor arguing fiercely about some musical point with such passion that suddenly we were conscious of a loud hiss and saw to our horror that the pair ahead of us had long since gone, were in fact but tiny figures in the distance and we had created a hideous hiatus in the rhythm of the ceremony. The major domo looked daggers at us. Mama took a pace forward. I, Unfortunate Child, was standing on her train and managed thus to drag her feathers and tiara smartly backwards half-way down her neck. With a Medusa-like glare at me she continued to hold on to the lot, do her curtsies and disappear. I, dreading the ghastly moment ahead when all the wrath of the gods would descend upon my misbegotten head, duly gave a sweeping curtsey to His Majesty (postponing the Awful Meeting as long as possible), followed by another one right to the ground to Her Majesty, and was somewhat comforted on raising myself to find her bestowing on me a very sweet smile. Trying to cling on to that small joy I rejoined Mama, by now chatting to a group of friends. As she turned to chide me the chamberlain, Jocelyn Godefroy who had given me such good advice, quickly intervened with a report from last evening's Court: we were standing at the buffet (provided by Messrs Lyons as I noted from the very visible wooden trays behind the tables). 'It appears', said Mr Godefroy (very elegant in knee-breeches and black silk stockings), 'that when the servants were clearing up the remains of the food at last night's Court they discovered in an urn full of flowers a set of false teeth embedded in a macaroon. . . .' That story has by now assumed apocryphal proportions, but that is where it originated and the telling and retelling of that terrible moment when the poor possessor of the dentures finding him- or herself lockjawed on that glutinous delicacy, resorted to tearing the lot from his or her gums and in total panic dropping them into the depths of the nearest vase, presents to all an image, frozen for a second in the paralysis of pure panic, followed by a gesture so frantic in its totality that the mind is ceaselessly exercised by the logic of it all.

All the way through *Parsifal*, to which Mama took me afterwards, hanging our feathers on a hook in the stage box, that macaroon haunted me. I only half-listened to the flower-maidens below and scarcely more to Frida Leider as Kundry, dragging herself along the floor of the Covent Garden stage in a cloud of dust, wailing like a beached porpoise while the flower-maidens, whose plainness attested to their maiden-hoods even while their flabby faces denied their youth, flapped around vocalising to what seemed to me (a Wagner-loather already) no particular purpose except that of keeping the curtain up as long as possible. To my delight, from the box where I was sitting right over the stage, I saw one of the lovely creatures dip into her capacious bosom draped in very unbecoming brown muslin and draw out a crumpled piece of music-paper, refresh her flagging memory and restore it to base as she gambolled off with the rest of her floral friends.

Whatever would I have done, reflecting still upon that macaroon, in like circumstances? Having listened to the Dresden Amen which I loved, I'd given no further attention to the music.

Neither Mama nor my two grandmothers having counterfeit teeth, I had little experience at that youthful age of what it must be like to endure such a traumatic moment when, dressed to the nines and surrounded by similar elegance, a fundamental part of one's bodily equipment fails one so signally. Did it happen to a woman? In which case she surely could have popped the lot into her reticule. But even then she would have had to face the assembly mumble-chopped and mute. No, obviously once the offending combination of macaroon-cum-dentures had been wrenched from the gums, one and the same passionate gesture must have swept their owner past the urn into which the lot was summarily dropped, out of the room, out of the Palace, into the car and home. There to burst into tears and to put the dentist's number by the bedside to be rung at first dawn.

I asked the chamberlain. The teeth were never claimed.

There had followed various balls and dances that season of 1930, mostly chaperoned by dear Goggo, my mother, having once experienced the burden of being chained to a gold chair the entire evening while I danced with a variety of boring young men, refusing to repeat the exercise. Goggo was an immense success and enjoyed herself hugely, the young men buzzing round her, entertained by her wit, her pussy-cat looks and on occasion asking her for my hand in marriage. All that dutifully done, I could honourably hand over the role to Griselda, who 'came out' soon after and was better suited to it than I, with her lovely blonde looks and her immediate sex appeal. The last thing I wanted was to be dubbed the 'Ballerina Débutante'. Like my mother before me I was totally professional in my attitude to my career and wanted no interference in my dogged pursuit of it. Moreover, in those days most mothers' ambition lay in getting their daughters married, so that from that time on I had to dodge proposals as deftly as though they were missiles dangerous to my progress, hiding love letters under mattresses and in odd drawers. On those dread occasions when the aspirant could not be hidden, I resigned myself to a few outings followed by a deft cut-off. Over the ensuing years, at least half-a-dozen of them were young men in the Foreign Office, many of whom became ambassadors (I am convinced because they married far more conventionally suitable women than I).

Thank goodness Griselda was able to deflect a good deal of the social scene from me, added to which my mother's musical activities and the Sunday musical parties she was beginning to inaugurate in Mulberry House were absorbing most of her attention. Not that every now and again she would not erratically focus on one or other of us to realise it was four a.m. and we had not returned. There was one memorable moment when I was climbing wearily up the stairs as the sun was doing the same behind the curtains in the early hours to find Mama sitting on the top step in her dressing-gown bewailing the fact that she had rung Scotland Yard giving my description, only to be comforted by the news, 'Not to worry, Madam, they always bring the bodies here and there's no one matching that description as yet.'

Poor Mama, the machine of her maternal feelings worked sporadically like some faulty engine and in ways that were rarely profitable to us. Passing Griselda in the hall, as the latter was on the way out with a young man and a suitcase to go to a hunt ball in the country, she suddenly flicked on the motor, demanding to know where Griselda would be spending the night. On being told that as was the custom they were all being variously put up at local country houses she retorted that she didn't know the owner of that particular house. Undeterred, Griselda, who had much more initiative than I, hastily kissed her goodbye and was gone, suitcase, escort and all.

A week later, Mama was giving one of her luncheon parties for about ten or twelve people at which both Griselda and I were present. She was a splendid hostess and always orchestrated the conversation so that it flowed naturally between all the guests. There was a momentary hiatus and we heard Mama's voice ringing out: 'Well, I suppose not having been brought up in England, I don't really know the expected decorum but I am sure you will all agree with me that when I discovered that Griselda [look of mute horror passes between the two sisters] was going to spend the night at the house of a total stranger for the ball, I really objected. Don't you agree?' In the somewhat baffled silence that ensued Griselda interjected: 'But, Mama, I was only going to be there twenty-four hours!' 'Nonsense Griselda,' said Mama, pat as a badminton racquet, 'they tell me Napoleon's love affairs took three and a half minutes!' The second of total disbelief was followed by a crescendo of incredulous laughter from all the guests, some of whom I hope realised our mother's complete innocence. How she produced three children in five years of marriage was always one of the mysteries of my youth.

For 'well-brought-up' girls, England was still an extraordinarily innocent place in which virginity for the most part prevailed, contraception was clumsy, pornography lurked under the counter, the young lived in the bosom of the family and abortion lay in the hands of dubious little men down dark alleys wielding dangerous instruments. Even had you not been the incurable romantic I was, all this was sufficient deterrent to keep you off the primrose path. Paris was quite a different kettle of fish and I early learnt that to go out alone with a man, even a family friend's son, was tantamount to offering oneself in exchange for a three-course dinner. It took me a couple of tough fights in a Renault and a Peugeot, and a long walk home, before I got the message in high-case and loud and clear. At that period I had little appetite either for food or sex; what I craved was company and conversation and that with men. Gossip bored me, girls' tattle even more, my friends came increasingly from among the ranks of writers, poets, painters (I often sat for them, still as a memorial in that heavenly smell of paint and oil and canvas), sculptors, budding politicians, diplomats or journalists. With them I could 'tire the sun with talking and send him down the sky'.

However, this coterie was gradually to develop over the ensuing years; at the time of my first season with the Markova-Dolin Company and the enjoyable summer holiday at the Hôtel du Cap, I had little spare time to cultivate friendships. Therefore that rather dotty, disorganised sunny summer spent with Pat and Bea and Bobby Peel did a lot to loosen the social conventionality of my mother's background, and I returned to Paris subconsciously short of a good many shibboleths (if all the same still a virgin).

Paris meant a sad and wretched twenty-four hours, a final talk with my grandmother's solicitor, a last night in that house I'd known and loved and longed to get back to since I was eleven years old. The twenty-first of August was one of the most sorrowful days of my young life to date. I was closing a chapter on that part of myself that might never have seen the light of day but for the great good fortune of that little second home. I lay there thinking of Guggan's only son, Gerard, the father I'd never known, wondering whether my deep affinity with France – deeper far than among the other members of my family – had not actually sprung from some source in him which I had inherited and I comforted myself with the fancy that had I ardour enough I need not lose this precious gift, this alter ego that had unfolded in me as naturally as the secondary shoot in a healthy plant. However shadowy the substance might become, now that its breeding place was gone, the essence, engendered by my unknown father, would accompany me throughout my life.

Heavy of heart, I returned to London and yet another tour of the provinces with the Markova-Dolin Company. Not that I didn't enjoy the work, the self-expression, the fulfilment that is so necessary and so elusive a part of that over-dependent profession. A painter can always paint, a writer write, a poet create a sonnet, but the wretched creature tied to the theatre must needs find employment before he can express himself. He cannot forever recite the soliloquies of Hamlet on an empty stomach to a naked light bulb, nor can the dancer eternally jump and turn in a classroom – however many *entrechats* he may add to his technique, or for her however many *doubles-fouettés*. We must needs find work, and I was extremely fortunate to be a soloist in this company for as long as it was to last. *Mirabile dictu*, Dolin announced that the Company had now engaged none other than Bronislava Nijinska, the sister of Nijinsky and one of the great choreographers of the day, who was to join us in the New Year. She would mount first *Les Biches*, the famous ballet she had created for Diaghilev to music by Poulenc with costumes and scenery by Marie Laurencin; and others would follow once she had assessed the strength of the dancers.

It was when we were in Bristol a few weeks later that Mama rang to tell me of darling Goggo's death; a final heart attack after several this year. Luckily she had been removed from her flat to Mulberry House so that valiant, sensitive, gifted creature did not die alone. She had been such a comfort and support to me, so loving and cheering, so witty and tender, scraping money from her slender purse to pay for massage for my muscle-bound legs, or to take us all to Lake Como for our first taste of Italy, or to buy us material for the dressmaker to augment our restricted wardrobes. There never was a more talented woman, nor one who better used her gifts as a blessing for others. She always remains enshrined in my heart, where I can talk to her from time to time.

8

Nijinska

Nineteen thirty-seven was the last really carefree year for those of us who, in accordance with much of Britain, put our collective heads into the sand, managing to breathe there somehow well into the summer of the following year. During 1937 we could still remain insularly attached to the *status quo ante*, pursuing our social and professional lives oblivious of what changes were taking place in Germany.

Griselda had the brilliant idea of reviving Mama (whose *remords de conscience* were biting into her uncomfortably after Goggo's death) by taking her to Vienna where she and her mother had shared so much joy and gaiety during lessons with Leschetizky in the last great years of pre-First-World-War Austria.

As Mama – always living encapsulated in her own world – had come to Vienna furnished with her oldest address book, our whole plot all but failed. After, for a few days, ringing front door bells which either remained unanswered or else presented us with a cross maid glaring with disbelief at Mama, snapping the Viennese equivalent of 'Been dead these last twenty years, *Gnädige*', and slamming the door, or else 'Never heard. Frau Pröglhöfer has lived in this flat since 1920', followed by another slam, we suggested to her that it might be wisest and most logical surely to go straight to the Zentralfriedhof, the great cemetery a few miles outside town. Of course Mama was outraged, spluttering with grievous indignation. Finally, however, she agreed and we set off in a taxi to the vast graveyard. Taking Mama firmly in hand we led her to what I suppose was the necrophilic Information Desk. Old friends' names in hand, we received the necessary advice on a slip of paper, furnished with which Mama set forth with unexpected determination, plodding down the frozen muddy, paths muttering '*Gruppe null, Reihe eins*', or again searching for a more recondite grouping in an effort to trace her friends of yore. Triumphantly she would stop before an imposing monument, finger pointing at the inscription: 'There he is!' she would cry in the manner of a hostess looking for an elusive guest at her party, whereupon, launching into a *curriculum vitae* of the bones, she would quickly cover them over with the flesh of her vivid memory. Half-frozen in the January wind, Griselda and I trundled on behind her as, heedless of the bitter weather, cheeks flushed, she strode down row after row, consulting her numbered paper, pouncing on the discovered tomb, relating the adventures, the quarrels, the musical experiences she, the adolescent Evelyn Suart, had shared with one and all. Numb with cold of body and spirit in those grim acres of the departed, turning up our collars against the arctic wind whistling down the great alleys heavy with brick and stone tumuli that seemed to function as weights to ensure no spirit nor soul should escape the serried graves, Griselda and I marvelled at Mama, unmoved by any thought of the terrible finiteness of it all, simply communicating with old friends.

However, Vienna was essentially light-hearted and there were balls in the Palace and outings in fiacres to Grinzing to drink the new wine, and concerts and opera. So we did bring Mama back settled in her heart and ready to continue her bird-song life.

Simultaneously, the Markova-Dolin Company was to enter into its most interesting and important phase. Nijinska arrived to start rehearsals at the beginning of February at the Stoll Theatre rehearsal rooms.

What quality is it that constitutes that elusive word 'presence'? Is it basically an evasion, a convenience designed to explain a characteristic that is too difficult easily to define, or is 'presence' an agglomeration of traits so subtle and for the most part rare that it must remain unfathomable and by nature not be analysed?

The moment Bronislava Nijinska walked into the rehearsal room of the Markova-Dolin Company this extraordinary gift of presence must have been felt by even the dullest spirit there. Small, cylindrical of shape, very compact in her dark–blue jersey and trousers with white cotton gloves on her hands (she couldn't bear to touch dancers), her dull-blond, grey-streaked hair, smoothed down in bandeaux framing the slightly pendulous cheeks, was caught in a neat chignon at the nape of her short neck, accentuating the big strong head, the high cheek-bones, heavy-lidded Slav eyes and the tall forehead. This head dominated the whole, seemed to me to constitute as it were the lighthouse of the entire body. Her hands, limbs, torso barely sketched the movements in the sparseness of her directions, but all were co-ordinated by this head whose tilt, whose angle moved like a gyro-compass as though keeping the balance steady and illustrated more clearly than would a dozen larger uses of all her members, her exact choreographic intentions.

The fact that she was almost totally deaf may have played a significant part in this appearance of self-containment, added to a certain aloofness, the wariness of those who are so cut off from easy communication they cannot even be sure that their own voice is loud enough to be heard. However, there was nothing cold about her; on the contrary one was conscious of banked fires within revealed by a sudden flash of the eye, a curt gesture of impatient dismissal at a badly wrought step and, blessing of all blessings, the surprise radiance of a smile when she was either amused or satisfied.

We all worshipped her, despite or perhaps because of her strict terms, i.e. one must not practise in the rehearsal room when she was working there; if one had exhausted one's body and the possibilities of doing exercises in odd corners of the dressing-room or adjacent passages one might sit on a hard chair not too near her, feet together, hands in lap and watch without talking. One curtsied when she arrived and again when one was dispensed with. All this, far from alienating us, rather enhanced a relationship compounded of affection, respect and ready willingness to work for someone so infinitely worthy, for once, of all those attributes. The ballet frequently demands obedience and discipline to be shown to those who deserve neither; it was wonderful to be able to give it with one's whole heart to Bronislava Faminitshna.

As she had, to my delight, conferred on me her own rôle of the Hostess in *Les Biches* (*The House Party*) which thanks to Diaghilev's invitation I'd seen as a child, I was only needed when she rehearsed my solo or other dances belonging to my part. Moreover, she had selected me to be her 'liaison' and her interpreter between herself and the other dancers. This comprised sitting on the edge of my chair all during rehearsals ready to spring to attention whenever she might summon me. Never for a moment during those long hours dared I relax. To complicate matters her 'signal' was an almost imperceptibly small beckoning movement of the index finger in its white cotton glove, most times not even raised from its position loosely hanging by her side as she sat bolt upright on her own wooden chair in the centre of the wide room. Often confused by the simultaneous brandishing of her cigarette in a long holder, I had to be very careful not to misinterpret the gesture. My duty was approach, curtsey and listen – listen with all my senses – to the mixture of Russian and French she imparted through half-closed lips and in that low drone which is the tone of those who cannot judge the volume of their own sound. Agonising. I would peer down anxiously into her face trying to lip-read and pray to God I had got it right. '*Mademoiselle Diana,*' she would intone in a buzz like that of an autumn bluebottle, '*Mademoiselle Diana, vous allez dire à cette jeune fille-là qu'elle danse comme un éléphant.*' Swallowing to gain time, I would tell the wretched girl that Madame would be obliged if she would try and dance with more lightness and grace, then bob and return to my chair to await the next call.

One fateful day our dear old Russian pianist, Foxie, who on occasion fell victim to strange habits that left her less than usually capable of knowing what she was doing or playing, was thumping away at the finale of *Sylphides*, her orange-grey hair nodding up and down like a pile of citrus peel, her kohl-ringed eyes peering glazedly at the music. The girls were prancing away for all they were worth when Nijinska called a halt, summoned me and ordered me to tell them that they must begin at the beginning again and keep their lines straighter. My job accomplished I retreated to my chair. To my horror Foxie launched gaily on into the second subject leaving the poor *corps de ballet* floundering hopelessly with the wrong steps to fit the wrong rhythm. Soon they would be forced to abandon the attempt and end in total chaos. Nijinska, it being one of her deafer days, was quite oblivious, hearing nothing. I hesitated, desperate; the girls looked desperate too. I took the plunge. While they doggedly ploughed on, I slipped behind Nijinska's chair, sidled up to the far end of the room where the cottage upright trembled and shook under Foxie's manic fingers, affected to lean casually on it as though in one mad moment I had been seized by a longing to feel its exciting vibrations and could no longer contain myself and, looking far into the distant rafters, hissed 'Foxie, you idiot, for God's sake wake up and play the *opening* of the finale, quick!'

I could feel her leering drearily up at me. I all but shook her arm under the cover of the back of the piano as the girls, thundering on wildly counting under their breath so as to keep together and to ignore Foxie's musical aberrations, were all too clearly reaching the end of their tether. 'Foxie, *please wake up!*' She shook herself once, focused a boiled black eye on me, swung it over to the girls, registered what was happening and long-experienced as she was, picked up the music exactly at the point they had reached with a toss of her head and in a shower of dandruff and fine hairpins. The whole thing could not have lasted more than half a minute but to me it had seemed a lifetime's agony. I breathed again and was preparing to complete the second half of my act as a casual crab when a peremptory voice rang out: '*Mademoiselle Diana, quand j'aurai besoin de vous, je vous le dirai, n'est-ce pas,*' accompanied by an arctic look. Flushing like a sunset, I crept back to my seat which seemed kilometres away. I was forgiven. However, I never discovered whether she had recognised the dilemma but felt she could never admit her failing without risking her power.

One day she dismissed the entire company for the afternoon announcing that she would only call me for a solo rehearsal. Trembling with apprehension I went down to the small café where I could barely swallow my lunch-time poached egg (Nanny had said that one couldn't poach a bad egg) and the dancer's usual litre of black coffee. It was a fiendishly difficult solo, full of intricate *batteries* (cross-beatings of the feet in the air) in all positions, added to which the upper half of the body had to remain completely relaxed, the shoulders turning this way and that in the classic Nijinska manner she had made her own, the famous '*épaulement*', a cigarette in a holder in one hand, the other free to gesticulate with the pearl necklace roped around the neck entwined in the fingers of the other clothed in a long elegant evening glove. To crown it all the costume, a clinging champagne-coloured affair, sported a tall ostrich-feather head-dress, the whole demanding a casual chic and an air of sophisticated nonchalance difficult to achieve, particularly while the lower half of the body was stuttering away with the pizzicato of fast and complex beats.

Nijinska kept me three full hours at it until I finally fell at her feet, bubbles of saliva coming out of my mouth and blood oozing through my shoes. As I lay panting, trying to pick myself up, her dear husband, Nicolai Nicolayevitch, bent to help me, gently remonstrating with his wife who suddenly focused on me, bestowed one of her rare smiles and said '*Bravo Diana – pardon*' followed by something complimentary in Russian, and with a pat on my damp shoulder declared the torture satisfactorily over for the day. Alas! For me, it was not over. A bursa had burst on my big toe joint and I hobbled about on a stick with a carpet slipper on my foot for a whole frustrating week.

Back at work again I was greeted with such warmth I realised that a real bond had been forged in those few weeks almost unnoticed by me, wrapped up as I was in the excitement, the total application, the long hard day's work, the very presence of this extraordinary woman who commanded respect and invoked discipline without ever having to raise her voice. There had been no time to consider personal relationships and my excessively romantic heart was so lost in worship that any reciprocal affection had never occurred to me; it would have appeared as *lèse-majesté* of the worst kind if it had. So it was with even greater fervour that I watched her every movement and noted how very spare and succinct they were, how she seemed to have reduced them all to an essence where a turn of her shoulder, a flick of an arm and hand, an angle of her head and the merest shift of her feet served to explain precisely the steps she wanted, after which she would return to her chair, take a long puff at the ubiquitous cigarette which a moment before had been describing arcs of great lyrical loveliness and grunt with satisfaction.

The Company adored her, even Tich, the sparkling Cockney wardrobe mistress, was to be seen, when we finally moved into the theatre, utterly bewitched, hanging on to the gallery up in the flies watching rehearsals. 'I don't know what it is,' she said, 'but she's a right marvel – can't take me eyes off 'er.'

Safely past the agonising first night of *Les Biches* and evidently not having disappointed her, or the critics, it was during a performance later on in the season when I was panting in the wings after that damnable first solo that I espied coming through the pass-door none other than Lydia Sokolova, Diaghilev's marvellous English character dancer, creator of the Miller's Wife in *The Three-Cornered Hat*, the Maiden in *Sacre du printemps* and many other rôles. Suddenly I recalled that she had been the only other one to dance the Hostess, besides Nijinska, *chez* Diaghilev. Before I had time to worry about what criticism she might offer, she tiptoed up to me (the ballet was in full spate and I was waiting for my next entrance) and whispered hoarsely 'Diana, whatever *has* she been up to, you poor devil? It was *never* like that – none of those *brisés volés* – nor those other beaten steps. She didn't have the technique – she was a character dancer pure and simple and that solo I inherited from her was straightforward, a matter of steps and strutting and a few small jumps – well I *never*!' Before I could reply I gasped, for at that moment, from behind the flat where I'd been waiting, none other than Nijinska herself emerged. Sokolova fled. '*Mademoiselle Diana,*' she said with cold anger, '*je ne sais pas ce que Madame Sokolova vous a dit, mais cela ne serait pas la vérité.*' I looked idiotic and murmuring '*Bien sur, Madame*', shot thankfully on to the stage. Of course her quick brain must have realised Sokolova's revelation and she was determined to deny it. As for me, if it suited her to have rewritten the solo with thrice as many technical difficulties, she had every right, even to the point where she didn't have to admit she herself had not danced them. Paradoxically, from then on I attacked it with renewed vigour and a stouter heart.

Partly, I suppose, owing to her deafness, and partly out of tradition, she kept herself separate outside working hours, only occasionally contacting one or other of us to make a point or offer a comment. One evening after the performance she paused at the door of the soloists' dressing-room on her way to her own, swept a basilisk look over the four of us and said: '*Il n'y a qu'une entre vous toutes qui connaît la passion et c'est Diana Gould!*' After which clarion call she swept on, leaving me part delighted, part dreading my new rôle as the Most Unpopular Girl of the Upper Sixth.

When her second production was due for rehearsal I saw, with that excitement and happiness only shared by those who know the agonising step-by-step climb upwards that is the ballet dancer's lot, that my name was down for the second leading rôle – the first of course being Markova's. This ballet would be *La Bien-Aimée*, starring Markova as the Muse and Dolin as the Poet. I was to be La Lionne, the beautiful *mondaine* dancing with four suitors. The music was Chopin, orchestrated by Liszt, gloriously romantic and the choreography in Nijinska's hands bound to be both musical and characteristically stylish. I could hardly wait for next morning's rehearsal on stage. For me it sealed the fact that I had in no way failed her in *Les Biches* and that this was an earnest of her faith in me. I thanked her as she stood there, back to the empty black auditorium, small, compact, authoritarian. She waved away my thanks, muttering, '*Mais, bien sûr, Diana, c'est tout-à-fait vous.*'

Rehearsal started and as far as I could judge went well. Nijinska's face, lighted from above, looked strangely like her brother's; very Slav. Those eyes heavy-lidded and slanting, almost reptilian except for their very human intelligence. Those quick, slight, sketch-like movements demonstrating the steps, the total concentration – all this after those first tentative weeks I now knew how to translate and above all how to relish. That night I danced Chiarina to Dolin's Eurebius in *Carnaval* which was always a joy. Next morning I came to class as usual, pausing by the bulletin board to find the times of rehearsal. I could not believe my eyes: another name replaced mine as La Lionne. Aghast, I plucked up my courage and knocked at Nijinska's door. Trying to hold back the tears of shocked dismay, I asked her why this change had been made, hoping against hope that there had been some mad mistake. Both she and her husband looked at me gravely. 'No,' he said, 'it is unfortunate, it appears that the rôle has been promised by Dolin to another dancer without consulting Bronislava Faminitshna, nor does it seem he is willing to change it. As she always has and always will cast her own ballets with those dancers she chooses, Madame is leaving at the close of the season.'

Then I did burst into tears. Nijinska comforted me and said nice things, but the bottom had yet again fallen out of my world. Somehow I got through that night's performance and myself gave in my notice. There was no point in staying on.

I left with a heavy heart. Once again the way forward had opened up, once again I had been chosen by the Russians, yet again Fate had intervened. Black Fairy?

Postscript.

The war was long over and I was married to Yehudi, with two small boys and now settled in London. I received a message: 'Nijinska is putting on *Les Biches* for the Royal Ballet and would very much like to see you if it is possible.' For once it was. I had entirely severed my ties with my old ballet life and albeit we now had a permanent home, still spent a great deal of the year touring with Yehudi all over the world. I told him I would love to see Nijinska after all those years. He was delighted and made time to come with me. We went to her Kensington hotel. Apprehensively, with what alien emotions towards a world I had so arbitrarily abandoned I could not clearly tell, we went to her rooms. She had changed very little. Grey-haired, more lined perhaps, a tiny bit stouter? But the same upright carriage, the same cigarette in its long holder, the exact way of turning all of a piece on the swivel of her feet.

We fell into each other's arms. Her smile was radiant. Dear Nicolai Nicolayevitch and Irina her daughter greeted me as though all those years had not passed nor left a chasm of forgetfulness. It seemed Nicolai Nicolayevitch was a great fan of Yehudi's and while she and I chatted about the far-off days, he told Yehudi how many records of his he had, discussed the violin repertoire and so on. I asked Bronislava Faminitshna how *Les Biches* was going. She replied '*Bien . . . très bien*' and then with a slightly wicked glance towards Yehudi, she said '*La danseuse qui danse le rôle de l'Hôtesse a un peu du tempérament de Diana!*'

Back in 1938, life had become more interesting outside the ballet too. With my Foreign Office friends I met politicians of every hue which added a dimension to a life otherwise devoted to a profession so demanding that it absorbed a good fifteen hours of every day with the exception of Sunday, thus confining me dangerously to a set of values narrow and unreliable. With too restricted a frame of reference one became the victim of the shallows of a theatrical career, of its inevitable disappointments, its intrigues, its shrunken horizons. More and ever more I recognised the pressing need for another strand to run concurrently with my dancing, to support or to underline my daily life and lift the mind above the bleeding toes and draughty theatres, mean colleagues and despicable plots, the inevitable underside of the theatre not so easily dismissed when it is the theatre itself that is the fount and origin of one's desires and hopes. With a broader view of the existence of other vocations, ideas, large problems, one's own professional concerns dwindled to a place in which they could be dealt with in accordance with their seriousness or their banality without recourse to those violent reactions where the only resolution seemed to be either to hang oneself from a convenient piece of scenery or shoot the dastardly rival through her hocks.

Sir Robert Vansittart was Permanent Under-Secretary (in other words Head) of the Foreign Office and stepfather of one of my closest friends there, and I would be invited by him and his lovely wife Sarita either to their London home or to their seventeenth-century house at Denham and would meet all kinds of politicians from Ramsay MacDonald, the first Labour Prime Minister and his daughter Ishbel, to various diplomats and Members of Parliament. In this way, listening and learning, I was able to broaden my thinking, to lift it out of my daily routine of bus tickets and banana skins and focus with less avidity on my career. Mulberry House, too, offered a variety of interesting people: Wilhelm Furtwängler, the great conductor of the Berlin Philharmonic, would lunch every time he visited London to conduct the *Ring* at Covent Garden (his '*Ritterdeutsch*', mumbled at great speed, was way beyond my capacity to understand and as his only subject was music these affairs became a dialogue between him and Mama and greatly boring to me); for Griselda, I imagine, somewhat less so, for his eye, always loosely anchored insofar as ladies were concerned, soon came to rest on Griselda, whose technique in charm and coquetry was far in advance of mine and who conducted his obvious *Schwärm* for her with as much skill as his with the baton. . . . Louis Kentner, too, the great Hungarian pianist, was at one of those luncheons. Did he also begin to fall for Griselda then? Nine years later they were to marry.

Meanwhile I was dodging various proposals, all of which would have furnished poor Mama with very worthy sons-in-law. I simply was not ready for marriage. The idea of giving myself, whether in or out of wedlock, to a man I did not love was anathema to me, nor could I be bothered with the hot and humid advances of those with whom I had nothing in common, but would despatch them summarily with a mephitic glare. Rather alone and my own person than be hung around with scalps of half-endorsed suitors. Arrogant and cruel though that may sound, to me it was honest and at least sincere.

My stepfather, finishing his two years as Captain of Destroyers in Australia, suggested that Mama, Griselda and I should travel out to Victoria on the Canadian west coast to meet him. We had the most glorious journey across the whole beautiful continent – albeit on the crossing from Southampton to Quebec Mama had decided there was only one plank between her and Davey Jones's Locker and had promptly retired to bed. Finding no one to sympathise or even to agree with her as to the actual amount of solid protection offered by the splendid liner she eventually rose like Aphrodite and thoroughly enjoyed herself. We picked up Cecil, returning via the States where one of my diplomatic aspirants valiantly met me off the train at Washington with a front tooth knocked clean out in a game of squash he'd just played. On the way back – the return journey of the new *Queen Mary* – another Unfortunate Child incident occurred. Working every day in the gym, I fell from a high bar when the ship rolled, tearing my knee badly. I was to be off dancing for the next nine months.

9

Fluctuations and Follies

Deeper into the sand went our collective heads for by now, 1938, unless one's ears were stuffed solid, one's nose choked and one's eyes muffled tight, there was no way of avoiding the unpleasant smells and noises blowing towards us from the Continent. Chronic muddle-throughers as the English are, lacking the passion of the Latins or the Slavs, settled in our comfortable way of life with a relatively honest governing system and an empire as our inexpensive supermarket, most of us enjoyed the conditions in which we lived. Food, clothing, travel, all were cheap. Inflation had not been thought of. The First World War had decimated the fortunes of my father's class, most of whose families had lost their bread-winners. We all of us lived in a kind of genteel poverty all the easier to bear as it was shared by so many. Perhaps then, it was the longing to enjoy a life that had barely emerged from the horrors of the 1914–18 war that made many of us grown to maturity in the Thirties strangely apolitical and as light-headed as we were light-hearted.

My mother used to relate an allegory about a German, a Frenchman and an Englishman to whom it is announced that there is a bomb at the corner of the street. The German immediately springs to attention, leaves the room intent upon doing something practical. The Frenchman reacts violently but none the less out of the apparent disorganisation of his mind, he also leaves the room with a plan already forming in his head; the Englishman waits till the bomb goes off and then is madly heroic and sensible about cleaning up the mess. This little parable tells it all. So we waited, hoping the Nasty Thing would go away while we averted our heads. For this moral turpitude we were to pay dearly. But at least we were to pay to the last penny which is some kind of sour comfort.

Above all the rumbles, London life continued. Furtwängler arrived again with the Berlin Philharmonic, coming to luncheon as usual, even more enamoured of Griselda, to whom he gave seats for his performance of *Götterdämmerung* at Covent Garden later in the season. I, tied by the leg, desperate and miserable, endured endless painful treatments of the mess I'd made of my knee, sat for various portraits, modelled for top photographers (Paul Tanqueray, Angus McBean, Norman Parkinson and Cecil Beaton) and went out a great deal, limping with a diversity of young men who activated me mentally but in no other way. I must have been maddening, wrapped up in my own self-sufficiency, 'clad in white samite, mystic, wonderful' and totally unstirred, like a Number Two Company 'Lady of the Lake'. Nevertheless I should not judge myself quite so harshly for this strange withholding of myself, when by now I might have been expanding emotionally.

Some years earlier a tragedy deep within the family had struck, scattering all the unrealistic attitudes upon which our behaviour was based, causing shock-waves that to this day still reverberate in my heart and mind. Dear brilliant Gerard, down from Oxford for a weekend, had without warning suddenly lost his reason. The terrifying sight of that familiar face possessed of the devil, above all of the bewildered look behind all that violence, shook for ever my unquestioning faith in goodness. I was seventeen. From then on I locked my feelings ever deeper within me. He never recovered.

One day, years later, Mama, Griselda and I were sitting on a bench in Kew with poor Gerard, for whose recovery our hopes were slowly dwindling. It was a lovely March day and he seemed to be fairly calm and happy. Down the glade, with the sun shining on their fair heads, came the entire Menuhin family, Hephzibah, Yaltah and Yehudi with his attractive red-haired fiancée, Nola Nicolas from Melbourne. Behind were the Menuhin parents. They passed by us, glowingly happy, handsome. 'Crowned with glory and honour,' I said to myself wistfully as they disappeared amongst the flowering trees. The bitter contrast stayed with me for a long time; the appalling tragedy that had befallen Gerard, the burden and sadness and growing hopelessness hanging over our young lives, the fathomless cruelty and uncertainty of it all, brought to a brutal focus by the passage of that golden family, was almost too much to bear. Even Mama, distanced by her nature from all reality, looked shaken. Griselda and I took Gerard by the arm and we walked back to the gates in silence. The commonplace phrase is that a shadow passes over one, leaving a sense of dread; what is the term when a radiance brushes one, leaving no warmth?

Dolin rang me and asked me to dine with him at the Savoy Grill. I had not seen him since I left the Company in June of last year; I had heard that it had gone out on tour for a few weeks, that Pat was disorientated and unhappy and that the whole splendid venture folded for ever. 'Will you marry me?' said Pat. 'Please, darling Diny?' And I, thinking it was again one of the many ploys he had used to tease and taunt me for nearly two years, laughed and said, 'Of course!' To my utter consternation he grabbed me by the hand, hauling me over to Bea Lillie's table: 'Bea! Isn't it wonderful? Diny's accepted to marry me!' Bea, who had been such a sweet friend to me when he was needling me on and off during our holiday at Antibes, looked at me with a mixture of astonishment and concern. 'Diny, dear, what splendid news,' she managed to say. I sat down, on her companion's lap probably, in an agony of embarrassment, kissed Pat wildly on the cheek and told him I knew he didn't mean it; that I was touched to the core; that I wouldn't dream of taking advantage of his moment of nostalgic affection; that I didn't intend marrying anyone for ages; that he must be and remain free as a bird; that I loved and respected him; that it was past midnight and would he or Bea or anyone please take me home? Pat, bereft of all his usual battery of 'acts', shorn of his habitual need to show off, of all the artifices which were probably a defence he was afraid to abandon, seemed unwontedly vulnerable and for the first time touching. I wished that all the time we had worked together he had shown me a little of the tenderness he now offered too late – it would so have helped me in my battle. . . .

London was filling up with refugees from Hitler, doctors, lawyers, professors, journalists, authors, theatre designers; Mulberry House was full of musicians from Vienna, Berlin, Frankfurt, Budapest, all of whom added an invaluable quality to the professional, intellectual and musical life of the city. Except for this all too vivid reminder of the upheavals taking place in Germany, life went on in its even tenor; there were Toscanini concerts with the BBC Symphony, lovely Olivia de Havilland came to luncheon with my mother; Aggie de Mille gave a remarkable recital at the Fortune Theatre and I, my wretched knee at last healed, finally risked going back tentatively to ballet class. I chose Mim Rambert because, knowing me since I was a child, she would discount the slow fumbling to recover my dormant technique and be merciful. Nine long and depressing months had passed since last I put on my ballet shoes, nor did the memories of all that I had suffered at the Ballet Club help me recover my spirits.

That very evening, Mama, Griselda and I went to the recital of Yehudi and Hephzibah at the Queen's Hall. They filled the place not only with their beautiful music-making but also with their presence, so utterly devoid of mannerisms, so undefiled by anything other than their closeness and the serenity this brought to everything they play. Yehudi's playing was unique, a choirboy's voice conveying a message that lies within the music and which you instinctively recognise as an integral truth. He is a medium through whom the composer's ideas pass untrammelled and pure. I felt renewed, less disheartened by the prospect of my long haul back to my former technique. In four weeks I was able to dance at a charity performance for the Mount Vernon

Cancer Fund, performing a very exacting rôle I'd created in the Markova-Dolin Company which further encouraged me.

Massine had formed a new company from all those dancers disaffected by the jungle arena of de Basil. A very strong roster of dancers: Markova, Danilova, Toumanova and none other than Serge Lifar himself. They were appearing at Drury Lane and I shared a box with Cecil Beaton and dear Tilly Losch. Alicia danced a most beautiful *Giselle*, one of the rôles she had really made her own, partnered by Serge who was depending more and more on his mannerisms and looks, the latter somewhat less saleable as his figure had expanded. I whispered to Tilly that his bottom looked like luggage sent by a later train. At the end there was tremendous applause, calls for 'Mark-Over, Mark-Over!' Again and again Serge kept flouncing through the curtain with her. Finally there was a longish pause, during which the curtain was seen to billow outwards, and could that have been a muffled sound we heard? At last Markova appeared alone to a crescendo of clapping and bravoes.

I went backstage to see my beloved Massine who greeted me as fondly as I could wish, and asked him what caused the pause. 'The only thing to do, Dininka,' he said, laughing, 'was for us to take Serge like this [a half-Nelson] throw him on ground and sit on his head!' Still, although Massine repeated his request, I hesitated about joining and indeed the Company did not last. The year ended on a downward note.

Aggie sent me to Myron Selznik's office with a view to film work. I had an interview with an absolutely charming man, his and David Selznik's London representative. 'My dear young lady,' he said with true American courtesy, 'please let me advise you. I know you as already one of the leading dancers here and I believe you've also acted in the straight theatre – that is where your career lies. Hollywood is a bear garden. You'll get nowhere unless you're willing to sleep all the way up. With your looks no one is going to dream of giving you a job in any other way.' A grin. 'They'd be odd if they didn't! Forget it and go on as you are.' Behind me rose the shades of battles with Korda;

running round and round the black-tiled bathroom of Tilly and Edward James's house chased by a famous American producer who finally skidded and landed on his backside, and how many similar encounters. I sighed, thanked that nice man and walked away down St James's Street wondering what it was about my looks and demeanour that made my hidebound virginity so obvious.

At the end of August my stepfather broke his holiday. He was recalled to the Admiralty because of the Czech-German crisis. There was a cabinet meeting. We listened with disbelief to the radio relaying one of Hitler's speeches to the great crowds at the Sportspalast – it belonged to a world we did not comprehend, a rallying and inflaming of people's emotions we, in England, had steadfastly refused to recognise in all their dangerous significance. The Navy was mobilised. Chamberlain addressed the nation in Parliament. I saw to the whitewashing and preparation of the big cellars under the pavements in the courtyard of Mulberry House ready for air raids. We queued up for gas masks, candles, biscuits and torches to store in the cellars. Chamberlain flew to Munich on 29 September 1938, to talk to Hitler and Mussolini. They reached an 'agreement' by one-thirty the following morning. The papers were full of pictures of Chamberlain waving a piece of paper: 'Peace in our time' shouted the headlines.

The dust settled but the feeling of the ground quaking beneath our feet was ever present. Rachmaninov played his No. 2 Piano Concerto at the Albert Hall to celebrate Henry Wood's jubilee. My good friend Aggie reluctantly told me that all this struggling time when I had been regaining my ability to dance, the very teacher with whom I had now taken refuge, who trained me from the age of nine, to whom I brought glory at fourteen by being chosen by Diaghilev and at sixteen by Anna Pavlova, in whose Ballet Club I had created rôles by Ashton, Tudor and de Valois, had been jeering about me all those long painful months of rehabilitation. 'How *fat* Diana's got!' Of course I'd put on weight in all those months of immobility. 'She'll never be *really* good enough again', or 'When I think of the poor performance she gave in *Squaring the Circle* and the marvellous one the present actress is giving', and so on and so on: unadulterated spite and calumny towards her earliest and most successful dancer. Why? Why did she pursue me with this hatred? 'Please, Diana dear,' said Aggie, 'don't go back. I just had to tell you, forgive me. I couldn't bear to think of you degrading yourself unwittingly.' I went, trembling with anguish and spiritual disgust, to Rambert, told her I knew all the unwarranted and cruel things she had been saying, collected my practice clothes for the last time and left for ever the place in which so many of my hopes were born and so many shattered. To this day I have never understood.

Knowing we were living on borrowed time Griselda and I took ourselves off to Paris on the ferry in December. Furtwängler was conducting the Paris Symphony Orchestra at the Salle Pleyel. It was a glorious concert: Beethoven, Debussy, Richard Strauss. No one who has not heard Furtwängler's interpretation of Strauss's *Ein Heldenleben* can conceive of that magical blend of the heroic and the spiritual, the sensual and the elegiac which he alone in all his essential Germanness could evoke. Griselda said I sat quite still, with the tears running down my face. As ever we had only a prescribed sum of money, it was therefore essential that we use all our most importunate skills to elicit invitations, especially those which occurred conveniently around mealtimes. My father's old friend, Miriam Rothschild, gave us a stupendous lunch including our favourite childhood pudding whose secret was known only to her chef: a soufflé half chocolate, half coffee with an invisible line of demarcation between the two flavours. That meal kept us going all day. Next day we cannoned into my treasured Diana Cooper. Her husband, Duff, the author and diplomat, was to give a speech on the political situation at the little Ambassadeurs theatre that afternoon for which she gave us tickets. It was brilliant and frank and brought the impending doom nearer. I called upon my darling Kschessinskaya with a big hydrangea. She was as gay and bright as ever. Griselda found an American suitor from London who fed her, while I once more and for the last time for years to come went to a Russian party at Kschessinskaya's. Lifar was there and Nemtchinova who lost no time in telling Mathilda Felixovna generous things about my performance in *Les Biches*. So far so good: we were not yet starving and the money was not running out. I got a call from London from a notorious cavalier. If he were to fly over, would I go out with him? Certainly, said I, counting on at least one good meal. He duly arrived, very handsome and with all the aplomb of the professional seducer. We had a superb lunch at the Périgourdine. Positively waddling down the stairs after three rich courses, Billy commented none too subtly upon the long zip at the back of my violet dress. 'That', he said in his richest voice, 'must be a very easy one to take off.' I turned to him with my most ga-ga innocent gaze and lisped: 'Oh yes, it's *so* comfortable,' smothering a slight belch. With a slightly frustrated look he walked me along the Left Bank, searching for a taxi (for him of course tantamount to an ambulatory bedroom). I chattered on with inanities interspersed with bright little trills, saying how good walking is for the digestion to say nothing of the figure (mistake that, it evoked a lascivious look sliding down my bosom) and prattled on about Paris, my grandmother (late), occasionally giving him the benefit of a great limpid look until we crossed over the Pont de la Concorde by which time he was limping slightly and looking decidedly chapfallen. Clapping my oddly adolescent hands, I suggested we go and have tea *chez* Colombin, nearby. A touch sullenly he agreed, possibly estimating that it was at least near the Ritz where he was staying and conveniently within navigating distance. Colombin was one of those old tea-restaurants full of tiny circular marble tables encrusted with the elderly greedy stuffing down their *feev o'clock* of *éclairs*, *mille-feuilles*, *palmiers* and *choux-au-chocolat* as though their very life depended on it. The wretched Billy looked nauseated, as well he might. I sat down still talking away and proceeded to gorge myself (praying my ulcer would not let me down), licking up the last smudge of custard cream from a mouth for which Billy was beginning to lose a certain fervour. Eventually, nausea brought me to a halt, I declared myself satisfied. With a slight weariness Billy paid the bill and I, clinging to his arm, trotted up the narrow street towards the back entrance of the Ritz, talking rubbish in the ecstatic voice I'd adopted ever since I'd decided how to handle this splendid meal ticket. Encouraged by my apparent closeness he put his arm round my waist, smiling down at my silly face with an obvious lift of the spirits. 'Well, Diana darling, are you enjoying yourself?' This accompanied by his best bedroom leer. 'Oh yes, Billy,' said I judging with finesse that '*ever so*!' would be just over the top.

I noted out of the corner of my eye that we were approaching the fatal door, the point of no return. The last *éclair* rose unbidden in my throat and with it the query as to whether the whole charade was worth it. I decided that it was: to trip up a man so conceited, so assured of his divine hold over women, so unused to failing, was to my mind a blow for all of us vulnerable young women belonging to a generation where in the aftermath of the Great War we were in a ratio of ten to one.

After he had pushed me through the door with growing impatience, we reached the lift. 'Billy,' I said, still the idiot *Backfisch*. 'That was a heavenly day – all that lovely food and being with you! You are *so* kind!' And as the lift arrived, I gave him a kiss worthy of the Sixth Form at St Trinian's, turned round and ran back to the entrance, afraid of looking at his face. God knows how he himself told the tale, or whether he preferred not to put so rare a failure on record.

Hunger thus assuaged and a nightmare of gastric agony following, Griselda and I assessed our common finances. We could afford about two days more, always considering we could find maintenance for the commissariat. Otherwise we would perforce sustain ourselves on croissants and thus enfeebled return home pale and attenuated. Our luck held. In the foyer we met John Lodge, the American film star, diplomat-Boston Brahmin and his striking wife Francesca. They took us to John's latest film wherein he struck at least four different attitudes with facial changes to match (two more than off-stage) and more importantly gave us lunch. John Walter, roving reporter for *The Times*, materialised in his best leprechaun manner (we met on a traffic island in the avenue de l'Opéra). That dinner was not embellished by the disturbing news from the Berlin he'd just left which much cut our appetites. He bought us some handkerchiefs with the sanguine legend

Viva Chamberlain embroidered on them in thick black thread (deliberate?). And the final day we ate our sandwich lunch while packing, for we were ensured of a splendid supper at Maxim's before which we were to be taken to hear Grace Moore, the most recent of Hollywood divas, in Charpentier's *Louise* at the Opéra Comique. Our host was Valentine Lawford, one of our fondest diplomat friends whom, having suddenly changed his name to Nicholas, it was irresistible to call 'Nicotine'. He had with him a very attractive blond colleague whom he introduced as Donald Maclean. We all sat in the front row of the stalls and behaved extremely badly. At Miss Moore's French accent, owing little to the Comédie Française and a great debt to the Bronx, we were hard put not to laugh outright; sitting there but a few feet from the footlights it would have been an egregious thing to do. However, as the big aria, '*Depuis le jour*', unfolded, sung with an ardour that, requiring all her vocal and emotional power, deprived her of what little mastery of the Gallic tongue she might have acquired in rehearsal, the farcical nature of the whole performance was more than we could abide and we exploded into giggles poorly muffled by our handkerchiefs or behind the ineffectual screen of the Gala Programme. Agony. Griselda and Donald Maclean were the worst, they did not even try to hide their glee and by now the whole orchestra, two feet away, was aware of our mirth and they, true Frenchmen, finding it all equally hilarious, ogled us, showing sundry other signs of disgraceful camaraderie. The opera limped on to the end. The applause was scattered and as we beat a hasty retreat, the orchestra, smiling conspiratorially, waved us goodbye. The supper at Maxim's, which lasted till three-thirty, was more enjoyable, as was the post-mortem on that misguided performance. Donald Maclean was charming, witty and excellent company. . . . What was revealed about his politics and his morals years later seemed totally at odds . . .

We, the Gould Gold-Diggers, chuckling at our first experiment in that particular line of hunting, returned to London. Griselda hopped back to Paris (refurbished financially) to hear another Furtwängler concert, while I dutifully returned to practise and to search for a new *professeur de danse*.

Nineteen thirty-nine could be described as the year when we all avoided each other's eyes; when the unmentionable remained exactly that and we felt our lives accelerating beyond our own wills. In such a libertarian society as my generation had known, this undercurrent was strangely destabilising. We continued, with a certain dogged obtuseness, to cultivate our gardens even though subconsciously we were not convinced that the perennials would see another year.

I started classes with Lydia Sokolova – that great character dancer with the Diaghilev Ballet. She was an inspiring teacher, full of cheerful and good-tempered advice – not perhaps one to seek out in search of a basic technique but definitely, like Kschessinskaya, one for the advanced dancer who needed both her experience and her knowledge of the infinite variety of challenges and pitfalls within the actual performance of a given rôle. Born in the East End of London, she had none of the stifling inhibitions of the middle-class English; full of the humour, spontaneity and cockiness of her class, she still spoke with an echo of the cockney twang which added a zest to everything she said colouring indelibly her Russian – which language she had quickly mastered – as well as her fractured French and the Italian terms with which the ballet abounded. Cheery, kind, full of zest, her classes were a delight. Slim and active, she could still demonstrate the steps themselves, an imperative element in an art which has no basic script; I would watch with delight as she spun and twisted in a manner known as 'marking' in the ballet, meaning sketching the movements to a reduction from the full dimension of leaps and turns and extensions – a kind of dancing stratagem where the intention is clear, only the engine is idling. With such a dancer as she had been, her illustrations were inspiring, for when Rambert could only follow the Cecchetti bible for each day of the week and never improvised – leaving me for one, very slow at picking up an *enchaînement* when I arrived chez Egorova or Kschessinskaya – Solokova, like them, created her own versions of adagio and allegro and even varied the *barre* if she felt so inclined, in that way subtly transforming a class into a performance so that one sublimated the technical even while studying the practice so eternally necessary to the ballet. It was a blessed relief to be for the first time happy in class and in London.

Television was in its infancy, installed in the enormous buildings of the Alexandra Palace in North London, and I was asked to do several programmes by the producer Philip Bate. Very restricted because of the lack of flexibility in the cameras of those days, each dance had perforce to fit into the confines of a tiny stage, and try to keep within focus. To throw oneself into a *grand jeté* wearing a long tutu would look like a storm in a pillow factory, and to risk getting too near the lens was likely to turn one's face into a caricature befitting a distorting mirror at a funfair. Not satisfying work, but interesting at least to be in at the birth of a new medium, and I was paid all of seven guineas – not to be sniffed at.

Musically it was a wonderfully rich season: Weingartner, Bruno Walter, Toscanini, Beecham, Schnabel in recital, Louis Kentner playing Liszt and Beethoven sonatas. I sat for yet another portrait by an RA, James Proudfoot (Yehudi unearthed it years later), and sat up two nights running to write a piece for Ernst Toller's *Die Zukunft* the German refugee paper published monthly. It appeared in July (under the title '*Frieden und Freiheit im Recht*'). I felt a little less unworthy of the times I was growing up in; on the other hand I had likewise come to realise that I might be full of qualities (even though that were better judged by others) but I certainly had few qualifications. So I took lessons in driving and duly passed my test. In common with most English girls whose parents had a staff, I was disgracefully ignorant about cooking, so I betook myself to the local Chelsea Polytechnic where a very prim lady with a forbidding face undertook to teach a dozen or so equally helpless females the rudiments of the art. If I say that Miss Bowlby's approach to all that was culinary was as far removed from art as is possible to imagine, you may surmise what those lessons offered.

To begin with, she horrified us all with the news that 'you will be required to eat all you cook'. Consternation spread among the rows of dutifully white-coated would-be cooks. My ulcer rose and hammered at my ribs in protest. However, away we went, working with a will at such *pièces de résistance* as toad-in-the-hole, rice pudding and Irish stew. Miss Bowlby brought to the teaching of cooking a kind of stern disapproval, rather like that of a father relating to his son the cruder facts of life. The only occasion – after we had obediently cooked these noisome dishes and tried doggedly to swallow them for upward of a week – on which I saw passion glow beneath her sallow skin was the one on which she arrived, brandishing an extremely dead rabbit. 'Oh,' said I guilelessly, 'was it run over, Miss Bowlby?' Daggers. 'Miss Gould, my brother shot it and offered it to me for demonstration,' whereupon she proceeded with indecent relish to deprive the sad corpse of its head and systematically rip its skin back as though peeling an overripe banana. One of my favourites among the ladies gulped wildly and headed for the door, never to be seen again. Miss Bowlby, licking her lips, her eyes glazed, continued her rôle of pathologist, accompanying each dissection with an obbligato of directions which we were expected to note down in our books. Finally, she sprinkled the grisly remains with flour in a kind of holy libation and shovelled the lot into a saucepan, there to transform it into something she called jugged hare. Slowly the glow withdrew from her face as the rabbit simmered away with a most hideous smell. Many converts to vegetarianism were indubitably made that awful morning.

One day I, feeling stifled with it all – the *reductio ad absurdum* of one of the basic passions of mankind – nearly threw in my tea-towel. But, wait, there occurred a better way in which to rebel! We were all to learn how to make that British basic: the steamed pudding. This version called 'canary pudding' was a pale-yellow sponge-like concoction – rather delicious in fact and in common with all its confederates, a very cosy lining for wintry British stomachs. Away we went with a will, filling our white basins, tying a neat cloth around the top and placing them on our ovens. 'Miss Gould, will you please lay the tables as usual.' I was evidently designated as knowing where the knives and forks should lie. Came the moment of fruition. We all collected our works of art, placing them on the long table at the top of the room where Miss Bowlby presided. One by one she untied them, turning the bowls sharply upside down and shaking out the contents. Nine fairly successful yellow mounds stood revealed so far; the tenth was vermilion. A gasp ran through the class like the susurration of autumn leaves in a high wind. Miss Bowlby gazed frozen in disbelief at this unbecoming intruder. Finally: 'And *who*, may I enquire, perpetrated this extremely unfunny joke?' said she, swiping us all with a withering look from behind her thick spectacles. I beamed artlessly and said not a word. There was no point in confessing, no one would be unjustly punished. My scarlet pudding looked divine, the negation of all the dreary dishes we had had to cook and, worse still, to eat. I longed to ask whether I might eat it all myself, but feared I could not have sustained my innocence. I threw away the little cochineal bottle I'd taken from the cupboard and felt infinitely better.

I had learnt not to put an empty pan on a stove because it would likely burn itself out.

The undercurrent was becoming more noticeable by the day. My stepfather was again called back to the Admiralty. The Italians had walked into Albania.

Sokolova put on a show for a project very grandly entitled the *Ballet de la Jeunesse Anglaise*, and in which I led a charming set of Russian folk dances called *Russki Plasski*. Great success at the Cambridge Theatre and I enjoyed myself even when some of my young men – who had incidentally backed the performance – complained that half the bouquets they sent me had been purloined by another dancer. . . . Quite in order. A little later at a ballet soirée in the Albert Hall for the Mount Vernon Cancer Fund, *Russki Plasski* was asked for again. I don't suppose I will ever forget living through one of the nightmares common to all dancers and which eventually, thank God, remain unmaterialised.

As always on such occasions, the arena of the Albert Hall is cleared of all seating and a large ramp is built joining the upper stage to the parterre down which one must move with as much grace and hidden determination as one can muster. Clad in my hand-painted Russian caftan complete with *kakozhnik* (the head-dress) I ran up the narrow backstage slope to the stage (surely one of the most exciting of all entrances as one emerges into the great vista of tier upon tier of boxes embracing three quarters of the vast auditorium), quickly crossed the stage and gingerly negotiated the slope down to the arena. The orchestra, seemingly acres away, were grouped in a bunch at the far end.

I waited. Not a note. Mystified I gave a long sweeping bow *à la russe*. Straightening up to applause, I made a slight movement to begin. Dead silence from the orchestra. Moored there alone with 6000 people staring at me I felt for all the world like someone waiting forlornly for the last bus home. A dozen questions passed through my head: the musicians had all been struck by paralysis? The conductor with his back to me had not registered that I was there? Should I put my fingers in my mouth and whistle? I had nothing to throw at them. Even then, thought I, getting wilder and wilder with nerves, it wouldn't reach them. Frozen with horror I decided to sweep round the whole arena in a kind of polonaise to the sound of my own chattering teeth, reach the orchestra and ask them, smothered with a honeyed smile between closed lips, what the devil they were up to? It was the longest pilgrimage I had ever made; under my caftan I felt the first itchings of a hair shirt and my satin slippers filled with dried peas. At last I got to the far corner shooting out my expletive at the wretched conductor as I passed by. 'Sorry, darling, couldn't find the music parts – okay now.' I doubled the speed of the polonaise in a fine bolt back to base and at last, a good four minutes after my entrance, heard the first liberating sounds to which I could begin dancing.

By now, there was a strange feeling of marking time, as though that current on which, young as we were, we expected to be borne, had turned sluggish; the future seemed as foggy as a London Particular in which we had lost our bearings. It was all the more welcome when Wendy Toye, that most generous of all colleagues, rang me up to say that Stephen Haggard (one of the leading young actors of the day) had just written his first play, *Weep for the Spring*, that it had been directed by the great Frenchman Michel St Denis with a star cast: Nicholas Hannen, Athene Seyler, William Fox, William Devlin and Peggy Ashcroft, had opened on its pre-London tour a couple of weeks earlier and, as it was on the short side, Stephen and St Denis had added as a 'curtain raiser' a slight comedy by Schnitzler; that the latter had proved a total flop and wanting to replace it they had appealed to her for an idea. Was I working and had I any suggestions? Time was of the essence, as there was only the weekend to devise something. Delighted, I told her I was resoundingly out of work; perhaps (working at top speed) she would consider putting a ballet together for Prudence Hyman, myself and two male dancers to the music of Mozart's *Eine Kleine Nachtmusik*? I would scribble a scenario, I still had the costume from the minuet of that lovely suite for which Dolin had written me the '*Romanze*' and we could get the remaining ones from Bermans & Nathans, the ubiquitous theatrical costumiers. Might we meet that evening? Wendy Toye agreed. I toiled all day collecting Pru and two male dancers, sketching the scenario and finally joining Wendy at eight p.m. to start work. That was Thursday, 18 May 1939.

Wendy was every dancer's dream to work for: precise, musical, flexible, with an inborn flair. We worked four hours that night, another eight the next day, five hours the following, so that on the Sunday the producer of the play and Stephen were able to come and watch the final four-hour rehearsal of which they approved heartily. We packed that night, caught the eleven-fifteen to Oxford on the Monday morning and opened at the Playhouse that evening, 22 May.

I revelled in that kind of tempo: challenge, application, arduous hours, no time for uncertainties or ditherings, the feeling of being a projectile hurtling towards a target and sure of no interjections. The play itself was a lovely one, sensitive and moving: the direction as sedulous and delicate as all things Michel St Denis touched and the acting, with such a superb cast, perfect. What made that all-too-short tour such a very special experience for me was the quality of all those taking part, including the understudies. With the exception of 'Beau' Hannen, and Athene, they were mostly young, so that as we went from town to town, from Oxford to Liverpool to Brighton to Scarborough, we would invent games in the train, organise picnics, find some way of enhancing the mainly ghastly digs, the abominable food, become more and more attached to each other, find shared tasks, share private lovings and loathings – in other words it was far removed in human terms from the desert of the ballet where there seemed never to be anything other than passion and persecution, pursuit or antagonism, relationships throbbing away at a most exhausting emotional pulse and total physical weariness. Those weeks remain enshrined in my heart as the first glimpse I had of the companionship of the straight theatre.

What made it possible to savour it to the full, of course, was the ease of the actual work: no *pointes*, therefore no bleeding toes, nor pumping lungs; a light practice hanging on to a piece of scenery an hour before performance sufficed to keep one in trim; the resultant lightness of weight and spirit, or responsibility, was pure heaven. Pru and I, finding ourselves in the same filthy pub in Liverpool where we had spent an imperishably awful week some four years earlier in the Markova-Dolin days, trying to sleep in tiny rooms, between sheets and blankets so impregnated with the all-prevailing stink of stale ale, only mocked at the squalor now that we had companions to share the sleaziness with us. We could giggle at the salad bowl of which the top half alone would be replenished with lettuce, cucumber and tomato while the bottom half, seen through the glass sides, daily assumed a growing mildew like seaweed clinging to the hull of a barge, which in those earlier years we had retched over and finally abandoned. When I quarrelled irremedi-ably with one of the most persistent of my Foreign Office suitors who had come up to see the show, it hardly affected me at all.

The impending war was beginning to intrude despite all our determination to push it aside like some unpleasant obstacle. The black-out was by now imperative, not a chink or glimmer of light permitted from any house. Ever light-heartedly having reached Brighton, our little group walked all the way along the front to Hove and back again in the soft summer-night air, guided by the moon shining on a sea of mercury and made a late supper of the lobsters the fishermen-stage-hands had sold us for a shilling each. I suppose it was all the more tantalisingly sweet because of the growing perception of the evanescence of it all. We knew instinctively that we were reaching a river in our lives which once crossed would mean the abandonment of our youth for ever. We savoured every moment of those last summer months.

Reaching Scarborough on the coast of Yorkshire, we learned the dismal news that our backer had run out of money, that the London theatre was too unsettled to risk booking a play of such uncertain popularity and that this would be our last week. To pile Pelion on Ossa the theatre was a broken-down Edwardian ruin with peeling gold paint, worn red-velvet seats reminiscent of the posteriors of certain monkeys at the zoo and not even a small orchestra for the Mozart ballet. A dreadful trio of piano, violin and cello made sounds so eldritch that it was well-nigh impossible to give a coherent performance, added to which the Unfortunate Child stepped yet again smartly on to a huge upstanding nail and had to improvise a very bizarre *contredanse* on one and a half feet so as to reach the wings with outstretched foot into which the nail was firmly embedded, make cabalistic gestures at the stage manager, who fortunately got the message and pulled the hideous thing out of my heel, so enabling me to glide back and finish my dance, leaving, of course, a trail of blood in my own honourable fashion. The digs were equally terrible and the food quite foul. Our four-week companionship now only served to add sadness to our wretched physical condition. Dear Billy Devlin, whose legendary Lear some years before at the OUDS had opened up the London stage for him, and with whom I had shared a love of sixteenth- and seventeenth-century English poetry all through the tour, came to my room, where I was resting before the final performance. In his hand was an anthology of John Donne which I cherish to this day. 'Diana, with all love, Billy, summer 1939', in his tiny, scholarly hand.

Stephen Haggard and Peggy Ashcroft came to the station and saw us off. It had been that kind of happy company. And although it was for me another end in a minor key, it had been one of the most joyful short spans of my life in the theatre to date.

I got back to Mulberry House on a Sunday to find nearly ninety people come to hear the music, for it was Louis Kentner playing and I sat on the stairs outside the packed music room and rinsed my eye, ear and soul clean of all the disappointment and tinge of nostalgia at both lost hopes and lost friendships.

On the strength of having passed my driving test, my stepfather had given me the handsome present of a £30 Morris Cowley with blistered windscreen, uncertain steering and an engine to match my own innards in caprice and discomfort. I would dread approaching a red light when, with a spiteful triumph, she would conk out, however hard I tried to coax her by revving up frantically between gear changes. Despairing, I would stroke her bleary windshield as I stamped on the self-starter hoping to get her going and quieten the cacophony of hooting behind me. I christened her 'Chi-Chi, la Marquise de Fla-Fla', an apt title for her unreliable temperament and a certain affected swinging of her back wheels befitting a tart with pretensions.

Cecil Harcourt was at the Admiralty as Director of Operations and as he liked his morning walk, I would be delegated to drive him as far as St James's Park, often picking up various very tall, very grand generals waiting at the Chelsea Town Hall for the bus. 'Stop, darling, there's old Shackerley-Ackers; we'll give him a lift to the Horse Guards,' and doubling up like a jack-knife a 6-foot-4-inch soldier, very smart in his uniform, would crouch in that dreadful little car. One evening after the theatre an impatient driver behind me bashed into poor old Chi-Chi's fancy hindquarters, nearly shot me into the Whitehall traffic ahead, causing me to collide head first with that spotty windshield. I was saved from concussion by a very chic turban I'd got on our last visit to Paris, a wonderful concoction of yard upon yard of Paisley wool designed by the then leading *modiste*, Caroline Reboux, and in this instance a perfect shock-absorber. Alas! Poor old Marquise de Fla-Fla was crippled cruelly and hauled off looking strangely obscene with her mangled buttocks. . . .

The de Basil Company was holding what was to be its last season at Covent Garden. One blessing of being temporarily out of work was that I could go there whenever I wanted, but the crowning glory came when one evening Gerry Sebastianoff, the very handsome general secretary who had always been a good friend to me, took me aside and asked me if I would care to join a new company they were forming (very obviously to get away from the present jungle). Irina Baronova together with Alicia Markova would be equal as *prima ballerina assoluta*, Alexandre Benois artistic director, Anton Dolin *primo*, Nijinska choreographer and I chief dramatic dancer. I was thrilled, but at the same time hurt that Pat had not invited me already. 'Go and see him and tell him I've invited you, otherwise you will only need Nijinska's permission and I know how much she admired you in the Markova-Dolin Company. I'll give you her Paris address. We should all assemble for rehearsals already in September.' I rushed round to Pat's dressing-room and scolded him for not telling me sooner. He apologised for the delay. I hugged him, adding that I would try to get in touch with Nijinska.

The following week I travelled to Paris, with Nijinska's address in my bag. I traced her to a dim little villa backed away as if in distaste from a strip of weedy garden, edged by rusty fencing and a wicket-gate. I opened the latter and without much hope walked up the mud path. Stuck to the front door was a torn paper bearing the message: '*Absents jusqu'a 20 heures.*' Forlornly I retraced my steps, banged the rickety gate and made my way back to the district railway. Imagine my incredulous joy when I found Nijinska, her husband and daughter Irina standing on the platform just about to board the incoming train to Paris!

I was as much a strange apparition to them and as out of context as they seemed to me. The anonymity of that open, raised platform, lined by its urban hedge of mile upon mile of high-shouldered skimpily proportioned houses, comprised an unlikely setting for one of the most famous and exotic of Russian choreographers still trailing clouds of Byzantine glory from the days of Diaghilev.

We all four squeezed into seats facing each other and discussed the new company. I told her I'd already been invited as dramatic ballerina and that there were many more dancers to be gathered by the coming autumn. '*Diana*,' said Nijinska, '*je voudrais que vous me trouviez tous les membres du corps de ballet de chez Dolin. Ils étaient marveilleux!*' It was true. The peculiar genius of the English for teamwork was exemplified by the precision and elegant lines of the girls wherever the old-style *corps* was used. I promised to do my best in the short time left. She told me there was also a film projected of Caryl Brahms's and A. J. Simons's book *A Bullet in the Ballet*, a travesty-thriller based on the de Basil Ballets Russes, which had been a best-seller. There would be a rôle for me in that too. We reminisced about the Markova-Dolin ballet which she had so enjoyed and in which she had entertained such hopes until the impasse between her, myself and Dolin had made her decide to leave. She asked me whether I indeed left at the same time. I affirmed, saying once she had gone I no longer cared to stay. What had happened to the Company? They had toured one more season and then, so I had heard, Dolin became dispirited (as I would have, had I stayed), and it folded. Sad.

For some peculiar reason I had always been looked upon as the Delphic Oracle in my family. Oddly, Mama and Griselda would from time to time hand me the crystal ball and demand to know what might be forthcoming.

This time, summer 1939, it was the unacceptable likelihood of there being a war. No question, I said, certainly there will be one, so Griselda dear, this is our last chance to go to the Continent and we'd better hurry.

Griselda in those days was full of initiative. She suggested a dash to Geneva, where there was to be an exhibition of pictures from the

Madrid Prado Gallery, and a hop over to Lucerne where Toscanini would be giving a concert. We could then go up to Denmark to the lovely castle where we'd spent two earlier summer and, I added grimly, be lucky if we made it. Toscanini conducted the *Coriolan* Overture by Beethoven, Debussy's *La Mer*, the *Vorspiel* and *Liebestod* from *Tristan and Isolde* and the Brahms Symphony No. 1, with a Festival Orchestra of which Adolf Busch was concert master and Karl Doktor the first violinist. It was an inspiring and elating performance in true Toscanini style. We then got ourselves to Geneva spending a whole day tramping round the extraordinary collection from the Prado until our feet were like medium-rare hamburgers, for there was, we discovered dolefully, no such thing as a season ticket enabling the footsore to limp home for lunch, soak their bunions in the bidet, and thus refreshed return to further joys in the afternoon; once you left the portals your ticket expired with cunning Genevan parsimony and only the talisman of further francs would unseal further joys. Fuming at such niggardliness, we kept going for nearly five hours gazing at such glorious pictures: Velasquez, Zurbarán, Goya, El Greco (for it was the Spanish school we particularly wanted to see) and a host of others, including the weird and wonderful Patinir, a dog-eared postcard of whose *Sodom and Gomorrah* from the Ashmolean Museum I'd carried in my wallet since I was a schoolgirl.

So on to Denmark, as hazardous a cross-continental trip as we could have contrived, no Swiss ever having heard of Fredericia our Danish port, and having to go via Basel and Hamburg, changing tourist cheques with great difficulty and making friends with very nice young German soldiers who asked us with a curiosity (tinged with future ambition?) to tell them all about England. Finally arrived in what turned out to be Friedrichshafen, I caught sight of a news-stand and bought both the *Berliner Illustrierte Zeitung* and some Danish magazine called *Ung Journalen*, in which there were pictures of charabancs (as they were still named) called London Coastal Coaches, bearing a poster cheerfully stating: 'Don't mind Hitler, book now.' When I reached the lovely Danish castle I wrote to Sir Robert Vansittart sending cuttings from the two magazines.

Mid–August. That pellucid Danish light spreading over the vast green field that stretched like a ceremonial carpet from the pink 'E' shape of Tirsbaek straight down to the silver-grey fjord. Huge old trees marching down each side in leafy walls. Not even an aeroplane to disturb the still air. Griselda and I and Ebba, the younger daughter of the house, lay under the great plum tree in the kitchen garden and gorged. One of Griselda's many suitors came to stay. I doubt we talked seriously. Someone came out of the house with a cable for me: a television date with Dolin on 6 September; rehearsals starting for the new company 28 September. Two days later, 21 August, serious war scares. On the twenty-fourth my stepfather signalled not to worry even though the German-Soviet pact had just been signed. The contract for *A Bullet in the Ballet* had arrived at Mulberry House. Restless, I said goodbye to our dear hosts and went up to see fond friends in Copenhagen, young people of our own age with whom we'd spent a carefree summer in their various country castles around. Danes have a genius for enjoyment, are very good to look at and handle their guests with an irresistible mixture of charm and grace that comforted my over-zealous, overly sedulous nature and gave me a blitheness I had by this time all but lost.

In Copenhagen, at the famous Hotel d'Angleterre, where on the terrace you could be sure of meeting everyone belonging to that close-knit pre-war society eating fresh shrimps accompanied by Tyborg beer, I put my burning question: 'How soon?' Adam Moltke, Niels Friis, Ulrick Ahlefeldt, Dannesjkølds, Rentelows – all laughed my fears away saying: 'Look, Diana, we all have German first cousins, of course nothing will happen here.' Unconvinced I turned to the inimitable Hasluv, a member of the shrinking confederacy of great concierges now nearly extinct, and begged him to give me his opinion. With no glimmer of expression on that extraordinary tortoise-like face, he said: 'I will get you a place on the next ship tomorrow, the twenty-sixth, Miss Gould.' Marvellous man, he had even got me a single cabin (under the piratical title of Lady Diana Gould), which I reached by stepping over the hordes of bodies lying on every available inch of the deck. Griselda and her young man managed to return to England on 28 August.

Anxiously every day I awaited the news that the rehearsals would begin. Silence. On 1 September conscription was announced, together with a complete mobilisation of all the forces. At six a.m. Hitler claimed Danzig and invaded Poland. The evacuation of all children, long prepared, began. Pa spent the night at the Admiralty and the next morning, 2 September, I found him breakfasting in the dining-room in his uniform. Nobody said anything in particular as we obviously could not ask Pa to divulge news. Britain sent that day, through Prime Minister Neville Chamberlain, an ultimatum to Hitler which, if not answered by eleven a.m. on the next day, would be tantamount to a declaration of war. In those days there was no television to speak of, only radio and under these circumstances only tight-lipped conjecture. We went to bed. I was glad that we were at least all together and back in Mulberry House, not scattered all over the Continent.

On the following day, Sunday, 3 September, Hitler having not replied to Britain's ultimatum, at eleven a.m. Chamberlain announced over the radio a state of war between England and Germany. At eleven-forty-five there was the first wail of the air-raid siren. Obediently we collected our gas masks. The all clear sounded soon after. False alarm. We set to sewing rings on thick black curtain material to ensure a complete black-out, stuck black paper round basement windows; large hessian sacks, full of sand I supposed, appeared at the bases of buildings. For the moment it would seem that all places of entertainment would be shut till further notice.

Long gone were my autumn plans: the film, the new company, my beloved Nijinska. The SS *Athena* was torpedoed and sunk. I did manage to say goodbye to Nijinska at Laura Henderson's, the old lady who backed the Markova-Dolin Company; she was as disappointed as I. I went to wave the de Basil Company farewell at Victoria Station.

They and Nijinska would all be going to the States. I felt totally bereft. Dolin as yet stayed behind and joined the ARP (Air Raid Precautions) unit near his studio in Carlyle Square; theirs would be the job of rescuing people from bombed-out buildings and getting them to hospital. I continued ferrying Pa's army pals, for poor old Chi-Chi's posterior had been patched up and she was no more erratic than she always had been. Griselda and I fumbled our way through the black-out on the district railway to where a suburban theatre had been allowed to open and Robert Donat, Stewart Grainger and many other stage stars were giving a wonderful season of Shakespeare and Goldsmith, which made the inspissate gloom, the endless stations now made nameless in a pathetic gesture to confuse a possible invasion, seem part of the indisputable argument. One did not complain about it as it was shared by all, which paradoxically enhanced the excitement and beauty of the plays and the acting. On 14 October 1939 the *Royal Oak*, our pride and joy, was sunk. Only 370 of the crew of 1200 were saved.

I was asked to double for a very well-known actress who had to be seen dancing in a film. Delighted to have a little work, I went down to Elstree with two male dancers. We had prepared what we proudly thought was a smashing ballroom dance. Film work for a dancer is pure hell. The delays, in those days endless, resulted in one spending hours in the dressing-room fully made-up in costume, clinging to anything steady enough to do exercises on, in a desperate attempt to keep one's muscles warm and ready, with the result that when the call finally came one had all the energy and vigour of yesterday's *banane flambée*.

Be that as it may, the daily pay exactly matched one's weekly earnings on the stage, so no complaints. The director was a Frenchman with whom I struck up a friendship which I can only call a kind of *contredanse*. Two steps forward from him; one by me, three by him; one backwards by me, which lasted all day through odd and dreadful meals in the cafeteria, incidentally offering me a great deal of happiness simply in speaking a language I so loved. The Star was not pleased. Not at all.

The ball dress, a copy of hers of course, was ravishing and I'd decorated my hair with a set of my grandmother's Edwardian moonstone stars. As I waited endlessly on the set (another actress was fluffing her lines interminably) the Star approached me where I sat at the director's side, hopelessly wiggling my toes. 'I like the things in your hair,' said in an icy voice, delivered through one blocked nostril. 'Thank you,' from me. Pause. 'I'd like to buy them off you. How much do you want?' her tone rich in layers of graciousness to an inferior, charity towards a pauper, with a covering of the sour cream of human kindness on top. She practically had her hand in her purse at the ready. 'Well?' she said impatiently through the other nostril. 'I'm so sorry,' I said, 'they're heirlooms and not really mine to sell without asking my mother,' and smiled sweetly. I heard a snort of laughter from my French flirt, the Star glared at me through both nostrils and flounced away. '*Va danser enfin!*' said the director, grinning broadly. So off I spun with my two handsome partners, determined, as an apology for my rather vulgar snub, to do her a treat as a dancer in the film.

I thought we were superb. However, when they'd finished swinging me around and tossing me about and we'd heaved to a breathless end, all the French director said was, '*Assez, tu viendras demain danser toute seule!*' My poor partners were dismissed and I got another day's pay, wildly improvising, moonstones and all.

So the year limped to an end while we all waited for what we did not or, more probably, dared not know. We accepted what work we could find, I always expecting to be called up. Our daily life, lived as far as possible normally, carried inevitably the undercurrent of our basic lack of liberty. It was like one of those three-legged races at school where one leg is tied to one's partner, comically hampering one's progress. Only this was not comic.

A rich Australian had bought the little Arts Theatre near St Martin's Lane in the heart of theatreland. Against the day theatres would open again, he engaged me as a kind of social secretary to make a list of potential subscribers to the ballet companies he would eventually engage and to dispatch them in readiness. Hardly thrilling, but he paid me the handsome sum of £4 a week. 'Better', as my grandfather would say, 'than a poke in the eye with a sharp stick.'

I sat for yet another portrait by Freddie Gore, a young and brilliant painter destined for a big career. Came yet another sign of altered times: dear 'Vava' Galitzine, Prince Vladimir Galitzine of the famous antique shop in Berkeley Street, closed it for good and all. He and his heavenly wife 'Mamasha' with their half-a-dozen languages would go into the BBC and the Postal Censorship respectively, while the three sons Nicholas, Immanuel and George (my close friend) would go severally into the Navy, the Air Force and the Welsh Guards.

In true Russian fashion there was a wonderful dinner to celebrate the closure – typically no regrets – after which I was hauled off in company with seven young men to the Players' Theatre, a delightful cabaret run by actors and actresses after curtain-down, in an old loft in Covent Garden and easily the wittiest set of sketches to be seen in London. We all sat at small tables, drinking, while satire followed farce, all acted and written by actors one had mostly seen playing Shakespeare or Shaw – Robert Donat had taken us before, but this night was exceptional. A gross creature dressed in a ball gown of puce organdie, a haystack of an orange wig on its head, its face smeared obscenely with make-up, trundled on to the small stage, followed by a pianist who took up his place modestly and patiently at the keyboard. The creature proceeded in a rich Central European accent to present itself as Frau Lieselotte Beethoven-Finck and for half an hour to describe the amazing discovery of a Schubert song with a rich absurdity reminiscent of all those numbing musical lectures whose arid seriousness must induce thousands of melomanes to rush for the nearest disco; at the end of which, rousing the dormant pianist, there followed a three-page introductory musical passage of a Schubertian nature terminated by the creature shrilling '*Es mus sein!*' thereupon announcing 'Dat vos der Fragment' and leaving the stage amid wild laughter and applause. It was the young Peter Ustinov, whose first play had just been produced at the Arts Theatre.

10

Finally Facing the Truth

Nineteen-forty and still this strange hiatus. It was as though we were being dragged backwards by our hair into an action for which we had little taste and were loth to turn our faces towards a responsibility we could no longer dodge. Our moral turpitude was beginning to smell and no amount of holding on to our nostrils could dismiss the stench. For so many of us German culture, music and literature had been part of our upbringing; we still wanted to believe that war between our two countries would never recur.

I always maintain that one of my countrymen's great strengths lies in their lack of imagination. Doubt stirs in the active, searching mind costing it its equilibrium; unruffled mind closed against the disturbance of too much thought does not have to entertain the idea of failure. An England based on its vast empire with all its riches offered a solid base; the apparently small island was but the tip of an iceberg of which the submerged foundations ensured its strength (as well as earning us from the French the soubriquet of *perfide Albion*, a nation of hypocrites maddeningly hiding behind the false modesty of being but a bouquet of offshore islands). The English, separated from the volatile Continent, are of a phlegmatic nature, tolerant, not given to passion, nor to extrapolation. 'Sufficient unto the day is the evil thereof,' they might say and turning away from disagreeable rumblings prefer to pursue their immediate tasks. Essentially apolitical, their two seventeenth-century revolutions had been relatively bloodless; once they had decapitated their monarch with due ceremony, and endured the dreary ideology of Cromwell long enough to do penance, they could return to their muttons; and when it seemed there must be further upheavals, towards the end of that century a Dutch prince was welcomed to rid them of another disobliging King. Above all, the English like order, so that they may pursue their individual lives, and above even that, to be left alone to do so.

All this led to their desire to dodge unpleasantness, their lack of enthusiasm for Great Causes. Their vision, if there were any, o'erleapt Europe into focus on the far-flung Empire. 'Over there' was where they would rather show their mettle, their heroism and their gallantry. Otherwise they preferred to agree with the great Lord Melbourne that 'Nobody ever did anything very foolish except from some strong principle' and consequently trimmed their moral obligations towards the necessity to recognise the darkness spreading steadily nearer and nearer until they could no longer escape either the terrible hazard or the ethical significance with which it presented them.

The dormant imagination finally awoke, and with it came the realisation of Burke's uncomfortable dictum: 'The only thing necessary for the triumph of evil is that good men do nothing.' Evil, by its very nature, is base, therefore hidden, remaining in the dark underneath of the soul, and only conscience brings it to the surface to be challenged.

To a certain degree we were relieved when this epochal stage had finally arrived; no more fudging, no more casuistic argument; finished with sophistry and quibble and, whatever the cost ahead, the war would at least prove a catharsis for years of evasiveness. Those who were too young to have lived through the war years tend now to discredit as sentimental myth the wonderful feeling of companionship and shared danger that evolved between us all. I, for one, can guarantee that it was true. Gone was the ghastly class-consciousness, the stiffness; the British 'keep myself to myself' that obtained in differing forms throughout all ranks.

Dolin, who had after a year or so gone to America (I had three separate opportunities to join various companies there but decided to remain in England and never regretted it) wrote asking me to tell him what it was like living in wartime London. I replied that it was in so many ways wonderful to be rid of all the silly fantasies, snobbisms and shibboleths and simply to be grateful every morning still to be alive; to be as shabby as the next one, to stand in line for one's rations, to be ashamed to grumble, in other words to banish pettiness and to be part of one essential whole.

Myra Hess, the great pianist, had instigated a series of lunch-time concerts at the National Gallery to which everyone who could manage went between their morning and their afternoon jobs. Harold Rubin, the man for whom I had been social secretary in order to raise membership for the Arts Theatre, decided to follow suit. He engaged three separate ballet companies, each to perform at lunch-time for several weeks in turn in the tiny theatre. The company to which I belonged was formed mainly of those dancers who had worked with the Russians ('dirty Russians' we called ourselves) and who had preferred to stay in England. These were Pru Hyman, Kira Strakhova (an excellent American dancer), Hélène Wolska and myself. The company was directed by Keith Lester, chief choreographer of the ex-Markova-Dolin Company, and Harold Turner with whom I'd given that first recital at fourteen years old. It was therefore a very strong and professional lot and one whose members had worked together often before. The other companies were one directed by Anthony Tudor with Maude Lloyd and Peggy van Praagh as his principal dancers and the third the Rambert group. Such were all three companies' success that Rubin then added yet another performance – after a quarter of an hour's interval used mainly to clear the house of its audience and the left-over sandwiches – and finally (anxious for still larger profits) yet another one, so we wretched dancers came to morning class at ten, followed by rehearsal, which left us time for a cup of coffee as we made-up for the first show from one o'clock to two o'clock; the second show two-fifteen and the third three-thirty to four-thirty, at the end of which we were given a large tray with the curled-up stale sandwiches no self-respecting member of the audience cared to pay for.

It was, above all, work. We were in no position to bargain and as we had all been through the Russian companies we were used to slavery and poor conditions. It meant that at least for as long as the job lasted the fear of the Labour Exchange loomed less menacingly, for every woman from eighteen to forty-five was conscripted, which would mean a choice (or not) of joining the Army, Navy, or the Air Force (in all of which services we would probably have been deplorably useless) and thereby no longer being able to keep up the technical practice compulsory for any dancer. So gratitude superseded resentment and I, for one, was delighted to have some lovely rôles created for me. Harold Turner wrote *May Collins*, a Cornish legend, in which I was the eponymous tragic heroine; Keith Lester wrote the rôle of the Moon in the ravishing slow movement of Mozart's C Minor Piano Concerto and I myself wrote the scenario and designed the costumes for a *Pavane*, with Keith Lester as my partner and choreographer, to Fauré's lyrical and melancholy music. Rubin became so enamoured of this work that he never missed a performance nor to send me flowers with a card to match the romantic verbiage.

I had always loved drawing and had had little if any time since leaving school at sixteen to draw, with the exception of the nine months of nursing my wretched rag of a knee. When unable to dance I took up my pencil again and 'practised' by copying every reproduction of portraits from El Greco to Renoir trying to regain what Charles Wheeler, the President of the Royal Academy, called 'an obedient pencil'. So that when Harold Turner wanted to produce another ballet, I suggested Hugo Wolf's *Italian Serenade*, wrote the scenario and designed the costumes and scenery, which I much enjoyed.

Otherwise the 'phony war', as we then called it, continued; theatres tentatively reopened, I gathered more and more men friends from all walks of life: actors, diplomats, painters, authors, politicians, those working in the arts and those few who did not have any particular work other than to administer their estates or look after their property. The very uncertainty of the future enhanced and deepened all friendships, adding a poignancy to those where the attachments were sentimental, an anxiety for those who would soon be called up. Gradually they all disappeared, swallowed up by the Army, the Navy, the Foreign and Intelligence services. Only those who could not pass the medical examinations, or those older men who served their own professions too well, who were of more value where they already were and conversely poor material for the military, were left behind. Many of those star actors who could be seen on stage night after night could not bear to accept this differentiation and simply enrolled themselves.

Griselda and I had long been dubbed 'the beautiful Gould sisters'; she was immensely popular and freer to move in society than I. Now that 'society' as such was fast dissolving, Griselda would need to prove herself capable of offering more than mere looks and even I felt it wiser in the event of theatres closing to join her in hastily casting about to find jobs. Firstly Griselda joined the Postal Censorship in the City of London, her fluent French being a valuable asset. Being Griselda she made great copy out of that and doubtless cheered her companions. Finding that the Postal Censorship was soon to be moved to Liverpool, she was determined not to leave London and found herself a job in MI5, the Military Intelligence, purely, I am convinced, on the length and strength of her eyelashes. Despite not being able to type, she managed to fit in very well and was very funny about that then rather messy department, writing a wicked lampoon about it which she inadvertently left on her typewriter (manipulated with two index fingers) and which was seized upon, copied and laughed at all over Whitehall, greatly to the discomfort of the War Office, which tried to arrest its further distribution.

After the war she told me she had found my name on the MI5 Black List, evidently for having innocently appeared in a thoroughly bad play written by an ardent communist acted by a very left-wing cast. It had only been for a Sunday night show in one of the drearier small theatres. I was about eighteen or nineteen I suppose, and quite oblivious of the political tinge of my leading man. All my senses were occupied trying to shut themselves off from his very rank body odour and I had little remaining to detect any reddishness in his ideology. I had been invited to take part by Lydia Lopokova, Diaghilev's ex-ballerina and the wife of Maynard Keynes, the great economist. I knew little about Bloomsbury other than its reputation as the intellectual enclave of such writers as Virginia Woolf and Lytton Strachey and had been touched that she'd asked me. I did indeed remember clambering again and again down one of the many customary stone stairs leading to the archetypal basement in which all our rehearsals seemed to have been held, from Bloomsbury to Kensington, and once coming upon a large poster of a very self-righteous-looking old man with a great deal of white beard, and innocently asking who it might be. I was greeted with shocked and incredulous silence, followed by a chorus of 'Karl Marx, of course' in such disapproving tones that, wickedly, I replied, 'Karl marks what?' The ensuing rehearsal was very frigid. I cannot remember another thing about it except that I never understood a word of my part as Eve (the ardent smell being Adam) nor tried to, for the whole play was written in a foggy vernacular of such pomposity and obfuscating wind that I could not rouse myself to tackle it. In retrospect, I rather enjoyed the strange eminence it had brought me when Griselda disclosed her secret – that I should be worthwhile identifying as a danger to the realm by reason of having taken part in that consummate tosh was a lovely black joke.

Gradually the handful of men friends dwindled away even more dramatically and our life was narrowed into work and the increasing and unavoidable restriction of most of our erstwhile freedoms. Clothes were rationed to eighty-two coupons per year – as a topcoat took the whole of it, the necessity of caring assiduously for every garment, mending, darning and resoling seedy old shoes, became paramount. Materials for décor and costumes were restricted, summoning a growing wiliness in our efforts to dress both on and off stage. Furnishing stuffs were as yet uncontrolled, so a great many armchairs and sofas and beds remained uncovered or shabby, deprived of the velvets, brocades and chintzes which now adorned our backs. The arts and crafts inherent in our lives became both artful and crafty and none of us were the worse for having to use our wits; to be jostled out of comfort and complacency altered our values as though a shake of the kaleidoscope had made new patterns of a quite different order and colour.

Because of the Draconian programmes at the Arts Theatre we were too tired for much else and were only fit to struggle home for our first meal of the day in the evenings. Occasionally, a friend long lost to a war job would surface on leave and the outing would be all the more worthwhile and treasured. George Galitzine, my closest Russian friend, now in the Welsh Guards for the past several months, called me up to dine with him. Delighted at the prospect of seeing each other again we made a date. It is a rule that in all the Guards regiments the new recruits pass through the lower ranks whatever their background socially or financially. Harold Nicolson, my guardian and one of the foremost English men of letters, had just written a very entertaining article on the extent to which clothes can affect the appearance, particularly of men.

According to Nicolson, clothes, however cheap or shoddy, never really affect a certain inbuilt distinction the average well-bred gentleman carries as his birthright. I was to prove, however, that nothing could have been further from the truth. The parlourmaid at Mulberry House announced George's arrival. I ran downstairs, excited to see him after all these months. For a fleeting second I thought there must be some mistake. Standing gracelessly in the hall, pinned down by the weight of his army-issue boots, as solid as a parcel in a thick khaki infantry suit, his red hair razored away to the top of his skull on which a tufty thatch lay incongruously like some temporary cover to keep out the rain, long neck sticking out of the ill-fitting collar supporting a pale face with protruding ears, the whole effect that of a lavatory brush with additional handles, was poor once-relaxed and elegant George Galitzine, a total oaf. 'Sparja, darling!' he called as I ran up to him, using my Russian nickname 'Asparagus', 'I beg of you don't laugh.' But I did, and it broke his self-conscious embarrassment at once. George had been a constant follower of the Markova-Dolin Ballet, often coming up to see us on tour; the possessor of a quirky sense of humour, he was wonderful company and I knew I could risk his laughing at himself. We ended up at the Four Hundred – a popular night-club in Leicester Square we could all be found in sooner or later. Very small and dark and cosy, the tiny tables squeezed along the walls made us all look like espaliered trees. In the centre was a minuscule dance floor with couples so glued together it was difficult to remember with whom one was dancing. George turned to a pretty woman, all but sandwiched to him at the next table: 'Good evening, Adèle.' He was greeted with that kind of cold glare reserved for the demolition of importunate males. Pause. 'Adèle?' Adèle Cavendish, erstwhile Adèle Astaire who, with her brother Fred had conquered London in *Lady Be Good* some years earlier, still froze this boring stranger. 'Adèle, it's George, George Galitzine,' by this time in an almost pleading tone on the verge of tears. 'My God,' she said melting all the former hostility with a spontaneous hug and kiss.

One day, he told me, at a dreaded inspection, all of the guardsmen rigid as poles standing at attention at the foot of their spotless beds in the long dormitory, eyes fixed straight ahead, the visiting general, gimleting down the rows as he slowly progressed, stopped dead in front of George and to his horror said 'Galitzine? Know your father, met him at so-and-so's,' and walked on. George waited in agony for the savage onslaught this must surely evoke. To his astonishment, once the general had disappeared the others crowded around him. 'You're a toff are you, then whatever?' they asked in their Welsh singsong. George, his ears tingling with relief, denied it saying his father kept a shop. . . . He had expected resentment and bullying, but the Welshmen felt neither envy nor the need to express it. When he got his commission George was much loved by his men and taught them to sing '*Auprès de ma blonde*' phonetically as they marched through the country lanes, with all the scabrous verses in their beautiful Welsh voices. I would love to have been a cow looking over a hedge listening.

Once our span at the Arts Theatre was over and the next company doing their stint, we were sent out on tour, mostly, as it was early May, to the coastal towns. Hastings was the first. We broke our strict code, swam (it was a heaven-sent summer), sunbathed, almost forgot the war that so far had only been a matter of loss of freedoms, covered ourselves with sun-oil, our only immediate problem being how to camouflage a sun-tan hardly befitting a moonlit Sylphide. Class and rehearsal every morning as usual. The door opened. Policemen. Gravely and politely they approached Barry Barcynsky, a young Pole, explaining that all aliens must for the moment be interned. Poor Barry went quietly. We resumed class.

May 1940: The German armies invade Belgium and Holland.

Deciding that behaving as though we were on holiday completely ruins the physical and mental concentration imperative to a dancer, we abandoned the *dolce far niente* of sea and sand and replaced it by long walks through the woods inland aflame with the gas-jet colour of bluebells, returning with armfuls of my most beloved of wild flowers, stuffing jugs and lidless coffee pots borrowed from our landladies to brighten the drably clean bedrooms.

Brussels and Antwerp fall.

Churchill made a wonderful, grave speech. His instinct for the nature of the British was unfailing. Just the right touch of warning as well as truthfulness, with faith in our ability to withstand. Three days later from our windows the sea appeared dotted with tiny specks, a rash sprinkled across the horizon. The sky was still blue, the water miraculously calm. I dressed quickly and ran on to the beach. By this time the specks had become boats of all shapes and sizes, dinghies, cockle-shells, small vessels of every conceivable kind, mostly with oars, a few with sails, obviously English and French soldiers cut off from the main armies and desperately rowing across the Channel to the nearest English coast. By this time large buses had assembled on the front. I asked if, speaking French, I could be of help and together with those in charge stood at the water's edge as they floated in one after the other, red-eyed, starving, ragged, soaking after God knows how long huddled on the Norman beaches and squeezed into any vaguely seaworthy object they could seize. Some with dirty, bloodied bandages, most without shoes, all dazed by the good fortune of being alive and on land again.

We handed out chocolate and I helped them into buses where they would be taken to various centres for hot drinks, hot water, clothing. It was strange for me to talk to the French again, to recognise even in such macabre circumstances their unquenchable intelligence; to see the routed look in their eyes – a kind of spiritual weariness matching their physical exhaustion. Most of them intended to join de Gaulle – in all their talk I detected the basic rationalism that informs all French thinking. They had no illusions, they knew defeat for France was not far off.

The ballet performances went on. We no longer needed to discipline ourselves not to go on to those beaches; anyway they were beginning to lay mines around the pier and cover it with a bird's nest of barbed wire. Later that night 'Patik' Thal (Strakhova in the de Basil Company) came weeping to our room. Her sister's husband, Captain Simpson, had been killed on the bridge of his ship, for by now the great retreat from Dunkirk had begun in earnest.

The German Army is at Boulogne. Amiens has been taken.

We went on giving our show, feeling less and less inclined. They were detonating mines found out at sea and the explosions rocked one off balance. Dancing seemed all the more absurd.

King Leopold of the Belgians surrenders to the German Army.

Away from London and the centre of things I felt afloat, longing to get back and not to be marooned here, ridiculously attired in a tutu with the sea as far as the eye can see full of our boats making for the coasts further up, where the distance from France is narrower. All day and night the anti-aircraft guns were going and Messerschmitts were dive-bombing the escaping boats.

At last London and Mulberry House. To fill up time I did another design for one of our soloists. The Sunday musical parties were still going on, only there were increasingly more refugees among the guests, as among the performers – a bonus both. Our Company went down to Tunbridge Wells, the spa near our maternal grandparents' much-loved little house, the scene of all our childhood summers. I spent all day searching for digs – for somehow, waiting for the Real Thing, one was not planning any more, simply leasing out the smallest possible amount of thought towards the practicalities of daily living while the rest of one's mind was in storage waiting to be summoned. I spent two days drawing the designs and the décor for the *Italian Serenade*, having found a comfortable double room in a hotel on Mount Ephraim overlooking the wide sweep of commons that would one day belong to our family as part of the inheritance of the Manor of Rusthall. It concentrated my mind wonderfully, looking from sketch pad out over the full June summer trees, the strange pachydermous rocks humped amongst them like a herd of strayed elephants, the wild flowers in the grass verges, the church spires of the town below, beyond the terrace of the 'Pantiles'. At least I felt fully occupied in a creative effort and not merely capering about interpreting nineteenth- and twentieth-century choreography.

14 June: The Germans conquer Paris.

What little peace of mind I had gathered, dissolved. The ache in my heart at the loss of my enchanted city was like a bereavement, in many ways worse, for it was not a simple loss, there was the sequence, the terrible anxiety over its ultimate fate. Fortunately the combination of the Germans' appreciation of Paris, together with the bargaining gifts of the pragmatic French supervened, ensuring at least its physical safety for the time being.

23 June: France surrenders, accepting the Armistice terms demanded by Germany.

And now the crux had been reached. We were really alone.

For the first time in my own life I felt the stirrings of a loneliness I had never known before. It was as though a crack had opened in my rigid attitude, a blend of unquestioning obedience to whatever the pursuit of my profession demanded, together with a certain emotional arrogance based on a romanticism that feared the anguish of surrender to anyone who did not measure up to my absurd criteria. All this, added to the inhibiting code of an Edwardian upbringing, encased me in an armour which I could not open but which at the same time had protected me. In the past months of the shifting of the very base of all that had stood for daily life, of the draining away of friends, of the revelation of varieties so sound and pure they could no longer remain hidden under a sediment of self-regard and irresponsibility, I felt I could no longer hide myself, nor suddenly was that self inside its protective covering safe. Unconsciously, I had been suffering from the pins and needles of awakening and was feeling the draughts of loneliness through that tin can. I was vulnerable in a way I had never imagined I could be. All around me I became aware of lovers, of companionships, of partners. I alone was alone – a solitary no longer content to be so. Was it the ever-presence of death that enhanced the quality of life, a life made all the more precious for its frailty, as in all beautiful things? I felt emotionally unsettled, yearning for closeness, for that loving concern of which I had received so little. I was at last tired of being Battling Gould the Wild Half-Caste, who could never battle for herself, who was too proud to beg for help, to admit to weakness and who cradled her pain to herself like the Spartan boy, loth to let anyone know how defenceless she really was. But there was still so much to overcome in me. No man so far had pierced that armour, nor kindled me.

And during that summer of 1940, as the war abruptly became real, as the Battle of Britain raged over the fields and hedgerows and little woods of Kent and Surrey and Sussex, I did meet someone with the courage and skill to break down all my defences. No matter that he was what the French would call *du métier* – a thoroughly professional seducer. No other lover could have conquered so frightened a romantic, could have cut so delicately through those layers of false sophistication, prudery, ignorance and sheer quaking fear, to reach that infant heart; no one else would have shown the infinite patience he showed nor cared for me in a multitude of ways I had never known. He arrived at just the right moment for us both. It was to last all of seven months and when he finally broke the heart he'd opened I suffered all the adolescent pangs for the death of a first affair with the anguish and emotions of a fully matured woman. As far as his over-exercised heart was capable, he had genuinely loved me nor, once I had recovered, do I regret what befell. I was slowly learning that nothing I ever received from life would happen without a high price to pay.

The first Blitz began and life took on a weird dislocation as though one continued one's job but with a wry-neck. The sirens wailed, the bombs dropped. We sat rigid in buses, stood frigid in queues. No one would dream of being shamed into lying flat on the pavement until the All Clear sounded, meaning that the bombers had gone and the raid was over, although we all longed to. The theatres and concert halls stayed open none the less and we hung grimly on to the principle that whatever happened we were all in it together, which of course was a great spiritual cement. Now at last, the class-conscious criteria were totally discarded. Furthermore, we actually talked to each other without being introduced. As the bus taking me to the theatre skirted last night's bomb crater in Piccadilly I asked the woman next to me how her night had been. 'Not so bad, dearie, 'ow was yours?' And we would wish each other another half-way decent one as we hopped off.

At last I felt less useless as I smeared on my make-up. Now that war was really here and the theatre crammed from one a.m. till six-thirty, I knew we were offering something of value, a welcome respite before the bombs would begin falling towards dusk.

The Company went up to Norwich. No porters. No taxis. Pru and I had to lug our heavy suitcases half a mile from the station to the squalid little pub masquerading as a hotel. I, who in London had been taking the Blitz in my stride, was now full of apprehension for the family left there. So many telephone lines had been destroyed that telephoning for civilians was forbidden. We were completely cut off. I worried myself sick, could not concentrate on my dancing, recognised suddenly one of those strange telepathic messages I'd so often received as a child. A letter came from Pa. Mulberry House had received a direct hit, blowing out most of the back and lower staircase, killing Wilson the parlourmaid and wounding our dear Winifred in the leg. Thank God Mama and Griselda had gone to the country to see Gerard and were safe and sound; Pa's own car had been blown up in the Horse Guards Parade where the Admiralty was also hit. Mama, Pa and Griselda – all three were safe, that was the equation, no material loss really counted.

I returned to London homeless. Mama went to her mother-in-law, Grannie Grace, my stepfather's mother at Hurlingham. Griselda and I found rooms in Lowndes Street. It was essential that Mama leave London. Most women of her class had joined the WVS (Women's Volunteer Service) and were doing multiple jobs of great value all over the city. The thought of finding Mama a job – she who could neither cook nor sew, multiply nor divide, drive a car nor roll a bandage – was dispiriting. Some dauntless soul did try putting her in an officers' canteen to serve, but she kept giving free buns to those soldiers she chatted up, with the result that the books would never balance, so she had to go. Many of her friends had gone to Bath in Somerset, a ravishing eighteenth-century town, a famous spa since Roman times and a highly civilised little city. A charming house had been found for her there; her three Bechsteins and whatever furniture she needed and had not been wrecked were duly despatched and Mama prepared to go.

There had been a little trouble at first as Cecil had got her a first-class ticket which she typically had tried to cash in and travel second. Cecil had a hard time explaining it came by courtesy of the Admiralty and she could not possibly do such a thing. She accepted grudgingly that a car would come from the Admiralty to take her to the station. Mulberry House had been patched up temporarily, an iron staircase replaced the first flights and Mama had to pack her clothes for the first time without the reliable Winifred, still in hospital. Griselda came to fetch her. Tableau: she reported Mama was standing on the steps that led down from the porch and the front door, two large suitcases at her feet out of which hung sundry extras such as ribbons, the foot of a stocking and the odd shoulder-strap or two; her hair was like an abandoned bird's nest on top of which sat at an uncertain angle her second-best hat. 'Mama,' cried Griselda, 'what do you look like, for heaven's sake!' Offended, Mama told Griselda not to criticise and she couldn't imagine what she objected to.

Griselda pushed open the front door and together with Mama dragged both cases inside. Kneeling down she got the cases open, wincing at the sight of the mangled clothes, quickly refolded them, tucking in all the extraneous danglers. Then she turned to Mama, removed the hat, did what she could with the recalcitrant locks, replaced the hat at a more becoming angle, secured it with its hat pin and raced her down the steps to the waiting car driven by the usual mummified service chauffeur. Arrived at Paddington, she got a porter for the suitcases and with Mama in tow and the reserved tickets in her hand proceeded down the corridor until she came to the carriage corresponding to their places. It was empty except for the monumental presence of a large lady occupying a rippling mink coat with hat to match, and possessor of a great many large rings on both hands, together with a face so daubed with make-up that it looked for all the world like a Hallowe'en turnip with the candle alight inside. This phenomenon took one look at Mama standing in the doorway and said with utter contempt: 'This carriage is *first class*!' whereupon marvellous Mama replied with great sweetness: 'Oh! Don't I look first class?' Griselda said you could hear the wind withdrawing from the *nouveau riche* lady like the hiss of a gas lamp going out, her face turned a delicate shade of purple and, fumbling with her gloves, she suddenly found the view out of the opposite window fascinating. Griselda settled Mama, plumped herself down and the train slid out.

I was relieved when neither of them was any longer in London. The Blitz was going hammer and tongs by now and Pru and I had managed to find two tiny top-floor bed-sitters in a very nice house in Lowndes Street in Belgravia – actually opposite the house in which we had, all three Gould children, been born. It had a single bed, a washbasin, a tiny wardrobe and chest-of-drawers, two chairs and I suppose some kind of table. The bathroom, shared, was on the half-landing below. Perfectly adequate, central and with a very nice landlady.

What was not perfectly adequate was the state of the ballet Company's morale at the Arts. After months of loyal and back-breaking work, both in London and in the provinces, one of those boring dilemmas endemic in the ballet had occurred. Our Company was the most vulnerable of the three engaged by Rubin in that, unlike Rambert's and Tudor's autonomous ones, it had started more or less *ad hoc*, gathering in all those leading dancers who had preferred to stay in England rather than go to the States with other companies; this made us prey to the whims of our employer, who suddenly decided to promote a totally inexperienced eighteen-year-old for whom he had conceived a passion. This being a classic in the history of ballet mores, we tried to argue with him that we could tolerate giving her a special appearance, but arbitrarily to place her at the head as a principal dancer, above a group of well-known and well-tried dancers, was not only ridiculous but detrimental to the good name of the whole Company which in those circumstances could no longer be taken seriously as first class.

Thus we bought time; she had her big 'number' with splendid Spanish costume (she was a thoroughly nice child) and the Company continued to perform, to survive on dog-eared sandwiches, to crawl home in the dark on erratic buses while the bombs fell and accept that on rare occasions the driver would abandon us and run for the shelter, leaving us to fumble our way through the darkened streets on foot to our respective dwellings, tired, hungry and now worried. For as the Blitz grew heavier the admirers for the later show dwindled and in the classic way of all managers we were made to bear the financial burden, not simply out of parsimony but because it might prove a subtle way of twisting our collective arm and forcing us to accept his determination to degrade us by promoting his little fancy. The new arrangement was that we were to be paid solely from the 'takings' of the week; on Friday night the accountant, having totted up the box-office money, would allot us the result. As a softener to this egregious treatment the salaries were guaranteed not to fall below the munificent sum of £3 sterling a week. Like most adherents to this Cinderella of a profession we were in no position to refuse and accepted the spiteful humiliation. From then on I, who had a horror of debt, counted every penny even more arduously than ever.

I worked out that as my rent was thirty shillings per week, I could only count securely on the other thirty shillings for transport and food (always given those sour sandwiches to stave off the worst pangs). I was too proud to ask my mother who, safely installed in Bath, had lent one Bechstein to the Pump Room and had the other two in her house together with the good Winifred, leg now healed, and the epileptic Mrs Battye, who had been found in her basement kitchen, covered with flour, shaking her fists at the skies, saying 'Bugger the Nazis!' in her best Irish accents. I managed to survive those weeks mainly because of my new-found lover who would whisk me away to his country cottage as soon as the last Saturday night show was over and feed me up till I returned on Monday morning for class, rehearsal and crumbs.

The full-moon nights were of course the worst. No amount of black-out could conceal a London silver-grey with trees still in leaf and the broad, blanched ribbon of the Thames winding its way, linked bank to bank by the bridges that were the chief target of the Messerschmitts. It was a week in which we were not performing. Foolishly perhaps and because there was some kind of unspoken rule of insisting upon leading as normal a life as possible ('Business as usual' proclaimed the small shopkeepers on the splintered boards across their shattered shop fronts), my lover and I were dining with friends at the fashionable Mirabelle restaurant in nearby Curzon Street. Very few people were there and the Cypriot waiters looked green with fright, as well they might, for the clatter of explosions well-nigh drowned the band, manfully trying to lift our slightly quaking spirits. 'I really feel a bit foolish in my pale-blue turban,' I said in a momentary lull to Teddy Hulton, the owner and editor of *Picture Post* (our nearest equivalent to *Life* magazine). 'Oh! no Diana, you're quite wrong, go on looking lovely and chic, it's such a boost to our morale.' At that moment the band stopped and the bandmaster seemed to be searching for someone in the room. At last his eye caught me: 'Oh there you are Miss Gould – would you go to the night-club off Bruton Street where your friend Prudence Hyman has been seriously hurt?' My stomach somersaulted. We had dropped poor Pru there as she didn't relish staying alone in her little room next to my empty one and I felt full of guilt. As I raced across the intervening streets into Berkeley Square and dived into the narrow alley where the night-club lay, I reckoned when I saw the damage that it must have been a direct hit from the same bomb that had knocked most of the glasses off our table about an hour previously. I was helped over piles of rubble and broken glass, and that awful stench to which we were becoming accustomed of escaping gas, brick-dust, blood and bodies, by the usual calm and friendly ARP wardens and guided into the remains of what had been the main bar.

There, on an improvised stretcher, lay poor Pru. Round her were various other victims, bandaged and patched with napkins and torn tablecloths. From the onset of the Blitz I had been with wounded people. I had never been able to understand the mentality of those who gathered ghoulishly around car accidents. Now, I had reached the dreaded moment of no return. Feeling the clammy fingers of faintness crawling over me, I shut my eyes, said a prayer, gulped, counted to three and to my enormous relief the nausea passed. I opened my eyes and went over to Pru, who seemed to me frighteningly to be bandaged all over: skull, arm, one leg (dear God, not irreversible damage please) but she was so brave and uncomplaining that I all but burst into tears. 'They're waiting for the ambulance,' she whispered. 'I'm lucky, the barman got all the bottles in his face.' The ambulance man arrived, lifting her on to a proper stretcher and I followed them out to the ambulance in the Square. Trying Mama's technique I said that I knew I was not allowed in the ambulance, that if all friends and relatives were permitted, their awful task on such a night would be impossible, that I was very worried as Pru was a dancer and I wanted to tell the nurses and doctors how crucial her leg damage might be and was there any way . . . ? 'Get in, dear, and don't worry,' the driver interrupted and off we raced, bells clanging, to St George's Hospital at Hyde Park Corner.

The stretchers were being carried up in a constant stream – like some macabre version of the return of Radames from his Egyptian campaign in *Aida*, I thought dislocatedly. There was hardly space to lay her down amongst the others in the long hall. After a time, an exhausted nurse came over with labels. I gave Pru's name and address and confided my worries to her. 'Oh dear,' she said, 'as all the doctors are with the gravest cases it may be ages till we reach her. We'll tidy her up and give her injections but you might have to wait all night and I'm afraid we can't allow that with the Blitz still going great guns and God knows how many more cases coming in.' So I wrote all the information I could on Pru's labels, waited till she got dopey, told her I'd be back in the morning (it was already one a.m.), that she was a splendid girl, kissed her and walked the few hundred yards back to my eyrie in Lowndes Street. Tired and anxious about Pru, I undressed and went to bed. My window opening vertically (what we call a 'French window') was at the head of my bed just beyond the built-in washbasin. I opened it wide, laid my head on the pillow and fell fast asleep.

I woke less than an hour later to a tremendous noise as though a squadron of jack-booted Mars-men were landing by parachute on the nearby cross-streets. My bed rocked from side to side, blessedly the glass from my open window fell like hailstones into the yard below. Clutching the bed with both hands, I saw the blocked-in fireplace turn first grey, then pitch black as the pressure of the explosions forced the soot up through the erstwhile chimneys from the basement storeys below, showering me with powdered grit. I counted five bombs in that 'stick' while clinging to my swinging mattress, and then silence. The rocking stopped; the house I was in had not collapsed. Not yet anyway. I got out of bed gingerly shaking the soot and a few pieces of stray glass from the covers and looked out of the empty sockets of the window. The adjoining street was brighter than daylight; one bomb must have hit the gas main directly. The next house of the terrace was fairly damaged, the last two as far as I could see were mostly gone.

I threw on some clothes and opened my door. The staircase was encrusted with rubble but negotiable. I slipped unsteadily down to the next two floors. There I was greeted by the remains of a car blown like a rocket clean through the front door and lying athwart the whole flight, obstructing my way. Gripping what remained of the banister I clambered on to the car's roof and hanging on to anything that might help brake my speed slid down it till I fell all of a heap into the front hall. The remains of the front door hung limply askew by one hinge; outside was a bright light and the sounds of digging and shouting. The ARP were hard at work on the huge tumulus that had once been numbers forty-three and forty-four. They had already got everyone out of the neighbouring house. Although it was worse hit than mine there were only minor injuries to the inhabitants, but the poor things were shivering with cold and shock in their night-clothes. 'You all right, ducks?' asked the supervising warden. 'Yes, quite. Can I do anything?' 'Yes, could you let us have a pair of shoes and a jersey?' 'Yes,' I said and thinking a little wistfully of my rationed wardrobe, sherpaed my way this time up the battered car which proved twice as hazardous, hardly feeling like mentioning the loss of my few remaining clothes to the warden preoccupied with so much graver problems. I got back to my tiny room by my now perfected climbing technique, shook the bedcovers as well as I could of their burden of rubble and soot, idiotically closed the glassless windows, dragged my suitcase from under the bed and packed my few things. Repeating my acrobatic tightrope act tossing my case before me floor by floor, I picked it up in the hall and reached the street. I gave the precious shoes and jersey to the warden. 'Look 'ere dear,' he said. 'Ta ever so, but you can't spend the night up there again, we're not sure if your house is safe either yet and we haven't got that fire under control. You must go to the air-raid shelter over there. Good luck,' and he turned to the sad little clump, shoeless and shivering, sitting on the broken steps and began to see whose feet would best fit my elephantine shoes.

I waited until his attention was otherwise occupied and, picking up my case, tiptoed away down the street in the opposite direction and into Belgrave Square. I sat on my case by the gardens, watching the battle continuing in the black void above me, Messerschmitt versus Spitfire, till at last the planes wheeled away towards the south-east, for the faint colour was creeping up the hem of the sky and dawn was not far behind. Before us would lie a few blessed hours' respite until the next night's cacophony would begin again.

I recrossed the Square and went back to Lowndes Street cautiously. Black-faced and weary, they were still digging away in their wonderfully delicate way at the rubble, listening for a cry for help, lifting each broken plank carefully, shifting the shattered stones, concerned not to dislodge an avalanche that might ruin all chances of rescuing more people alive. Satisfied they had not noticed me, once more I negotiated the battered car lying like some monstrous insect killed while trying to crawl through a jungle, and regained my room. Wearily I undressed again, flinging myself on the gravelly bed and fell asleep too depleted, too worried about Pru, to care whether that night's supply of bombs was finished or not, and with the roaring of the flames slowly dimming in my ears I slept at last.

A handful of hours later I woke, found to my delight that there was still running water, washed and dressed and for the last time gave my performance, by now honed and polished, of the descent of the stairs. The first person I met in the street was the valiant chief warden. 'Did you go back there, you naughty girl? Well you won't be there tonight and that's flat!' Flat's the word, I thought and wondered what I could do as I went to see Pru in St George's Hospital. She was, they told me, in the big ward on the first floor. It was nine-thirty. There were roughly fifteen beds on each side of the long room. I walked down peering at each face on each side as I went. Three-quarters of the way down I was just about to pass by a bed where the patient sitting up had two small grey pigtails sticking out from under her ears, her whole face covered with what looked like cheese-cloth and her arms in bandages when, thank God, something in the uprightness of her carriage and the holding of her neck spelled 'dancer'. Just short of the corner of the bed I stopped dead. 'Pru,' I said brightly to the mask. 'Diny,' she cried and cautiously I hugged her. 'How was the rest of the night, darling?' 'Oh, they passed me out finally and I'm all stitched up and this,' pointing to her poor face 'is because they discovered that my face had been burned when the electric lights were hit and the whole thing flashed in our faces.' Cheerful and quite convinced all would repair itself. I gave her grapes and some night-clothes and went off to rehearsal, the bus going all over the place dodging bombed buildings and the odd crater.

Every morning I called in, every day she improved with that extraordinary speed common to all dancers. She flat refused to be moved to the country. The young doctor was very attractive (and so was Pru).

After a couple of nights sleeping on the mattress on the floor of the digs of some kind members of the Arts Theatre Company I finally found a solution. Far away though it was, I could settle myself in Granny Grace's empty Hurlingham flat and sleep in the basement where in the cellars of each square block's inner courtyard they had organised a shelter. For a solid month I travelled by whatever means available the six miles to Hurlingham after the performance, boiled myself an egg (there were still a few then), opened a tin of sardines or made a cheese sandwich, washed, put on trousers and a jersey and went down to the shelter where the inhabitants were forced to spend the night on mattresses, a few lanterns casting weird shadows adding to, rather than lightening, the gloom. Most of the flat dwellers, being elderly like Grannie Grace, had already left London, so we were not overcrowded. Every morning we got up at seven and climbed back to our respective flats.

Afterwards when anybody praised me for being 'brave' I would immediately demur, saying with absolute truth that I was not afraid, only angry, outraged at the disruption, the interruption of life; those who were really brave were the frightened ones like the young woman sleeping next to me in that shelter who would get up shaking at two a.m. to drive her ambulance through the bombs to the horrible and heart-rending scenes that greeted her night after night. I would whisper encouragements to her as she fumbled her way into her uniform, face white and tense, hands unsteady. She really was brave.

At last the nadir of that October month was over. Through a friend's friend of my mother's I learned that a lovely flat in Sloane Square could be had for four pounds a week plus the cook-housekeeper's wages, for it appeared that the old lady to whom it belonged wanted it to be occupied, thus ensuring the morale of her temperamental domestic. The old lady vetted me, I vetted her, the flat, and the deal was made. The fact that she changed her mind and nearly sent me out of mine the very next day was assuaged by her changing it back again after the weekend, and joyfully I packed up that suitcase yet again and left the shelter for ever, settling into this sumptuously lovely flat high above Sloane Street, unable to believe my good fortune. Lying in the French *directoire* boat-bed in clean linen, contemplated by a pair of gilded swans, served excellent coffee and toast in bed by Leah, the Austro-Hungarian treasure, wallowing in really hot water in a marble bathroom, could only be a dream from which surely I would rudely awake.

After visiting her every day I was finally allowed to collect Pru from hospital, perfectly repaired: face clear as silk, hair grown luxuriant once more. Feeling horribly greedy alone in the flat, Griselda only coming up on occasion from Bath, I offered her the other bedroom and she joined me.

Leah was a marvellous cook, creating superb dishes out of the rations which were becoming more and more stringent, with the dubious benefit that none of our men friends any longer wanted to take us out. They preferred savouring Leah's meals. Griselda, bored stiff in Bath and wishing to be in London to keep an eye on Gerard whose affairs she had taken upon herself to administer, got a job in the Signals Section of the Admiralty. As it was top secret they always employed women who were related to officers in the Navy, knowing they would never be tempted to betray even involuntarily any smallest item of their work, so it was a foregone conclusion that she would come and share the flat. Pru went back to her family and Griselda came to join me just after Christmas.

I suppose there was some vague celebration on Christmas Day 1940, but we were still dislocated, still torn between guilt at the reluctance with which we had finally entered the war and an uncomfortable feeling that festivities might seem flippant. Besides, there could be no real plum pudding.

11

Struggling Against Odds
and Other Oddments

Was it overly optimistic to hope that the reality of war –
bombs, rockets and the growing uncertainty of survival –
might have produced in personal behaviour a growing of
goodwill, a desire to harmonise relationships in contrast to the
disruption of our daily lives? Admittedly there did exist a genuine
closeness in shared fear unspoken, in a sort of reticent kindness towards
one another that strengthened bonds otherwise missing in the highly
competitive world of the theatre. However, such empathy was sorely
absent from our boss, who continued to punish us for baulking his
wishes, until in a fit of final fury he gave us all the sack. Forced to collect
for ourselves the last salary we found it to be exactly £2.3s.6d and, sick
at heart, we tried to find some dates elsewhere. Furthermore, he
refused to talk with me, refused my request to borrow our costumes.

Forlornly, I took a sapphire ring and diamond bracelet in the form of
a snake I'd always disliked to a jeweller. He blithely offered me
£4.10s.0d, so I put them back in my bag and produced another piece of
unwanted finery, a hideous necklace of navy-blue lapis given me by
some kind Rothschild friend of my Paris grandmama. The jeweller
stuck his tiny sawn-off telescope in his eye, grunted disparagingly and
said, 'What stones are these?' Stung to anger, I retorted, 'Victorian
gallstones' and swept out with my unwanted swag. I earned a little

modelling for *Vogue*, until we went down to perform in Bath for a week in the dismal damp Pavilion sunk like a swamped boat in the fields by the river. At least I did not have to pay for digs, as I was to stay in my mother's house. We had brought what scraps of old costumes we owned and Winifred, my mother's maid, and I dipped a hastily run-up crepe skirt forlornly in thick black coffee in an attempt to recreate my beautiful costume for '*Danse Arabe*' in *Casse-Noisette*. The result was very weird, long, muddy streaks interspersed with a greyish slate tinge looking like a bad case of varicose veins. But we had no choice as we turned and jumped and cavorted despondently to a few rows of frozen people whose very presence reeked of eccentricity to the point of masochism.

26 March 1941: Yugoslavia signs a tripartite agreement with the Axis.
Prince Paul flees to Greece: King Peter takes over with a pro-British Premier.

We continued dolefully to do another week at a seaside resort, where the wind wailed like a banshee and the sea behaved like stirred porridge. Then came Harrogate, a tidy resort in Yorkshire, where we battled on, losing with every performance in those wretched costumes the pride we once had had. Pru and I had brought a large sausage of meat and herbs made by Leah, a '*Falscher Hase*', which I put on the mantelpiece of our shared bedroom, marking it in disciplined sections to last us for lunch for seven days. At the end of the week, going to the box office to ask for a pair of seats for the last performance, I noticed great stacks of tickets stamped 'Yehudi Menuhin' dated for the following week and sighed, comparing his splendour with our tattered, woebegone condition and the future waiting blank and empty with only the bombs and rockets as security. One more grisly date followed in a Midlands industrial town tramping all day in search of digs. Having finally decided we would have to spend the night in the theatre the kind manager took pity on us and drove three of us to a small and dingy house where the landlady offered us one room – and that her parlour. It was after ten p.m. and we were exhausted and cold. Two girls shared a sofa and I put three chairs together with a cushion smelling of beer and cheap cigarettes on top. I undressed, covering myself with my overcoat and using the odoriferous object as a pillow, and fell fitfully asleep.

The Blitz was raging with renewed force in London and I was longing to get back to help Griselda find a more pleasant flat than the one lent us by the kind old lady (whose less-kindly daughter was constantly putting up the rent). I arrived to find that Mulberry House had been ransacked, but nothing of value stolen. That night the noise was violent, as though the sky were full of giants tossing thunderbolts at each other. Added to the whine and crash of the rockets was the staccato chatter of the anti-aircraft guns. Impossible to sleep much but at least I was back, sharing it all with Griselda and my beloved London. Next day we managed to get round the odd craters in Piccadilly to the Queen's Hall to hear Moura Lympany, a protégée of Mama's and a brilliant young pianist (now a leading virtuoso). We were confronted by a smoking ruin out of which the firemen were trying to rescue what orchestral instruments had been spared. Moura sat cheerfully on a truck amid what had been scavenged, surrounded by members of the orchestra. Determined to give some sort of concert they drove off to the nearby Royal Academy of Music's small Duke's Hall taking us in tow and there, with as many of the audience as could be crammed into the space a quarter the size of the Queen's Hall, sitting, standing, squatting, Moura gave a shining performance of the César Franck *Variations Symphoniques*.

Had I known that that beloved hall – where Toscanini, Furtwängler, Bruno Walter and Mengelberg had conducted; where pianists like von Bülow, Paderewski and Rachmaninov had played; where we heard the great cellists Suggia, Casals, Piatigorsky, and violinists from Ysaÿe, Heifetz to Yehudi Menuhin – would never be rebuilt I would have wept, imagining the ghosts of those already gone lying among the ashes and ascending in the smoke still rising as we passed it on our melancholy way back, a sad memorial to the most perfect hall London ever possessed.

11 May: Rudolf Hess lands by plane in Scotland to meet Lord Clydesdale and is first reported as a 'refugee'.
24 May: HMS Hood *sunk with all hands.*
27 May: Battleship Bismarck, *after a long chase, is at last sunk.*

Against all those cataclysmic events life limped on. Every week we stood in obedient queues waiting for our few ounces of fat, our single chop, rasher of bacon, ounce of cheese cut from a huge boulder that sweated like wet soap and tasted much the same – plus the bonus of an occasional egg with shell so thin that one carried it back in a knotted handkerchief and contemplated it for long minutes like some icon demanding worship, unable to decide whether to boil, poach or fry it or add it to the ersatz powdered egg in a brave attempt to redeem the powder's truly awful taste of cigarette ash and scramble the lot. We would chat each other up as we stood, comparing the previous night's experience, I for one learning from the cleaning ladies various ways of making the best of our meagre meat ration.

10 June: Italy enters the war.
22 June: Germany invades Russia.

There were small bonuses, tiny delights. A naval officer friend of mine brought a bounty of marmalade, stockings, butter, tea and even scent from wherever the ship he called; also I had been engaged to join a small revue, which supposedly would reach London should it meet with success. We were all still young, hard-working and optimistic and rehearsed with goodwill. Oliver Messel, the great stage designer who had done the costumes for *The Miracle*, offered to make me a crown for one of my numbers. Like all really gifted men of the theatre he used his imagination to create extraordinary beauty out of most unlikely materials. Producing a large packet of furry white-wire pipe cleaners at the dressmaker's, he proceeded to twist and bind and join them, until suddenly as though by magic an exquisite little coronet seemed to spring from his hands. He set it excitedly on my head, burst into tears and said: 'Oh! darling, you look so beautiful!' Small tributes such as this

191

helped to lighten the fact that the revue lasted a whole week and folded quietly. I earned five pounds and some more experience.

From OFLAG VIIC in Germany, one David Campbell wrote to ask for a picture of me as his pin-up. I heard from the Russian designer George Kirsta, who had done the costumes for a Nijinska ballet with Markova Dolin and who had admired me, that he was putting on the Mussorgsky opera *The Fair at Sorochinski* and he wished to incorporate the *Night on the Bare Mountain* as a short ballet and for me to dance the 'Venus of the Inferno' in it. Hooray, said I, and went to meet the ballet mistress, an erstwhile character from the Bolshoi Theatre in Moscow, Catherine de Villiers. A very suspicious name for the totally Russian figure I met. Short and stoutish, somewhere around sixty, with the ramrod carriage of the Russian-trained dancer she had a large whey-coloured face in which were buried, like small currants in a mass of uncooked dough, two very shrewd black eyes. Her hair, black and drawn up and back from her face like a turban, was marked in the centre by one thick white streak (shades of Diaghilev's badger mark? I wonder), the cheeks hung loosely in well-packed pouches each side of a wide scarlet mouth, and from one supple hand dangled a long cigarette; a fine down like the ash from her cigarette lay across her upper lip. A commanding presence and in those early days of her reign one illuminated with a dry humour and a certain Slavic warmth.

She did not strictly belong to my category of Russian-Parisian ex-ballerinas, though she had spent a brief spell with Diaghilev, then gone up to Berlin to join the small band of White Russians. None the less she spoke fluent French and we got on famously. Rehearsals would start towards the end of August. Meanwhile I got another of those peremptory proposals from a diplomat. Would I please say yes or no as he is being transferred soon? 'So sorry, John dear, no good, love Diana,' I cabled him. However uncertain and harsh my life, I didn't want to marry yet.

The backer of the new company was a Russian with plenty of nice whisky money who typically chose to put it into the theatre. His name was Jay Pomeroy (originally Pomeranetz) and he was warm and kindly and generous. There was naturally a strong Slavic element in such an opera cast: the soprano, the Polish tenor and several other voices. In some, the thicker accents of Central Europe could be detected, struggling with the diphthongs of the Russian vowels, but we had the indestructible old singer Oda Slobodskaya to coach and tease and trim and the young Walter Süsskind to look after the chorus; Anatole Fistoulari and George Weldon were to alternate the conducting and the orchestra would be the London Symphony, one of the four major London bands. So far, better than good. Excellent. The ballet company was as usual relegated to the dingier rehearsal rooms. This particular one, buried in the maw of Soho, embraced by sleazy night-clubs and sex-dens on one side and the weekly market on the other so that one was embedded in both human and vegetable detritus – slowly rotting humans and faster-decaying cabbage leaves – seemed sempiternally earmarked for the dance. Its long room and steamy mirrors were impregnated with decades of sweat, tears and toil, the floors sticky with rarely cleaned rosin; the greasy light bulbs shed a reluctant glow as though they were ashamed of revealing so much shabbiness.

Here, to an out-of-tune upright thumped by the indomitable Foxie, de Villiers choreographed the *Night on the Bare Mountain* and other sundry scraps of mime and dance for the opera. That she depended mostly on a dog-eared catalogue from her long years' experience soon became obvious, but the steps and combinations were perfectly serviceable and I worked away with a will. Before two weeks were out the classic rows had erupted like the first burps of lava in the ever-boiling volcano pit that is the Russian Theatre, be it ballet, opera or whatever.

So Kirsta and de Villiers took over the production of the opera from the first director (who had fled) and we rattled on towards opening night like a coach over cobblestones. I got paid one pound per week which just about covered my bus fares and a sandwich and coffee at midday. All the good male dancers had been called up or were already employed in older-established companies, so I had been left with an overweight gentleman of dubious age and even more dubious technique, who managed to drop me on my right leg in a fumbled lift, which accident confined me to a couch for six days, there to contemplate a foot slowly turning black right through to the underpart of the instep and the hideous possibility of missing the opening night. Black Fairy again, no doubt. Luckily there was no point-work so I somehow managed the first night, sparing my barely healed foot and compensating with a great deal of dramatic undulating which befitted the Venus of the Inferno, or so I hoped. 'Diana,' shouted Katusha from the stalls at rehearsal 'more *un*decent movement, please!'

It was all a great success, thank God, especially the Gopak finale, while dear old 'Pom' would emerge from the wings at the end of every performance to beg the crowded house to pray for the deliverance of his fellow Ukrainians in the siege of Kiev. Mrs Churchill brought the Russian Ambassador, Maisky, and his wife to a special evening to raise money for the Russian Red Cross and after a successful three weeks we went out on a gruesome seven-week tour of the provinces.

7 December: Japanese bomb Pearl Harbor.
8 December: Japan declares war on America.

The inexorable current suddenly flowed faster and deeper, gathering momentum and with it the relief of no longer struggling alone in the war, coupled with fear that its expansion might bring retribution of an even starker nature to our battered island in the forefront of the battle. Exhausted and still heartsore at the collapse of my first love affair, I was left with a tangle of broken ends, shattered patterns and the shock of a shame that would not go away. The kindly doctor who came to see me at midnight in the dreary digs of some Midland town, to whom I'd finally appealed for help over my fainting and fits of ice-cold shuddering, diagnosed complete nervous collapse. Seeing my unwillingness to admit to such weakness, he looked me in the eye and said, 'You've been through some deep emotional crisis and tried to handle it all alone, haven't you?' Simply the unwonted sympathy and perspicacity helped me out of the slough of despond, even though New Year's Eve was spent still in harness in a dim hotel far from friends and family.

In an effort to defy the constant setbacks and fateful frustrations with which my professional life seemed to be strewn, I seized the chance to do everything within my power to make a success of my opportunity when Pomeroy announced that he would dump the opera and develop the balletic side of his Russian company, to be called rather ostentatiously the New Russian Ballet. I became not only the leading dancer but virtually directress, partly by force of circumstances brought about by the somewhat loose hand of our Katusha (de Villiers) whose dependence upon whisky, while improving her mood, tempered her ability to govern with any degree of coherence. We moved into the Adelphi Theatre in the Strand and into rehearsals of a ballet to the music of Ravel's orchestration of Mussorgsky's *Pictures at an Exhibition* which furnished her (by nature of its serial form) with an easy solution to obscure her lack of real creative talent.

All kinds of scraps of choreography were welded together in a sort of archaeological dig from her memory and coupled with the zest and goodwill of dancers pathetically grateful to be in work, a fair success was made of it. Again the Maiskys lent their presence. The cachet offered by an ambassador constantly in the news who, ever since the shock of Germany's breaking of the Nazi-Soviet pact had been keeping the government on tenterhooks refusing to sign a pack of non-aggression with the British, paradoxically helped our box office.

Still flat-hunting and in our Sloane Street apartment, Griselda now doing a gruelling stint of night duty in the Signals Section of the Admiralty which entailed twenty-four hours on duty and forty-eight hours off, I permitted myself a Saturday supper after the evening show with my current diplomat friend, for at least I could lie abed on the Sunday morning. We went to the Mirabelle. It was a quiet evening free of bombing and I, having decided to dress up a bit was fortunately wearing my lovely diamond wing-brooch given me by my Paris grandmother Guggan, together with the little diamond-studded watch and pearl-and-diamond ear-rings and the pearl necklace given me by my maternal grandmother Goggo, all of which detail I relate for the simple reason that when a telephone call came from a distraught

Griselda asking me to return at once as we had been burgled, for once I could claim good fortune as all my small collection of jewellery was hung on my person.

Abandoning our half-eaten dinner, I raced back to the flat to find poor Griselda bereft of her brooches and rings, while two policemen showed her how the burglars had defeated two safety locks by inserting a sheet of mica, entering the empty flat, opening unlocked drawers till they found what they wanted, and slipping neatly away. They had obviously been 'casing the joint' for days as the Americans so graphically put it, seeing my name on the Adelphi Theatre's posters revealing my absences, watching the comings and goings of Griselda, and on Leah's night out they had duly 'broken and entered, Miss', said one of the policemen. 'I have to tell you there's little hope of catching them, for now the flat-racing season's on and we are so understaffed they can pick their choice with impunity.' This said with the lugubrious, triumphant tone peculiar to the Cockney, they tipped their hats and were gone. Leah flung her apron over her head and howled helpfully in true Central-European style and Griselda and I went sadly to bed.

15 February 1942: Churchill announces the fall of Singapore.

To add to my rather meagre salary I modelled some clothes for the couturier Lachasse, walking up and down Bond Street being photographed by Cecil Beaton. Meanwhile I tried sturdily to improve the standards of the Company, often taking over the teaching of the morning classes (now in one of the rehearsal rooms at Covent Garden) when Katusha's hangovers prevented her arriving in time. Steadily, my relations with her were deteriorating, her fondness for me soured by the sight of the homage of at least two of the men in the company and various suitors who took me out; her frustrated jealousy prompted her to all kinds of petty manoeuvres, from trying to reduce my position by hiring other dancers to being very unpleasant during rehearsals. I was sad, for I had been fond of her. Although she could hardly match my beloved Karsavina, Egorova or Kschessinskaya, she nevertheless evoked a faint perfume of their inimitable Russianness as the stopper of a long-finished bottle of scent will still hold the tantalising echo of its former contents. I struggled on, more and more convinced that I would never be able to achieve my design for the Company with her obstructing it all, however hard I tried to please her, carrying out the title she'd conferred on me of *charmeuse de serpent*, which being defined simply meant that on tour I would somehow manage to procure her the bottles of whisky on which her engine ran. . . .

14 March: The Battleship Electra *is sunk.*

By the end of that month Pomeroy had rented the Cambridge Theatre and the plan was for de Villiers to create a couple more ballets for a projected opening in May. In search of good dancers I dragged her with me to ballet schools and the one or two companies that were also holding their heads above the difficulties of the Blitz with its shortages of materials for costumes, of wood, canvas and metal for scenery. At one such matinée Katusha, bolt upright by my side glaring at the two *petits sujets* who emerged from the *corps de ballet* to dance a short duo in the lakeside scene of *Swan Lake*, pronounced in a stentorian tone with her strong Russian accent 'But who ginger *monster*?' (one of the unhappy girls being a redhead), thereby calling down a shower of remonstrance from the surrounding audience. After that embarrassing episode I went alone to search. I engaged another of Hitler's many gifts to the arts, the great German designer Hein Heckroth, to do the scenery and costumes for a ballet called *Audition*, with choreography by Wendy Toye, in preparation for the expanding of the company to include other such innovative choreographers and thus attract some really good dancers. I had never wanted to be the big frog in a little pond, but to prove myself as an important artist on my own merits.

On 27 March 1942 I lunched at the Foreign Office with the kindly diplomat who had shown me so much compassion during my misery after the breakdown of my first love affair. As he was on duty, he was watching the news as it came in. Suddenly he signalled to me that there had been a big Blitz on Bath. I telephoned our flat: a telegram had come from the cook, Mrs Battye: she and Winifred were all right but the back of the house was blown out. Mama was fortunately staying with her mother-in-law in London. Abandoning both the diplomat and the dubious food I raced back home. Griselda got leave and the following day we took the train to Bristol, the nearest available station, queued up for a bus which would get us, jam-packed like canned goods, to the outer fringes of the city from where we saw a pall of smoke rising as from an incinerator. With hearts heavy with dread we picked our way over the rubble, swerving round half-collapsed houses looking as though they were sorrowing for the demise of their battered neighbours, and found that numbers one to seven Rivers Street were an unrecognisable pile of broken stone, glass and splintered wood sticking up like so many rotting teeth, but thank God the front of number eight, Mama's house, was still complete. We rang the bell which did not work, banged the knocker and poor Winifred and Mrs Battye appeared grey with fatigue and fright. Beyond them at the end of the hall daylight shone in and all was covered with a pall of dust and débris as though the poor, pretty little house were wearing mourning weeds.

The first thing was to find accommodation for them both for the night. We stood for hours in the queue for, unlike the stalwart, resigned Londoners, Bath was in a state of shock and everyone, dreading a second such dreadful night, was planning to escape, even to sleep in the surrounding fields and caves rather than go through more terror. Eventually we found shelter for them and sent them off by bus, arranging to meet next day to take them back to London.

The sight of that beautiful, small, eighteenth-century city, the only totally planned town in England, with gap-toothed crescents and gaping terraces was inordinately painful. Turning our backs on it we proceeded to pack all the clothes, linen, silver, everything movable, into trunks and cases and then went in search of transport. Bath was a ghost town: most shops and all businesses closed, the station deserted. Flummoxed, we went to see if Sir Saxon and Lady Noble were by any happy chance still in their lovely house in nearby Royal Crescent. To

My maternal grandmother (née Katherine Lester), nicknamed 'Goggo'

My paternal grandmother (née Constance Rawson Reid), nicknamed 'Guggan'

Third from right: my maternal grandfather William Henry Hodson Suart, nicknamed 'Gannerwanner', with his polo-playing fellow soldiers of the Royal Horse Artillery

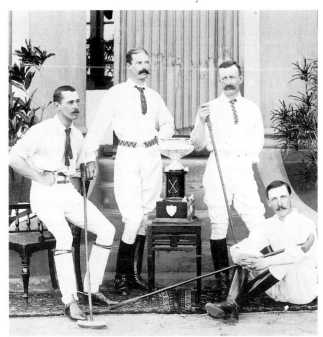

My paternal grandfather Gerard Gould

Underneath the grapevine

On the terrace

The House at Mykonos

In Yehudi's practice room

'On the rocks'

our joy the Crescent was almost intact and they were trying to decide what their next move should be. Delighted to see us, they begged us to stay the night as caretakers and fled, glad to escape and we only too glad to have a roof over our heads. We found some food, took off our shoes and outer clothing and camped ourselves on the sofas in the drawing-room, sleeping fitfully, full of sadness and the feeling of the futility of this cruel mutual destruction.

We woke stiff and tired, thankful that the bombers had after all not returned, and managed to haul over the trunks and cases, dumping them on the Nobles' billettee, poor man. There was only a little water and no gas, so we tidied as best we could, nibbled some stale bread, collected Winifred and Mrs Battye and got on the crowded bus to Bathampton, where we had been told there might be a train going in the direction of London. The platform resembled a bad film from a Russian novel, a crowd of ill-washed crumpled creatures at least 300 strong standing shoulder to shoulder in a sort of precarious alliance right up to the very edge. The only item missing was the heaps of sunflower seeds to complete the Dostoyevskian picture. For two solid hours we stood, gradually welded into each other unwillingly as though fate had removed our identity and lumped us casually in a series of pathetically unwanted heaps.

At last the train arrived and we surged towards it, flattened against the carriages by the force of those behind, groping for doorways through which to enter more or less singly, to invade already congested corridors in an unwelcome swarm. Eventually, suffocated and stiff, we got to Swindon, were decanted and at last found a train that was bound for London. Mrs Battye went to her sister's, Winifred we sheltered at Grannie Grace's – where our mother took the whole tragic affair as a personal affront and was totally ungrateful to us for having brought her her furs and jewels.

Cheered, on reaching our flat, by the first square meal we had had since we left, we were even more comforted by a bombardment of worried telephone calls from Robert Donat, Louis Kentner and all our closer friends, anxious to know how we had fared and what we had found. Griselda and Winifred returned next day to Bath, which was stirring into some kind of life, to rescue and store the furniture and Mama indulged in such a bout of hysterics that in order for both of us to get back to work the only expedient was to put her into a nursing home for a spell.

Weary of body and mind, I returned to rehearsals in a company further reduced in morale by the behaviour of Katusha, who was busily creating another of her pastiches, this one based on Snow White and the wicked stepmother, which latter part she gave me with glittering eyes. Even she could hardly present herself as the innocent victim in the dreary drama that reached its height a few days later when, unable any longer to contain her enmity towards me, she slapped my face at rehearsal in front of the entire Company. That this assault was dictated more by the bottle than by her own genuine emotions, once so full of fondness towards me, made the whole sorry scene the sadder for it confirmed in my reluctant heart the ineluctable fact that I could never make a successful company with her at its helm. Trained to obey, I finished rehearsal without comment and only then went to telephone Pom and tell him I doubted I could carry her much longer. To add to the misery, a silly tug-o'-war ensued over the dressing-room which had been allotted to me, at stage level as befitted my rôle as leading dancer, directress, chief cook and bottle-washer and holder of all the myriad strings governing the Company from the wardrobe to the orchestra and the youngest member. Furiously, battling like some old rooster, Katusha finally demanded that I hand over my carefully detailed lists, my address book and Company notations (this after eight horrible days of cutting me dead in a way peculiar to the Russian ballet world wherein one's closest friend becomes an implacable enemy overnight and all the minutiae of shared delights and disasters that should forge indissoluble bonds melt into nothingness in the heat of Slavic passion). I had no resource other than again to appeal to Pom, saying that the morale of the whole Company was lower with every day. He agreed that I should have number one dressing-room, and was to keep all my papers and so forth.

Somehow out of all this stew the first night arrived without further disaster on 9 June 1942 and I got through my various roles in all three new ballets, the last being quite a witty rendering of Prokofiev's *Lieutenant Kijé*. Even the ensuing success could not restrain Katusha's persistently wayward behaviour. Despondent and utterly spent, I finally told her I was heartily sick of her, her malign treatment of me, heartily sick of the whole messy situation and ready to leave at the end of the season, defeated in my efforts to present her with a worthy company. Meanwhile, as I was tired of the farce of classes either conducted with dull ill-will owing to boundless hangovers or taken over by myself, I had engaged one of the most gifted of all Russian teachers, a retired dancer I had met at Sokolova's, Vera Volkova (later to teach at the Royal Ballet and after that to be chief ballet mistress of the Royal Danish Ballet, but as yet my own discovery). Schooled in the best of St Petersburg style she was an encouragement to the least gifted dancers and an inspiration to the best, so my spirits lifted a little as I watched the discipline and goodwill which she soon revived in us all.

Late one night, weary after the long week's work, I got a call from Pom. He apologised for dithering and told me he had at last sacked Katusha. The way ahead cleared as though an impenetrable fog was finally dispersed and I could move on with my plans unhampered by her curious enmity. Determined to the end to extract what shreds of sympathy and drama she could evoke in a thoroughly demoralised community she bade farewell in a flood of tears, which to my embarrassment was not echoed by anyone else, and walked off the stage and out of our bemused lives.

On 29 July my stepfather, Cecil, was promoted to Rear-Admiral, which should bring cheer to Mama whom we had by now installed in her own flat in the same block as her devoted mother-in-law, with all her furniture brought from Bath. Fortunate woman, oblivious of the homage she had always been able to summon.

Unwilling to lose any time while the season was still continuing I engaged several choreographers, more good dancers of both sexes, eminent designers and discussed the libretti of the various productions to come. Evidently delighted, Pomeroy signed them all up. The season at the Cambridge came to a successful finish and we were all set after a final week at Brighton to start rehearsals.

19 August: Raid on Dieppe.

The failure of that ill-fated venture was reflected in our half-empty houses at Brighton and we returned to London depressed by the bad news, only to find that Pom had suddenly and inexplicably decided to decrease the money he had promised for the new season. Miserably, I had to sack the weaker dancers in order to prune the Company and fit the new finances. It was one of the most heart-wrenching duties of all the unhappy situations in which I had found myself in my career and I performed the executions with self-loathing and as compassionately as I could. By the end of the month I understood why Pomeroy had acted so strangely. He had been suddenly rushed to hospital with a heart attack that had been threatening for some time and which he had chosen to ignore. I tried frenziedly to raise money, turning from one agent to another producer, from Anthony Asquith to David Henley of Selznik, all to no avail. I could not believe that, after all my struggles, my work, my projects, this cruel blow of fate should kill a year's hopeful planning. I visited poor Pom and begged him as gently as possible to give me a chance to go ahead. Sadly he told me he couldn't; his business, as he was the sole progenitor that earned the money, could not be put in another's hands and so long as he was in hospital all his sources were sealed.

The only pleasant interlude in all this dislocation was my being taken down to Hove by a literary friend of mine to meet Lord Alfred Douglas in his little flat. Of course I had been brought up on the notorious Oscar Wilde case and knew how his passion for that exquisitely beautiful young man had led to his undoing and his squalid end. I had also read some of Douglas's sonnets and was looking forward to meeting a man who had been a legend.

If it were at all feasible to substantiate one of my pet theories, i.e. that the thoughts you have entertained are indelibly marked upon your face as the years proceed so that in most old faces can be traced the entire psyche of a human being, then indeed Alfred Douglas was a sad proof of my contention. In place of the blond beauty with its perfect features and serene expression I saw a crumpled, wizened face like a badly baked apple, watery blue eyes peering irascibly out at one – eyes that bulged slightly as though self-absorbed arrogance coupled with suspicion thrust them forward in a ready defence against any rude intrusion. A few sparse grey hairs clung to an undistinguished head and his whole appearance was somehow petty, both physically and figuratively. He greeted us with the sort of hasty dismissal usually reserved for the postman asking for a signature on a package, and bade us come in. I suppose he accepted me as neither quite plain nor stupid or simply as an audience worth talking to about himself and the importance of his position in the world of letters. After finding out that we had a few mutual acquaintances, he demanded that I approach the most powerful among them to try and extricate his 'work of genius', *In Excelsis*, written during the year he was incarcerated in Wormwood Scrubbs for libelling Winston Churchill. ('Shades', thought I, 'of emulating Wilde's moving *De Profundis*, his cri de coeur from Reading Gaol.) I promised I would do my best and, disappointed with the faded image of an individual of almost historic rank in the literary world, returned to London.

Returned to find that all hope of keeping the ballet together as a unit by going on a projected six-week tour had crumbled into nothingness and that Pom from his hospital bed had summarily dismissed the entire Company without compensation. I was deeply sad on many levels: firstly about the repeating pattern of defeat yet again just as I seemed to have success within my grasp; secondly the humiliation of having offered so much hope and work to so many colleagues, artists, friends who had trusted me; thirdly because Pom had become a close companion and a kindly boss and I hated to see him ill and forced to abandon, apparently without compunction, those who had for the most part worked hard and faithfully for him for over a year. The only cheering news at this negative and troublesome time was that Griselda had found a pair of flats in Belgravia, one suitable for us and the other linked by a corridor to an adjoining building for Mama, whose continuing nervous state made it risky not to have her within reach.

At the end of October we moved in, discreetly declining Leah's request to come with us. We had weighed carefully the respective merits of exquisite *Apfelstrudel*, *Sachertorte* and *Tafelspitz* against the vicissitudes of the Austro-Hungarian temperament with its thunderstorms and showers and tears like the weather of her native Salzkammergut and decided that the Blitz furnished us with enough danger and uncertainty without adding more to our daily lives, and that we would have to survive on our own dubious culinary gifts.

The flat was lovely; at last surrounded by our share of the Mulberry House furniture and thus comforted by the fond and familiar, we settled into our first home since the autumn of 1940 so that when, by 2 November 1942, the last vestige of hope to resuscitate the Pomeroy Company died in a terminal shudder, at least I was consoled by the comforting presence of inanimate but symbolic objects I had known most of my life.

5 November: Rommel withdraws from Egypt.
8 November: The USA invades Morocco and Algiers.
9 November: Capitulation of Morocco and Algiers.

As the tide of war seemed slowly to be turning in our favour lifting one's flagging spirits, and as I was anyway out of work, I took the opportunity to go down to Hove again to visit Alfred Douglas and have lunch with him. He was more relaxed on this second visit and talked arrogantly about the superiority of his sonnets over those of Shakespeare who, said he scornfully, did not even follow, as did he, the strict Petrarchan form. I hesitated to suggest that genius could well dispense with such corsets. He gave me a couple of his books.

27 November: The French scuttle their fleet at Toulon as the German and Italian armies march in.
3 December: My stepfather, Cecil Harcourt, sinks six ships in convoy.

Griselda and I were beset by newspapers and photographers as though we could add anything to the news.

The next day to my apprehensive delight I was called to the film studios at Denham to read the part of the young lead in James Barrie's play *What Every Woman Knows*, and to my joy I got the rôle for a coming London production. Fears of the Labour Exchange calling me up were thus dispelled for a time.

At the end of the year, still heartsore and emotionally spent, I was persuaded by George Galitzine to go to a party in Berkeley Square. A very Russian party it turned out to be, crammed to the ceilings and walls with people enjoying themselves and each other with that especial brand of humour and malice, sardonic goodwill and the priceless capacity to savour the moment, that is the secret of survival in every Russian emigré I have ever known. I felt pleasantly absorbed into the warmth and chatter and ease of an undemanding crowd and therefore resisted George's request to come and talk to the Irish fortune-teller half hidden in the far corner of the room. 'Come along Sparja,' he pleaded. I absolutely refused. 'Are you afraid, Sparjenka?' Challenged, I suddenly realised I had *nothing* to lose whatever nonsense might come, for I had felt so empty for months that nothing further could change my mood.

I went over and found, amid the noise and cigarette smoke and the chatter of voices in several languages, a tiny, crumpled woman in a stained grey flannel suit, with the rubicund face of a faithful devotee of the whisky bottle, reeking of spirits and stale ash in equal quantities. Very unprepossessing, and I made to move away when she seized me by the hand and ordered me to sit on the sofa by her side. Staring from my palm into my eyes she announced in a strong brogue, 'You've been through a bad time, my dear.' Too easy, I thought. 'But you have had some help, I believe. It was family trouble, wasn't it?' Feeling slightly antagonistic, I said it was my mother. She frowned and said, 'That's funny, I could have sworn it was a man who helped you.' Encouraging her I said, 'Why, do you have a name?' 'Yes, it's Louise.' 'How do you spell it?' I asked. 'L-O-U-I-S,' she replied. Intrigued, I told her it was indeed a man and that it is pronounced with a mute 's'. Louis Kentner had been enormously kind and compassionate.

She moved on to give me a rough sketch of the collapse of my love affair and said that I will marry a man who is some kind of an artist and that she sees him on the stage; that he is smallish and fair and bites his lip. At this time I did not even know Yehudi, but years later I recalled her words which were an exact description. 'You will have one child with great difficulty, and another one, but . . .' and here she stopped, saying 'Come and see me, dear. Here is my card and I'd rather continue privately.' Probably with that inexplicable vision she'd seen that my third child would die an hour after birth. How does one fathom such extraordinary gifts? George came over towards the end of the party crying, 'Sparja, she says I'm going to marry someone I've known for a long time and loved too. It's you, isn't it?' 'No, darling George, it's your lovely hostess, she answers the description far better than I.' And indeed he did marry her.

12

Consoling Work
Amid Continuous War

We entered the fourth year of the war, 1943, by now reconciled to being part of a life not of one's choosing, of abandoning all idea of liberty of choice. Small private emotional corners, rescued and cherished out of the general seriousness and drama, became all the more vivid and precious. There was by now no pretence: life was hazardous and uncertain, had to be contended with, not disavowed, taken not as doom but as destiny. This larger dimension made things easier; life was quite simply reduced to basics, the priorities existing in a simple gratitude for remaining alive, for the air raids had begun again in earnest and concentration was narrowed to survival and the daily job.

Rehearsals began for *What Every Woman Knows* which had a wonderful cast: the *grande dame* of the London stage, Dame Irene Vanbrugh; the leading character actor Nicholas Hannen; Barbara Mullen famed for her Scottish rôles; John Stewart the hero; and myself the 'young lead' Lady Sybil Tenterden. They were all kind and helpful and encouraging, especially Dame Irene and 'Beau' Hannen (at sixty still renowned for his good looks) from whose long experience I gained confidence and learned many lessons. I had already acted in a few straight plays and more and more, having always been regarded as a dramatic dancer, longed to abandon the insecurity, the physical pain and exhaustion and the malevolent atmosphere of the ballet companies, to become an actress. Even though this would mean no longer interpreting music with my body, I would still live within the theatre, working with material so much more distinguished and interesting than that offered one by those few choreographers whose muse one could aspire to become; or the dreary choice of what the Russians used to call 'the oldy-poldy' ballets – the classics of Petipa and Fokine taken out of storage, shaken and dusted and pressed into service according to the funds available. For me the decision was not altogether a difficult one.

A skeleton of social life still staggered on. Puffin Asquith gave a series of dinners in a private room at the Savoy to entertain his unique mother, the notorious Margot, Countess of Oxford and Asquith, widow of the one-time Liberal Prime Minister Henry Herbert Asquith, renowned for her fearless wit. At her request I was always to be invited. 'Diana,' said she, as reported to me by Puffin's secretary, 'is the only beautiful girl in today's deplorable society who is also witty.' Hooray. There would be eight or ten guests, always carefully chosen and interesting: playwrights such as Terry Rattigan, designers like Cecil Beaton, film producers such as Anatole de Grünwald, or Puffin's half-brother the High Court Judge Cyril Asquith; European journalists who had fled through the war lines. Wonderful conversation flew across the tables like arrows from a bow, caught deftly and returned with wit or passion as the subject demanded. A feast I shall always treasure. I would be entrusted to accompany Mamma Oxford back to her house, thereby enjoying a special *envoi* to the evening.

Added to these dinners I remember a lunch given at the Savoy by the Foreign Press Club to honour the exiled King George of the Hellenes. Sitting at Mamma Oxford's table for six, arguing with the brilliant but imperious ex-editor of the *Frankfurter Illustrierte Zeitung*, I noticed that Mamma Oxford had gobbled her lunch, was looking impatiently at her wrist-watch and making fretful clucking noises as she glanced over her shoulder to the top table where the King sat with the official party. Abruptly she rose to her feet, pushing back her chair, strode over to him and leaning across the carnations and cutlery said: 'Your Majesty, this is very boring, it's high time you delivered your speech and put an end to all this.' Whereupon the startled monarch, after a short pause to recover from this shot across the bows, promptly rose and delivered himself of his prepared statement. Mamma Oxford fell asleep after the first sentence or two and awoke at my nudging to thump her elegant stick on the floor and shout 'Bravo!'.

Her mould is alas broken for ever.

We had reached the final week of rehearsals for the Barrie play when I awoke one morning with a raging temperature and flu. No question of going to the theatre for a day or two (the limit for all dancers to indulge in illness) but Black Fairy had other ideas and by the second day I developed jaundice. The doctor came and confirmed it, saying that it was an epidemic all over London due to an imbalance in our frugal diet and gloomily foresaw ten days in bed. Given my wretched disposition as a Professional Dyspeptic I suffered agonies of stomach pain and could only eat mashed potato lovingly cooked by Griselda. A few days later they sent me the alarming news that tomorrow would be the dress parade. Filled to the gills with tots of whisky, painted like a desperate whore in an effort to hide my complexion, I staggered into a taxi, still looking like an elderly lemon with the good Griselda propping me up. Somehow I got to the Cambridge Theatre dressing-room where the wardrobe mistress got me into my first-act dress which, to her horror, slipped right off me and fell to my feet in a hiss of crumpled taffeta. I had lost about ten pounds in five days. She pinned it hastily all down the back, while I tottered on to the stage. 'God God!' called out Pomeroy whose venture it was. 'Whatever's happened to Diana Gould?' I hastily minimised my wretched condition (ill-health is anathema in the theatre), showed off my other dresses while managing to faint only off-stage and got home and back to bed where I could allow myself two more days' ill health before returning to the last rehearsals.

'Why, Diana, are you playing the love-scene looking down?' the sympathetic director Clifford Evans complained. Plastered with bright-pink make-up, I could do nothing about my golden eyeballs and had been squinting unromantically at my knees. I was forced to raise reluctant eyelids and give him the full yellow flare. He was very compassionate and resisted treating me as the leper I was.

Yet another of my diplomatic friends presented me with an ultimatum. No thank you, dearest Algernon, I said, and he went off in tears to marry someone else and live happily ever after.

Came 'train-call': Euston departure ten a.m. Still very groggy I got into my carriage and collapsed wearily against the antimacassar. The Russian wardrobe mistress, a relic from the original Pomeroy Company and a good friend, poked her head through the door laughing and in her thick Slav accent said, 'Diana, you know what? So-and-so [the actress daughter of one of the players in *What Every Woman Knows*, who was furious she had not been offered the part of Lady Sybil] sees you and say that you looked *terrible* and will never make the first night *tomorrow* and she had better get on train and come to Glasgow. So I say to her, "You don't know Diana Gould, she Russian-trained. She play tomorrow and perhaps die after!" '

We did not reach Glasgow until eight-forty-five that night and my digs were fairly comfortless, but everyone was so kind and so supportive it had almost been worthwhile to suffer that miserable disease.

Pomeroy's fortunes had obviously by some mysterious means been restored, for not only was he financing our play, but also Bernard Shaw's *Heartbreak House* with a star cast including Edith Evans, the young Deborah Kerr and Robert Donat, as well as Turgenev's *A Month in the Country* with Michael Redgrave and also a strong cast. Robert's play opened in Manchester on the same night as ours in Glasgow so we sent each other heartening cables, while at the close of the second week in Edinburgh on the train southwards to London Beau and I, finding that Robert's lot were on the other platform on their way to follow us in Edinburgh, raced over to hug each other, tore back to our platform only to find our train slowly edging out. Beau grabbed at the nearest door, I tumbled in after him and as the train gathered speed, ran down the corridor to regain our carriage, only to find the communicating door locked. Consternation in the Company, who were convinced we had been left behind. Hours later the train reached a station and we hared along the platform, regained our proper seats and relieved their hearts.

I returned to London on the first night only to find poor Griselda had succumbed to the disease and was looking very seedy. The opening night was at the Lyric Theatre, amongst the pleasantest of all London playhouses. I died of nerves but acquitted myself adequately enough to get very good reviews. Light of heart and happy for once, well employed and surrounded by a very friendly Company, I laughed when one of them said, 'You never seem tired at the end of long rehearsals or the eight shows a week. Why not?' I asked them if, when they watched a ballet, it had ever occurred to them that the wretched dancers had been working full out since nine in the morning with a two-hour class followed by interminable rehearsals which could last up to an hour or so before curtain-up; that statistics showed that the physical output of the ballet dancer equalled seven times that of the workman wielding a pickaxe on the road in terms of muscle strain and pressure on the heart, whereas walking up and down a stage using my jaws with maybe a little fancy arm gesture thrown in for good measure was to me an exquisite conception of work, a whimsical wonder after the grim toil through which I'd pounded all my life so far.

However, this paradisiacal state was not to last long, for two days later I was serving Griselda her breakfast in bed and put down the tray on an upholstered chair to go and plump her pillows. Unbeknown to me there was a loose castor underneath the valance, the tray slid, crashed, and my bare feet were covered with boiling-hot tea. Anybody who has experienced scalding will agree that it is infinitely more painful than a dry burn. By the time a doctor was found I had two enormous long blisters on each foot stretching from my ankles to my toes and was still in agony. That night I got to the theatre in bandages and bedroom slippers belonging to my stepfather and shuffled to my dressing-room put on my make-up. 'Oh Miss!' said Ethel, my darling dresser. 'Wot 'ave you done?' Ethel would sit in the armchair at the end of the room in a clean white apron knitting away serenely and regaling me with tales of sex–life–as–it–is–endured–south–of–the–River–Thames, till my eyes bulged with disbelief and my heart yearned to help her. Laconically she would describe her various strategies either to keep her husband off her or to abort herself with anything from a fork to a button-hook, poor lamb, at such times when her efforts to avert him failed once too often. Her quiet voice, the absence of emotion as hideous experience followed grisly story, interspersed with directions such as 'You'll find your false hair in the left-hand drawer, Miss', or, after a particularly horrendous story of being picked up haemorrhaging in the street by a kindly policeman who took her home in a taxi, 'Would you like a cuppa in the interval, Miss?' opened up a whole world to me of selfish and brutal men and indomitable, stalwart women.

They carried me down into the wings. I'd sliced some soft satin slippers in slits such as Henry VIII wore to ease his gouty feet, propped myself on two sticks till I heard my cue, dropped them and walked on. Luckily the period of *What Every Women Knows* is around the early 1900s so my dresses were long and swept the floor. The difficulty with pain is that it gnaws away at one's concentration, summoning the brain to pay it attention. However, long training on ever-sore toes helped me conquer the faintness and the nausea and I got through without missing a single performance, perhaps fortified by the comic fact that the hungry actress longing for my rôle had materialised yet again and could be seen in various parts of the theatre greedily awaiting my collapse. Thus strengthened, I even carried on through the frightening weekend when one of the biggest burns decided to turn a nasty shade of green and I was warned that unless it cleared up within twenty-four hours I would have to surrender and go into hospital. But it did relent and I went on to enjoy three months unhampered at last by either flu, jaundice or scalded feet.

Not that the true course of a theatre career – like that of love – is ever entirely free of friction, simply that its protagonists are less inclined to behave like denizens of some remote jungle than those in the ballet. None the less I did suffer small unpleasantnesses from the leading lady who was irritated that *Picture Post* showed three pictures of my face and one of her ample behind, and took umbrage. I was learning that it was impossible to win: either one was a success and an object of contention or a flop and an object of contempt. Anyway she had a laugh like faulty plumbing and was fearfully smug.

Pom's three companies flourished, so he decided to hold a party for all three casts; there was a very jolly evening during which Michael Redgrave came up and said charmingly: 'I was in love with you when you must have been about sixteen,' and proceeded to tell me that he had come to see me dance whenever he could. Nice. 'Would I care to come with him to see a *Heartbreak House* matinée tomorrow?' Indeed I would and did. Together with Laurence Olivier and John Gielgud, Michael was part of the leading triumvirate of the English theatre. It was a marvellously acted show and he and I had a merry tea with Bob Donat after and then raced off to our respective theatres to give our own performances. That was to be the beginning of a long and tender relationship of great value to me.

Gradually spring was opening up the ruined streets, fireweed shone purple amongst the rubbled heaps, the bushes in the squares leafed over with green and early blossoms cheered the vistas where the broken profiles of bombed buildings, jagged and forlorn, lost a little of their mourning. Griselda and I went to yet another concert given by the valiant Yehudi, who had flown over curled up in an army bomber to play and raise money for the *Amis des volontaires français* at the Albert Hall. It was packed and the beauty of the slow movement of the Brahms concerto was like a benediction to our tired souls.

8 May 1943: Tunis and Bizerta fall.

What Every Woman Knows continued contentedly. The Queen and the Princesses Elizabeth and Margaret attended, in aid of a charity for the blind. I was receiving offers for film tests and Ivor Novello, the popular romantic star, stopped me in the street to tell me I was the only young actress on the stage who moved with grace. Hooray. Such a change from the pain and strife I had floundered through most of my professional life. And then all collapsed. The leading lady was

213

'expecting' and did not wish to continue, so the notice went up after fourteen successful weeks. My film test, I was told, was the best the studio had seen in a year but the rôle would be given to an actress already under contract and ahead loomed the dreaded Labour Exchange and possible conscription. Added to the gloom was the sadness of a last night, to have to part company with so many colleagues become friends, and lose a new family forged in that uncertain and unstable element that is the theatre, with its hopes and fears and passions shared and made sharper by the tensions inherent in acting; to know companionship and even love created by proximity. For a time all my stage friends tried to help me find another job, and I was signed up for a film called *Don't, Mr Disraeli*, which held out some hope. Drearily I served at a charity stall with Deborah Kerr at the Dorchester Hotel and the war rumbled on.

5 July: General Sikorski and Victor Cazalet MP killed in a plane crash at Gibraltar.
10 July: Invasion of Sicily by the British and Americans.

And I was faced with a most distressing task: Pomeroy had been summoned by Equity to stand trial for the dismissal of his Ballet Company without the statutory two weeks' salary last November. I was called to the meeting and waited miserably for the moment I would be invited to bear witness. There was a long table with the chairman and chief officers of Equity seated in judgment, Pomeroy sitting at one end. To my dismay he embarked on a long paean of praise in my honour not only as an artist but also as someone who had done everything within her power to make the Company a success. 'In fact,' he declared, 'Miss Gould was virtually my directress as well.' He had presented me with an unpleasant challenge, for when I had begun to supervise everything for lack of anyone else doing so, I had eventually had to beg him to authorise that very position and to hoist my salary, as that would both strengthen my hand and help my purse, depleted by dozens of telephone calls, letters and other costs. Pom had refused. Now he was admitting belatedly what should have been, perhaps trying to flatter me in the hope that I would prove a sympathetic witness; added to which he chose to insist that there never had been any definite plan or promise for another season and he was mystified to think that the Company should have entertained such an idea. Praying that he would not think I was taking revenge on him for his failure to have been generous to me, I had no choice but to present my own and the dancers' case against him. I therefore related all the efforts I had put into presenting him with a strong Company, the hiring of new dancers, choreographers, designers, librettists, most of whom he had actually signed up, to say nothing of several weeks of rehearsal. 'Furthermore,' I concluded with a flourish, 'I cannot, nor do I, imagine Mr Pomeroy was supporting all our prodigious efforts with a view to offering us a couple of weeks in Raynes Park bandstand,' and sat down.

The chairman smiled appreciatively. Mr Pomeroy would have to pay two weeks' notice to every member of the Company or go to a higher court. My triumph was tinged with real sadness, for I loved Pom, but so had I loved the wretched boys and girls thrown arbitrarily into the streets without warning. 'I would like to add that I wish to waive my two weeks' salary as a gesture to a boss who otherwise had been exemplary,' said I and, avoiding Pom's eye, left that dismal office with all the emptiness of a Pyrrhic victory. I was very hard up and unemployed.

25 July: Mussolini resigns. New Italian Cabinet headed by Badoglio under King Victor Emanuel.
3 September: British invade Italy.
8 September: Italy surrenders unconditionally.
15 September: Cecil gets the CB.

Autumn seemed to rush in. The leaves on the trees turned, dried out and fell like burnt paper on to the dusty pavements. Ahead lay months of cold, darkening days and the war dragging on endlessly. My only hope of a job, *Don't, Mr Disraeli*, would be postponed till next May. Abysses stretched before me and close at hand that sombre woman with her bare, stripped face and her ledgers at the Labour Exchange. Out of the blue, Cyril Ritchard, whose chameleon gifts had developed from a career in musicals to one of the most admired of comedy actors, suddenly rang me up. I hardly knew him other than from the audience side of the footlights, but it appeared that he, like Michael Redgrave, had been a fan of mine since I was a very young dancer suffering the onslaughts of Rambert. Oh, thought I, why did not either of them come backstage and pay me the homage I was thirsting for? He asked me to join him in a new musical show he was planning. Thrilled, relieved, overjoyed, I agreed to meet him to discuss plans. The following day he rang to say that it is all off; Beatrice Lillie, that great comedienne, had persuaded him to join her and do his duty by ENSA, the organisation to which all stage performers were expected to give some of their time for entertaining the troops in whatever part of the world they happened to be. Shocked with disappointment and despair, I thanked him for having thought of me, wished him and Bea luck, hung up the receiver and, gloomy of heart, went apprehensively to the Labour Exchange. To my relief the usual robot was not in charge; whether she had died of hardening of the arteries or was in hospital undergoing treatment for a haemorrhage of acid I could not tell. What her absence did offer was the presence of a much younger, less misogynist type who allowed me a permit of seven weeks, taking me to the end of that year, 1943. I bounced along Marlborough Street, light of heart albeit light of pocket, took the bus back to the flat and the train down to see old 'Bosey' Douglas at Hove.

By now we had established quite a friendship; I had evidently struck the right note of respect for his self-styled genius without abrogating in the process all claims to be considered as relatively well-read and intelligent (even though he dismissed those sonnets I'd submitted to him as lacking the virtue and purity of his own). For one enticing moment, bending down, he dragged out from under his sofa a large Foreign Office-type red tin box, full, he said, of Oscar's letters. I tried to find the right expression of encouragement, tense with anticipation. Should I goggle at him with greedy eyes full of unbridled appetite or would it fit the occasion better to assume a look redolent of quiet reverence, of a holy respect that only silence could portray? Even as I was juggling with the problem, Bosey shot one of those mischievous slightly viperish looks at me, tempered by the wateriness of his faded blue eyes, chuckled and shoved the lot back under the sofa like an unwanted footstool. I could have slapped him. I suppose he sensed my disappointment for he gave me a picture of himself, half-photograph half-drawing, in which his beauty is so compelling it raises pity and forgiveness in one's heart both for Oscar Wilde and for Alfred Douglas. Even though I had to report to him my and Puffin Asquith's total failure to convince the Government they should let him have his *In Excelsis*, he also gave me several more books. That was the last time I was able to see him, that small, shrunken figure unrecognisable from the picture. He looked, I thought, musing on the train back, rather as though he had been captured by the Igorots, the Philippine tribe who shrank the decapitated heads of their enemies to a quarter size, only in his case the whole being had been processed.

Two weeks after Cyril Ritchard had first raised, then doused, my hopes he rang again. He is not accepting Bea's idea, he is improving upon it and is planning to take the whole show of Lehár's *Merry Widow* which had been running concurrently at the time of *What Every Woman Knows* and offer it to ENSA as the first and only full, top-class entertainment that melancholy, ill-organised institution had managed to engage for the troops. Would I play the role of Frou-Frou, the French dancer? And would I meet him to discuss it? Would I indeed? Cyril transpired to be the most enchanting, warm-hearted, funny, gifted man I had ever met and from that auspicious meeting on and off for the following two years he and his lovely actress wife, Madge Elliott, were to give me the happiest years of my life in the theatre. Black Fairy must have folded her exhausted wings and taken a nap.

We had a riotous meeting, the next day after his evening show, in his tiny flat in Grosvenor Square. Running into a somewhat loose-tongued female playwright on the landing outside who swept a malicious, well-oiled look over us, Cyril said with a grin, 'That's torn it.' He explained that there was acting, dancing and even singing in the rôle. I said I could manage the first two but I was known in the theatre as the 'gravel soprano' and could not promise much in that line, would *chant parlant* do? Cyril complied and I took a deep breath saying, 'Would it be frightful cheek if I were slightly to alter the script?' It was quite sterilely awful, a sort of static bleep no amount of delicate modulation could warm up from its tonelessness. 'How do you mean?' 'Well Frou-Frou was obviously a Parisian whore and should have spoken the original German with a strong French accent – to say nothing of her choice of words, which would have sprung from the gutters of Montmartre, don't you think?' Cyril gave me *carte blanche*. I went to see the eminent Binkie Beaumont, casting director of the prestigious H. M. Tennant's, and signed up for the lordly sum of twenty-five pounds per week. I also went to take singing lessons and discovered I could rely upon about two and a half octaves in the middle register which, together with prayers, cheek and chicanery, might get me through.

Two days dancing on a film called *Fiddlers Three* helped pay the groceries and rehearsals soon began – of course in a scruffy room above a den in Soho. I had never done a musical show and Cyril was a marvellous help showing me the totally different technique, extrovert as against the introversion of the ballet, wherein the dancer must absorb the music and then transmute it into movement expressive of the choreographer's intent, subjecting his or her personality according to the needs of the rôle. Now I had to learn to throw myself, as it were, to the audience, to consider them as a mass of individuals from whom I should encourage an immediate response; it should be more of a conversation, an exchange – even those parts of the rôle that bore no words should carry this broader and closer co-operation. I enjoyed every aspect of this widening of stage learning and was so grateful to Cyril for the care and generosity he showed me.

Rehearsals began to sour a little as we prepared for going abroad. 'You must have ten injections,' said the dour head nurse at Drury Lane (requisitioned by ENSA as their GHQ). It was not so much the prospect of being used as a pin-cushion as the relish with which she announced this debatable pleasure that irritated. In the lunch-break we would have to go to wherever the requisite poisons and their accompanying needles were awaiting us, roll up our sleeves, be stabbed, sticking-plastered and return to rehearsal. There was a particularly horrible injection known as 'TAB' applied in three stages containing typhus and assorted fevers. I can remember, after submitting myself and my sore arm to the final shot, returning to rehearsal, dancing on increasingly rubbery legs, trying to focus on Cyril, who had inexplicably become twins and whose voice sounded like a fog-horn from a far-away bay, and coming to propped up against the wall. 'Gould,' said Cyril, 'go home and give up.' Gratefully I took my blazing face home and fell into bed with a temperature of 101 degrees Fahrenheit.

One day dear Cyril, after the manner of most men, belatedly excused himself in the middle of taking me through my *pas de deux* on the Drury Lane stage, at last having decided to go and have one of his injections in the mini-clinic set up in the quondam royal box; after an unconscionably long time he returned to the stage sheepish and bright green. 'Are you all right, Master?' 'Oh dear me,' said Cyril, 'as soon as that rapacious creature stuck her needle into me I threw up.' 'Oh, Cyril!' 'And what's more all over the doctor's felt hat.' 'I hope the doctor's hat was suitably sterilised,' I said, 'otherwise it had no right to be there in the middle of a hygienic area – so serve them both right.' Cyril grinned and we continued with the leap *en arabesque*, into my partner's uncertain arms.

On the last week of the year we opened at Oxford and despite swollen glands beneath our arms and sundry other injection-produced ailments, it all went very well. The English automatically find a foreign accent droll beyond words and only an occasional hoot of laughter betrayed an undergraduate studying modern languages who had understood the gutter French.

13

Uneasy Paradise

By now four years of war had passed, bringing a slow but steady displacement of normality; a shift from the habitual routine of daily life and work to an almost unwitting acceptance of the exceptional and irregular. Paradoxically the hazard of the bombing had brought its own version of the customary by the very token of its constancy, rather as though wakening from a nightmare in which there was a blaze, one found that the house was indeed on fire.

But ahead, for those of us in *The Merry Widow*, in 1944 a pale sun shone, still qualified because of the tight security that kept us from being absolutely sure of our destination; as far as we were permitted to know it would be vaguely at the far end of the Mediterranean. Somewhere around mid-January, on an icy black night, we were called to Drury Lane for a security talk. 'Back to school,' I reckoned (looking at the official gentleman from MI-something-or-other with his permanently locked face and accusing eyes), 'only with the additional discomfort of finding oneself on the headmistress's mat, guiltily apprehensive.' Whereas the results of misbehaviour then would have been a hundred lines and no outings for a week, now we were warned of consequences varying from imprisonment to death. We were sent on to Kingsway to surrender our books (rationed in number) to be vetted. I was on my best behaviour and refrained from taking *Ulysses* or *Les Liaisons Dangereuses*, hoping they would find nothing subversive in the Shakespeare sonnets, my complete John Donne, Somerset Maugham short stories (surely nothing too reprehensible in straying wives in the steamy tropics), Stefan Zweig's *Beware of Pity*, Connolly's *Enemies of Promise*, and Dickens's *Our Mutual Friend* to be reread yet again, and I wavered between Wilkie Collins's *Moonstone* or one or two new Agatha Christies.

Told to pack one large suitcase and one small and to have a coat and raincoat all at the ready, we more or less sat on the lot in our respective halls till one evening three days later an abrupt telephone call ordered us to Drury Lane within the hour. Dear Cecil, at home for a term, stopped me by the front door (my mother having focused just enough attention to kiss me goodbye as though I were off to a hunt ball): 'Diny darling, do take care, won't you? I know for you it's an exciting adventure, but you'll be going through very dangerous waters. Do exactly what you're told and then only you may be safe. God bless you,' and kissing me he helped me into my taxi and away. Away for nearly five months had I but known it.

It was dark and cold when I got to the theatre where the Company was assembled on the bare stage in varying moods: apprehensive, wary, stolid or, as I, excited. Bundled into buses, we were driven to a blacked-out station through the blacked-out streets, hustled into carriages, four a side, and after half an hour, with a snort of evil-smelling steam and a bad-tempered jerk, the train rumbled off into still more blackness.

I extricated myself from the lap of the chorus-boy opposite into which I had been catapulted and regained my seat. In the carriage there was a lovely soprano, Nancy Evans, myself and a covey of chorus-boys, incidentally the best and funniest company in the world. We chatted and joked and rolled about in the penumbra of that squalid carriage, quipping and quizzing in the peerless idiom special to their ilk, irreverent, outrageous and totally comic. As the gentlemen of the ballet take themselves far more seriously on the whole, this was my first experience of that rare hybrid, the musical comedy male chorus, trained in singing and dancing, sexually ambivalent and marvellous

221

company. However, even their wit and ebullience slowly petered out; one after another heads dropped, wilting in the icy stuffiness and all was quiet except for the odd snore. All night we rattled on, till a pale dawn showing a feeble light to match our own weariness leaked beneath the blinds and the slowing of the train announced our arrival. Where, we had no idea.

'Diana,' said Nancy, 'you're maddening. You haven't even got bunged-up eyes.' I explained that as I had already lived through God knows what tough conditions and ghastly discomfort, spending eight hours bolt upright in a freezing train was hardly worse than my former miseries and to my romantic mind the excitement of the journey ahead, of getting out of wartime England, obliterated everything else.

By now we knew we were bound for Egypt in general, Cairo and Alexandria in particular, and that prospect alone levitated me above and beyond any petty inconveniences.

It was six-forty-five on a cold, wet, northern January morning. The platform, picked out by thin pencils of light, shone stickily like black saliva; cramped and stiff, we were herded into a large shed, so many cattle in quarantine, where for half an hour we shuffled, hungry and shivering, through customs and passports, were pushed into lorries and driven off into that sombre wetness peculiar to the English north, which seems to be almost palpable in its impenetrability. After a time we were decanted at a place where, from the smell of salt and oil, the sound of clanging metal and clanking chains, the added chill of a stiff breeze, we could at least deduce that we had reached some dock. Obediently we staggered towards a gangway and clambered on to what seemed in the growing dawn to be a fairly large ship. Georgina, the talented soprano who sang second lead, and I were apportioned a small, stuffy cabin amidships not too far below decks, which was to be our home for fifteen days. To both of us at that moment it was second only to the Ritz; its stuffiness was warmth, its worn mats and threadbare blankets on the two small bunks a dry haven. We shed our damp overcoats, collapsed on our bunks in relief, forgetting for a while our aching stomachs.

At long last we were marshalled into the dining-room and consoled with pitch-black strong tea, so strong you could not detect the bottom of the cup and preferred not to, and wedges of rather stale bread tasting of woollen gloves, both of them in our famished state transformed into nectar and ambrosia. 'All is relative,' said I, with my mouth full. The dining-room soon filled up with a regiment of Lancers, very elegant on their way to somewhere, together with other officers of the Army or Navy, including David Milford Haven whom I knew and who managed to break all protocol and join me at our theatrical table.

Next day we sailed and most of the chorus-girls promptly turned green, declaring graphically that they 'could keep nothing down'. I pointed out, as we rolled into the Bay of Biscay, that this was a great pity as the boat was loaded with irresistible young gentlemen belonging to a crack regiment, whereupon I dragged a few sickly creatures up to the main deck to prove my point, callously telling them that if they insisted, the means of ridding themselves of breakfast were still at hand on either side at the rails. Curiously enough, seasickness disappeared as if by magic, nor were there any further reports of rejected meals. I seriously considered patenting my cure for a while, but was distracted by being called by the Officer Commanding Troops to combine with the Leading Wren and Chief of the ATS (female troops) to organise 'tea fatigue'. The ship was full to bursting and we had to eat and drink in relays, sitting on the floor of the smoking room for want of chairs, munching unrationed biscuits to our heart's content, our 'Mae Wests', as our compulsory life-jackets were jocularly called after the fulsome shape of the famous film star, always near at hand.

I could never fathom why I particularly should have been chosen to represent the non-Service category of passengers aboard, as there were many older and soberer than I, nor why OC Troops summoned me one evening to submit me to a truly wonderful exhibition of verbal obfuscation sprinkled with 'ums' and 'ers' and orchestrated with short coughs and loud swallows and other signs of that kind of embarrassment long now a moribund part of the sexual taboos of yesteryear, which for a time made me fear the dry old soldier had lost his wits and gone a-rambling, until a few odd words rising to the surface like an emission of gas finally gave me the clue. The poor old dear was trying to tell me that all sorts of jolly goings-on were taking place in the lifeboats slung along the upper deck, where the heaving and grunting beneath the tarpaulin covers betrayed sports of a kind not consonant with quoits, badminton or ping-pong and must, ere they spread irredeemably, be brought under control. With which the good man wiped his forehead and cleared his throat in a final trumpet of relief. . . . Restraining a desire to ask him by what means he thought I would be able to bring about the stifling of human behaviour at its most natural – would he consider my poking at the heaving mass with a harpoon or swinging the boats over the water and tipping the ardent couples into the drink, for example? I told him I would do my best and left him exhausted, looking despondently at his shining boots.

I organised – very reluctantly – a night patrol which unfortunately succeeded in quelling the joyous Bacchanalians.

The fifteen days were a wonderful change after years of bombing, rations and other restrictions, of which boat drill every morning was now the only one. There was plenty of company and those kinds of sentimental relationships born of proximity, danger and uncertainty, adding a bitter-sweetness and spontaneity to all attachments; open-ended, starting from nowhere, with nothing to offer other than the warmth and fragile tenderness of the limiting time ahead; like flowers in a vase, but none the less heartaching when, after escaping the torpedoes that sank the ship ahead, we finally reached Port Said and the end of the voyage.

The ship came alongside a dusty quay rimmed by rusty iron fencing, whorls of barbed wire like so much metal tumbleweed and a gaggle of extremely unpalatable humans dressed in dirty galabiyas out of whose rents and tears peeped a knee, a shin, an elbow, all now serving as battering rams. A confused yelling rose from this unappetising crowd in parody of a welcome. All visions of an Egypt of sunsets, golden sand and pyramids sank rapidly.

'Oh my!' shrieked one of my favourite chorus-boys. 'Number Two

Company *Desert Song*; would you believe it, duck?' 'Duck' had no choice but to believe it and together with the rest of the Merry Widowers sadly bade farewell to our particular flames and tottered down the gangway heavy of heart. Following the interminable official obligations, we were stuffed into two rickety buses and after minor explosions and much black smoke trundled off towards some God-forsaken place called Ismailia, where we were offered quite the most awful meal of all the awful meals I had been faced with in my life. Shovelled back into our old rattle-bags, with the same rude orchestration to herald our departure, we finally reached Cairo towards evening.

Before us a large bright hotel dispelled the blackness from which my war-dimmed eyes recoiled; so much light, uncontrolled, dissipated, wicked, extravagant, dangerous light? However, I was fit for nothing, longed for nothing but bath, bed and dark . . . but I had not reckoned with Egypt, with Cairo, with a fantasy lifestyle so totally alien to seriousness and order and dull rectitude, nor indeed with the enormous handsome proprietor who swooped upon me and together with a gaggle of his pals dragged me to his gloriously vulgar suite, where I was showered with champagne, platters of food and revived with chatter till three in the morning. It was also wonderful to see Madge and Cyril again.

Next morning seemed total unreality. Assailed by the sounds of the beggars' and vendors' ceaseless cries, of hooting cars outside, bewildered by my room piled with masses of flowers and an actual laundry basket full of fruit, I went out on to the balcony, looked up in wonderment at a smoke-blue sky and at the whole huge expansion of everything after years of shrunken appetite and locked-up longings of every kind.

The following day, still giddy with transition, I reeled across to the Opera House (built in six weeks and falling down ever since, now alas! gone for ever), and discovered in my splendid dressing-room more flowers and piles of letters from friends I thought never to see again ever, since one after the other they had disappeared into the Army, the

Navy, diplomacy. Suddenly life became lively, not just a matter of managing to remain alive.

I laid out my things in my dressing-room and we rehearsed for the following two days under the paternal eye of Solomon Bey Naguib, the intendant of the Opera House (soon to become 'Sammy' Naguib to all of us), who sent out coveys of doe-eyed seven-year-old small boys to bring back an assortment of orders for coffee, tea, sweetmeats and drinks that would have confused a waiter of twenty years' experience, and who never failed once.

Came opening night. Up went the curtain upon a glitteringly full house: up went one's spirits at seeing people well and elegantly dressed. What I had not recalled was that French being the court language, all my gutterspeech would be understood to the last and lowest vulgarism. Howls of delighted laughter greeted Frou-Frou's repartee and I had to invent a whole lot of 'business' until I could bring out the next (and possibly even more unrefined) phrase. To tumultuous applause I shot into the wings, the first-act curtain came down and I was making for my dressing-room when Solomon Bey stopped me and said, with the requisite air of solemnity, 'His Majesty King Farouk wishes to see you in his box,' and led me there. I was confronted by what looked like a plum pudding stuffed unceremoniously into a white uniform. Solomon Bey retreated. I curtsied and waited, watching the rather handsome face not yet quite blown up to match the bloated body. He smiled. 'How is it you speak French like that?' 'I apologise, Your Majesty, for the coarseness – my French is generally somewhat cleaner, my family has lived in France since 1800.' This said demurely, as I watched his eyes travelling professionally all over me, longing to ask him how much he felt I'd fetch on the market, but I thought better of starting my Cairo *séjour* on such a risky overture. We chatted on about France and Egypt with all the depth of two waterflies skidding over a pond. His eyes, focused now on mine, looked, I considered, like a pair of half-sucked peppermint humbugs. Forcing myself to listen to what either of us was saying, I suddenly realised he had asked me something twice over. Grabbing at the tail end of the sentence I gathered he had been inviting me to supper with him after the performance. His weight may more or less have anchored him to his immediate surroundings, however his reputation had flown on wings to the four corners of the world. 'Majesty,' I said, 'you flatter me, but I am already late for my next appearance, you will excuse me,' dipped a speedy curtsey and backed out, before the rising spleen on his face could explode in mine. The fact that I did not actually appear on stage again till the final act must have made him very cross.

There followed a marvellous time, four weeks of such excitement, such colour, so full of old and new friends, of parties and luncheons, of flowers and tributes, it was like an awakening from a nightmare, like taking off a tight shoe so that the restored circulation of blood to one's whole system made for a giddiness of delight. Again I felt like Beerbohm's Zuleika Dobson as I picked and chose among those swains who in London had always been so passionless and spoilt. The rapture of coming through the foyer at Shepheard's on Marmaduke's arm, apologising fraudulently to Archibald for having forgotten the promise to dine; to dangle Algernon's box of chocolates before his imploring face, shaking one's head sadly at Percival for the umpteenth time, now that they were bereft of all the girls they had once treated so cavalierly and stranded with a poor choice of female company among the valiant but anaphrodisiac ladies of the services, was something to be savoured with unashamed relish.

I suppose the *coup de grâce* was a huge bouquet from none other than Rubin, accompanied by a card so flourishingly flattering as to make the bile rise in my throat. 'Too little and too late,' said I, and tearing up the card, gave the flowers to my dresser, remembering those weeks of overwork and semi-starvation and the final sacking.

The days sped by full of interesting new friends, both cosmopolitan Egyptians in various governmental posts, secretaries at the British Embassy, Englishmen in various wartime jobs among whom were a few old friends. They gave luncheons for me, supper parties, came again and again to the show. They were for the most part wonderful company, two out of the three secretaries of the Embassy wrote poetry and short stories, others among them teaching in Gizeh University. For the first time in my life I was fêted, free of the cruelty and petty intrigues of the ballet world, liberated from my own melancholy breed of disappointment and loneliness, breathing a new air among people I could trust and who showed me care and concern, homage and love. Slowly I unwound, loosened from the tension created by fear and the anticipation of the next blow to fall. It was like coming into the sun and light from a shivering dark corner and I relished every moment. Bliss it was indeed to be young and alive and to be with all of them was very heaven.

Nevertheless stricken with guilt, I bought silks and brocades in the souk, adding packets of dried fruit, posting them weekly to Griselda still stuck among the bombs and black-out; visited the hospitals; argued with the charming British Ambassador (a friend of my stepfather's) about the appalling poverty and illnesses of the fellaheen (minimum four diseases per capita); spent late evenings after the show with writers and painters, poets and journalists, all of us waiting and watching apprehensively the Allies' slow progress up the Italian peninsula. And it was out of that joyousness, that light-hearted swirl where nothing and nobody bore any particular outline that on the crest of the wave, as it were, one figure emerged and I understood by that emotional collision what the French mean by *coup de foudre*. It is not only the lightning that strikes, but the electric shock which carries both along on a single current so intense that all else dims into insignificance. It began by his attacking me bitterly at a crowded party and my sending him off to sober up so as to make the battle worthwhile, that betrayed that, on previous meetings I must have got under his skin. I continued dancing and talking to various friends around me. He returned, tried to pursue his antagonism which I countered, but I could tell that only half or even less of his heart was in it and by now none of mine; both of us knew we were helpless before the elemental. For two wonderful days of floating we went everywhere together, out to the pyramids to watch the dawn rise, to Shubbra to see the ravishing little Turkish baroque palace and I would come off-stage to find him in my dressing-room.

We needed very few words in that rarity of close feeling that is the drawing together of two hearts. I would go to the theatre and find messages pinned to my mirror: '*Pour moi une rose inconnue a été mon pays vainqueur.*' I danced my *pas de deux* with added lyrical feeling. As I came off-stage Cyril said: 'That was lovely, darling. By the way we leave for Alexandria early the day after tomorrow. . . .' We spent every golden moment we had left together, gathering what we shared to store away; sat in an Arab café surrounded by babble and chatter, the clatter of coffee cups, the haze of Egyptian cigarettes; and finally didn't have to speak at all. The masses of bouquets, the heart-warming reception, the fond farewells from fans and friends were very moving on that last night. R and I went out to the Pyramids once more. At six-thirty in the morning I returned to the hotel to pack. At nine-fifteen I was in the train to Alexandria. We had had three days.

Installed in a comfortable hotel overlooking the harbour, Georgina and I still had to share a bedroom, the luxury of one room each being beyond the overcrowded conditions of Egypt in wartime. Seven South African officers gave us a jolly lunch and I tried hard to put my heart into a locked safe. Almost impossible with loving cables arriving and heart-to-heart telephone calls all through the empty nights. I received an invitation to lunch from the British Information Officer to whom I had written at R's suggestion. I accepted it in a lacklustre way, saying I would meet him in the hall of the hotel at one o'clock. As I went down in the creaking old open-cage lift I saw below me a great poll of shining golden hair. 'Wasted on a man,' I thought in imitation of Nanny and when I got out, I found it belonged to a stocky man in the middle-thirties with a witty nose like a big toe and an enchanting smile. 'I'm Diana Gould.' 'I'm Lawrence Durrell.' 'Not the poet and author?' 'Guilty. You wrote me one of the most surreal letters I've ever had,' he said, with a quizzical stare. 'Oh, did I? It didn't seem to me to be anything out of my usual style.' 'Good,' said Larry, 'that's a splendid start. Let's have a drink and then go to lunch.' And then, without another word, we went out through the swing doors and got into the gharry and talked about – what? It could have been anything, the other poets in Egypt at that time, the curious light in that great empty ancient sky, *The Merry Widow*, the palimpsest of smells around us which grew so overwhelming. When I suddenly realised we weren't moving, I opened the box of chocolates just handed to me by a persistent admirer, picked out the hard ones and pelted the horse's behind. The driver was outraged, not so much by the extravagance as by the fact that the animal, deaf to his yells and impervious to his whip, yielded at once to the blandishments of confectionery and with a delighted snort started off at a trot which he maintained until the supplies were exhausted. Where else but in Alexandria could that reaction have happened, where else would even the cab-horse enjoy perverse pleasure?

After one of those delightfully interminable lunches in an Arab café, I got to the theatre by the skin of my teeth; Larry said, 'I think I'm coming to the show tonight, but my nice English landlady is a week late with the birth of her baby.' So I said bring her and her husband too and I'll dance it out of her. So he did and I did and the baby was born that night when she got home. Larry took me afterwards to a restaurant, impressing me vastly with his fluent Greek and his Arabic and that unique mixture of cleverness and kindliness so rare in Englishmen. I looked at him across the table over my couscous and thought, 'somehow Cromwell has bypassed this one.' He was more like Englishmen must have been in Elizabethan times: ribald without sniggering, erudite without conceit, sensual rather than sexy, the whole informed with a charming diffidence that in no way detracted from his alert mind and sharp eye. He turned out to be a heavenly companion and we talked for hours, arguing, agreeing, disagreeing, chuckling and I still absorbed by that nose, that prehensile nose that seemed to me the clue to his whole nature – solid yet sensitive, always on the qui vive. When he turned his head it was as though he swung round by courtesy of his nose, and I saw him going through life like some very evolved animal through a jungle picking up scents, tracing and following them, sometimes losing them, on occasion stuck on a false trail, but always an original one, for where other writers and poets were using their ears and eyes only, Larry was using his nose as well. The bliss was, of course, that we had words in common.

We talked about everything, jumping like happy antelopes from Bradshaw to Stendhal, Donne to railways, England (which he called Pudding Island), the metaphysical poets and cooking, dancing, coins and *cacahuètes*. It didn't matter. A day or so later when after a rehearsal I went to pick up Larry at his office, he was sitting behind his desk with two deep red parallel scratches down each side of his rubicund face. He said 'Have you read Stendhal on *L'Amour*?' I said no. He said, 'I have reached the stage he describes as crystallisation,' and looked quizzically at me. 'The evidence on my face is the handwriting of my current girlfriend who thought it an effective way of demonstrating her objection to you.' And off we went to eat.

Later we drove out over the pot-holed road and past Pompey's Tower at which I stuck out my tongue because I hate all things Roman, and on over the dry, dandruffy landscape to Lake Mareotis lying magenta-coloured in a hollow beneath that empty Egyptian sky and I said, 'I've never seen a sky with so much room in it before,' and Larry said, 'I'll write you a poem for that.' And later he did. There was never a companion more receptive or more responsive or more fun and he would come to the show most nights and send me round absurd messages on small scraps of paper, with odd drawings and metaphors that would give me heart. For this, after all, was the war and I had arrived tired in Egypt and also by now torn of heart – had come from England half-starved and needed just that attention and concern that he was showing me. One night I had twisted my rib muscles badly and had been strapped round like a mummy with those vast strips of plaster to be found in a John Bull puncture outfit for bicycle tyres, and at supper Larry was so funny that I had to go up to my room and tear the whole kilometre and a half off because the agonising constriction was too much for laughter.

At that time I had already read many of his books and his poetry and felt he was the first writer in English since the Victorians to write (until the *Nouvelle Vague*) as the French have always written, with sensuality and passion and colour and with the cognisance of the tension between man and woman, which is the whole structure of life. To this he added humour and ribald wit and his own especial gift for describing a setting, a surrounding, as surely as a great landscape painter. Here was suddenly a writer who didn't bore or burden one with his endless metaphysical ratiocinations, his intellectual gastric troubles, his high-falutin despair. Here was no German philosopher thinking head foremost downwards into a tunnel of his own digging, no French intellectual fragmented into brittleness in between political theory and sexuality, no American taking 800 pages to work the last speck of murk out of his id, but '*l'homme moyen sensuel*' at his most poetic and articulate.

And so in Larry's company the Alexandria days offered me yet another image of Egypt; Alexandria of the centuries-old Jewish and Greek enclaves, with their culture and character, lively, intelligent, sophisticated and elegant, both overlaid with a Mediterranean finish like some beautiful varnish. Lunching with Larry or together with his charming friend, the Welsh poet Gwyn Williams, in the tiny Greek cafés, taken to beautiful Greek villas after the evening show where, at one gathering, a very boring Greek naval officer, who had been pestering me all week, made a violent scene and had skilfully to be removed.

Next day Larry showed me his Alexandrian flat, a wonderfully eccentric tower atop a large rather ordinary villa looking like a rakish hat dumped on a solemn head during a festival. Sitting on the floor of Larry's tower he suddenly noticed my sadness. 'What's the matter, Diana dear?' 'I am sick of an old passion,★ dear Larry.' He clapped his hands to his forehead. 'Oh what a fool I've been all along – I see now. I'll try and get R over here from Cairo for a lecture.' And so he did, and once again my *coup de foudre* sat in my dressing-room that night and once again fate intervened. I'd been told that very afternoon that we would be leaving the following morning at dawn. R watched from the wings and neither the standing ovation nor the masses of flowers, the

★ From the poem *Cynara* by Ernest Dowson

endless curtain calls nor the shouts of 'Frou-Frou' could lift my spirits. We had had exactly twelve hours in Alexandria together. By five in the morning I was in the train to Port Said crying all the way, hoping to empty my aching heart.

14

War *à l'Italienne*

The boat bound for Italy, small and packed tight with Polish female soldiers who were sick all over their boots at daily boat-drill, rolled and pitched and tossed its way like a drunken sailor for the next six days. At last, at six-thirty on an icy March morning with the famous bora wind howling down the Adriatic straight at us, we landed at Taranto and were left standing on the quay huddled together till noon signalled the arrival of two very old buses of the same vintage as the Egyptians models of six weeks ago. Too battered to complain and with only the familiar mug of tea and lump of bread to fortify us, we squeezed ourselves in, to be bumped and rattled northwards up the coast until six in the evening. By this time the officer appointed by ENSA to look after us revealed that Vesuvius was in full eruption and that, the incommodious natural event having put Naples out of commission, we were to be taken to Bari instead, a God-forsaken town on the eastern coast, a port which having won Mussolini's prize for the highest birth rate in Italy had been rewarded with extensive housing development. A town, I reckoned, as we entered its soulless streets of barrack-like blocks, built entirely on copulation. Down with sex in all and any form.

It was by now dark and extremely cold. We were deposited at a fairly large house destined for the main Company. Already suspicious of the offhand domineering manner of the ENSA fellow designated to look after the Company I felt I should, in the absence of any other authority, supervise the place. Telling the coach to wait, I followed the girls and boys up the stairs. The first lot on reaching the filthy bedrooms, had collapsed on the bumpy beds, near to tears. I pushed open another door. The cockroaches rustled away like dried leaves. There was no heating. Furiously I turned to the ENSA man: 'Where is your superior officer? The girls and boys can't stay in this dump.' It appeared that it was too late to do anything. 'Then where is the Quartermaster General's headquarters?' This in my best Services manner. 'What is this ghastly rooming house?' No answer. (It turned out to have been a vacated brothel recently made out of bounds to the troops.) Stalled for the moment, I consented that we be taken to a fly-blown little hotel, Il Moro, for food. It was totally disgusting. Meanwhile leaving the Company there, Georgina and I were driven to our own 'superior lodgings'. By the look of it – a series of rooms piled one on top of the other for five storeys – I reckoned it to have been Bari's tonier brothel. Georgie and I looked at our rooms. Two iron cots covered with grey-white sheets the colour of wet newspaper nicely decorated here and there as though by a random hand with dark-red specks which, on closer inspection, transpired to be the blood of squashed bugs. The floor was of chipped encaustic tiles and a dirty net curtain waved a sarcastic welcome to us, stirred by the wind gusting through a broken window-pane.

Livid with fury, I dumped our luggage, ran down to the effigy in uniform and demanded to be taken at once in his own jeep to HQ. Reluctantly he drove me there. I came into a small office where, with his boots on the desk, sat a fair-haired something-or-other in uniform. 'I must see the Quartermaster General, please.' The Khaki Thing sneered at me as though I were a beggar asking for Buddha. Finally he put out his cigarette and said insolently, 'You can't.' 'Why not?' 'Because he ain't here.' However, he had made the mistake of looking over his shoulder at the door behind him. Quick as a flash I pushed past him and before, jerking his legs to the floor he could recover, got the door open.

An Aladdin's cave hailed me: a vast room lined with shelf upon shelf of supplies: blankets, tins, boxes, bottles reaching to the ceiling, before which putative Trimalchian banquet sat a scholarly looking officer at an imposing desk, outraged at the intrusion of a crumpled virago advancing towards him uninvited. . . . 'Henry!' I shouted in disbelief. 'Henry Croom-Johnson, by all that's miraculous.' I heard the door behind me close sharply as my enemy, the Khaki Thing in full pursuit, retreated hastily.

To find a friend in high places at such a moment of extremity was beyond all imagination. 'What are you doing here, Diana?' He could just as aptly have asked me why I looked such a dishevelled tramp, but he was an extremely gentle and kindly man, and after I had rapidly explained both the reason for my presence in Bari and our plight, he gave me *carte blanche* to take what I needed. We piled blankets and tinned food on to the jeep. Seizing two large bottles of brandy in a final flourish and accompanied by the good Henry I returned in the jeep to the Company's rooming house where I distributed the blankets and tins all round to cries of joy and handed over one of the bottles of brandy. Further ecstasy.

Henry, already shocked at the conditions there, was totally speechless when he dropped me at our salubrious quarters where poor frozen Georgie waited. One look at the beds and we decided discretion required us to sit on the floor where we passed our bottle round, rejoicing as the strong fluid burnt our unaccustomed throats and brought back a little circulation. Henry left, promising to try and extricate us somehow. Georgie and I, already tipsy, swallowed one more swig each, took off our shoes, rolled ourselves in our two blankets and with our folded overcoats as pillows fell asleep on the floor, at last oblivious of the cold.

The next morning, heavy of head and aching in body, I found in my determined quest for help yet another old pal in Wakey Chandos-Pole, aide-de-camp to General Nares, Commander-in-Chief of 2nd District Southern Italy, and marshalled them both into finding us somewhere to live. Someone mentioned the existence of a YWCA (Young Women's

Christian Association) tea shop. Hot water, hot tea and biscuits. Oh joy! Found Joyce Grenfell installed in the only big hotel, grandly called L'Impériale, and wallowed in her boiling bath; adding yet another friend, a colonel, to give weight to my plight. By the time I'd had lunch with Henry and dinner with Wakey, I was feeling temporarily better. However, when he dropped me back at brothel number one and saw my squalid bed the dear man took off his overcoat and laid it across it, declaring I could not possibly spend another night on the floor. Eventually the ENSA rations arrived: bacon, bread, jam. I shared a filthy lunch with the Company, all of whom were screaming in various keys and, at last finding the billeting officer, blew his head off. He left in pursuit of it and I had another bath in Joyce's room and found yet another friend, Edward Astley, in the hall, who after tea walked me back to my sleazy room and was duly horrified. A friend of Larry's gave me dinner and joined what I now named my 'shocked troops'. Reinforced by their consternation and determined this third night would be my last in that repulsive place, I bearded the Colonel in Command and told him Georgie and I would move into Joyce's vacated room the next day and to hell with his fear of our being raped by the officers whose lascivious eyes were, according to his arguments, bound to lead us to a Fate Worse than Death. I resisted adding that I was mistress of that Fate and not at all sure it was Worse than Death.

At last the murk cleared, after three days and nights so cold and dirty and comfortless that I felt I must in some strange way be paying for that recent excursion into a paradise of the heart to which I had no right. Belaboured everlastingly by the conformist moralising of one part of my nature, the other wild and passionate for which the dance had been my sole outlet, I could never really feel unfettered, relish the rapture of the entirely carefree, for long enjoy uninhibited any emotional flight that might carry me up and away at liberty to forget anything other than the warmth and joy that love can bring. It was as though that very strong pagan part of me had long since been stifled by the strictly moral religion in which I had been brought up, clipping my wings for ever, burdening me with a fear of retribution like some horrid wagging finger blocking my vision, chiding me for excessive spontaneity.

Sickened by his lack of gallantry, I refused to argue any more with stuffy Colonel Billetteer. Gathering my military chums, Henry, Wakey and Edward, Georgie and I packed up our few bits and pieces and got ourselves driven across town to the haven of the Impériale where we wove our way between tough-looking Yugoslav women resistance fighters, mute Russian officers who seemed to have locked their faces for good and thrown away the key, unobjectionable Britishers and gigantic Canadians, to our small double room at the end of a corridor blessed by a bath and an inspiring view of that kind of desolate concrete block native to Italy where the empty eye-sockets of the windows seem encrusted with the sores of cracked cement and rusty metal stains.

'*Vivat l'Impériale!*' I yelled and felt the beds. Quite firm and the sheets were dry and clean and – *mirabile dictu* – neither bugs nor cockroaches to be seen. . . . Above all, Madge and Cyril had arrived at last, the black chasm had closed and relative comfort was within sight. I had a bath, went to a concert with one of my chums, had another bath, got into a night-dress for the first time in four nights and slept the sleep of the Redeemed from Hell.

The following day we all went to the huge Opera House to find that there was no glass in the windows and large holes in the roof, the result of a very successful New Year's Day bombardment by the Nazis, blowing up most of the supply ships and blasting open all doors and windows for half a mile inland. I had noticed I could not close our door properly in the hotel last night but was too blissfully comfortable to worry. My dressing-room's empty window had a large paper poster nailed to it, through which the bora blew vindictively. Shivering, I watched my name on it shimmy back and forth in a cataleptic dance and laid out my things. Next day it rained soot solidly. The wind, banshee-like, had swept up all the ashes from the still-burning Vesuvius and was scattering them in swarthy largess across the whole country. Armed with an umbrella and bundled up like a mummy I ran to the YWCA to read in peace over a cup of tea and two buns. Lunch consisted of dehydrated meat and potatoes. Chewed you never so hard, it was impossible to swallow that lump of undetectable animal, so we all decorously returned it in sad little mounds to the side of our plates and were grateful for the dandruffy potatoes.

Cyril was determined to get the show on without further delay which entailed spending all day working in the icy theatre rehearsing among other matters the 'extras' for the final act '*Chez Maxime*' – a hazard poor Cyril had not foreseen. In Cairo he had had the pick of attractive girls to sit at the tables which encircled the stage. Here in the teeth of the war he was compelled to use the ladies from the lower ranks of the Army serving in the canteens and albeit they were indomitable as soldiers and invaluable in dispensing food, it has to be admitted they lacked that certain grace and glamour requisite to their rôle as fashionable Parisiennes. In despair Cyril tried to show them how to enter the stage and sit down as though they were not marching through bog in heavy boots or parking their bottoms on the seat of an army truck. All to little avail. It was already seven-fifteen in the evening, the house was packed with soldiers and the curtain had to go up. Exhausted, he abandoned the attempt to teach them to walk gracefully and with his usual good humour allowed the show to begin.

How I envied those soldiers out front, buttoned up in their greatcoats and mufflers and warmly shod, as I danced in my flimsy tutu with random flakes of snow falling through the chinks in the roof on my bare shoulders while my teeth chattered like castanets during my dialogue. Madge, elegant as the Merry Widow, could sing her songs with her mink coat slung across her shoulders, but even had I owned one I could hardly have appeared looking like an animated teddy bear *sur pointes*.

Cyril and I stood in the wings as the curtain rose on act three, '*Chez Maxime*'. He had finally decided not to risk the extras clumping across the stage and had dumped them soberly at the tables. Clad in very fetching evening dresses out of whose décolletées rose square, muscled shoulders like bentwood chairs, their satin bodies embracing a weird variety of bosoms ranging from the flatness of shoulder-blades to large bags of canary seed, they looked for the main part like unsuccessful drag queens, but at least the lamps adorning the tables had been turned down almost to extinction, so that the knobbly elbows supporting the large utilitarian hands in turn propping up a manly chin (which device despairing Cyril had adopted in the effort to prevent their placing threatening fists among the cutlery and napery) did give a vague air of sophistication, until that time when, to our horror, we saw the most prominent one thrust her vast paw into her frilly bosom and extract very slowly an enormous khaki cotton handkerchief into which with a flourish she trumpeted, triumphantly rising above the sound of the orchestra. Cyril collapsed and I, shaking with laughter, could hardly control my legs as I swept on-stage in my partner's arms to the strains of the 'Gold and Silver Waltz'.

How wonderfully worthwhile it all was when at the end, as the curtain fell, we heard the roar of delighted acclaim from the 3000 soldiers out front, raising what remained of the roof in their welcome. . . . The bugs, cockroaches, soot and cold all dissolved before their vindication of our being there. We knew that within twenty-four hours they would be leaving for the front, where less than a hundred miles north the enemy was putting up tremendous resistance at Campo Basso and that few would return. It was a minor hardship to munch our way through our dehydrated diet, all the more so when, invited to lunch with General Nares, we sat shivering in his unheated flat chomping away at exactly the same inedible food. '*L'union fait la force*' say the French and the shared adversity strengthened our will as it did our jaws.

The Americans, typically generous, began to shower me with trays full of delicacies from their Liberty supply ships, all of which I carried back to Madge's and Cyril's room for plundering after the evening show. 'Gould,' said Cyril, 'tell your American fans to drum up some caviare!' I did not quite manage that but did contrive a three-inch steak dinner followed by a marvellous party in a villa pulsating with heat where, to the accompaniment of an officer playing superb jazz piano, we danced till dawn and went back to L'Impériale loaded down with grapefruit. . . . I thought of General Nares planning the strategy for the coming campaign huddled in his greatcoat, trying to ingest the dehydrated meat. . . .

Everything in life being relative, the change in our physical fortunes still remained sovereign even though every night we returned from the theatre, Georgie and I had to choose our moment to dodge the huge armchairs in the hall being flung about like shuttlecocks by gigantic drunken Canadians, skid into the lift, apply a sharp kick to the shin of one trying to impede our upward journey by inserting his boot in the door and race down the corridor to the safe haven of our room. However, it has to be admitted the word 'safe' was a euphemism, for the same successful raid that had blasted most of the glass from the windows had also, as I mentioned, contrived to contort the doors, making it impossible to lock them.

For a whole week it had not seemed to be of any great importance until one night Georgie and I were shovelling down the contents of one of that day's Liberty ship trays on the bed, when I heard a strange shuffling in the passage outside. Georgie, turning white as a piece of cod, leapt to her suitcase, dug out a huge Mauser, the gift of one of her many admirers, and waggled it before us. 'Put that thing down!' I whispered and moving to the door I peered outside. Nobody to be seen. Unfortunately we were in a cul-de-sac and on our immediate left was the room at the end of the passage. With what I fondly hoped were stealthy footsteps I crept towards it and heard heavy breathing behind the half-open door. Seizing the door with all my might I crashed it back against the thing from which the stertorous sounds were emanating, thumping and whacking away in the forlorn hope that I might knock it out, I suppose. But his strength was far greater than mine and after a few grunts and groans he sent me staggering back against our door and emerged to present himself as the six-foot-four husky who had been prowling around suspiciously wherever we had been all day. Fortunately he had primed himself over-liberally with strong drink for whatever purpose his hunt intended and was therefore not quite Master of his Fate; swiping at me with flailing hands, he toppled towards me with a bibulous leer. Evading the dubious embrace I slid under his arms, pushing him lurching backwards down the narrow passage, hitting him till his wind gave out, and left him staggering away down the main landing.

Dusting my hands, I returned to Georgie and the remains of our supper. It was midnight and we were tired and wanted to get out of our clothes. I peered out again. I heard a noise – the damned man was back in the empty room again awaiting his chance to pounce. Furious, I told Georgie to run and find some superior officer while I applied my slamming door technique as long as I could hold out. Just as I was losing, Georgie returned with an embarrassed major who hauled him off by the collar. She and I, feeling the urge to shake off the unpleasantness of threatened rape, went to Madge's and Cyril's room to join their party and jollied ourselves sufficiently to be able to return to our own, satisfied that the menace had been dealt with.

What lurking paranoia made me decide not yet to undress I cannot say, but at around three a.m. I heard the drunken shuffle yet again and by this time I was so furious that when I found him about to open our door, neither his height, his strength nor the really sinister glare in those glazed and drunken eyes, nor the wave of whisky-sodden breath in my face, deterred me for one moment. I leapt at him shouting, pummelling, kicking with all my dancer's strength (lethal on occasions) and while his hands grabbed and his arms waved like windmills and I ducked and dodged, I managed to get him backwards on to the landing where with a final assault I toppled him over the stair-rail and heard his head crack on the floor below. I did not dare look; tottering back I at last undressed (as he had got most of my jacket buttons this exercise was swift) and crawled into bed, wishing Georgie a pleasant remainder of that night.

The following day I was visited by the Monster's commanding officer bent double with apologies, so my fear that I might have broken his neck was allayed; albeit because the reluctance to allow us to stay at the Impériale had been unfortunately justified, I had to beg the commanding officer not to say a word to Colonel Billetteer. Georgie and I continued to dodge the flying divans in the hall, but were otherwise left unmolested. The icy bora retreated, the sooty rain ceased, the American trays supplemented the dehydrated fodder, while the acclaim and gratitude of the audience and the unforeseen arrival over the next weeks of yet four more London friends, amongst whom was dear Billy Devlin, the actor, enhanced a period that had begun so blackly.

At last three letters from Larry Durrell also from R and Gwyn Williams* arrived, full of affection and warmth, bringing me joy tinged with *Sehnsucht* and Cyril announced that Naples was at last ready to receive us.

So after four and a half weeks we left ghastly Bari, were put into buses as dilapidated as ever but were compensated by a miraculously beautiful drive over the mountains right across to Naples bathed in the setting sun and misty light of a Vesuvius still surlily smoking.

This time we were billeted, Madge, Cyril, Georgina and I, in a very pleasant flat in a quiet residential street. I thought guiltily of the wretched people from whom it had been commandeered (a moral tribute only of a few seconds' duration) and we sorted out our things. Two bedrooms with a bathroom at the end of the passage had a view on to a garden below and thick, fairly firm mattresses on the floors. The bathroom was one of those exquisite 'designer' ones all tricked out – bath, loo, bidet, floor and half-walls – in shiny powder-blue, a veritable harem of a bathing place. The only hindrance lay in the fact that there was little or no water. After our long, dusty drive from the Adriatic coast we longed for a bath – only a sullen, rusty trickle dripped from the gorgeous taps. Worse still was the loo which, far from ingesting the contents, deposited them with an angry gulp like a seasick passenger; it regurgitated all its burden over the lip and on to the glossy floor. Grimly, I started cleaning it up. Cyril, ever good-humoured, dug out a buxom maid who helped amid gales of laughter, obviously finding

* see Appendix

herself at home in the farmyard once again, and who promised to get a plumber by next day to induce the water to run. We slept the sleep of the righteous who yet know their good fortune – no bugs, no cockroaches, no brutal and licentious soldiery. We could well disregard the drought.

A fearful hammering woke us in the early morning, as though a hundred horses were cantering through the flat. Cyril's door opened and he appeared resplendent in a short red silk dressing-gown covered with a pattern of guardsmen, below which his elegant legs showed heron-like. Stalking down the corridor towards the noise, he found it emanating from our maid cleaning the floor vigorously by performing a tarantella on her wooden clogs to which were tied threadbare cloths. '*Silenzio, sordida,*' yelled Cyril in his best Italian, and 'Sordida' the poor girl remained for the rest of the stay.

Into the streets we plunged and found them a-snarl with traffic. Naples is built on three storeys, its roads coiling up snake-like between the closely packed buildings stacked against the precipitous rise, as though only by huddling together could they avoid sliding down into the harbour. The Americans were in charge with their usual and most modern equipment: jeeps and trucks galore choked the way, together with the battered cars and ancient trucks of the locals. The women clattered about in wooden shoes wedged two inches high in an effort to look fashionable. After the dreary vacuum of Bari, all seemed lively, busy, purposeful, full of cheer despite the continuing war.

We took a taxi to Vesuvius and walked up as far as possible to where the lava still smoked and sent off waves of heat; we went to our theatre, the Bellini, a dirty little place sporting one light bulb per dressing-room; in the evening we heard *Carmen* at the splendid San Carlo Opera House with a divine tenor, Augusto Ferrauto, such as only the Neapolitans can produce – and finally we gave the first show for the soldiers; a wonderful, grateful audience, and now that it was mid-April we received great masses of spring flowers to take back to our somewhat arid flat where still only driblets issued from the taps. The British and American war correspondents gave us a jolly supper after the first performance and we learned that we had been lucky to arrive during a hiatus, for the city was usually bombed every night.

Indeed, the following night during the show down came the bombs and out went all the lights. After sitting in our rooms wondering what to do next, the ever-resourceful Cyril groped his way back on-stage, asked the men to shine their torches on to it and we sang all the last-act choruses to them.

Night after night there came these swift raids, the planes diving like birds of prey to drop their bombs, the Americans turning off all the lights and tearing up and down the winding streets with huge canisters of smoke attached to their jeeps trying to camouflage the town; the anti-aircraft batteries chattered back – the din and the stench and the dark combined to make it frustrating to say the least. On one very bad night a US officer ran into the theatre ordering us all to go to the cellar. He must already have seen the show, for he said to Cyril and Madge, 'Where is Diana Gould?' Cyril looked at him witheringly, 'If I know her, like all ballerinas she is in her dressing-room darning her tights by candlelight.' I was. And he left, baffled.

Some nights the raids would be short enough to resume the show, but when the lights remained extinguished, Cyril again would resort to having the soldiers shine their inadequate torches on to the stage. I all but missed my invisible partner's arm one grim night as I dived in a run from one end of the stage to the other, only managing to save myself from crashing into the orchestra pit by twisting in mid-air. My ribs hurt for days. That same night, wearily and very late, we returned to our street, only to find it barricaded. 'Sorry,' said the soldier, 'there's an unexploded bomb in one of the back gardens.' 'Which one?' 'Number ten.' It was, of course, ours. We waited till he resumed his patrol at the other end, slipped under the barrier, ran up the street and fell on to our mattresses too tired to care. One bonus was that as it was three a.m. we found the water plentiful and hot and we had our first baths for eight days. We were lucky. They defused the bomb the next day.

The military regime decided we needed a respite after two weeks of raids, sirens, infernal noise and disrupted shows and sent us four 'stars' rattling over pot-holed roads, dodging bomb craters and burnt-out trucks in a springless fifteen-hundredweight truck across the Bay and over the headland to Amalfi and the Tyrrhenian sea. The pains and aches of bruises fled when I opened the shutters of my small whitewashed room and looked out over the sea, standing on end like the chimerical backdrop of an opera. The great mountains that guard that peerless coast drop straight down to the water, a sea so violet blue in the last rays of the sun that I realised for the first time the meaning of the Roman Tyrrhenian purple.

The peace that passed over me filled every corner of my being with the most extraordinary solace – only a sudden surge of emotion for that part of my heart turned off and left behind in Egypt rose from where, in all the hazards of the past weeks, it had been buried and I found myself weeping for that lost love in the loveliness of the scene before me. Forty-eight healing hours later we were crashing and thumping back to our job at the insalubrious Teatro Bellini in Naples. The raids continued, as did the US Army's travelling smoke-kitchens, the rattling staccato of aircraft batteries and the sudden black-outs. But we were whisked as compensation in ex-King Umberto's launch to the ex-German ambassador's beautiful villa on the island of Ischia, where we dabbled and paddled in the hot springs and I innocently picked armfuls of pretty mauve flowers which turned out to be garlic. Back in Naples we visited the slightly dilapidated Villa Emma on a promontory just beyond the bay; visions of Nelson and Lady Hamilton amongst the tall, cool salons and the titillating views of that most romantic of all bays. What a perfect setting for an idyll.

At the end of three weeks the chorus began to mutiny, keening for the grey skies and dripping rain of Durrell's 'Pudding Island', quite oblivious of the dramatic beauty of Naples, of the light, sun and colour. Admittedly the war had somewhat distorted the image and certainly at night the aphorism 'see Naples and die' took on a more sinister connotation. Cyril submitted regretfully. We had in fact been away since 15 January – nearly fifteen weeks – and to point out that we would most likely be returning to more of the same in terms of battlefields would not hold water so long as fish and chips and the understatements of an English summer beckoned them so seductively.

So, on 10 May 1944, we gave our last performance to the soldiers. There were fifty bouquets on stage, one of mine came from the heavenly tenor whose performance in *Carmen* and *Aida* I had contrived to slip away and hear from the stage box of the San Carlo whenever I was free – together with a photograph: '*Con ammirazione profunda, Augusto Ferrauto.*' Next day, as a final gift to us for having brought the only complete West-End production to the troops, we were sent, Madge, Cyril, Georgina and I, in that infernal truck back along the coastal road, but this time to Positano, then totally unknown except to painters and poets. Invisible other than for one brief flash from the coastal road far above as one drove along, it consisted of a collection of small white-washed houses, among them ancient arab hovels huddled in a narrow ravine like nuts in a nutcracker. Perilously perched on either side of terraces of orange and lemon and fig reaching down to the tiny lava-grey beach, there, on the sand, stood a small cathedral, its yellow-and-blue encaustic-tiled dome dominating the scene as though it alone could serve the double purpose of preventing the houses tumbling headlong while at the same time keeping the sea from engulfing them. Two grand lions reposed at the head of the steps adding authority as the waves lapped teasingly towards them. Positano can only be approached on foot, leaving the car at a piazza half-way down; the rest of the descent is made down a winding cobbled path, skirting walled villas thick with jasmine and bougainvillaea, until finally one reaches a small open space where the tiny hotel of Giulio Rispoli stands.

The halcyon beauty of the place in contrast to the grime and noise and danger of Naples censured my joy, presenting me with a dilemma. How to determine which of the two scenes was true to life: the horror and pain, the irredeemable nature of man's inhumanity to man, or the serene loveliness here offering an escape into the empyrean? That irrepressible Protestant conscience at work again, forever judging, qualifying and spoiling delight. Giulio had been a well-known photographer in London before the war and had turned the house behind the cathedral into an ideal small hotel. The floors red-tiled, the walls whitewashed, the furniture spare and simple. From the balconies of the top floor huge swatches of wisteria plunged, turning each room below golden violet in the late sunlight. Giulio's sister cooked in the small enclosed terrace looking out seawards; cooked as only Italians can cook the simplest things, even transforming shortcomings into dishes of character and subtle taste.

We threw our few things into our rooms and went, ravenous, to the tiny dining-room. After weeks of suspicious tinned salmon, a few weedy vegetables like the scrapings of barge bottoms and the everlasting mashed potato, the fresh tomato soup, followed by a perfect omelette apiece with salad, was all part of this dream. . . . Suddenly from the corner of my eye I saw Georgie drag a large bottle of ketchup from her all-purpose sack and prepare to shake it over that superb omelette. 'Georgie, for God's sake!' I yelled, and hit the bottle a resounding slap which sent it skidding across the marble table with a crash to the floor. 'Gould!' said Cyril, 'you've gone too far again.' 'But I've succeeded in getting dear Georgie to taste the first real omelette in her young life,' I retorted.

Five enchanted days followed, as did several of our friends, for the British had astutely purloined Positano as their 'leave place'. We rowed in the dinghies, explored the tiny Arab houses (left-overs from the time of the Mussulman), made friends with the local painters, happily stranded by the war, German, Dutch, English; walked in the moonlight amongst the scented terraces, said goodbye to those who would be going back to the war (somewhere I have lost the Royal Fusiliers badge in diamonds I was given with 'For Diana' engraved on it, but to this day I have the lovely Malaysian sarong, a present from a very close friend who returned to the front to be killed). We left, still bewitched, to go back to Naples, to gather our things, make the last of those journeys in trucks to the harbour and get on the ship; the same kind of old P & O (Peninsular and Orient Line) bucket on which we had left Liverpool seventeen weeks before. Georgie and I grimly watched the trunks being hauled up in the claws of huge American cranes, to be dropped from a height of twenty feet like so many lumps of sugar higgledy-piggledy into the hold, and retired to our cabin.

That night we sailed, all set to retrace our route through the Gibraltar Straits and up the Bay of Biscay to Liverpool, or so we fondly imagined; however, the German submarines had other ideas, chasing us out into mid-Atlantic and some very rough weather. The Officer in Command of Troops, this time a charming retired army officer who reminded me of my beloved grandfather, summoned me to his cabin: would I please superintend the Maltese mothers and babies at their daily boat drill? Restraining myself yet again from asking why Frou-Frou of the *Merry Widow* should be thought suitable material for such a job, I did ask him what this particular ethnic category was doing on board a boat crammed with soldiers at last being returned after the Egyptian campaign to England. 'Ah, my dear,' he replied drily (totally dissimilar from the OC Troops I had served on the way out). 'You see there was, about a year or two ago, a draft of British infantrymen who passed twenty-four hours on Malta on their way to the battlefields of the desert. They used their one night to good effect, if you can call it that, and the result is with us now. Some Whitehall boffin came across this liability in his pigeon-hole and decided it should be dealt with forthwith and here we are. Be a good girl and see they do what they're told.' Darling man, I would have walked the plank for him. I left him proudly putting on the brand-new discs of *Oklahoma*, just issued. 'Come in tonight with the Ritchards and listen to this show — it's divine.'

So twice a day I mustered a hundred mustard-faced women with babies to match, got them into their 'Mae Wests' and drove them like a herd of goats to the various points on deck where presumably they would take off into the water. 'Women and children first,' I muttered. What did mystify me was the absolutely anaphrodisiac quality of the mums. . . . Could there have been a pitch-dark black-out that fateful Maltese night? After a week, packed like sardines below decks and longing for home, the troops began to mutiny. 'I say,' said OC Troops, 'do you think you could help in some way – dance or sing, or something?' So Georgie and I went down to the hold to the sugarbowl of trunks and, with the sea rolling like a drunken clown, staggered about on top of the unruly mound until we found a corner of a familiar case, got it hauled out, opened it, extracted a possible evening dress each and tottered back to our cabin.

From then on we all put on a show for the troops in the big dining-room for an hour and a half. That it compensated in goodwill for what it lacked in smooth performance was none of our fault. I would not wish on my uttermost *bête noire* an attempt to waltz on a plunging ship, whose decks fell without warning in a ten-foot dip, only to rise again in a sickening lurch accompanied by a shudder. (Indeed, after a few shows my poor partner tore his Achilles' tendon, never to dance again.) Gone was our evening meal, replaced by an unappetising offering of tinned meat and ship's biscuit at nine o'clock. But it cured the trouble below decks.

At last, on the seventeenth day twisting and turning away from the U-boats, we crawled up the west coast of Ireland and over the north coast and finally made Liverpool on 2 June 1944. Catching the train to London, that same night I was back home with Griselda. I had been away seventeen weeks. Every moment of it had been worthwhile, phenomenal in all senses, from the horrific to the sublime. I felt stretched, enlarged, deepened, freed of many tight little values and silly criteria.

6 June 1944: Invasion of France by the Allies begins at dawn.

So also did the enormous rockets that destroyed whole streets of small houses, postponing our opening date at His Majesty's Theatre and forcing the Company out 'on the road' yet again as the only solution to keep us earning till the time London might, as it had with the earlier bombs, come to terms with conditions and continue its theatre life. That postponement was to cost me dear.

Several new people had joined the cast, so for two weeks we

rehearsed before going on tour. Cyril had decided to change my 'Gold and Silver Waltz' and to give me two partners instead of one, engaging a well-known choreographer, Freddie Carpenter, to create the steps. We were all three pounding away to the statutory out-of-tune upright in a studio in Archer Street, just off Regent Street, when above the sour sounds from the piano I suddenly heard a much more eldritch one, a hiss turning into a roar somewhere above us. Shouting 'Lie down', we all fell flat on our faces with our hands uselessly covering our heads; the rush of air was appallingly painful, I was sure my ribs would cave in as all the breath was knocked out of me. As I began to black out, there was a tremendous crash about a hundred yards away followed by the familiar sound of tinkling glass as all the shop windows in the big stores of Regent Street blew out in a thousand fragments on to the pavements. The building rocked and then settled. Feeling very groggy I sat up, shaking brick dust from my back and hair. We had been very lucky; the ceiling which was one big glass skylight was wired and although cracked and riven had not splintered, so we were not cut. Propping ourselves against the walls we strove to recover our breath and still our shaking limbs. From outside came the familiar sound of ambulance horns, of shouting voices, fire engines and the trucks of the ARP.

We dressed again and wobbled out into the street: the Regent Palace Hotel at the far end had received a direct hit and, fortunately for us, had fallen in the opposite direction. Too jolted even for long-suffering dancers to attempt to go on, we each of us found our way home where I sat on the sofa in our empty flat trying to control the tremors that shook me like a rag doll.

Before we started our tour, I went dutifully to Nicholson and Watson, at Larry Durrell's request, to meet Tambimuttu the Singhalese poet and editor, there to discuss Larry's idea that I should write a short book on the *Merry Widow* tour of Egypt and Italy. Flattered at the idea, I told Tambi (a very eccentric character) that I would probably call it *Feet across the sea*. He was delighted, the contract was decided on, he hauled me to his watering hole, the Hog in the Pond, nearby, drank inordinately while still talking in a kind of waterfall as though the alcohol regurgitated itself in a perpetual verbal stream, and I escaped just as his bright-brown eyes were beginning to lose focus. I never did get around to writing that book, too many circumstances pressed upon my time. This recollection of that unique time in Egypt and Italy is but a truncated version of that extraordinary period, as clear in my mind now and perhaps better defined by the distance of the years.

The great rockets continued to crash down and we started our tour from town to town. The war reached a climax of horrifying reality that made the refuge of the daily work wear very thin and did nothing to settle minds made restless by deferred hope. Then came blazing news when we were performing in a particularly dreary Midland town.

23 August: Paris falls to the Maquis.

I will never forget the joy of that day. It was as though the door behind which I locked all emotions too nostalgic and insoluble to be dwelt upon had of a sudden and with a tremendous force been burst open and out tumbled a chiaroscuro of past delights, of childhood excitements and girlish passions, of Guggan's beautiful hands and torpid face, of a hundred smells: the morning's bread, the Métro and the sulphurous lake in the Bois, the redolence of cooking emanating from the very pores of every building at midday, the dusty, vinegary smell of the Seine, the illusion that the huge chestnut tree after a shower of rain actually smelt green – and a thousand other tiny things all shining like motes in the beam of the sublime sunlight of that news. The chorus-boys and I bought packages of fish and chips and danced along the cheerless streets singing the 'Marseillaise' with our mouths full of bones that night. A pathetic little celebration but the best we could manage.

The new *pas de trois* in the last act was going very well and my first-act scene stopped the house, as it had on every night since the première in Cairo and the dubious tribute of the admiration of King Farouk. I was longing to get back to London to perform my Frou-Frou. By now I had polished both acts and felt that they could only succeed. All the more brutally unexpected then was the letter I found in my dressing-room in the middle of the performance, announcing that the producer thanked me for my work and was presenting me with the statutory two weeks' notice legally necessary to dispense with my services. Somehow I got through the last act and stumbled into the wings after the long applause, bursting into tears I had had to control. The chorus, men and women, were outraged and came to tell me they were prepared to go on strike as a support for me against this unexplainably ruthless gesture.

In shock and despair I went to Cyril. He revealed that he had been fighting for me for the past weeks, had insisted that the producer came to see the show and the huge reception I got twice a night – all to no avail. It was the old story. The producer had acquired a new girl-friend who wanted my rôle and he had promised it to her. From that moment on, darling Cyril nicknamed me 'Busy Mrs Ibsen'. 'Busy' because he had never seen anyone work so hard, and 'Ibsen' because having followed my career since I was a girl he had never seen anyone visited with such ill fortune.

5 September: Brussels Falls.

Sadly I gave my last performance in *The Merry Widow*. We were all in tears. I tried to think of the eight and a half months of wonderful companionship I had had with Cyril and Madge, of all the fun and dangers we had shared, of the invaluable theatrical advice he had given me to store up for the future. Above all, not to dwell on Black Fairy who had yet again struck.

The show opened at the Coliseum without me. I was told that Freddie Carpenter, my choreographer, came storming into the wings (on leave from his RAF base) demanding to know where I was. 'That girl can neither dance nor sing – where the devil's Diana Gould?' he shouted at Cyril, who was standing beside the producer. The last act was even worse. Cyril told me the producer approached him asking if I would consider coming back. 'She wouldn't touch you with the butt end of a barge pole,' said Cyril, 'after what you did to her.' Anyway I had irretrievably lost the first-night reviews, the culmination of all my work.

★

Bleakly, September stretched ahead, jobless and with the black shadow of the Labour Exchange. I took myself to see Michael Redgrave in *Uncle Harry* with his wife Rachel Kempson and Beatrix Lehmann making up the cast of a very sinister play. Michael, as the wretched, flaccid brother driven to murder by his two awful sisters, gave one of the most memorable performances of his whole career, holding hysteria just below his pathetic, pliable demeanour till at last it bubbled over and exploded into violence. Elated by his wonderfully orchestrated acting, I plucked up my courage and went round to see him – something I am always loth to do for fear of sounding insincere. As he received me very warmly I took the plunge, telling him that Yehudi Menuhin had just rung my mother and would be coming to luncheon on the twenty-ninth, would he care to come? Michael wiped the greasepaint off his face and said 'Oh darling, but I don't know that I dare . . . he's a genius!' 'Come off it,' I said, 'after that performance you're not far from that yourself. I'll ask Puffin Asquith, too.'

So came about the most portentous day of my life: 29 September 1944. Mama had gathered all our coupons together to make an acceptable lunch. We assembled at her flat. 'I've just had a call from Yehudi Menuhin to say he's been delayed and will get here as soon as possible,' she told us. As a matter of fact he did not turn up till five minutes before poor Puffin had to leave. In my diary I wrote: 'Menuhin rang to say he would be late, Puffin had to leave before food served. Tremendous success. Menuhin dropped Mike and me at Piccadilly Circus. Went to dentist.' This arid account was all that a five-line-per-day diary could contain. I knew I for one had found him enchanting, enviably healthy and well-fed against our pale-faced skinniness – particularly poor dear Griselda upon whom the strains of her Admiralty schedule were beginning to show. There was a simple straightforwardness and warmth of manner that defused all self-consciousness, easing the way to happy exchange and friendliness.

My mother, at all times *Madame Sans-gêne*, was in her element. Yehudi says his recollection is of me sitting on the big leather pouf at the end of the long drawing-room and of his determination then and there to have me to himself as the embodiment of all he desired. When he confessed this to me years later, I remonstrated: 'But Yehudi, you were married. It was your little daughter Zamira's fifth birthday that very day!' But then I knew nothing about Cloud Nine, that rented place in Outer Space from where Yehudi's Extra Self operates, irrespective of what may transpire on common earth.

Further signs of climbing up the slippery slope out of the Slough of Despond appeared. Michael rang me the next day to thank me for that 'exhilarating lunch' and asked me to come to his theatre between shows. He handed me a copy of a French play by the famous Porto-Riche, *L'Amoureuse*, one of Sarah Bernhardt's greatest triumphs. 'Would you translate that with me, Diana?' Delighted, I said, 'How do we go about it?' From then a very happy companionship developed, I doing the groundwork, Mike the delicate fingerwork to shape it into good theatre dialogue. After my first two hours of slogging alone I wrote him a despairing note: 'Oh, Mike, I find I'm breaking the butterfly of the French language on the wheel of the English tongue!' But he was marvellously pliant to work with, although it took a little time to break down his reserve (a compound of nerves, self-consciousness and fear). 'Mike,' I said when on the third session he arrived very withdrawn. 'Look . . . when you first came here, you gave me the usual theatrical kiss on the cheek; last time you shook my hand; if next time you're going to address me through your lawyers, just let me know in time to shut the door in your face.' He swept me up in a bear-hug, roaring with laughter, and from then on we shared the fondest of *amitiés amoureuses*.

After one three-hour session, Mike gave me lunch at the Hyde Park Hotel and from there, says diary, 'we go to the Albert Hall to collect two tickets left by Menuhin.' Lalo's *Symphonie Espagnole* and the Beethoven concerto was what we heard, joined by lovely Rachel Kempson, Cecil and Mama. Diary holds no other comment. Those were a happy few weeks spent sometimes at Mike's theatre, sometimes at the film studios, occasionally at their flat where I first met the ravishing child Vanessa and young Corin – around six and seven years old I suppose, and we all 'listened to Menuhin: Bartok 2.30. Mendelssohn 4.15 on the radio' (Diary).

Cyril rang me and asked me to join him again as he was going to take *The Merry Widow* to Paris, Brussels and possibly Holland, depending on war conditions – and would I please come for the last two weeks at the Coliseum and restore my Frou-Frou to the show? How could I say no to such an invitation, or show bitterness of spirit and meanness of heart?

L'Amoureuse was nearly finished to both Mike's and my satisfaction. From Cairo I received a copy of *Personal Landscape*, the literary magazine edited and published by all the authors and poets whose company I had so highly enjoyed. In it were, to my delight, three of my clerihews. In mid-November, the raids having started again, the Prime Minister announced that the 'pilotless planes' are known as V1 rockets. Not that giving them a title helped in any way to come to terms with the sight of whole streets wiped out or to help me forget the one that had all but annihilated me.

7 November: A Big Push on a 400-mile front begins.

In December I was back in *The Merry Widow* at the Coliseum, getting the same ovation I got in Egypt and Italy. Mike Redgrave took me, Madge and Cyril to a celebratory supper at the Savoy Grill and the next day came to see the show, sending me flowers, and before he went back to his own play sent his dear old dresser, Lobb, round with a book of Valéry poems and a lovely inscription about my performance. The wound was almost healed, but the scar would always be there.

15

Back at Last in Paris

The compulsorily secretive arrangements were again *de rigueur* for our journey to Paris, added to which, because of our proximity to the enemy lines, this time we would have to wear uniforms. The penalty, if you were caught in mufti, would be death. I said goodbye to the family and, armed with Mike's farewell present, Cyril Connolly's *Unquiet Grave*, and a suitcase full of coffee, chocolate, cigarettes, jam, soap and whatever I could collect as presents, joined the Company. We were put in some God-forsaken train to come to some blacked-out port, there to be decanted on to what seemed, judging by the dreary saloon amidships, to be one of the old cross-Channel steamers of my childhood. In the dim light a kind of food counter could be discerned round which a bedraggled queue of soldiers was forming. It was about eleven o'clock and we were very hungry so we joined it. We were soon able to assess the genuine strength of our hunger when, holding out our plates, we resignedly accepted a thick piece of corned beef, a slab of bread, a smear of margarine and another of plum jam all slapped on them indiscriminately; perched precariously in the middle of the lot sat the ubiquitous mug of mud-brown tea. Georgie and I had already taken possession of a pair of sleazy bunks that lined the walls by dumping our cases on one of them, to which divan we retreated with our dubious feast. Eating as much as we could stomach (the corned beef tasted better with jam on it, we decided), we got rid of our plates, our cups and our shoes in that order and lay down.

The lights were further dimmed, the engines had started up long since, but for some reason we seemed to be hove-to half-way across the Channel. I thanked God for a calm sea – the food was bad enough, the conditions bleak, but the prospect of seasick passengers was truly nightmarish. I lay down gingerly on the dirty blanket, Georgie's toes just ahead. Suddenly something skittered across me; as I sat up I saw two red eyes glaring, a flash of whiskers and then it was gone. But that halted all sleep. Better sit up all night than let the rats run over you. You could hear their claws, see the scarlet flash of small eyes as they streaked in and out below the bunks seeking bits of food, pulling at the blankets as they raced for the choice morsels of that awful corned beef.

At last we thought we heard the ship docking as dawn showed through the chinks. Not a bit of it, we were anchored three miles out at sea. By eight-thirty we were given another dainty plateful and more mugs of hot, sweet tea. There was no water. Dirty and aching, we sat amongst the droppings till three-thirty, when we were finally allowed above deck. We had evidently docked somewhere in France. Eventually rescued by some kind officers, we were taken to a villa (in Boulogne?) to wash and clean up. I shook the past night out of my mind. I was in my beloved France again after a break of five years.

After an hour we were packed into army trucks and driven through battle-scarred land for ten solid hours of jolting and buttock-breaking discomfort until at two the following morning we entered Paris. Nothing mattered any more, neither the filthy rations, nor the dirty bunks, nor the evil rats, nor the bone-shattering drive. Before me were the lovely lines of the boulevards again, the Seine wriggling along like a playful serpent under its myriad necklets of bridges, the great open spaces, the smooth brow of the streets that met the sky so harmoniously in those days before the rude interruption of tower and skyscraper deprived if of its serenity.

At the little Hôtel Vendôme on the edge of the Place Vendôme we found Madge and Cyril. Georgie and I installed ourselves in our little suite while I got into bed, black and blue and happy as a summer bumble-bee, and fell asleep. It was three a.m. and I had a room to myself . . .

I woke with a start. It was daylight and standing at the foot of my bed casually clutching the brass rail was a man. My curdled brain struggled to orientate itself – where the devil was I? My eyes swivelled round the unfamiliar little room with its nondescript wardrobe, table and chair and suddenly it all fell into place. It could only be France, only Paris where the waiter would coolly enter my room to enquire about breakfast. He had probably knocked, got no reply, walked in and had been watching me wake. . . I grinned. He grinned back. '*Bonjour Mademoiselle.*' '*Bien le bonjour, Monsieur le garçon,*' said I and with him still hanging on to the rail we had a long discussion on what Paris had been like under the Occupation. By now he had brought my ersatz coffee and rather rubbery roll but did not dream of breaking the dialogue. Paris had been free about four months by then, so my waiter had had a taste of all the varieties of soldier. The British he brushed aside as not worthy of serious analysis I suppose; the Germans: '*Ah, Mademoiselle, les Allemands étaient au moins correctes.*' '*Et les Américains?*' I asked tentatively. '*O,*' he said, his hands raised in horror, '*les Américains!*' In trepidation I awaited tales of rape and ruin, steeled myself to try and counter them. '*Les Américains!*' he repeated with a mixture of repulsion and indignation, '*Mademoiselle, imaginez*' (here I gripped my breakfast tray hard), 'with the soup they drink *beer* and with a *soufflé au chocolat whisky*! They are barbarians, total savages – no other word!' Whereupon he swept up my tray and was at last gone.

I laughed till I cried: only a Frenchman would condemn the race that helped liberate him from years of domination on what were to him basically important matters – those of taste and style . . . Delicious.

I flung on my clothes and ran to the nearby Tuileries and the Place de la Concorde. It was quite simply breathtaking, the whole Champs-Elysées stretched before me right up to the Arc de Triomphe as clear of traffic as it might have been on an early morning a hundred years ago before the carriages and horses were about. Not a car, not a bus, marred its beautiful length. As I stood transfixed at the magic of it all, far away up at the Ront-Point two jeeps crossed in opposing directions and were gone. I nagged at a poor liaison officer till, glad to get rid of me, he lent me a truck for the morning. Arming myself with goodies, I had him drive me to Kschessinskaya's studio. She was not there. I got him to drive on to their little villa in Auteuil. Alas! They were not there either. Forlorn and disappointed, I left my presents with Ludmilla, the fat Russian cook, who greeted me with cries of joy and a strong whiff of alcohol: two pounds of coffee, two pounds of marmalade, one hundred cigarettes, soap, Lux, chocolates – all I could pack in my small suitcase – and sadly drove back to the hotel. I washed the rats and dust out of my hair and was just trying to dry it by the electric fan when there came a knock at the door of our suite. As the Ritchards and Georgina were out, I ran to open it, dripping all the way. There standing before me was my beloved 'Lucy', the Grand Duke André.

How salutary separation can be when it raises such an intensity of feeling. He looked worn and thinner but just as handsome, with that sweetness of expression that never seemed to leave his face. He and Mathilda Felixovna and Vova were well and yes they would all come to lunch next week. And thank you, darlink, for all those lovely things. As he went away I wondered which of us had had the harder war.

Just as we were getting ready to open at the Théâtre Marigny, the order came for a curfew. In the last few days there had been far too many parachute drops nearby and we were all to be indoors by eight p.m. We were confined to giving daily matinées only. Very boring. A day or so after, Madge and Cyril and I were in our little sitting-room when we were knocked off our chairs by a loud explosion nearby. We picked ourselves up somewhat shamefacedly, each saying our version of 'What the devil was that?' We soon found out; we had contrived to arrive in liberated Paris at exactly the time when the only two bombs ever to be dropped on that sacred city had hit the Tuileries gardens at the end of our street and, more seriously, a hospital train in the siding of the Gare St Lazare. This had coincided with the beginning of the

Battle of the Bulge, the last effort of the German army under General von Rundstedt in the Vosges mountains.

Meanwhile we continued our dreary matinées. There were moments of brightness: my dearest Kschessinskaya came with her Grand Duke to lunch and was as gay and full of light as only those unique Baltic Russians can be. I had a profitable time in the rue de Castiglione bookshops slipping in after dark to exchange the remains of my coffee beans for some 2000 francs' worth of beautifully produced books. Unbelievably, it was drawing towards Christmas and we were entertained, wined and dined, or rather lunched for the confounded curfew kept us locked in our cages like disgruntled animals at a zoo.

One evening, utterly frustrated, I was emboldened to risk dining with a friend whose apartment lay in one of those beautiful seventeenth-century *hôtels particuliers* (the great private houses of the seventeenth and eighteenth centuries) across the river in the St Germain district. I changed into mufti, wearing the Caroline Reboux turban I had earned from Miriam de Rothschild for acting as her courier to her agent in Paris. Reboux was the *première modiste* and had made me a ravishing concoction of Paisley material only half as tall as the confection I noticed on other Parisiennes' heads (a riposte to the Army of Occupation's rationing of two metres of cloth for the making of a dress). Outraged, the Parisiennes had retaliated by using most of the material to wind and bind into the craziest monuments on their heads. Typically French. So long as every woman wore those clownish creations no one could be selected for punishment. Mine was comparatively modest and very elegant.

I reached my destination on foot and without incident. The streets were almost empty and very beautiful in the wintry twilight. It was a charming flat exquisitely furnished (it had been commandeered from a shocking old Pétainist). I had a delicious dinner and amusing conversation and, at about ten o'clock, prepared to walk home – alone, as my host could not risk breaking the curfew. I had just reached the broad avenue of the Boulevard St Germain when to my horror I saw at the far end an entire line of police stretched right across my path.

Cursing myself for being so foolhardy, I was trying to resolve whether I should go straight on, greet the police with a jolly smile and hope to get away with being a Parisienne (albeit without any identity card), fearing they might take me for a tart, when all of a sudden there was an ear-splitting whistle and the whole posse was momentarily routed by a huge truck that hurled through them. Giving chase in one swoop, shooting wildly, they all thundered straight towards me.

Desperate, I looked for shelter. There it was, right before me, only a few paces away: *vespasienne* to my rescue – the kiosk-like street urinal so necessary to the supposedly incontinent male. I shot in. The trickling water round my best shoes did little to allay the appalling smell – but what matter? I could hear the running feet of the police, the furious shouts, the volleying shots as they gave chase. They pounded and panted past me. For one awful moment I realised that my pride, the Reboux turban, must be sticking out way above the urinal. Then they were gone, tearing round the corner beyond me. I poked my head out gulping for fresh air. Without a moment's thought I pelted helter-skelter in the direction of the Place da la Concorde, streaked across it, down the rue de Rivoli, up the rue de Castiglione and finally reached the hotel, broken-winded but safe.

I flung myself on to my bed and only then started laughing. I had been very naughty and had I been caught without papers would have been spending the night in a police cell with further dire consequences.

We took the show to the dilapidated old theatre at Versailles where the RAF were stationed. We were greeted by a small horse in the stage doorkeeper's cubby-hole at the artist's entrance, all very Magritte and a warning of worse things to come in the dressing-rooms, I supposed. But no matter, the audience was wonderful, compensating for the city cold. Only one incident marred the evening. The great entertainer Maurice Chevalier, under a shadow for having been an alleged collaborator, had asked if he could tentatively test his position by singing a number following my waltz at Maxime's, giving one of his more popular songs. There was indeed a chilling cry of '*collaborateur!*' which shook him, but he recovered and thereafter was a great success.

As a matter of fact to make any categorical judgement was extremely complex, as I had quickly learned in the short time I had been in Paris. Life had had to be led under the prevailing conditions, jobs retained, situations maintained. Only the grossest and most obvious of moral betrayals, those that brought special comforts and advantages, cushioning those hardships which the greater part of the population endured, could understandably be deemed as corruption. It was a sad revelation. This smudged line of demarcation troubled me. How much simpler 'my' war had been with so few moral choices and a shared danger.

Cyril and I went to High Mass at Notre Dame cathedral on the morning of New Year's Eve. He was a devout Roman Catholic. As I explained to him I was simply a Believer which being in itself a state of grace needs to be constantly maintained and honoured. The service brought us both a cleansing, a beatitude that only that great cathedral with its history and beauty could bestow. As we walked back, I felt less bewildered.

That night, New Year's Eve, we got into our wagons-lits *en route* for Brussels. A drunken American officer grabbed me as I walked down the corridor. Tired and disgusted I hit him and slipped into my carriage. He banged and beat against the door for two full hours till a large crack ran down the panelling, at which juncture the indifferent conductor hauled him off, bored to death at the sight of the Conquering Hero's behaviour.

On the first of January 1945, I woke to find the train had stopped. Faint light was drifting through the blind. Baffled, I poked my head round the door, and was greeted by the uninspiring sight of the conductor slumped asleep on his stool, so no news from that quarter. Half an hour later, with one of those jerks that throws every socket out of joint in one's body, the train started up again. I raised the blind. It was dawn and alarmingly clear why we had stopped; we were passing slowly through a snow-covered RAF airfield on which practically every aeroplane was ablaze, men were running like distractd rabbits from one pyre to another – total panic in what looked like total destruction. I caught sight of one or two agonised blackened faces as we gathered speed. The raid must have happened a half–hour or so before; we were extremely lucky not to have been part of it. A happy augury for New Year's Day, maybe?

We were rushed to the Palace Hotel, bathed, had a filthy lunch (British Officers' Club) were driven to the big theatre and gave the first performance that very night. The theatre was large and pleasant and clean and Brussels itself appeared intact. The cold was bitter, the heating nil. I found yet another of my London chums who took me out and gave me my first square meal since Paris. I discovered the Officers' Tea Room. Oh! blessed British institution, always miraculously ready to supply tea and buns and a modicum of warmth. Spending my mornings there, I sat gobbling and writing reams of crumb-filled letters: to Larry Durrell, to Mike Redgrave, to R, and to other close friends, and in between I went to the opera when I was free. Just off to my evening performance when the floor-maid dashed in to announce '*Mademoiselle, imaginez-vous!*' They had caught a Nazi general in British uniform in room 528. Bad luck for him, I thought. When will this beastly war end and the complex question of loyalty and valour be clearly qualified, and from whose particular perspective?

Meanwhile the raids on Brussels continued sporadically, but with none of the sound and fury of either London or Naples. It was as though the heart had gone from the Nazi armies, the early dynamism petering out, the bombing was now token. What was self-evidently not token was the heart-stopping sight of those airmen we went to dance for in the clinic where they were having their burnt faces and hands slowly and painfully rebuilt. To be confronted by those inhuman masks, some noseless, all patched with a mosaic of minute sections of newly grafted skin, the sad, sometimes frightened eyes staring unblinking out of the wreckage, pleading to be taken for normal, was a terrible challenge. I took a deep breath, swallowed the unsummoned nausea and stared back, finding a common purpose in the exchange. With a few whose faces were well on the mend after God knows how many operations I could talk, get through the stiffened, expressionless screen to the voice and its intonations.

The battle, for me, was to hold back the tears, not the revulsion at the sight of the young faces bearing through their courage the masks of gargoyles. I returned whenever I could. One particularly distorted boy would be brought night after night to the stage box overhanging the footlights and I would focus my dancing towards him, give him my final curtsey, watching the glow of delight spread on his maimed face, for I knew he was one of the most psychologically damaged among them and was a little consoled that by the only means I had to offer I could help. The doctors reported at the end of our time there that he had improved immensely and was no longer bitter nor depressed.

After three weeks of buns and bombing we all agreed to go up to the front line in Holland where they desperately needed a little cheer as it appeared no other troupe at that time was willing. On a pitch-dark, icy winter morning, barely re-inforced by a hot drink that was something indecisive in its brown muddiness between strong tea and weak coffee, we were packed into two large buses and by eight o'clock started off on the glacier-like road to the front line, part of a long column of army trucks carrying ammunition and food and such odd supplies as chorus-boys and girls and hopeful entertainers like ourselves.

We averaged twenty miles per hour, slipping and skidding and slithering, averting our eyes from the dispiriting sight of lorries less fortunate than ours (so far) lying in the ditches on either side, their mud-and-snow-encrusted bottoms revealed, wheels in the air, strangely indecent in their involuntary abandon. After some five or six hours the chorus began to plead for relief. 'Nonsense,' said Cyril. 'Diana and Madge are holding out; so can you.' Diana and Madge and Cyril combined, however, after two further hours could themselves no longer sustain their image of Paragons of Bladder Control and begged the bus to stop, all guilt as to holding up the army convoy dissolved in the general fear of possible incontinence. We poured out of the bus, lemming-like leaping across the snow, ignoring the signs everywhere warning us that we were in a minefield. Even British inhibitions were scattered to the four winds in that moment of blessed relief crouched only partly hidden behind an abandoned cottage. Never was there a clearer proof of nature in its functions overcoming all barriers of sex, class, beliefs or customs. Blissfully we clambered back on to the bus, ignoring the various cat-calls from the military trucks behind us and at four o'clock arrived at Eindhoven in Holland.

The thermometer was at ten below zero, the wretched little two-storey building in which we were stored (apt words) was totally unheated, all glass had long since been blown out of the windows. Hungry and cold, Georgie and I stared dismally at the one hard bed we were expected to share. Galvanised by despair I managed to wheedle a camp bed which we could use alternately. My good stepfather had insisted upon giving me the pyjamas he had worn on his Arctic cruises. After a scratch meal we took off our clothes with chattering teeth, I shuffled into the pyjamas, added two pairs of socks, mufflers and woollen scarves and crawled between the rough, icy blankets, falling into a fitful sleep. What we had not taken into account was the snow blowing in a steady blizzard on our faces, freezing our noses protruding like periscopes from the submarines of our bed-coverings and signalling us to awake whenever they reached zero. Rubbing them till they glowed in the dark we cheered each other up, debating whether there was such a horror as frostbite of the proboscis and dozed again, repeating the exercise till a wretched icy dawn decided us to give up and get up.

Outside on a long rail track coal trucks were slowly passing, while the soldiers in charge were pushing odd lumps off the top of the enormous piles to the skinny children running after them in the snow, fighting wildly for each piece. We were taken to the canteen and given some sort of breakfast, driven to the little theatre built by the electrical firm Philips, for their workforce. There for a solid week I had to strip, put on my flimsy costumes, silence my chattering teeth, control my shivering limbs and do my best to bring cheer to the rows of soldiers buttoned up like parcels in their overcoats, boots and sundry woollens, cheerful, receptive and jolly. The realisation that, judging by the omnipresent sound of the nearby guns, a good half of them might not be alive the next day made light of our discomfort. Girls in the chorus began to fall like ninepins, struck by pneumonia; one silly one ventured out in a jeep with a soldier, never to return. It was harsh; physically it was utter misery, psychologically a salutary lesson in endurance.

At the end, so hardened by the cold and perpetual low hunger, I remember running out only in my shirt sleeves under a light shower of snow to bid Madge and Cyril goodbye as they went to catch the plane home. It had been understood, and was one of the bonds between them and myself, that I would not take advantage of proffered privileges and would stay always keeping an eye on the Company and doing my utmost to prop up morale. As this in great part consisted of trying first to maintain my own I must confess there were many times – such as our subsequent journey of all but twelve hours in unheated buses to Ostend – when I found my upper lip in a rictus of effort and all the Kipling I could remember summoned to my flagging aid.

We spent next day sitting in the hostel alternately refilling hot water bottles and looking out to sea (thick boarding house gruel) praying for deliverance. One more dismal night and a whole morning spent sitting on our suitcases on the quayside brought us salvation when at last, at two p.m., we were crammed together with a mass of people as amorphous and miserable away from the snowbound Continent homewards. Aboard, we once more queued patiently and were rewarded with a half-tin of the unbiquitous corned beef, four biscuits and the regulation cup of blackish-grey strong tea. The next day found us moving up the Thames to Tilbury reinforced by more corned beef, rebrewed tea and the prospect of home.

16

The Magic Mountain

What a magnificent sense 'home' assumes in those circumstances we all underwent during the war ... like a palimpsest of feelings, line upon line criss-crossing in recollections, symbols, affinities deepened and clarified by the changing focus brought by absence and return. I distributed all the small presents I had managed to gather in Paris and Brussels in return for my chocolate and coffee: books, *couturier* jewellery, little artefacts, and was asked by Mike Redgrave to 'hold his hand' on his first day's shooting of the film *Dead of Night* at Ealing. I brought down my two-foot Reboux turban, stuck it on my head at lunch in the local pub, to Mike's delight and the outraged astonishment of the clientele. Given a different context it did admittedly look monstrous. Armed with a letter from Mike, I made the dreaded trip to the Labour Exchange and was grudgingly given an extension till the end of the following month as a reward for the gruelling work in the service of my country from which I had just returned. Yet another aspect of my country's gratitude was the demand from the Inland Revenue kindly to return fifty per cent of the £10 fee offered to ENSA's top performers. I learned later that my Russian colleagues had been decorated with medals that weighed down their tutus and awarded all manner of special benefactions. So much for the honour in which England holds the Arts.

The next two months were downhill all the way: the rockets crashed with less frequency but shattering results. In such circumstances work was all but impossible to find. Bosey Douglas died aged seventy-four; Griselda's declining health caused even more worry; I got my 'final permit' from the Labour Exchange: twenty-eight days or call-up.

12 April 1945: Roosevelt dies.

On yet another anxious visit to yet another doctor, we learn the ghastly news that Griselda has TB, a hole in the apex of one lung which should have been diagnosed months ago. Determined at all costs not to be called up, as now it was of prime importance to stay by Griselda's side, I persuaded Michael to let me play the small part of his lover Cosette in *Jacobowsky and the Colonel* which he was putting on. 'It will be bad for your career, my dear,' he protested, 'to appear in such a small rôle.' I explained I did not give a damn so long as I stayed out of the greedy clutches of the Labour Exchange and was free to handle Griselda's illness.

27 April: Peace offered by Himmler to the United Kingdom and USA.
29 April: Mussolini captured and shot by Italian partisans.
1 May: 'Hitler Dead' announced by Admiral Doenitz.
2 May: Doenitz declared Führer. Unconditional surrender by Italy.
3 May: Berlin falls, Rangoon falls.
5 May: German surrender in Denmark, Holland and North-West Germany.

In all that disintegration I took Griselda to a hospital, far away in the south-west of London and visited her on the two following days.

8 May: At last VE Day. Victory Europe. The war is over.

We were rehearsing at the Phoenix Theatre (strange and apposite omen?). Begging Michael to free us, we walked through the crammed streets to Trafalgar Square to join the cheering crowds in that great catharsis of the mind, the soul and the body. All but six wasted years of the destruction of the young, the brave and the promising; of great cities; of codes of behaviour; of a whole pattern of life to which no one on either side would ever return. Admittedly many false demarcations, useless shibboleths, over-used attitudes, were swept away for ever but at a cost that did not bear close scrutiny. Before us finally lay a definable future, definable only in the sense that the smoke of battle had cleared figuratively and literally and one was more or less free to extricate oneself from the bonds of the past years, to try and restore some private patterns to life lived as an individual.

That night we celebrated by dining together: Puffin Asquith, his mother Lady Oxford, my dearest Madame Ta-Ta (Tamara Karsavina) and her husband Benjy Bruce to listen to King George VI's very moving speech. There was little if any exultation, simply an enormous sense of relief and deep sorrow at so much loss, such irredeemable waste.

Meanwhile *Jacobowsky and the Colonel* had opened at the Picadilly Theatre and I had gritted my teeth, playing my short scene with Michael as well as a vignette as a silent tango-dancing tart in a night-club in the last act. That little scene I enjoyed more than the rather conventional love scene, for I could express the comedy with more licence, to the strains of '*La Cumparsita*' dressed in a tight black satin skirt, dreadful white organdie blouse and a pair of black stockings carefully laddered into cobwebs.

It was already June and one day Yehudi Menuhin rang me up. (Diary 6, 1945: 'Menuhin rang. Back in Claridge's to do the sound-track for a film on Paganini.') Mama brought him to the show one night and we had a hilarious dinner with champagne afterwards. Mama could always be relied upon socially to bring gaiety and warmth and her own slightly dotty humour. I suppose it was after that that I allowed myself to call him Yehudi – not that the inhibition had been based on convention, simply on a basic dislike of intrusion followed by false instant friendship likely to wither. From then on Yehudi fetched me often after the performance greatly to the dismay of the stage-door keeper (a special breed now long gone who knew all the actors and actresses, their friends and foes, their successes and failures, and were an intrinsic part of backstage life), who would remind me reprovingly of a date I had promised some other friend for that particular night. 'Mr Menuhin is here,' the good Frank would say. 'Miss Gould, you haven't forgotten you're going out tonight with Mr X, have you?' And I would wait till X came and combine him with Yehudi if need be. After a time, however, I realised that Messrs X, Y, Z needed me far less than did Yehudi, alone and strangely lost, his utter simplicity and modesty bewildering to anyone who, like myself, knew him only from the immense stature that he had gained so early in life. So I no longer bamboozled dear old Frank, refused all the Algernons and happily kept myself free for the long talks in which, after a hesitant start, Yehudi slowly unfolded himself as someone who, with all the good intentions of an artless and elevated nature, had lost his sense of purpose and somehow his way.

I was content to listen, touched that he trusted me. Ever since I was seven years old and received my first proposal from a nine-year-old at my brother's day school, I had felt a bond with men, was drawn towards them as the true romantics of the two sexes and enjoyed their manner of thinking; while they for their part seemed to recognise this companionable quality in my attitude, to realise that neither conquest nor seduction ever entered my head, rather the enjoyment of men's minds, the exchange of ideas refreshingly free from those twittering topics beloved of many of my female contemporaries that ranged from the A of male mastery all the way to the B of fashion and back again in one deep, dreary furrow. If this sounds smug, I apologise. I simply cannot account for a taste that manifested itself early and remained an immutable choice. From small childhood I can recall being sent again and again to deal with recalcitrant male members of the family, from a distant relation (whose temper was ruined along with his digestion by resorting in the American gold rush to eating his leather razor-strop), to temperamental male dancers indulging in hysterics on the floor of the Ballet Club and tough managers refusing to offer the *corps de ballet* a decent wage.

Most nights Yehudi and I would spend having supper at the Berkeley, comparing the early aspirations we had both known when very young, the subsequent way onwards; his a comet's flight, mine always earthbound and filled with obstacles, challenges and heartbreak and yet with sufficient experiences in common to be able to offer him an empathy he told me he had never known or ever imagined he might find. His total lack of conceit, of even a trace of arrogance or vanity despite such a triumphant career, I began to find disquieting, for without the support of a certain amount of self-esteem he surely risked finding himself in precarious situations which would demand of him that firmness of purpose and clarity of vision that can only be based on a modicum of self-respect and assurance. It was as though his vast renown, the speed of his upward soaring, had unmoored him, leaving his integral character behind, undeveloped and mainly unexplored.

The propinquity that we found with such delight grew with every day, lifting me above and away from the unsatisfying work in the theatre and bringing relief from the perpetual worry of Griselda's illness. As for the first – the play – a sad solution was at hand. Peter Daubeny, our valiant producer, begged us to take a reduction in our salaries so as to enable him to 'nurse' the play (whose reviews had been less than enthusiastic) until such time as the audience could be built up; however, Michael Redgrave was unwilling to accede and we were told that after the statutory two weeks the show would close. As for the other and far deeper worry, poor Griselda had already undergone during her weeks at the hospital two operations in an effort to collapse her lung, both unsuccessful. I made the long journey again and again, taking her what food I could find to supplement the awful hospital fare and tried to hide my unquenchable dread in the face of her poignant courage. Returning by tram and bus from the distant part of London where the hospital lay, my heart felt as grey as the charmless streets about me.

July 1945: Churchill loses the election to the Labour Party and goes into opposition.

Two slightly brightening events happened: full street lighting was at last restored – bliss, after groping for six years – also cancellation of the need for permits from the Labour Exchange was announced. Double bliss to be released from permanent fear. I found a further lifting of the spirits spending a whole day starting at six-thirty taking Yehudi to the Lime Grove film studios where he had been recording the sound-track for a film on the life of Niccolò Paganini. Wickedly, and with no intention of accepting the part, he had agreed to try his hand at acting a love scene between the famous violinist and his *inamorata* at the suggestion of the producer, who scented a marvellous box-office gain should Yehudi prove both capable and willing of accepting the leading rôle. All the way down in the hired car I fed him his lines, trying to instil a little warmth and colour into the monotone of his replies with precious little success.

Arrived at the studios, he was whisked to the make-up room, suitably daubed and fitted with a large, over-curled brown wig which reached his shoulders, making him look like a cross between a bewildered lion and a brunette Lorelei. Bundled into a green frock-coat, knee breeches, stockings (which I will admit did show off his shapely calves) and buckled shoes, he was led to the set where the test was to take place. There, a sweet but profoundly uninspiring young woman awaited him. I hissed a final injunction in a wild effort to introduce a little of the passion requisite to the situation in which a Genoese musician is offering his heart and hand to the object of his desire. Alas! to no effect. Poor Yehudi using one string (and that open with not a touch of *vibrato*) intoned the words with all the ardour of a born deaf-mute. I pitied the poor young actress who tried to respond to this liturgy, got irrepressible giggles and had to retire behind some arc lamps.

It did not take long for the producer to realise that Stewart Grainger would be better for the part as a whole, so we cleaned up and went home, Yehudi having thoroughly enjoyed his attempt and not in the least nonplussed.

Next evening we went to some party or other at a South American embassy. I changed afterwards into slacks and a shirt and we walked along the nearby Embankment on a balmy July night with the tugs hooting through a slight mist and the water lapping against the wall on which we leant. Suddenly, unexpectedly, Yehudi kissed me and told me he was in love. I was caught off guard, knowing he was married, not wanting to take advantage of our close friendship, nor disturb the delicate balance I had tried to maintain. I chose not to tell him that I loved him deeply and decided to grant him whatever he wanted, free of any obligation. . . .

In the few days that were left I went with him to his sitting for the bust Epstein was making. At the end of the seance, Yehudi told Epstein that he was going off that afternoon to Germany with Benjamin Britten to play in the recently liberated concentration camp at Belsen and could only manage one more session six days later, on the day he was due to fly back to the States. Epstein looking at me, turned to Yehudi and said, 'Bring her, Yehudi, because you look quite different when she is here.' A little comfort for me in the empty days that followed, when *Jacobowsky and the Colonel* finally closed and the visits to Griselda seemed ever more filled with anxiety.

Yehudi returned, we went to Epstein. Disaster: the wonderfully promising clay head had been knocked to the ground by the importunate cat locked all night in the studio. Epstein would have to start again. Yehudi gave him as much time as he could; we dashed back to Claridge's, I packed for him and with heavy heart watched him get into the car for the airport to return to America, wondering if I would ever see him again, to the last reluctant to buy myself a stake in his feelings towards me by declaring my own love.

As though they knew I was available again, all my close men friends rang me in the following days, but I had no heart to see them. A producer gave me lunch together with an offer to perform in a new revue he was getting up in the autumn and I was glad to be working again even that far ahead. Next day a long and loving cable came from Yehudi, which allayed my sense of utter loss a little. I wrote him the first of the hundreds of letters I must have sent in the next forty-five years.

6 August: The atom bomb is dropped on Hiroshima.
10 August: The Japanese surrender with the proviso that the Emperor remain.

14 August: The Japanese surrender at last.
15 August: VJ Day. Victory Japan. The crowds mill around in the rain.

At long last all the murder was over. I wrote to Yehudi again. On the twenty-first, after I waited for the announced call so anxiously all morning, Yehudi came through from Alma, his Calfornian home, begging me to wait for him as he planned to return, asking me if I could consider marrying him. I told him never to use that phrase again until he was free to do so, but my unguarded heart leapt. Two days later I got his first letter which I read and reread in the tram and bus and all the way to Griselda for days on end till I knew it by heart. On the twenty-fourth, listening to the BBC nine-o'clock news, we learnt that Cecil Harcourt, my stepfather, was to become governor of Hong Kong, which he had just liberated from the Japanese. Cheering news.

The following weeks were mainly desolate. Griselda had to move to a sanatorium in Kent, an hour and a half's train journey away and not all the comfort and good company that Puffin Asquith gave me during those September weeks could bring me joy. I visited Griselda twice a week, standing up all the way in a crowded train, taking a bus to the gates and walking the mile-long drive on my one pair of brogues which slowly split, the soles parting company with the uppers so that they gaped like adenoidal mouths. As we were rationed to eighty-two clothing coupons a year there was no question of buying others so I resorted to welding them together hopefully – with massive straps of sticking plaster (bright pink). By the time I reached the building most of my handiwork had succumbed to the intrusion of pebbles, small leaves, bits of twig and pellets of dried mud and grass. Griselda was putting up with all the cheerless loneliness with her usual brand of sour wit ('vinaigrette' was her sobriquet for herself). I would sit chatting by her bed picking the detritus out of my shoes and sticking them together again for the journey back.

The only bright spot in those dark weeks was another of Puffin Asquith's Savoy dinners, the guest of honour being Léon Blum, the French ex-Prime Minister whom the British had just managed to help escape. A fascinating evening discussing the moral meaning of the war so recently over. Lord Justice Cyril Asquith, Puffin's half-brother, sitting next to me, joining in the arbitration said that the effect it had had on him was to transform him from an agnostic to a believer. 'For', he said, 'there was no utter reason why we should win, unprepared and reluctant as we were, before the organised might of the German army. Rightly, we were made to pay for our moral turpitude, forced to undergo bombing, years of death and attrition; it seemed to me as if, having earned absolution, the Powers that Be had, against all odds, spared us inexplicably from invasion and after six years allowed us to emerge as conquerors. There can be no logical explanation other than a metaphysical one.'

Seven long weeks and neither letter nor telephone call from Yehudi. Returning from the sanatorium for the third time in a week, heavy with anxiety and heartache, to our flat where I embarked on cooking a chicken kindly offered me by our local grocer, who was very concerned about Griselda, the bell rang. Irritated at the interruption I went, greasy-handed, to the door.

Standing there, beaming, was Yehudi. Everything dissolved in immeasurable delight: anxieties, longings, lonelines, all lifted to a level where they suddenly seemed soluble. He explained he had been resolutely planning a series of concerts to be played in England so that he could get back to me and he had not wanted to raise my hopes in case he failed. For the two ensuing weeks we shared every moment we could, I still refusing to declare my love, unwilling to raise any obligation in his mind or heart, trying not to think of the time when he would be gone again and my life even bleaker.

Meanwhile I was more than ever determined to get Griselda to Switzerland; it was becoming increasingly obvious that there was no other hope of saving her life. Every obstacle lay in my path: her doctor refused to admit he could not cure her; Louis Kentner, having obtained his divorce, could not marry her until he got his British naturalisation, being stateless; Griselda's passport had expired; we had no Swiss money to pay the sanatorium in Davos, nor visas to go there. I began my long battle on all fronts, a battle that was to last through the next four months while I anxiously watched Griselda getting thinner and paler, being put through yet another useless operation. I heard the relentless beat of time paying out the days and weeks and months, sounding like hooves chasing me ineluctably onwards to a post I wondered I would ever reach in time. Yehudi came to the rescue on one score, promising to arrange concerts in Switzerland with Kentner in the spring, telling his Swiss agent to pay for the Schatzalp sanatorium as soon as we could get there against his coming tour. That meant one huge obstacle overcome.

I went to a glorious concert in the Albert Hall where he played the Brahms concerto. He was due to go to Prague for the first time since before the war and suggested I stay with mutual friends in Paris if I could get a visa; he would meet me there on his way back. It would only be a few days and it would do me good, he said, after this long period of strain and hard living. I managed to extract a month's visa out of the reluctant paw of the official at the French consulate and bought my train and boat ticket to Paris by the time Yehudi had left for Prague. On my way back from Cook's a couple of days later I happened to meet Winifred, my mother's maid, in the street. 'Biss Diadda,' she said, 'Bister Beduidi is id your bother's flat!' I rushed there to find dear Yehudi dirty and tired. He told me the Russians had approached him in Prague and practically kidnapped him, insisting he go straight to Moscow from there – the first musician to be invited since the war – and that he had told them he had to come back to me first and would then promise to go to Moscow in a few days . .

Next day we went to Epstein's for Yehudi to be photographed with him and the finished bronze; three days later he at last got the visa and ticket for the flight to Moscow. On the same day I made a somewhat more civilised journey than the last rat-infested voyage to Paris, the only adventure happening in the Calais–Paris train when a man opposite me, seeing one of those ubiquitously nosy officials with whom our lives had been burdened for years, begged me to put a wad of money inside my shoe. I had no time to protest, slipped it under my instep, assumed a most innocent look offering my Simon-pure handbag with its miserable regulatory sum of francs to the official and breathed again when he declared us free of skulduggery and went on down the corridor. I handed the money back (slightly warmer than it had been) to the grateful man.

Paris held the unfailing delight it always had for me. Waiting for Yehudi, I delivered the stores I had brought to my beloved Kschessinskaya and the Grand Duke, went to a Casals concert where he played both the Elgar and Dvořák concerti wonderfully and on to the British Embassy to a party in honour of Winston Churchill on whom the French were bestowing the Freedom of Paris together with many other tributes, no doubt to show him that their gratitude surpassed that of the ever *perfide Albion*. As the incumbents were Duff and Lady Diana Cooper, I had a jolly, carefree evening trailing on till six in the morning, after visiting several night-clubs with his daughter Mary (twenty-five years later herself to be ambassadress in that lovely house). None the less I was all the time straining after news of Yehudi. Just over a week later a cable came saying all his plans were aborted and he must now return directly to London.

Dreadfully disappointed, I went to Cook's to book my return as soon as possible. There were great crowds milling around the *Assemblée* because of the sudden rumours that de Gaulle had definitely offered his resignation, which dramatic situation was at that moment under discussion. I went out to Le Bourget airport and sat and sat hopelessly. Fortunately I found a friend, an English businessman, just the right ally at such an obstructed moment. Abandoning all hope of a plane, we got a taxi, raced at Gallic speed to the Gare St Lazare, bought the last two tickets, caught the train by our fingernails, the boat and the further train to London, and I returned home eventually gasping, only to find no sign of Yehudi at Claridge's. Neither, more worrying still, was there any sign the following day when he was due to play at the Albert Hall, no less. I went immediately down to Griselda in the sanatorium, having rung her original London hospital and begged them to let her return there, promising it would only be temporary as I hoped to get her away soon to Switzerland. She was of course much heartened by the news. I made what I hoped was my last walk up the mile-long drive through the half-frozen mud of a late November evening, my brogues reinforced with fresh sticking plaster.

Arrived back at the flat, I was horribly disturbed to find still no news of Yehudi. What could have happened in Russia? Were they keeping him there? Had his aeroplane had an accident in this winter weather of ice and snow? It did not bear thinking of. Alone in the flat, tired and footsore, I was beset with *idées noires,* could settle to nothing, could neither eat, nor read, nor think of anything without my restless mind returning to the obsessive fear as to Yehudi's whereabouts. It is at such moments that loneliness is at its most powerfully cruel. It was too late, too dark and cold to put on my coat and go for a walk; there was no escape from the weight of worry.

The bell rang, and ready for any relief, even a few words exchanged with someone delivering a late package, I went to the door. There, yet again, was Yehudi, dishevelled and scruffy, clutching an enormous drum of caviare, together with a large green, gold-lettered volume entitled *Nash Ballet* (*Our Ballet*) slipping from under one arm and various packages at his feet. Again the joy, that release from pain and strain (that, had I known it then, was to become a regular pattern through the decades ahead and which I was never to learn to conquer). We tidied up cursorily and went to dine at our old post the Berkeley, where he told me the familiar story of the impossibility of ever getting any definite information from the Russians, of his days waiting in the hotel and airport. However, all this had been compensated for by the wonderful concerts, the dinner given for him by the American Ambassador, Averill Harriman, where he'd met Shostakovich for the first time, the touching welcome of Moscow audiences added to which was the tale of how, finally one morning, he had slipped his Intourist guard and run to a bookshop where he had found this fascinating old book full of the early ballerinas whose history was part of every dancer's pantheon.

And what could I tell him? Only the continuing struggle to overcome those barriers in getting Griselda to Switzerland and my besetting fear that I was running out of time. Yehudi again begged to be allowed to help in any further way he could and I felt a little comforted.

Another beautiful concert – the Elgar concerto, so much Yehudi's own – at the Albert Hall; one of Griselda's many adoring admirals drove down to Midhurst with me, giving her at least the small comfort of returning by car to London and the King's College Hospital; Yehudi came to greet her; at the final concert at the Albert Hall he played the Mozart D Major and the Bartók concertos; the following day there was the private view at the Leicester Galleries of the Epstein bust . . . and it was all over.

I drove down to Hurn from where his aeroplane, a Skymaster, was to take off for New York. It was a dismal wartime airport. In the Quonset hut, suspended from everything human and warming, surrounded by rather overly vocal Americans, Yehudi stood beside me looking more forlorn than I had ever seen him. Armed with a large crate of Crimean wine from his mother's birthplace, holding my hand, there was nothing to say that would not have been banal in that alien setting. Even his naturally hopeful spirits seemed doused. Perhaps sensing our sadness, the kind airman in command invited me to come in his own bus with Yehudi to drive to the airfield where I watched him, mute with pent-up feeling, climb into the plane and fly off, as far as I knew for ever out of my life, back to his family and a five-month tour of the States.

To the bitter end I had never told him how deeply I loved him, nor that I was ready to wait for him should he really want me. I will never know if I made a wrong decision. I wept, desolate, all the way back to the empty flat and to my battle for Griselda's life.

Yehudi rang from New York at two a.m. the following day. They had had to make a crash landing, but he was all right.

My good Puffin Asquith proved a marvellous friend. Through various relations and political friends of his my pleas for Kentner's naturalisation had reached the Home Office and the news came that given Louis Kentner's invaluable contribution to music in England he would immediately become a British citizen and get his passport. Yet another obstacle overcome. Yehudi rang again from New York at five a.m. And again two days later. The calls were a great comfort; he was very loving and concerned and that brought him closer again.

At last I got Griselda's passport. Obstacle three surmounted.

On 19 December 1945 Cecil Harcourt was knighted.

I meanwhile was gathering papers, passports and beginning my assault on the minister at the Swiss Legation, to which I was to return again and again, pestering the poor man until finally I might force him to give in and allow me the visas without which I could not get to Switzerland.

A long cable came from Yehudi: he had had a talk with Sir Alexander Fleming who would send the newest tuberculosis cure to us in England. I tried to feel that this latest discovery would indeed be of use. Then came an alert from the Overseas Exchange: would I please stand by for a call from Mr Menuhin? For four long, anxious days I sat by the telephone, hardly daring to leave the flat as on and off the announcement would come through, only again and again to be cancelled. New Year's Eve arrived and I was still waiting, alone and utterly depressed. I did not even celebrate the New Year but fell asleep, worn out and praying that 1946 would bring some change in our fortunes both for Griselda and myself.

For ten long and longing days I awaited Yehudi's proposed call, meanwhile moving Griselda from the hospital back to our flat, hoping to make her as comfortable as possible and raise her sorely tried spirits. At last Yehudi's voice came through, full of loving sympathy, begging me to join him on his US tour. As I told him with a breaking heart that there was no possible way in which I could leave Griselda the line went dead, and with it a large part of my hope that we would ever really come together again.

10 June 1946: The first meeting of the United Nations Organisation.

An American rang me from the Savoy. He had parcels for Griselda and Louis and me from Yehudi. On opening mine I found a pair of brogues (farewell, sticking plaster), my first ever crocodile shoes and six pairs of nylon stockings. What bounty! In Griselda's there were many tins of food to help her flagging appetite. Oh! blessed Yehudi, who, for the next week, managed somehow to ring me nearly every day as he travelled from town to town, knowing that I was growing ever more desperate in my battle to get a permit for us to leave England. Dear Cyril Ritchard, addressing the audience at a Swiss film première, made it known that whereas sound and healthy people were getting away to ski, I had so far been refused a permit to take my sister on the point of death to a sanatorium in that country. His words were publicised in one of the dailies and, comforted by the publicity and an early call from Yehudi, I again assaulted the Swiss Legation, shuttling between it and the French Consulate for transit visas (why there, unless it were that the plane might crash inadvertently in France and we all be considered illegal corpses, I never knew) and at last, triumphantly, I got those Swiss visas. However, the following three weeks I was baulked again and again; the bank required more 'evidence' before they would give me the necessary 'free sterling' currency: Griselda's pet admiral promptly wrote to the Governor of the Bank of England. I spent all day ringing Cook's and the bank hoping to get our return tickets. Always to no avail. And oh, wonderful moment! I collected our passports duly stamped; the application had at last been granted. The two seats were booked for 13 February and Yehudi got through again from New York. Beside myself with joy and excitement, I took the bus to Airways House where after an hour's wait they told me, with that kind of satisfaction peculiar to all petty officials, that they had no confirmation – *ergo*, no tickets. Distracted, I went back again to the Swiss Legation where, after an hour's tussle, I was finally told that anyway the plane of the thirteenth was full. On the verge of tears, I produced my trump card, the admiral's letter to the Director of the Bank of England. That, added to my long battle and possibly my tears, must have melted them, for relenting they booked us for the nineteenth. Dear Puffin rescued me for lunch and took me back to Airways House where, after a long and agonising wait, I got my tickets. Gazing at them, at our visas and passports, I could hardly believe that after all these months of fighting I had won, even though my joy was tempered by the fear born of watching Griselda wasting away and the dread that I might yet be too late to save her.

For the next week Yehudi rang me every day, giving me support and loving concern, detecting in my voice not only the exhaustion my long battle had wrought but my apprehension at the verdict we would face once we got to the sanatorium. Maybe it was the same fear that caused Griselda, as I tucked her into bed on the eve of our departure – all cases packed and the precious papers in my pocket – to turn on me and accuse me of having shown little warmth or affection, of having been bossy and unfeeling and generally wanting in those expressions of emotion that she said would have been preferable to anything else all these nine long months. Shocked and hurt, I went to my room and cried for an hour, pouring out in those tears all the pent-up anguish I had controlled, always fearful that had I indulged in too much overfeeling I might have revealed to Griselda the forbidden dread she must never suspect, to say nothing of weakening my own determination. I fell asleep finally, riven with distress at having so evidently failed her. Yehudi never felt so far away nor the future more hazardous.

Next day, 19 February, Yehudi rang from Chicago to wish us Godspeed, heartening me for the journey ahead. As we rose into the air on this my first ever flight, I looked at the distancing land below me hardly able to believe I had at last won the first half of my battle; before us still lay the long journey to the mountains and the doctor's verdict.

When we landed at Zürich an ambulance awaited us. As they tried to help us in, I had to explain that despite my haggard face, it was my sister who was the patient. Griselda, outwardly at least, had regained some of her loveliness.

We spent the night in Zürich and the next day travelled through the whitened country and on up to Davos, arriving in snow packed so hard by the fourth month of winter that we were put on to a sledge, wrapped in rugs and, to the sound of horses' hooves and ringing bells, carried along to the funicular. Griselda's spirits rose: 'Anna Caramelina,' she said delightedly.

The Schatzalp Sanatorium (now long since gone) was the original one in Thomas Mann's *The Magic Mountain* and its head doctor, Maurer, was a formidable little man; the building, bleak and antiseptic, coldly furnished with little decoration and no colour. But through the big window of Griselda's room the superb view of the white wall of mountains opposite, the trees weighted with snow stretching in clumps and patches all the way down to the town in the valley below, compensated for all the barrenness. The pure and icy air, the light – crystalline in the sparkling sun – drove away for the moment the apprehension inhabiting my heart for so long and now reaching its apogee.

Griselda's ironical brand of courage stood her in good stead through the ensuing examinations as it did through the weeks ahead when they were repeated. That first night I wrote my thirty-third letter to Yehudi, as I was to write him every single day for the next ten weeks. The good food, the clean air, the glorious view and finally the wonderful news that the cavity in Griselda's lung was closed (but would take a long time to strengthen and be sound enough for her to return to normal life) were like a gift from God. Slowly we were mounting the slope from the slough of despond. Griselda after her usual fashion had conquered most of the more interesting males in the sanatorium, including Dr Maurer himself, so her life took on some colour and shape after the terrible months she had had to endure.

Occasionally Yehudi got through by telephone and his beloved voice cheered me. He had just sent a furious cable to J. G. McLure, the American official in charge of Germany, begging him at least to allow Wilhelm Furtwängler the right to his 'Purification' trial (which should absolve him from any collaboration with the Nazi regime). He had already been passed by the French, English and Russians. On 16 March 1946 Churchill gave his famous speech at Fulton, Missouri, warning the West of the might of their recent ally Russia and the dangers inherent in Stalin's policy. I read Stalin's Machiavellian riposte in *La Suisse*.

One sunny day, those patients well enough were packed into sledges to go on a 'trailing party'; fifteen-strong, balloons tied to the harnesses, bells ringing all the way between the hedges of snow to Monstein, there to lunch in the open air and drink litres of red wine. On the way back there was a tea-dance at Davos. Oh! the wonderful escape from sickness into the normality of healthy people's lives, the flight into the carefree. Returning in the late afternoon, we tumbled out of the funicular, laughing and light-hearted, and went to our rooms. Griselda's nurse came with her remedies. The little Turkish boy we had left behind had died in our absence. Suddenly the shutter that had lifted descended again, expelling all light and warmth. I went back down the long corridor to my room in the nearby chalet reserved for those very few relatives who accompanied the ill, noting as I passed by what I had tried so often to avoid – tried to expel from my mind – the occasional door that had once been open and that was now sealed betraying a recent death; of someone one had spoken with in the dining-room perhaps, had seen in the hall, had known to be as full of hope as ourselves. The appalling precariousness of the whole terrible illness bore down on me like a wet shroud and I shivered in my little room, praying that Griselda would have no relapse, yearning for someone to talk to, to share my dread. As usual I wrote to Yehudi, so very far away.

17

Reluctant Reckoning

It was April, the loveliest month in the high mountains; the snowing was almost over, the sun shone day after day and the snow seemed full of diamonds. Every now and again its heavy burden on the trees, loosened by the warmth, fell with a plop off the branches as though they were shedding winter; small, bright, intense-blue gentians appeared where the cover was thinner and the night sky's blackness, pierced by a million stars, seemed a reflection in negative of the day's brilliance.

Soon Louis Kentner, his naturalisation papers in order and his passport in hand, would arrive and he and Griselda would marry. On 15 April a cable from Yehudi from New York simply said: 'Just leaving.' I scarcely slept all night. When the wall telephone in the corridor outside my room rang, I went at once to answer it, knowing it would be Yehudi. His voice was blurred with tiredness and full of longing, my throat so full of heart I could hardly speak. He was back in London. Nineteen long weeks of separation at last to end. 'Darling, I was to come over this afternoon only . . .' here he hesitated, 'would you be patient for just one more day?' It appeared that by the most incredible stroke of destiny Nola and the children, after months with her family in Australia, had chosen not to return to their home in Alma where Yehudi had been waiting for them for the past two weeks, but to arrive the very next day in London. 'I will meet them and settle them in and fly over to you the next day. Only just one day more, darling, I promise.' He had been speaking in French as we often did in those early days and I remember choking on my words: '*Yehudi, j'ai peur, j'ai peur . . .*' 'However can you fear?' he asked. 'Tomorrow we will be together.'

With my usual apprehension I had feared that should he meet with any sudden impediment in his intentions (intentions he had long ago made perfectly clear, without my knowledge, to Nola who had for some time been in love with another man), neither he nor I would by character be equipped to deal with any serious impasse. He by the very nature of his approach to life, one low in self-esteem and inimical to strife; I confined inescapably within a code that forbade me to propel a situation in which I held no moral claim.

Yehudi's touching refusal to consider there were any grounds to justify my sudden betrayal of fear at that moment we had both waited for with such longing made me feel ashamed before his loving trust and I apologised, refraining from telling him of the ever-hovering Black Fairy who had destroyed so much hope so often in my life.

Alas, my fears were well founded. His simple trust, built on so much fulfilment in his life to date, was to be mercilessly destroyed by the bitter implications with which he was suddenly and unequivocally faced by Nola. She had had a change of mind. He would not be free. His duty lay by her and his marriage. With one skilful movement based on her astute knowledge of his nature and his readiness for self-sacrifice, Yehudi had been summoned to return to the fold forthwith.

Louis duly came over, and he and I went to get his marriage licence together in Zürich. Griselda and he were married on 29 May at the Stadthaus there. Yehudi and Furtwängler were best men. Griselda needing me no more, by June I returned alone to our flat in Chesham Street, helping the good Winifred move all Griselda's possessions to the charming house Louis had found in Chelsea.

I went to Paris in an attempt to pick up my dancing again, but dispossessed of all significance in my life, I fell very ill. When I was able to leave the clinic, I went back to London where my kind stepfather, returned now from Hong Kong, together with that admiral whose invaluable help had supported me throughout my battles to get Griselda to the sanatorium, fetched me from the airport, still very weak, and took me back to the flat, now bereft of all furniture except for my bed and chair.

Months ago – in another world and time – I had bought myself a ticket and got a visitor's visa for the States. Sitting on a crate I looked round at the empty shelves, at the light patches on the walls where once the pictures had hung; my mind wandered through the rooms where Yehudi and I had grown to love each other, found comfort in the healing and marriage of Griselda and decided that utterly depleted as I was, with no home, no job, no hope, I would use the one thing I had, my ticket to America. To live in London would be unbearable. With the strange courage and purpose that is born of a total vacuum and occurs only when one has reached a nadir in life, I confirmed my flight to New York, packed up my few remaining possessions, told my parents and Griselda I was leaving and waited in the limbo that my life had become.

Rachel and Michael Redgrave had learnt that I was sitting in the empty flat – for my plane was delayed for three days – and, dear friends that they were, insisted I stay with them until I left. There in their lovely riverside house I felt a curious peace. What had been must be buried for ever as one buries a stillborn child. One day perhaps I might dare recall a glorious hope to which I could lay no claim, nor blame anyone but myself for believing it. Now I must go forward into the *néant*.

On 23 September, Mummy and Griselda saw me off on the bus from Airway House. Mummy, as I turned to look through the window, wearing her usual vaguely disapproving look; Griselda with tears pouring down her cheeks.

In those days, a long journey in a propeller plane was hazardous and after endless stopovers and hours spent flying between a closed-in New York and a beclouded Boston, the pilot decided Boston would be the lesser risk. It was the evening of the next day and a kind man who had befriended me on the aeroplane took me to the station where I got a ticket for New York, arriving after midnight to find the room I had booked given to someone else and the hotel full. They apologised, led me to a small banqueting room redolent of stale cigarette smoke and alcohol. I emptied a dozen ashtrays into a waste basket, wiped the beer and whisky stains off a long table, took off my shoes, spread my coat on it and tried to sleep. It was three a.m. I had thought to have reached the nadir in London. I had been mistaken: there were further depths to plumb.

I awoke stiff and sore the next morning, to find that the kindly manageress, who happened to be English, had retrieved my room. I had not even got Yehudi's address as I had no intention of seeing him again nor getting in the way of the marriage he must have felt that after all he could not abandon, even though it had had no significance for either him or his wife for years.

Anton Dolin and Alicia Markova were with the American Ballet Theatre; Toni and Klari Doráti were there, he conducting the de Basil Company; Lucia Chase, directress of ABC, had invited me to join just before the war broke out and I felt fairly certain that I should be able to find a job with one or other of them. Meanwhile I worked hard and thanks to a long-time friend, Ana Ricarda, a dancer whom I had known as Ann Simpson and whose mother was a friend of my mother's, I was able to join her private classes given by an ebullient Italian called Celli who whistled and stamped and sang his way through his own somewhat singular *enchaînements*.

I went to a handful of auditions from which I fled after the sundry lascivious fumblings common to such interviews, spent whatever time Pat Dolin could spare with him, but although he told me that Sol Hurok, the leading ballet and concert impresario, spoke of me as 'Dolin's beautiful girl', neither offered me any work, and I would have starved rather then return to the mad jungle that de Basil's company had increasingly become. I was as a matter of fact already reaching a state of acute hunger, for my money was gradually dwindling and the few introductions I had been furnished with by the kindest of friends (Ivor Newton the famous accompanist), when I could at least stuff myself with cocktail biscuits and salted almonds and even enjoy an occasional square meal were, after a few weeks, expended. Breakfast was coffee supplemented by a few biscuits from a packet sternly apportioned; lunch a sandwich; supper a piece of cheese and an apple in my small room. I had long since abandoned the dining-room. Edward James, met again at one of those introductory cocktail parties, took me out to dinner where we talked long and longingly of his Ballets 1933, while I filled myself up with two days' worth of food.

All too quickly that welcome paralysis of the mind and heart that had motivated my plunge into this untried world was vanishing and gradually, like pins and needles in a limb that is returning to circulation, I was becoming aware of my plight, conscious of my loneliness, my penury, the ticking over as it were of time lived from day to day, with neither purpose nor vision – a life such as an animal might live, waking in the morning to move through the hours in an unthinking rhythm. The ever-kind Klari, giving me lunch one day, told me that Yehudi was back in New York – she had disclosed I was here looking for work – and he was wanting to see me. In my earlier numbed state, or had I found work and some life of my own, I would easily have been able to refuse. But now, anchorless, hungry, jobless, with both lessening hope and augmenting dread, I agreed. We met a few times but he knew there was nothing he could say, nor could anything have brought me to disburden myself of all the shock and anguish that might only seem like condemnation. He did bring his little daughter Zamira to see me, however, a strangely lost child with something very touching in her tentative and wary approach. I remembered the first day I had met her father at Mulberry House had been her fifth birthday; by now she would be all of seven. After that first meeting she would ring me up every morning, beg to see me, we would go for walks or to the ballet or I would cook dinner, for by now I had moved to an inexpensive flat.

Came the night when I could bear no more, the perpetual half-hunger, the lack of money and last but not least an anticipated job on which I had set my heart falling through. I felt that especial loneliness that only uprootedness can bring. My seemingly inextinguishable hope died out with a final flutter. Walking out on to the street, I looked all round at the figures about me with a kind of terror; everything and everybody was alien and nothing belonged to me nor anything of myself to them; nothing held any significance any longer. I had been seven weeks in New York – seven humiliating weeks living from hand to mouth, subsisting on the charity of a few acquaintances for a square meal, slowly losing faith in my usefulness to anybody or anything. A wayfarer in a strange land, whose value was nil. It was a chilly December evening when I walked on to Fifth Avenue, moving through thinning crowds as I went downtown. All my life I had sought to solve the seemingly insoluble by walking. Somehow the rhythm creates a current which loosens the most stubborn obstruction, carrying it away from that choking centre where even breathing is difficult. I seemed to be surrounded by strangers all of whom were hurrying towards a person or a place awaiting them; I alone was expendable, taking in nothing, unaware of anything other than my own pain. After two hours I found myself near the harbour. The squalid buildings around were like piles of shabby clothing dumped on each side of the narrow street. I felt no fear, even though part of me knew I was in the most sinister and criminal quarter of the city. I had walked fifty blocks. I was leaning on the parapet watching the filthy water swirling below. After an hour or two I began to feel a shift in my muddled head, a new perspective as though the very dirt, the dark and squalor around me had rekindled some light and lightness in my heart. Turning back I trudged up the Avenue as the first light spread behind the skyscrapers bringing them into being like huge plants sprung up overnight.

The next morning the mail brought an invitation from the 'Boys', Frank Ingerson and George Dennison, to give up struggling alone in New York and to come and stay with them in California. I packed a few things, got a ticket with the remains of my money and by 14 December reached that paradise of a countryside and fell into the welcoming arms of the two old friends of my grandmother and mother whom I had not seen since I was about twelve years old.

The Boys' house lay amongst huge live oaks and fruit trees at the foot of the hill in the Santa Cruz mountains where Yehudi had built his house. The young Menuhin family and they had been close friends for years. In fact it was they who had suggested that Yehudi's father, Aba, should buy the ninety acres on which Alma stood. It was they who had written the never-to-be-delivered letter of introduction to my mother; again it was they who had finally given Yehudi her telephone number two years ago. After a few days it appeared that Yehudi himself had arrived at his house above, and one morning he came down to the valley and asked me to come and meet his parents who lived, as they had since 1936, in the little neighbouring town of Los Gatos. In the strange confusion of heart in which I now lived, feeling like some cheap clock that had to be rewound every day in order to keep ticking over, I consented.

Yehudi's father and mother were a legendary pair renowned in the musical world for their separate and very vivid characters: Aba volatile, emotional, worshipping his son with a fanatical devotion more passionate than wise; 'Mammina', his mother, who had been a great beauty, very Russian, very imperious, didactic, a veritable Sybil insofar as restraining her feelings was concerned; in other words a conjunction of natures basically incompatible, held together by their own brand of moral conviction, Aba's unquenchable love and their total consecration as parents. Not very conducive to domestic harmony perhaps, as I was to discover – the daily round of small battles rattling like grapeshot across the dining-table – but basically totally integrated. Aba, a convinced liberal, lectured his children on the Human Condition in capital letters, always concerned in trying to improve the lot of mankind; Mammina deliberately confined her rôle to that of the archetypal mother, albeit with a matriarchal demeanour that subtly gave her precedence over Aba in nearly every field except that of politics and the economics of the household. Fascinating I found them, but as potentially explosive as sodium dropped into water.

I met Yaltah, his younger sister, a pretty young woman with her mother's golden hair. A few days later Yehudi's beloved sister Hephzibah arrived from Australia with her husband Lindsay and two small boys, Kronrod and Marstie. Yehudi and she had been separated by the war for nearly six years and the joy and excitement of their reunion was wonderful to see. A whole facet of his nature seemed to come alive as though a new current ran through him. The Boys had told me of their ineradicable companionship, not only the shared music, but the shared jokes, their delight in being together, of Hephzibah's childhood longing for her beloved brother so early separated when he and their father were away on tour – all this was so palpably alive, it eased my heart to realise that even were he never to free himself for me, there was someone else close to him who would cherish him and bring him comfort.

What to my surprise brought me further consolation was the warmth and support I received from both Hephzibah and her husband Lindsay, Nola's handsome brother, who at this moment of spiritual and mental atrophy took me under his wing and henceforward, at first unbeknownst to me, pleaded my cause – a cause I myself had all but buried. The Boys, having with their slender means bought me a fourteen-dollar black dress and a jersey to augment my tiny wardrobe, were planning to take me down to Hollywood, as they had taken the young Olivia de Havilland nearly a decade ago, to introduce to their friends in high places and relaunch me professionally. Lindsay, I learned, had all along looked with disfavour at his sister's involvement with Yehudi, knowing her high-spirited waywardness; he was deeply musical himself and doubted that she could ever undertake the onerous and responsible task of looking after a career of such magnitude as Yehudi's.

As the year came to an end, they – Hep and Lindsay – drew me ever closer back into Yehudi's life, showing me an affection and a welcome so unforeseen that my feelings were thrown into a turmoil. I had, I hoped, amortised all despairing longing and would if no job transpired in films eventually return to London. I felt I must accept that what I had once perceived as destiny had been but an episode in Yehudi's life.

By hindsight the New Year, 1947, imperceptibly brought a change in my fortunes. The Boys, kindly and determined as ever that I should regain independence, drove me down the coast to Carmel for lunch with the beautiful Joan Fontaine, Olivia de Havilland's sister and her equal in cinematic fame, hoping perhaps that the contact might lead on to my finding work. Lindsay had flown to New York to see Nola, the sister from whom he had been separated for six years – also, as I afterwards learnt, to beg her to release Yehudi from this dead marriage, whose end as far as she herself was concerned she had frankly announced to Yehudi several years before, choosing to tell him so when she met him off the train. The ruthless shock had made it the saddest homecoming of his married life and had obviously contributed to that increasingly enclosed and distracted manner I had perceived, the reason for which I had withheld from asking him directly.

On return, Lindsay and Hep and the children swept me up with them to fly to Los Angeles where Yehudi was to play the Elgar concerto. In my few days there a vivid recollection remains of true Hollywood vintage. Yehudi had arranged a working breakfast with one of the big moguls from MGM, who was intent upon luring him into the film world. Waxing eloquent over the vast salary Yehudi could expect, the wide publicity, the glittering honours and so on and so forth, the poor fellow, chain-smoking as though to generate the engine of his own enthusiasm, ploughed sedulously on, watering his dried tubes with cup after cup of the peculiarly filthy coffee provided by the hotel. I began to feel a glimmer of sympathy for the man beating his beak (rather prominent) against the *tabula rasa* of Yehudi's face. At last, oblivious of Yehudi's oriental inscrutability, he asked with a flourish of tin trumpets for his opinion. Whereupon Yehudi said politely that he had absorbed all the advantageous perquisites so graphically cited in the last half-hour; however, he did feel that it was a very contrasting world to that of the musical one to which he belonged and in which he had worked for some twenty years to – in all modesty – his joy and satisfaction; that – if he could be forgiven – there were certain risks inherent in appearing in a medium such as film, for instance the likelihood that he would be powerless to control many aspects he might find contrary to his taste or even – forgive me – dangerous to his image as a – forgive me again – serious artist.

The MGM envoy looked aghast at the suggestion that Hollywood might lack the sensitivity to recognise distinction or style. 'Why, Mr Menuhin!' he expostulated. 'You know the famous pianist José Iturbi, who has just completed his second highly successful film for us? Well he has a clause in his contract protecting him from ever appearing in a *sailor hat!*'

'How very interesting,' said Yehudi, 'Now if you will excuse me, I'm already late for rehearsal,' and shaking the crestfallen gentleman warmly by the hand we bolted, leaving him thunderstruck that anyone could turn down a million dollars so casually.

We returned to Alma. Yehudi went off to conduct the Dallas orchestra for the second time. Hep and Lindsay, concerned as ever, talked at length with me, persuading me to remain with them till their return to Europe in six or seven weeks; it appeared Yehudi had meanwhile taken a small house by the sea in a quiet, unfashionable part of Florida. I said I would only come if I could be of service and cook for them all. I flew alone to New York where I stayed on the twentieth floor of a cheap hotel on the West Side – an eyrie among the bird-droppings – escaping after a week to join the family on a train grandiosely named 'Orange Blossom of Florida' and the modest villa on the beach.

At the villa there were two ebony-skinned, good-natured maids, one paradoxically called Blanche. There, with the nearest grocery store seven miles away, I cooked for five weeks for six adults and three children (for Yaltah and her small son Lionel had joined us) – a task encumbered by the Australian contingent demanding all food to be cooked to a frazzle and Yaltah's nervous habit of creeping down in the middle of the night to raid the icebox of food carefully predestined for the following day's menu. Once-full soup bowls would suddenly appear inexplicably drained; jellies oddly disfigured by large gaps, fish mousses become suspiciously pockmarked, while cheeses nibbled all round would make me wonder if I had unwittingly allowed mice inside the refrigerator. By the end of that holiday everyone except myself looked blooming and I was living on amino-acid powder.

On return to New York, Yehudi and Hephzibah found their beloved George Enesco there and rehearsed the coming programme for their first recital together since 1938 at the Metropolitan Opera House where they were 'touting' the tickets at astronomical prices on the steps outside. I persuaded Yehudi to shave off the orange-red beard he had sprouted in Florida, at sight of which poor little Zamira had burst into tears. Yehudi teased her by shaving first one side, then next day half the moustache on the other and so on until he appeared clean-shaven for the concert on 16 March. Needless to say it was a great occasion and for the siblings a wonderful renewal of their old close partnership. To me, who had gone with dear Cyril Ritchard and Madge Elliott, it brought consolation of heart to see Yehudi once more joined to a love that was steady and trustworthy and deep. Four days later we all sailed on the *Queen Elizabeth*, I sharing a cabin with Marstie and the governess who were dramatically and incessantly seasick.

On arrival in London I, now homeless, went to stay with my mother, the others at Claridge's. Mama and I went to Yehudi's and Hep's recital at the Albert Hall. It was extraordinarily moving: nearly 8000 people who would not let them go and finally the police holding back the crowds outside to make them a passage to their car as they shouted: 'Ye*hu*di, Ye*hu*di, *Hep*zeebah!' I returned to Mama's flat feeling elated at the love and admiration in which he was held, and increasingly disorientated. Try though I might not to think of that flat adjoining this one where once so much had been born and had grown – so much that was so beautiful – of my three nightmare months in New York, of the whole failed six months in America, of the subsequent limbo in which I was living, I was still struggling to wrench myself from the wreckage of a dream in which I had had absolutely no right to believe. Now without home or work, seeing Yehudi with that great adoring crowd around him, restored to Hephzibah, I could find no further rôle for myself. The moment of agonising reappraisal had come around yet again and I could not shirk it, only comfort myself that at least I was not this time facing a bleak moment of truth utterly alone in an alien land. I was back in my own country in which, whatever painful dead hopes lay about me, there were threads to pick up, friendships to rekindle and my abandoned career to bring to life again.

Lindsay rang and asked me to lunch with them at Claridge's the next day. Hiding my own sadness, I agreed. Everybody seemed happy, the glow of that Albert Hall concert still enveloping them. After the meal Lindsay took me aside; within a few days they were off to the Continent to give concerts from Paris to Prague via Budapest, Holland and so forth as I indeed already knew. Would I please come? No, I said with aching heart, it was good of him to ask me, his affectionate friendship had upheld me wonderfully over the past months, for which I would be eternally grateful, but I felt I had reached the parting of the ways. Yehudi was now so much happier, the playing was going well, he had found his beloved Hephzibah. I felt he was back in the saddle again. I only hoped that I had been of some use, some help in his achieving that security and now I must pick up my own life again which Griselda's dangerous illness and my own foolish hopes had totally disrupted.

Lindsay looked at me with disbelief and surprise. I hastened on, fearful of his trying to make me change my mind. I pointed out that here back in my own European haunts I was hardly unknown, that it was humiliating for me to give the impression of hanging on like some importunate fan, a rather undignified member of that gaggle of self-appointed acolytes whom so many famous artists have to endure, an appendage never quite belonging, a sort of spare tyre, a guarantee against possible malfunction; that I could no longer dabble with my life nor dupe myself that it was otherwise than the way in which I myself now perceived it. 'If', said Lindsay angrily, 'your pride is more important to you than the fact that Yehudi needs you as much as he ever did, nor can you realise that we will soon be going back to Australia and I dread the thought of what is to become of him, then you're not the person I had thought you were. You alone can help him; remember I have known both him and my sister Nola for longer than you, and I will do all in my power to persuade you to stay by him and help him.'

'It is not simply a matter of *amour propre*,' I replied. 'You are asking me to risk rekindling in myself something it has taken months of struggle and anguish to bury, if not to destroy. I am sore of heart but resigned and know a sort of peace. Can you understand, dear Lindsay?'

'I'm begging you to come with us, Di. That's all. Please.'

I had bought Hep an anthology of John Donne, the great Elizabethan poet nearest to my poetic feelings, as a farewell present. 'Please listen to Lin, Diny, he knows exactly what he's asking of you and its serious significance to us all,' she said.

I tried to reason with myself most of the night, fighting that hovering fear that never seemed to be out of sight, always ready to ride alongside every happening in my life, which by now had wearied me till I no longer had the courage to resolve any problem and had lost the instinct that had once seemed to be one of my strongest guides. I had never pursued a man, not for a job, nor as a conquest, nor for any imaginable advantage. The very idea was abhorrent. At the slightest sign of a diminishing relationship I would be gone like a leaf on the wind. Was I now, after so much suffering and uncertainty, to prolong some vision seemingly long since dead of attrition, by now all too clearly revealed to have been an impossible and absurd dream? How to balance the moral values with the emotional ones, the guilt with the devotion? What was honest and what self-deceptive, merely a longing to cling on to the extraordinary wonder of that first opening of love and with it that curious sense of destiny that had carried me through so much? Was that too an illusion?

I had once been so sure and so strong and so ready to wait. Now I only felt there might be nothing to wait for and only indignity to expect.

Yehudi's London cousin 'Aunt' Edie, a sweet woman who had become a close friend from the beginning, got in touch with me. Her daughter Sonia had been invited to go with the Nicholas–Menuhin family – would I please go as her chum? I decided to take this as an opportunity to spend their last weeks in Europe with the Australian family and through them deepen my knowledge of Yehudi's early life and not to think beyond.

The tour was to start in Paris, my erstwhile second home, so that to book myself into that small hotel I had stayed in ages before with Griselda still left me with a modicum of independence. Anyway Paris was so much part of me that I never felt I belonged to anyone but myself and my early years there. I brilliantly managed to fracture my foot leaping out of bed to grab at the telephone (one of those old upright ones with the ear-section dangling at the side on a clip, standing on the far chimney-piece way across the room), without discovering that my whole leg was fast asleep and as capable of use as a boiled banana. As it gave way under me with a dull crack I knew, as all dancers do, what I would go through when the pins and needles wore off and the excruciating pain began, leaving me only one leg and foot of any service. Furious, I confessed to Hep at the end of the wire what I had so cleverly achieved and crawled back to spend the next few days in bed, missing Yehudi's recording of the Lalo *Symphonie Espagnole* with Jean Fournet and receiving in somewhat shabby ceremony such special friends of Yehudi's as Pierre Bertaux, the young tutor of their early years at Ville d'Avray – since then one of France's leading Resistance fighters and what is so elegantly entitled '*une grosse-tête*' (so infinitely more graphic than 'great intellectual'); and dear old Gabrielle, her face yellower than ever, like a large lemon in the setting sun, but now furnished with a firm set of piano keys in her mouth in place of those ever-loosening almonds I always feared would drop one by one into her mending. '*Merci, merci Mademoiselle Diane*,' she murmured when I slipped Mama's fat packet into her old purse. The sight of her evoked so very much of a happier, securer past, as when a blind, its cord loosened too fast, rattles up to reveal an overwhelming view. The flood of youthful memories, of aspiration, of purpose and of hope undeterred by doubt fed by that kind of divine energy that drives all young artists, now seemed altogether vanished. I felt suddenly all the more desolate, rudderless, becalmed in a river without a current.

The caravan rolled on to Brussels, Amsterdam, Strasbourg, I living out of the top of my mind and the edge of my heart, like someone who holds her nose in order to avoid an unpleasant taste. Yehudi and I made a swift run up to the Schatzalp where Griselda had gone for a check-up and he gave a concert with Louis Kentner in the sanatorium. I held before my mind's eye – as a screen against all the other painful memories – the wonderful fact of Griselda's healing.

May had come round again and we were all in Vevey on the Lake of Geneva. Yehudi having only met Furtwängler and his wife briefly the year before at Griselda's and Louis's wedding, rang him up at the nearby Niehans Clinic where they were living and asked them to lunch. Furtwängler thanked Yehudi deeply for having secured him a fair 'Purification' trial in 1945, which had freed him from the cabal determined to block his further career. We dined overlooking the lake. It was the first time they had actually talked with each other. He came with his lovely blonde wife, Elisabeth. I felt more than ever dislocated for of course he recognised me from the many times he'd been to my mother's house before the war. But it was a moving evening and good to discern the affinity that they shared. Furtwängler, dignified, reticent, very much the German *Ritter* warming towards Yehudi, the gentle, artless, genial, still young man whose genuineness never failed to set the tone for all those who became acquainted with him. This was the beginning of a musical partnership that was to be one of the most valuable and significant factors in Yehudi's life, linking him in turn to his affinity with German literature and the culture that underlay most of the music he had played since early childhood.

From there Yehudi and Hephzibah and the ensemble rolled on into Central and Eastern Europe to visit those cities he had known before the upheavals of the war, to play day and night concerts – pre-arranged and improvised – raising money for causes of every kind, initiating as it were the way of life he had subconsciously always wanted to follow, part troubadour, part crusader, always trying to identify his music, his playing, with the common cause, at last escaping for a little from the harness of those rigid tours travelling for months from town to town, rehearsing, performing, moving on in clockwork repetition as though he were a useful commodity to be distributed on the assembly belt of High Culture.

From the very beginning of our friendship, when he haltingly revealed in the unlikely setting of the Berkeley Hotel dining-room his conception of music from early childhood as a message, a voice given him to bring bliss to heal all the trouble in the world (this said very shyly as the rather absurd, overly ecstatic ideal of the four-year-old), I had sensed that this moral seriousness he was hesitatingly trying to explain was what informs all his interpretations and makes him totally separate from any other violinist; that his vision of the artist as a servant of his public aiming to prove that art was a source of imperishable significance in life was acturally the significance that was Yehudi. I had also realised that that was what made him so achingly vulnerable, so lost and without weapons in the professional world he must needs live in; from there had been born my desire to be of use to him and the foolish, undefined hope that I could occupy some position in which I could fulfil this ardent wish. Hubris, perhaps? After all that had ensued I found myself torn to shreds and no longer clear of head or heart, incapable of discriminating right from wrong, caught in a thornbush in which every move only brought self-condemnation.

Prague in itself, despite the deprivations of the war and its very recent liberation, was a tonic. The splendid buildings, the musical life, revived me and brought Yehudi the kind of companionship and music-making of which he had never had enough. Rafael and Ludmila Kubelík's apartment was the centre where everyone gathered and where Yehudi met David Oistrakh again, playing chamber music with him and Jacques Février, the French pianist, or with Hephzibah and many other musicians, of whom in that wonderful city there was a plethora of choice. They would play till the small hours, sight-reading Martinů or

Spohr and there it was that Yehudi and Oistrakh first went through the Bach Double Concerto which they were to play in so many cities together from then on. Although the structure of much of this extraordinary spell must have been pre-arranged there was an enchantingly improvised quality about that tour.

No sooner had we spent three packed days in Prague than we took the train to Budapest. It was only late May but the journey was hot and dusty and Budapest bore all the marks of the long weeks of battle it had gone through. The beautiful Elizabeth Bridge lay in the Danube, a tangle of torn metal and twisted wrought iron, curiously supine like some lovely, half-drowned creature neither defunct nor rescued. All the buildings alongside the river were pock-marked with shell and bullet holes as though a plague had swept the city leaving its face scarred for ever. But despite the evidence of a battle far worse than Prague had suffered, the lively spirit of the Hungarians was everywhere to see, to hear and to marvel over, from the German-speaking taxi driver who yelled imprecations over the Russian 'Liberation', to the manager of our little suite, the paucity of good food, the Soviet straitjacket which was slowly and inexorably closing round them, restricting their own ability to recover. 'Why didn't the Allies liberate us?' was the cry. 'Why did you leave it to the Soviets?' Unanswerable, now that the meeting at Yalta had come and gone with irreversible decisions. How could I explain as an Englishwoman that Churchill had been overridden by Roosevelt and Stalin?

Workmen sat on the piles of rubble they were clearing away, eating huge hunks of bread and sausage and swigging at wine and beer. Somehow there was always food produced in that magical Magyar way that heeds no laws, obeys no edicts but simply manages to get what it wants. There was no moaning, only irritated anger, and an extraordinary recklessness disregarding the risk of the dangers inherent in airing their antagonisms and their opinions of the regime. It had been quite different in Prague, where anyway there had always been a sympathy towards communism and its ideology. Here there was revulsion and impatience; small wonder that when Yehudi and Hephzibah gave their recital they were mobbed both trying to get into the hall and leaving it.

Yehudi gave the first press conference to be allowed a foreign visitor in a crammed and seedy room in the hotel. A half-hearted attempt was being made to restore some of the worst damage to the outside of the building; from the scaffolding workmen hung in through the windows to look at Yehudi as though he were some phenomenon. He spoke in German and English, occasionally a reporter would translate into Hungarian. They were elated, it seemed, at the news that there was some small liberty they were to be offered to sweeten the sourness of the grid of laws imposed by the new regime, a tiny loosening of a knot in an all-important skein of petty rules. Did Yehudi not agree that this was a useful sign, something to be grateful for. 'Nonsense,' said Yehudi. 'Never forget you were all born free. It is not within their power to tender to you what is already and irredeemably your birthright. No gratitude is necessary, simply acknowledgment that they do seem to recognise that you are human beings and what you expect.' Roars of delight from the scaffolding after this had been translated. Typically, the Hungarian papers printed the whole interview including this declaration.

Old Gundel, the great restaurateur, was still alive and gave the most extraordinary banquet I had ever seen, worthy of pre-war days, at his garden restaurant. Goodness alone knows where it all came from. I remember a particularly delicious giant brioche filled with sweetbreads and herbs and the delight of the old man as he hugged Yehudi with tears in his eyes. This inimitable Hungarian gift of making the most of the moment was intoxicating and reminded me of the similar approach to life of the Russians. And there was the all-night music-making, the *musizieren* that is the enviable way of life of the musicians of Central Europe, of which my mother had so many tales to tell. There would always be someone with money and an apartment who would throw open their doors, supply food, welcome a flood of players till, utterly fulfilled, they would release their exhausted hosts in the small hours and crawl off to their various homes.

It was the breath of life to Yehudi, who had always been a marvellous sight-reader: both the companionship, the high level of musicianship and the fact of making music for the sheer joy of it fed him, reinforced that core of his whole being to which music was essential and from which his career relentlessly drained so much.

Sadly, the crammed five days came to an end. We drove to the station to find half the town there bearing cardboard boxes full of the most Parisian of *petit fours* and tiny *pâtisseries* from the historic Gerbeaud. Lindsay absent-mindedly took snapshots of a group of Russian soldiers and had his camera summarily snatched and unloaded. There was a moment's discomfort and then the hiatus filled up with the ebullience of the crowd; we climbed into the carriage, clutching our pastry cartons, I carrying an enormous silver bowl engraved with Yehudi's name and multiple parcels of Hungarian embroidery. There was nothing in the shops to buy except for some books and a few antiques, probably pawned in exchange for food, but the bright faces above the shabby clothes, the appreciation that flowed from them like a warm current, made me suddenly ashamed of complaining of my lot and doubly so as the train moved off so easily into the freedom we took for granted.

Prague seemed very self-contained, almost prissy in its cool demeanour, after the Hungarian experience. We had lunch with David and Tamara Oistrakh and were joined by Shostakovich and his wife. Having met the composer in Russia, Yehudi had warned me of his reticence and shyness. William Walton and Alice Wimborne, who happened to be in Prague, joined us and we all went in a bunch to the concert that late afternoon in which David and Shostakovich and other musicians gave a whole programme of Shostakovich's works: a quintet, a piano and violin sonata and a piano trio as far as I remember – a music all rather understated, I found, wandering and shapeless as though the composer were uncertain of what he wanted to say – or maybe unsure of what Josef Stalin and Zhdanov wanted to hear? Afterwards there was yet another long and lovely evening's *musizieren* at the Kubelíks' till the small hours, and the following day a concert with orchestra at which, among other works, Yehudi and David played the Bach Double Concerto for two violins for the first time in public, conducted by Rafael Kubelík. It was a glorious concert after which Jan Masaryk, the foreign minister, gave us a late dinner talking, with all his brilliance and experience, at length and very apprehensively about the political situation. Neither quality would stand him in good stead, alas. Not long after, he 'fell' out of a high window of that great castle that was the seat of Government. His 'suicide', gravely deplored, removed a man carrying a great name and awkwardly a great part of the independent Czechoslovakia no longer of use to the new regime.

Amsterdam and the Bartók concerto with van Beinum finished the tour and we all returned to London. I, still homeless, to stay with Mama, the Nicholas family to return to Australia.

It was June 1947. I was more than ever uncertain of my situation. The very fact that I had been able to share such extraordinary experiences with them all had not helped solve my personal problem, rather exacerbated it. That dreary code in which I had been conditioned, which insisted upon rewards being earned, happiness only justified by honest investment of labour, tributes to be accepted only by the most spotless of hands, inhibiting spontaneity, spoiling ecstasy, dragging me down from every flight on which I had started with such *envolure*, that leaden code was again foremost, admonishing me for having enjoyed something to which I had no actual right; the problem was no nearer solution than when I had accepted Lindsay's and Hephzibah's and Aunt Edie's arguments and prolonged my stay with them all.

Now there could be no further dallying. I saw how much restored Yehudi was in himself and in his playing; how he had emerged from that limbo in which I had first heard him two infinite years ago, the limbo I had already detected long before I got to know him when he had come to London to play for us – it seemed to me in an almost somnambulistic way. All that dislocation in him had nearly dissolved. However, I had not detected any sign of his being able to find a way out of the *status quo* insofar as our relationship was concerned, nor did I ever raise the question to him. His nature was not equipped to fight for himself; he had been told by his wife in no uncertain terms where his duty lay. It was not for him to decide. That much had been made abundantly clear to him that day in May 1946 when he had thought only to delay his return to me by one day.

Yehudi rang me. Before Lindsay and Hephzibah's departure it appeared that Lindsay and he had again approached Nola, begging her to tidy up a ridiculously untidy situation. She had, it seemed, drawn up new divorce papers more advantageous to herself than the earlier ones Lindsay had, unknown to me, tried to persuade her to accept, but she had made no further move. She had given as an excuse this time that she could not leave the children for the six weeks necessary to obtain a divorce in Florida, where it could be got with descretion. Yehudi had promptly suggested sending them both over to him in the summer and quite extraordinarily she had accepted. Krov and Zamira would arrive in Paris on 13 June. Yehudi was convinced I would look after them. Typically he had not asked me.

I was caught on the horns of a dilemma: had Yehudi come pleading to me to undertake this really onerous job for him I might have demurred, but his absolute certainty that I would accept it added to his obvious trust in my managing to bring it off made it, to my mind, impossible to refuse. It might look like pettiness or retaliation. Again there was to be an extension of this unsettling relationship; I felt added bewilderment as I tried to analyse Yehudi's actions and reactions *vis-à-vis* my own illicit position and my growing fear of imposture.

18

The Core
Had Remained Constant

June 1947. Paris. A concert ahead with Enesco, and Yehudi and
I awaited the children's arrival. The day had started inauspi-
ciously when he had taken me out to lunch at Prunier's, near the
hotel. With his customary zest for food so long as it is in
accordance with the law of the Medes and Persians (in Yehudi-speak
organically sound and exquisitely cooked) Yehudi had ordered and
eaten a dozen oysters, three quarters of a large St Pierre fish, a
voluminous salad and a selection of cheeses, mostly goat and definitely
vociferous, finishing off with one of those terrible tisanes concocted of
very smelly hay with a tinge of the kind of roots only eaten by desperate
animals on bare mountains (or so it seems to me) and which he swears
by as an unequalled digestive. As he has an interior system that would
make an ostrich's appear dyspeptic, it was useless to argue that particular
point. Came the bill, large, being Prunier's and taking into account the
heartiness of the meal; came also the fumbling in every pocket in search
of the non-existent money, with which I was to become familiar and
learn to pre-empt.

Finally, with an airy gesture he asked the waiter, whose face had
assumed that polished contempt special to the French, for a pencil.
'*Pourquoi, Monsieur?*' '*Pour signer l'addition,*' said Yehudi blithely. With a
curl of his lip the waiter informed Yehudi that the idea was both mad
and unacceptable. Irritated by now, for he always expects others to trust

him in the same way he trusts all and everyone, Yehudi suggested that the bill be taken to the Hotel Raphael in the next street, where he was staying, and the concierge, Yehudi's paternal banker in every city, would pay it at once. And what name should be given, even were he to do anything so absurd (*saugrenu*)? As Yehudi always hates giving his name and mumbles something that sounds like 'Mumbrumbrroin', I felt it was my turn to intervene, even though my share of the lunch had been one quarter of the fish, about the same of the salad, a corner of the least noisy of the cheeses and no oysters (I always think the repulsive and overvalued things look as though they have already been eaten), and in ringing tones said 'Yehudi Menuhin'. This declaration only served to raise the sarcasm of the waiter to unscalable heights. '*Et moi*', he suggested, '*mois, je suis Jésu Christ.*' I looked at Yehudi's crumpled suit and had to give the disagreeable waiter a point or two. Reluctantly I fished in my bag. Our lack of perfect grooming was due to our having just flown overnight from New York where Yehudi and Hep, after a television interview, had been presented with two beautiful pens inscribed with their names. I found Yehudi's and, as languidly as possible, offered it to the waiter. He looked at me acidly, peered closely at Yehudi for the first time (at Prunier's they don't look, only serve condescendingly and with distaste), recognised him, muttered an apology and handed him the bill to be signed. I longed for Yehudi to withhold a tip, but that is not, alas, his style. We got up. '*Eh bien,*' I said, '*on aurait pu la voler, la plume, non?*' and swept out as the waiter's jaw dropped at the suspicion I had aroused that we could have stolen the pen and Yehudi was but a look-alike.

The children arrived safely. I spent the next few days overhauling their clothes, taking them to the doctor and dentist and to hear their father play the Bach Double Violin Concerto with his beloved Enesco, as well as the Beethoven and Bartók concerti in a marathon of a concert with the Orchestre Colonne. Zamira, intensely musical, loved it, but Krov flew into a paroxysm of irritation kicking the box with frustration till I sent him home at the interval.

Yehudi's agent had found us a car which, so he triumphantly

declared, was a paragon of its kind; a white convertible with plenty of room for the four of us plus baggage, a vehicle fit to take us down to the Côte d'Azur, to the pine forests stretching down to the sea, where Yehudi had rented a converted farmhouse belonging to a friend.

We set off for Lyon in high spirits on the road to Sens, where we had a marvellous lunch of snails and other delicacies while waiting to have a puncture mended – admittedly a slight nuisance but the cathedral was beautiful, the food delicious and our spirits undisturbed. We picked up the car from the garage and sped on to Saulieu to fill up. There the self-starter, after a few whines and a series of gurgles, died. We left the car at the garage to be repaired and ourselves repaired to the nearby hotel renowned for its restaurant. Having ordered dinner I looked around. So short a time after the end of the war, France had few tourists and was swarming with the remains of the Resistance which had been composed of as many insalubrious characters as of heroes. The dining-room was deserted except for a handsome American officer and his ravishing girlfriend at a nearby table. The children demanded their evening serial, an interminable and dramatic story which I had invented to keep them happy at supper time. For some peculiar reason known only to my subconscious, the hero and heroine were called Jerry and Hepatica. My recital, unbeknown to me, was going to reap us a great benefit.

While I kept the children engaged, Yehudi was engrossed with his exquisite *foie gras* and awaiting his next dish with happy anticipation. My choice was as prudent as it was unimaginative and did not intrude much on my story-telling: soup and grilled sole. Once again Yehudi paid the bill, we traipsed across to the garage, collected Dégé (named after my initials), paid an astronomical ransom and set off at a fair pace towards Lyon, already a good few hours behind schedule. The landscape became more and more empty, twilight was spreading long, melancholy shadows across the road, the last sign of habitation had been some miles back – an enormous abandoned *château* coquettishly to the right followed by a glissade to the left – and, as Yehudi struggled to bring the car to a halt, she emitted a loud, rude hiss, subsiding to port. I leapt out; Yehudi followed. This time it was a back tyre that was flat, lying obscenely and wrinkled on the macadam. As the car had been designed around 1938 by a pretentious madman, all four wheels were covered right over with heavy metal eyelids like some old tart.

We dug the jack out from beneath the multiple suitcases, heaved up the wheel, shoved it under one of those irremovable covers and Y, good-tempered as ever, had started pumping away valiantly when there was a kind of low-pitched vindictive growl and the whole jack disappeared for ever beneath that voluptuous eyelid, sunk deep into the tar softened by the long summer heat.

A chill breeze blew while the night fell faster than I have ever experienced before or since. After twenty endless minutes a car passed. Ignoring our wildly waving arms, it accelerated and fled past us, as though we were lepers. Half an hour later, chilled to the bone, we saw the headlights of a large American car and again semaphored desperately. To our joy it slowed down and out got the handsome American officer. 'Hi, there,' he called, 'what's up?' One look at Dégé gave him the answer. 'Now look here,' he said, 'I was fascinated by your story at dinner. I didn't miss a word. Trouble is I'm not allowed to take anyone, military orders' (his eyes shifted towards his *petite amie* and I nodded solemnly), 'but after that story I can't leave you all here. I'll take you and the kids as far as Chalon-sur-Saône and I guess you'll find a car there.' We abandoned poor dear Yehudi guarding the luggage, I grabbed the violin case, hugged him and we jumped into the car. An hour and seventy kilometres later we reached Chalon. It was only nine-thirty, but the whole small town snored. Provincial France was abed. I begged the kind American colonel to drop us at the police station and we waved him goodbye as he shot off.

I went tentatively into the main room of the police station with Zamira, Krov and the violin case. It was straight out of *Tin-Tin*. Three very young blond cops, still wet behind the ears, stared at us. I explained our grim situation. 'Madame,' said the eldest (at least twenty-three), 'you will never find a car to take you out on a dark night like this, the whole region is alive with bandits!' Suddenly I had a ghastly vision of Yehudi alone with that horrible car and his throat cut from ear to ear. 'I beg of you, please at least try and ring one or two garages and see if you can find out what they can do to help.'

New misfortune: the telephone operator had already joined the chorus of snorers. There followed a proper pantomime of crossed wires and misplaced sockets which under any other circumstances would have made us howl with laughter. Finally they managed no longer to connect with the local loony-bin or the kitchens of the Hôtel de Paris at Monte Carlo and succeeded in getting one of the garages in the vicinity. 'What kind of bloody fool do you take me for?' was the succinct reply and the proprietor hung up.

We were all chums by now and desperate. Then one of the policemen cried out: 'What about trying that *Pied Noir*, that Algerian? He might just risk it.' And indeed, ten minutes later the man arrived in a car at least more viable and trustworthy than miserable Dégé. Casting an eye on the case containing Yehudi's Stradivarius and his Guarnerius, I made a quick decision and said: 'If I leave this case with you all meanwhile, would you take the greatest care of it? It contains two irreplaceable violins of great value.' The three blond heads bent over the case and read the label under the handle with curiosity. '*Mon Dieu,*' they cried in unison, '*c'est Yehudi Menuhin!*' Three cheers for French culture that three country policemen in a small town long before the advent of television knew exactly who the bearer of this strange name was . . . 'Quick, Madame, get into the taxi at once.'

'Children,' said I, 'will you stay here or will you come with me?' Splendidly, they both said in canon, 'Of course we'll come with you.'

Putting them in the back of the car, I jumped in beside the driver, a nice, responsible-looking fellow in his thirties with a headful of black curly hair like astrakhan – but what was this metallic object under my right buttock? Before I could cry out he slipped in the clutch and we were off at a cracking pace. Without a word he passed his hand under mine and closed it over the revolver on which I was unhappily sitting while visions of rape at pistol point and those two poor children kidnapped passed through my head. Adding menace to black comedy he muttered: 'Not a word in front of the cops.' As we accelerated he explained that he had no right to carry arms but that his best friend, also a taxi driver, had been attacked by a gang of thugs and murdered only two days before. I breathed more freely, promising not to say a word, suggested to the children that they try to sleep a bit and we plunged on through the murky night, I trying my best to indicate where roughly I thought we should find Yehudi (please dear God) at the roadside. The driver was sceptical. I felt sick with worry, praying that the children's French was not up to understanding his Cassandra-like prognostications delivered in a thick Algerian accent.

After more than an interminable hour we crested a hill and began to descend on the far side. Thank God, there was dear Yehudi standing just ahead of us in the glare of our headlights, bang in the middle of the road, hands on hips, obviously expecting a horrible fate and trying to give the impression that he was a cross between this year's prize-winning heavyweight and Tarzan. We yelled, 'Yehudi, Daddy, it's only us,' and flung ourselves on him.

As for dismal Dégé we were ready to abandon her, lop-sided and leering old whore that she was, with little or no compunction. However, our good driver managed skilfully to change the wheel and we all returned at top speed in tandem to the police station where Yehudi received a royal reception from my police pals. We rang poor distracted Pierre Bertaux – who insisted that he must send his own car to ensure no further transport dramas – thanked and rewarded our brave Algerian and finally, after what seemed an eternity, clambered into Pierre's very grand Delahaye, thanked heartily our fond policemen, and with old Dégé driven by a man of Pierre's at last arrived at the Lyon *préfecture*, dirty and crumpled and exhausted at four o'clock in the morning.

Two days later (somewhat cleaner and refreshed by the company and conversation of the brilliant Pierre (incidentally now the youngest mayor in France), we entrusted ourselves once again to Dégé who, contrite, got us quite demurely down to Aix-en-Provence and finally to the Mediterranean coast at Sainte-Maxime on the following morning. There we got thoroughly lost trying to find our farmhouse, wandering amongst a tangle of scented pine trees for nearly two hours, until at last sliding perilously down a track we came upon it sitting solidly in a quiet clearing. And quite firmly locked.

Inured to disaster by now, we resignedly unpacked the car, dumped our cases, raincoats, violins, books, straw hats, toys, scarves, nougat (from Montélimar on the way) by the back door, deciding we were famished and would try to find something to eat at St Tropez. Lo and behold, a stalwart figure of uncertain age and sex, black hair and eyes, walnut skin, dressed in old blue trousers and shirt and battered straw hat that looked as though it had been stolen from a donkey, came panting up the road, apologising and announced herself as Madeleine, hauling a nice young boy with her whom she introduced as Jean–Marie. The house she proceeded to open up proved delightful, we dumped our luggage and apportioned the rooms, by which time Madeleine had got lunch ready.

Too excited to nap we drove down the barely cleared track, rutted with winter rains and veined with the roots of oak and pine trees, to shop for stores at St Tropez. Needless to say, Dégé's tender organs were ruptured by the time we reached the main road. She limped into a garage to which, had we known it, she was about to make as many visits in the ensuing weeks as a hypochondriac to a clinic. We shopped, picked up old Dégé whose current complaint had been dealt with to his satisfaction, said the *garagiste* (we never managed to decide whether he treated one symptom and contrived skilfully to engender another to ensure her return within a few days) and got back safely to what proved to be a perfect haven.

We swam, walked, slept, helped put out forest fires, explored little deserted bays all strung along that lovely part of the coast, bays still entangled with the barbed wire of the military defences, avoiding those with warnings of mines, mostly choosing one particularly beautiful beach where a big white villa stood battered and empty, cloaked with a cascade of purple bougainvillaea. No one but us – free to spend all day royally in command of those exquisite white sands, warm blue water

313

and perfect skies. That Dégé would fairly regularly throw a fit on the way back and start making weird braying sounds was the only shadow in that whole sunny month. We simply got her to her doctor, the *garagiste*, or if she lay in epilepsy by the roadside, trudged back to him and telling him to collect her, clambered through the forest to the farm, a delicious dinner and bed.

After four and a half weeks, Yehudi, ever the optimist, declared Dégé perfectly fit to take us on our next venture; following Hannibal's route up the Rhône valley to Montana in Switzerland. By now it was getting too hot in the Midi, suffocating nights, the air thick as lentil soup just off the stove and with huge *bouderagues*, flying beetles, crashing through the open windows and meeting one head-on at terrifying speed.

With great regret we left dear old Madeleine, who armed us with a couple of bottles of red wine, which took the lining off one's throat, from her own vineyards and set out early in the cool of the morning for Nice, where we toasted our coming campaign, if I remember correctly, at the Negresco with a very strange combination of toast and cheese and champagne, starting off along this glorious valley with its twists and turns, its narrower slopes covered with trees, occasionally opening up to fields and crops and late summer flowers. We bought honey and cheese and sausage and ate by the wayside, spending the first night in a primitive but clean little hotel. Up early next morning to climb higher all day through pass after pass while the trees changed from deciduous to evergreens and grew even sparser; past smashed and ruined towns, witnesses of the recent war, we lunched sitting on the last threadbare patches of grass, revelling in the pellucid light and thin, pure air, with that wonderful feeling of being on the very summit of the world and ready like a bird to take flight.

Finally we coasted down to Val d'Isère to a very pleasant small hotel where we made the gross error of putting Dégé in the tiny garage. Up at five-thirty the next morning and ready to go, Yehudi discovered that Dégé was in one of her sulks and refused totally to be driven out of the garage which we had not been observant enough to notice had a damp earth floor and a wooden rim at the base of the doorway. Dégé had spent a comfortable night with her old rump embedded in the warm soil. Yehudi revved and revved until she smoked with resentment; there was no way of persuading her to make the small leap that would entice her from her nest. After two hours and with helping hands we got away, gliding gracefully all the way downhill to Chamonix where, with a sigh, we took Dégé to the nearest garage for yet another check-up and ourselves went up the glacier and put her out of our minds, cavorting about in that marvellous combination of hot sun and freezing air and snow.

It was the fourth day. Up early again and over the frontier to Switzerland, climbing up the vertiginous Col du Fauclas holding our breath collectively, and saying every prayer in the canon, sighing with premature relief when we made the top of the pass and began coasting down to the now broad and beautiful Rhône, lying shining like pewter in the wide valley below. As though sensing our relief Dégé, vindictive and selfish as ever, began knocking in a curious way as though she had acquired a pair of badly handled castanets somewhere in her innards. By common consent we none of us said a word. One look at Yehudi's set jaw was enough to convince us that it would be politer not to question the origin of this odd percussion. However, by the time we had reached Martingny on the valley floor, Dégé, possibly enraged by our attempt to ignore her, changed her tune and started the most heinous noise imaginable, a sort of passacaglia of wild rattle overlaid with a shriek. In order to accomplish this aria she slowed down to fifteen miles an hour.

It was more than Zamira, Krov and I could stand and we yelled with laughter. The sight of Yehudi hanging on to the steering wheel with set face and dignified air driving this demented old hag shrieking through the town at a stately pace, trying to ignore the gaping people on either side, was such pure farce that I felt all that was missing was sawdust underfoot and the Big Top above.

Wearily we got her, screaming and rattling all the way, to a garage where the owner diagnosed Dègè's hysteria. She had burst her oil pump and must of course be left in his charge. We hired a taxi, put in our luggage and its accumulations and drove up the mountains, where an hour later we reached a tiny chalet, beautifully placed at the edge of a forest, isolated from the village of Montana below and with one of those Swiss views across to the Matterhorn that looks so like a postcard you long to put a postage stamp on it. It had been hired for us by a Swiss girl who had served as secretary to Yehudi on and off and who must have thought it would do us good to rough it. There were four tiny rooms, no bath, no shower and only cold running water in basins in two of the rooms. The longing for a hot bath was never so heartfelt. We did have, incongruously, the couple Yehudi had had at the Villa Karma: Edouard the butler and Clara the cook. I would willingly have disposed of them both for a little running water and one tub. . . .

Clara boiled kettles of water and I filled the children's basin, standing the poor mites on a chair and sponging them down; Miras, through chattering teeth: 'I wish some of my friends in America could see this and realise how lucky they all are!'

I gave them an extra-long serial story at supper that night.

Yehudi was gone the next morning with the dawn, down to Salzburg to play the Brahms with Furtwängler conducting, happy as a lark at the wonderful prospect. I longed to go, but of course could not. Determined to compensate for the upholstered hut in which we found ourselves, I crawled out, hitting my head on the lintel, and walked towards the woods hoping to get a perspective of its surroundings. Behind the chalet a long grassy field sloped down to a belt of trees, not a house to be seen. Good. On the left was the country road bordered by shrubs overlooking the Rhône valley with its backdrop of mountains, back of me was the forest. It was indeed a covetable position, isolated, peaceful and with only bird-song and the rustle of leaves to be heard. If only the spartan Vaudois had felt that beauty is even more appreciable with the possessions of a minimum of comfort. Shuddering, I shied at the prospect of a wet day, huddled inside, with the mountains obscured by a curtain of rain busily rattling on the shingled roof, of myself dragging the wretched children out to slosh their reluctant way through the dripping forest and to return, longing for a cosy room, a log fire and a hot bath. There was no way of improving the Hut, no fireplace, no bathroom and the living-room was a shoe box – and that for size four-and-a-half slippers. And we would likely be here for a good six weeks. One must pray for good weather, buy more books and games. I would ask Yehudi for one of those exquisitely designed small Swiss sewing machines and run up the cotton dresses and overalls Zamira needed and would start each day with a French lesson, out of doors hopefully, for the risk of being stung by a wasp was to my mind far less of a hazard and a hindrance than the dismal claustrophobia of the dull brown planks that constituted the walls. We would picnic as much as possible, taking long walks through the woods to eat our hard-boiled eggs, carrot sticks, sandwiches and fruit on one of those rocks with which Swiss woods abound. By now there might be wild raspberries and tiny strawberries, and later blackberries and mushrooms. That would still leave plenty of time for Yehudi to practise, for supper and the serial story. I got so carried away with my extrapolations that I failed to hear a wail from the children, calling woebegone and at a loose end after that glorious month of sun and sea and sand and the beautiful comfortable farmhouse.

Disobeying all Yehudi's dietary strictures, I took them down to Montana half a kilometre below to explore its amenities and eat *pains au chocolat* and *mille-feuilles*. Much restored we climbed back to the frugal Hut, our appetites ruined for lunch but our spirits restored. We soon fell into a happy enough pattern and, blessed by almost perfect weather, my optimistic scheme was by and large achieved. Yehudi came and went, going down to Lucerne to play the Beethoven with Furtwängler and to record it afterwards. Again my longing heart went with him.

In between, the Archetypal Optimist would plan splendid adventures, driving us down to the Rhône and all the way up that magnificent valley to Andermatt perched at around 2000 metres in its narrow pass as an eagle might alight on a peak and survey the whole wild scene unrolled below. The children were very excited by the glacier although it was not looking its best, covered with summer detritus and needing a good wash.

So far, Dégé had behaved like the lady she was not, but the effort was evidently too great to maintain. In the precipitous descent her clutch broke and while Yehudi shot her into bottom gear it was left for me to hold on to the gear lever, clinging for dear life when it jerked out of the '*couronne*' every so often and tugging it back into place desperately. It was hours before we arrived in Sierre, my arms and shoulders ached so much that I had not the strength left to smack the old thing as we crawled into the garage and yet again found a taxi to take us up the mountain and home.

When Yehudi returned from Lucerne and Dégé from hospital, nothing daunted he proposed driving up to St Luc just below the Matterhorn. I, sick of playing Cassandra to his Polyanna, joined in the general joy.

We had not yet explored the opposite side of the valley although we gazed at it every day. Off we went, all four of us, in beautiful weather, Dégé proudly showing off the total success of her last operation, and climbed up to St Luc getting out to inspect the tiny hamlets with their mushroom-like chalets, their stilt-like bases clinging on to ledges all the way up. The sun was sliding behind the mountain when we reluctantly clambered into Dégé for the descent. Like any cross creature who has been kept waiting too long, Dégé was evidently determined to pay us back. Half-way down, the gear lever stuck sullenly and adamantly; Dégé was sticking out her tongue. Nothing would budge her. Yehudi drove her close up against the rockface to prevent her sliding us further and with hideous result into the ravine on the farther side; we got out, braced ourselves against her and waited submissively.

It was almost dark and we were huddled together against the growing cold when the last Post-bus came down from Zermatt, took pity on the four waifs and rescued us. Arrived at Sierre, this time we walked along to the garage without the Invalid Phenomenon, dolefully arranged for her to be fetched from her bed on the bare mountain and ordered yet another taxi. The children were as ever sporting and equable. Poor Yehudi was trying so hard to hitch up the drooping skirts of his chronic optimism that out of compassion and kindness we heaped all the blame on Dégé, who by now had assumed an identity purely separate and sovereign, a kind of *monstre sacré*, demanding obeisance and sacrifice.

The mountain holiday was drawing to a close. Thanks to the blessing of good weather it had been a happy and harmonious time, despite the rigours of the Hut into which hardly anyone extra could fit for so much as a cup of tea. Fortunately the Hindemiths were both small (although as solidly round as pouter pigeons) and had fitted in reasonably neatly at luncheon, Yehudi and Paul taking themselves off for a walk afterwards, while Mrs H, commandeering the jigsaw puzzle, drove Miras and Krov and me to distraction arrogating to herself the right to push and shove utterly unlikely pieces into the wrong places while the children and I kicked each other under the table. Otherwise it cannot be said that the Hut resounded to the cheer of gay chatter nor the clinking of champagne glasses: beer – and that in smallish glasses – and a very proscribed social life had been its Calvinist style. But the children's cheeks were rosy, the muscles of their legs stalwart, their French much advanced and their lungs filled with fresh air. Miras looked adorable in the little pinafores and skirts and night-dresses I had made and Krov's nervous energy had been canalised so that he was now a lively, spontaneous, bright small boy.

Early one perfect morning Edouard piled the big luggage on to a horse-dray and sent it down to the valley; we bade fond farewells to him and Clara who had done much to redeem life in the Hut, packed Dégé with the smaller cases and, waving goodbye with a mixture of affection and relief, prepared to drive down to Sierre. We had spent six and a half weeks up there – good, fruitful if frugal weeks – and now the children would be taken back to their mother in New York – and I? I felt as though I had been put to some kind of test – not a deliberately planned one, but as so often in these last attenuated seventeen months I had had to acquiesce in a way of living improvised and insubstantial in which every situation arose from chance circumstance, the way seeds blown by a wayward wind will implant themselves in a rock face, sprouting a few flowers.

With these thoughts in my head and the sun rising gloriously over the extravagant mountains we drove for the last time down to Sierre. The air was pure and still so warm that I wound down the window – more exactly, I tried to wind down the window – but Dégé rebuffed me. So we drove her to her home-from-home, the garage, and had the handle fixed, waving goodbye to her 'doctor' as we took the road trustingly on to Lausanne. However, Dégé had other plans and came to a stubborn halt a few feet away; the gear was jammed. After a long hour in which the *garagiste* explored the old prostitute from every angle, crawling underneath her, sticking his head deep into her bonnet, jiggling and juggling around on the front seat, he triumphantly called out to us (walking up and down the road) that all was well and *en état de marche*.

We inserted ourselves once more between the boxes and cases, shot off down the road singing . . . and came to a dead halt. True to the end Dégé, in typical French fashion, had revolted . . . And so had we. At last even Yehudi, who had shown her so much patience and faith, had had enough. The children and I in a chorus of fury begged him to discard the charade, relinquish the belief that Dégé was anything other than an ancient monument in an advanced stage of vehicular syphilis and must once and for all be abandoned. We telephoned a good friend, Monsieur Burger, who piled all our paraphernalia into his car and drove us at a tremendous pace to Lausanne where we scrambled into the train by the skin of our teeth, stacking our myriad boxes and bags on to the racks.

Sadly I ceded my beautiful big white Paris hat as too impractical to manage amongst the welter, calling out to M. Burger who standing on the platform still held it in his hand to give it to his wife . . . Dégé had had the last word.

A few days after, the children returned to their mother. We had had a very close and happy three and a half months together and become very used to each other, sharing so many different experiences, from their

father's concerts and rehearsals to the sunshine and sea of the farmhouse
on the Côte d'Azur; to the tiny cold-water chalet on the edge of the
forest overlooking the Rhône valley. They had seen more of their
father for longer than they would ever be likely to see him again in their
lives; suffered the total unreliability of Dégé with sporting good
humour; walked the wood picking flowers, finding mushrooms;
submitted to their French lessons with grace; avidly followed their
supper serial without which they refused to go to bed. I saw them off
feeling both sadness and loss. They had bound me once again closer to
Yehudi, whom I had been convinced I had lost for ever, and by the
same token had left me all the more adrift and anchorless. For fifteen
weeks I had been able to forget anything other than the joyful necessity
of looking after all three of them: to jettison all the nagging torments of
my own position, expunge all the self-inflicted calumny that had
plagued me so ceaselessly and there, in the blessed anonymity of La
Berle and the Montana chalet, create and dwell in a small and happy
world *à quatre*.

However tenuous was the base on which this tiny paradise had
rested, at the very back of my mind there lurked an unbidden feeling
that there had been a shift somewhere in the direction of my life. Not
daring to analyse it, in case it were just another illusion born of the past
months' harmony, I went with Yehudi to Berlin feeling that if this were
to be the final period we could share together it was of such intrinsic,
almost historic importance in his career that I could allow myself to be
part of it and share it with him.

On 27 September 1947 we were put on the special first KLM flight to
go to Berlin since the war. Landing at Tempelhof airport in the early
afternoon we were met by the American Military Branch in charge of
Entertainments and driven through a city that to me, used though I was
to the bombed streets of London, looked like a lunar landscape. By
now the rubble of demolished buildings had been cleared on either
side, making a grim causeway through canyons edged with the jagged
profiles of those few houses that still retained one or two storeys. Going

down these streets was as though in some nightmare one was passing through a cemetery after an earthquake. It was so horrifying that it suspended imagination and feeling in a kind of paralysis of disbelief.

Shunting away towards the suburb of Dahlem where the devastation had left an untouched area of villas, we were unloaded without further ceremony at the Titania Palast, an old cinema which did duty as the only concert hall left in the whole city, where the rehearsal of the Berlin Philharmonic had already begun with Furtwängler conducting. Yehudi had a little time to warm his fingers and then go through the Beethoven concerto which he had recently played with them and recorded in Lucerne about four weeks before. We dined afterwards in the villa reserved for visitors with the US Musical Association, joined by the remarkable Romanian conductor Sergiu Celibidache who had somehow miraculously held the Berlin Philharmonic Orchestra together throughout the war after Furtwängler's flight, and with whom Yehudi had played the previous year.

The following morning was Yehudi's first concert in Berlin with Furtwängler. That performance was earmarked for British and American soldiers and administration who made a wonderful audience. It must also have been the first time we met the US Ambassador, Robert Murphy, who had invited us to lunch. He turned out to be a man of such warmth and courtesy, humour and bright intelligence that it was impossible not to fall in love with him after the first five minutes.

There was a crowded press lunch chaired by Stuckenschmidt, the leading music critic, a meeting at which the dilemma created by the presence of Yehudi crystallised. He was the symbol of so many disparate factors: the great musician who because of his Jewishness had not returned to Germany since his adolescence; the man who, American by birth, typified the opponents; who for himself had seen the horrors and reality of Belsen; and finally the human being who despite all this had chosen to come to Germany to try and heal the rift the Nazi aberration had torn across the whole fabric of German culture.

Yehudi's entire perception of mankind's significance in the world, his *Weltanschauung*, had been an indivisible one: man as soul and body, an organic whole in tune with Nature and Time, the Platonic conception of man as artist, the highest expression of his being within whatever circumstances he finds himself. He himself fortunate, born with his great gift, equipped to translate this personal philosophy as best he can, has always done so, whatever the cost to him in terms of misunderstanding, criticism, wilful mischief and actual danger in the pursuance of his career. It has been a long and running battle in which he has had to defend his terrain again and again whenever he has felt challenged into action. There have been many fronts, political, social, professional, in all of which he has fought without belligerence but with a steadfast courage that is stronger and more effective. The extraordinary trust in which he is universally held stems, to my mind, from the total lack of the pharisaical in him, recognised instinctively by everyone.

The press conference proved a catharsis to many of the German reporters, who must have brought much apprehension to this meeting. Yehudi's frankness and humaneness gave them an opportunity to express the inexpressible, to divulge shame without hypocrisy, gratitude without cringing and the hope that Germany would be allowed to restore her own shattered dignity irrespective of the condemnation she had earned and with some of the desperately needed compassion which Yehudi was offering.

The next day, 20 September, was a concert which will remain enshrined in my memory for many reasons. Not solely because Yehudi and Furtwängler's interpretation of the Beethoven Violin Concerto is the most perfect meeting of two minds over the most beautifully expressive work ever written for the violin, but also because the presence in the orchestra of many players who had taken part when Yehudi had played as a boy added to the intensity and quality of the performance; but above all because this audience was a German one, composed of people defeated and in a destroyed city, to whom music must have stood as the one unblemished thing amongst the ruin of their lives. The packed, silent audience was like an identity with but one mind, one heart. I held my breath as the music unfurled, seamless, pure, serene, carrying its healing message through Yehudi's voice.

At the end there were several seconds' total silence. Then the applause broke out in a great well of sound and continued right through the twenty-minute interval till Furtwängler returned alone and raising his baton began the opening bars of the Fifth Symphony of Beethoven.

From morning till night for two days Yehudi played for every possible cause: the Jüdische Gemeinde, the Hochschule für Musik, hospitals, children's homes and, one morning, at a large cinema for the inmates of a Displaced Persons Camp. These sad places were a kind of catch-all wherein were herded all those people whose lives had been torn from their moorings by the war; mainly Jewish but also gypsies, Asiatics, all those who had somehow survived elimination as unworthy of the *Herrenvolk* and for whom some kind of future had soon to be found.

We were met at the stage door by a large benevolent-looking American-Jewish officer in captain's uniform. He took me aside and with great embarrassment confessed that there were about fourteen people out front. 'Why?' said I. 'Well, you see, we've had a man in the camp for the past week who's been stirring them all up, telling them Menuhin's a traitor and shouldn't be here at all and they'd be traitors if they came to his concert. I can't do anything with them. He's made a mare's nest out of the camp. He is in fact an *agent provocateur* and wants to get them all to Israel, which is OK by me, but why pick on Yehudi?' Poor fellow, he looked desperate.

I went straight to Yehudi and told him. We decided he had better go out and play for half an hour to those few stalwarts who had braved the others. I went out there swelling the ranks to fifteen and listened to Yehudi playing a Bach solo sonata. Then we asked the Captain if we could come and visit the camp. We could just squeeze in an hour early tomorrow morning, if he would like. 'Wouldja!' he said, cheering up vastly. 'D'ya know what you're letting yourself in for? Those poor wretches are brutalised by years of appalling treatment and hardship and are hardly human any more, and this fellow has brought out the worst in them. I'll have to get the Military Police to handle it.'

Next morning Yehudi and I, accompanied by the Captain, drove through the camp gates and were immediately engulfed by a swarm of yelling, gesticulating creatures clutching at the car before it had time to stop. Enormous military cops with white helmets cleared a path as though they were sweeping aside ants. I opened the car door and stepped out. In the gap they had made, well surrounded by a hedge of hating faces, stood a small man with a mean face and a club foot. He was also glaring. I held out my hand (I had found out his name), '*Herr Jonas, Guten Tag.*' He looked as though I had fetched him a fourpenny one across the face. Also as though he had lost his script. Reaching for his hand I shook it and repeated my words. Yehudi and the Captain were out of the car by now and added their greetings. The yelling had diminished to a growl. The police led us into a long, low room with narrow pillars and a platform at the far end. It was like coming into a zoo with a dozen different animals howling and barking. It was above all deeply distressing. Yehudi was taken up to the platform bolstered by a policeman on either side. Herr Jonas joined him and one or two members of the American Cultural Team who were in charge of Yehudi's visit. It made an unalluring frieze.

The people were lining the walls, had crawled half-way up, clinging to the pillars from where they bawled. They looked inhuman in their concentrated hate, bruised beyond redemption, the poisoned fruit of years of cruelty, neglect and hopelessness; the frightening example of the power of man to animalise his own kind. These wretched lost creatures looked like something painted by Hieronymus Bosch. They needed redemption, not condemnation. Above all they did not need to be inflamed by loaded propaganda.

Yehudi stepped forward, held up his hand to quell the noise and spoke, explaining his reasons for coming to Germany, addressing them as the rational human beings they had once been. 'We Jews never were and never must become beggars, holding out our hands for alms to compensate us for cruel treatment, demanding payment for our wounds. We should go forward into the world reclaiming our honour and dignity as the foremost tailors, furriers, financiers, scientists – even violinists,' he told them. 'No circumstances can extinguish us, nor rob us of our talents. This is what we must show the world in whatever capacity we can!' and much more beside. A great cry broke out, clapping, calling Yehudi by his name. When Jonas angrily got to his feet shouting, 'He's the kind of man who says how terrible it is to see so many buildings in Berlin destroyed! I say how terrible it is that even *one* is left standing, they should all be rubble!' They shouted him down, rushing up to the platform, surrounding Yehudi as he clambered down and was swept to the door. They implored him to give them another chance to hear him play. He explained regretfully that we were leaving that very day.

I shall always remember their worn faces stamped with long suffering and now with a little light in them as they followed the car to the gates. 'Thank God, Yehudi,' said the Captain. 'I shall have peace and quiet in the camp now.'

That evening Herr Jonas called on us to apologise. He had misjudged the situation badly, he said, and let his rhetoric overrule his reason. He now knew he would achieve what he wanted by continuing with the means Yehudi had shown. It was decent of him to have come. There was no compulsion to have done so.

The army plane flew us to Frankfurt, strapped into parachutes and belted to the steel benches on either side. We were taken to the Reichsbank and shown rows of large pails full to the brim with gold teeth; lying hideously among them was a handful of little brooches, pins and rings, the detritus culled from thousands of humans who had known the misfortune of being born into the wrong race. Only God can forgive, only time can hope to forget.

Two more planes took us to Copenhagen and thence to Stockholm where Yehudi's long-time accompanist, Marcel Gazelle, met us. There would be a few recitals there and in other towns in Scandinavia, ending up in Copenhagen. For me it meant the winding-up of yet another of those passages in and out of Yehudi's life, like scenes in a badly constructed play in which I could never know what rôle I should act, nor be sure of the propriety of accepting any of them.

The Stockholm hotel was called the Castle. The suite was rather dark and I was desperately tired after the experiences in Germany and three flights in one day. Too weary to think of the future, I turned to unpacking: Yehudi to the batch of mail awaiting him. I looked up suddenly and found him standing there with an unfathomable expression on his face, tendering a sheaf of papers towards me. 'These are my divorce papers. The decree is absolute,' he said tonelessly. Again the separate versions of privacy in both our natures – his reserved and a trifle phlegmatic, mine based on discretion and the wariness bred of a hundred disappointments – stifled what should have been a wonderful moment of catharsis. A little sadly, I realised that the momentum of this news had to work its slow way through his system, cleaning away goodness knows what clogging in his psychological arteries, righting the balance and clearing his mind's eye for the future.

I would have to wait, to find the patience somehow till he had reached his own conclusion: all I could assume was that he was free, free to choose for himself.

It was a full eight days later in Copenhagen that he at last emerged from his inner turmoil and asked me if I would consider marrying him. What searching and sifting of his heart and soul he had laboured through I would not ever know. I said I would marry him if he were quite certain; that my love had never altered over the years. He replied that whatever appearance to the contrary his love had shown, the core had always remained constant; it was the will that had failed before the moral onslaught, the allegations of lack of duty and responsibility and above all the irreversible feelings that what he longed for most was beyond his reach and his rights.

Suddenly full of joyous energy, Yehudi suggested we try to marry here in Denmark, to avoid the inevitable publicity with which his life was plagued. I had spent several summers in this lovely country with Griselda before the war and had many friends. I rang up Adam Moltke, having found out through the inimitable concierge at the Hotel d'Angleterre that he was now Mayor of Copenhagen. 'Diana,' he replied, 'of course I'll waive the banns and arrange for you to marry Yehudi. How wonderful!' Meanwhile, Yehudi got in touch with his ambassador and arranged to lunch with him that day. Josiah Marvell (direct descendant of my favourite poet Andrew) proved an enchanting man, witty, enthusiastic, full of energy and ready to help in any way. 'But, my dear,' he said to me over the shrimps and Tyborg on the terrace, 'there is the little problem of *your* ambassador. The British one. I will clear Yehudi, Count Moltke will accept you both as far as the ceremony in the Town Hall goes, but you have got to square your own position.'

As always apprehensive, I read something greyish in the tone of his voice. He made an appointment that afternoon with His British Excellency. As soon as I saw His Majesty's representative I, who had been a Foreign Office moll, recognised the type with sinking heart: a bundle of bureaucratic sticks tied tight with frayed red tape.

I put the case to him. He demurred. It was not really a matter for him. I should have applied to the consul. 'Why good Mr Blank,' I expostulated, 'isn't it totally obvious that I know I am asking for a stretching of the law such as Mr Marvell and Count Moltke have already willingly offered, and that I therefore come to you who have the power to use your own judgment and the leeway as ambassador which is not the prerogative of a consul? What is obstructing your willingness to help?' A clearing of his throat betrayed a diet of rusks for breakfast, accompanied by a great deal of blinking of his eyelids up and down over opaque brown eyes.

'Well, Miss Gould, there is the *reason* for banns, to ensure there is no bigamy.' Exasperated and beyond control, I flapped my spinster's passport for the fourth time in his face. 'Mr Blank, if that is not sufficient evidence will you be so good as to ring my stepfather, who happens to be Second Sea Lord at the Admiralty, and ask him whether his stepdaughter, Diana Rosamond Constance Grace Irene Gould is married already, or not. He should know.'

Unbelievably he declined, still wavering. Then asked for time. We told him we were due to leave tomorrow morning for London and the whole grounds for our perfectly reasonable plea was to be enabled to arrive as husband and wife. We left, I furious, he probably to bite his horny nails. Dear Josiah Marvell and his beautiful wife came to the concert that night, held in an enormous hangar of a place filled with 6400 people and a dozen or so pigeons who flew around ecstatically to the music Yehudi played. We had supper afterwards with the Marvells. Josiah told me he'd argued with the costive British Ambassador and even typed out a statement similar to the one he had written to clear Yehudi, for him to mark, learn and inwardly digest; the only outcome of which was that he was to bring Yehudi and me to the British Embassy at nine o'clock tomorrow morning when he, Mr Blank, would give us his final decision one way or the other. That should leave us just enough time to go through the ceremony at the Town Hall and get to the airport to catch the plane. Blessed man, I hugged him.

Next morning, all cases packed and in the taxi, in company with Josiah we drove to the British Embassy. Full of banked-down hope, we went into the Ambassador's office. There he sat, looking gloomily at a typewriter in which was inserted what was obviously the statement suggested by Josiah; he looked at it with a mixture of dread and loathing as though it held some hidden menace likely to undermine his entire moral constitution. Josiah broke the tension by expressing his conviction that the Ambassador would indeed and of course sign, had already certainly signed, the document and set us on our way to the happy legal union. The dull eyes Mr Blank finally raised to us contained all that is most unattractive in my countrymen: priggishness, obduracy and puritanical self-righteousness. He had consulted his Consul who had advised him not to tamper with the accepted law even though the circumstance was an unusual one, given that the Danish Mayor and the American Ambassador had already committed themselves in our favour. He was very sorry but he could not do the same himself.

I had rarely come nearer to assault – not merely because he had refused something of enormous importance to us, but because he represented, to my shame before Josiah, the meanest and most unlikeable qualities too often encountered in the middle-class English: lack of love wedded to lack of imagination. I glared at him, turned and left, afraid of bursting into tears. Josiah, too much of a gentleman to say what he felt, embraced us, wished us good fortune and saw us of to the airport.

As we had feared, London airport was full of cameramen. I dodged and ducked, finally making my way to Griselda's, where she hid me for the next four days. Mama was being assailed by importunate reporters and was proving quite hopeless at fending them off; Griselda, an accomplished prevaricator, handled them skilfully. I managed to creep undetected to the Chelsea Registery Office, a few hundred yards down the road from her house where, for the sum of £2.13s.4d, I obtained a licence for marriage and pressed the need for privacy on the two gentlemen in charge of legal coupling: Mr Marsh and Mr Stream. You need not believe me, may suspect that my admiration for Charles Dickens has stimulated me to lend colour to their names in order to brighten the deadly leaden office where they held sway, but it is the plain truth and I can add that they showed me all the willing sympathy and understanding the British Ambassador to Denmark had withheld. 'Don't you worry, Miss,' said Mr Marsh, 'we've handled many a sensitive case the likes of yours.'

'Indeed we have,' said Mr Stream. 'There was the case only a few months ago, wasn't it, of Lord Knitting? It would he his fourth marriage and he was very anxious to keep the news to himself and his bride if possible, and no further.'

'So how did you manage?' said I.

'Well, like this: we have to put your and Mr Menuhin's name down in the public ledger with the date of the ceremony, time etc. The press come regular of a Saturday to look through the next week's list to pick out anything of interest to a newspaper, see. What Mr Marsh and I did on that occasion was to take their attention off Lord Knitting's name, flip the page over and point out some other name on the following one.'

'We'll do the same for you, dear,' said Mr Stream. 'I'm sure it'll work a treat. So you both come with your witnesses etc., at nine-fifteen on Sunday, 19 October, the day after tomorrow. We'll slip the names in now, they'll only have tomorrow to have a peep, and not to worry.'

I ran back to Griselda's, lighter of heart than I had felt for a long time. Yehudi and Louis spent the evening playing Beethoven sonatas late into the night. Yehudi returned to Claridge's, where they too were doing their best to keep the press at bay. The following night all four of us went to Benjamin Britten's opera *Albert Herring* at Covent Garden and had a bumper supper afterwards at Boulestin.

Sunday, 19 October 1947, at nine-fifteen a.m., Wedding Day.

Epilogue

I suggested in the short prologue to this book that telling one's own tale might lead to the same distortions as would leaving it in the hands of another; that the events lived, enjoyed and suffered by the narrator herself, preserved as they were within her heart and mind, might by the very fact of this enclosure have lost shape, deprived of the larger boundaries of time and space. Repeatedly to stick the thermometer of memory down one's throat to measure the separate temperature of a myriad experiences would produce a reading like the contour of a mountain range.

Conversely the task of the biographer equipped with the facts alone would be a much simpler one, free as he is to assemble them with his own assessment, apportioning importance to some, discarding what seems desultory in others, painting a portrait whose salient features represent what he conjectures to be the significant likeness. Between the biographer and his subject lies the paintbrush; between the autobiographer and his, there is only the self. Perhaps there will always exist the two tales: the one that of the lived-through; the other that of the observed – the subjective and the objective. And yet something of each must lie in the heart of both; for it is impossible to be totally objective about oneself. Any sensitive biographer passionately engaged in his work must find an empathy of its very nature subjective.

Therefore I have offered my tale of many years as truthfully as I can, but nevertheless restricted, reduced, boiled down, for nothing is more boring than a self-important saga wallowing in a soup of its own self-esteem. Why embark upon an autobiography at all? That is easy to answer: because I was asked – not once, not twice, but many times till finally I wrote *Durch Dur und Moll* (*Fiddler's Moll*); and why did I embark upon this one? Because I was asked for more . . . And so I decided this time to start at the beginning of my own beginning – to give roots to what I had already told. In it I hoped to be able to follow a thread through a rather harsh childhood nourished by one great aspiration, the dance, through the painful battles that the profession demands, through World War Two and into my meeting with Yehudi, and on to that strange feeling of destiny that together with an immutable love would withstand the obstacles that, finally overcome, led to our marriage. I found that on looking back my tale had, from the outset, been one full of passion and pain, of struggle and ecstasy, battles contrasted by moments of quiescence, of great anguish balanced by inspiring love of varying kinds throughout my private and theatre life; my experiences had all proved a trial by fire in which my impatient soul had gradually learned to accept the ineluctable: that I was fated to lead a life of eternal challenge. Even as a child and a young woman it seemed that my destiny would always consist of climbing one precipitous ascent only to tumble yet again into a pit of disappointment and despair, and yet it was just that experience that was to train me for the inevitable demands endemic in a life shared with such a being as Yehudi. There would be, however, one great difference: the personal, petty conflicts of my career would be transposed, transformed by one overwhelming inspiration – the dedication of all my efforts to looking after and serving him.

London, 19 October 1991.
Forty-four years have passed since that dismal ceremony in the Chelsea Register Office; years of a variety and richness fit to choke the arteries of any system; years taken at a speed that left one breathless and at the same time proscribed any indulgence or self-pity or grieving.

No sooner were the children born, wherever the violin happened to be on the ninth month – Edinburgh, 23 July 1948 at the Festival for Gerard; San Francisco on 2 November 1951 for Jeremy; San Francisco again on 10 August 1955 for Alexis (who did not survive) – than we uprooted ourselves from the Nirvana of California where I felt the children would never grow the necessary antibodies to sustain them through a life full of mental, physical and psychological germs and settled in Switzerland, in what was then a simple village in the Berner Oberland known mainly for its excellent schools called Gstaad.

No sooner, again, had Yehudi, the All-Purpose Progenitor, set his foot in the comfortable hired chalet than he was approached, beseeched, by the local *Kurdirektor* (seduced might be an apter word for a tale of such woe), depicting a winter season so short as to fill the hotels for only a few months, followed by a summer so doused with rain as to send the tourists scampering to the Riviera or the Caribbean clutching their raincoats around them, which final tragedy caused most of the hotels to close with a whimper that brought calamitous tears to such as himself . . . Now (wait for it) if Herr Menuhin were to give just two – only two – concerts in the lovely 1607 church at Saanen everyone would remain, soused or not, to attend such musical delights.

It was 1956 and Benjamin Britten and Peter Pears happened to be staying with us. They and Yehudi leapt at the idea; two concerts were given in each of the following two years with them and other musicians. From then on, to prevent the little church from bursting at the seams with the clamouring public, more and more concerts were added till the Menuhin Festival (now in its thirty-sixth year) had so expanded Gstaad culturally that, acting as a magnet, there developed a dozen other projects, attracting whole cohorts who built, as finally did we, their own chalets and despite the immutable paucity of winter snow and the abiding menace of the rain found Gstaad an exceedingly pleasant place in which to establish a base. Out of gratitude to Yehudi they offered him, myself and our two boys genuine Swiss citizenship which honour will continue through generations to come, bringing to us both comfort and delight.

Alone I, the ageing Matriarch, feel the loss of my summer holiday. *Eheu fugaces*!

A creak, a crack and a thud from the neighbouring room, such as would awaken the deepest sleeper, propels one unwilling into the morning after too short a night, and one rises Minerva-like out of sheer habit to open the shutters; for the noise proclaims that Yehudi has descended from his headstand and another day has inexorably begun.

The sun has just climbed over the Eggli (or the Kuegli) and the whole lovely valley is warm with light. Visions of a picnic on top of the Hoernli (or the Spaetzli) with the children melting great gobs of cheese over a wood-and-dung fire, rescuing charred Wiernerli from the ashes and getting merry on red Dole, flood the mind with pleasant anticipation and one is just rushing downstairs in one's night-dress, counting madly, to tell the cook to order four dozen sausages, three kilos of Gruyere and four bottles of the local red Biddy, when one is stopped in mid-air by a ring from the front doorbell, accompanied by the vision through the hall window of a large young man equipped with thick eyebrows and a violin case. Clutching one's night-dress around one in outraged frustration, one beats a hasty retreat to the bedroom muttering imprecations against hair and music generally.

Safe behind the door, above the loud beating of one's heart, one can hear Yehudi's footsteps as he slips down the stairs, his lusty welcome, a muffled conversation and, as one eats a lonely breakfast lightly tinged with adrenalin, distant strains of a somewhat depressing nature. Time elapses and Yehudi appears, beaming, and settles to his breakfast without a word.

'May I ask *who* that was?' This from me in a controlled voice.

'Of course, darling. It was a violinist.'

'Yes, darling,' voice breaking slightly out of control. 'I do recognise a violin when I hear it.' Tensely, 'Even at seven-forty-five a.m.' Pause for further information. When none forthcoming, I continue, 'Who, may I ask, and where from?'

A vague blue eye shifts its gaze from the yoghourt and tries hard to focus on myself. However, a light veil of sheepishness seems to hamper the visibility and he says, clearing his throat, 'Er, I don't quite know . . . it might (brightening) be that nice young man I saw backstage in Budapest, or the one M asked me to see, the French one who'd just left the Conservatoire.'

'Well,' from me. 'What language did he speak?'

Panic fills the eyes for a moment. 'I don't remember . . . I think French. No [triumphantly] German!'

'Then it was most likely the one you scribbled on your schedule for seven-forty-five *tonight*: Hans-Knappert Katzenellenbogen.'

Look of tremendous relief and affection floods the clouded face, as towards someone who has fitted the last recalcitrant piece into a difficult jigsaw puzzle, and with a final swig of his tasty dandelion tea and a hearty 'Of course!' he is gone to warm his fingers for the fifteen minutes left before leaving for rehearsal at nine-twenty a.m.

This latter detail is not a vouched one, one simply deduces it from long habit, working back from the scheduled hours of rehearsal through the time needed to get there, subtracted from the number of minutes required to circulate the fingers and finally to that present moment that somehow never exists as a point in time, as it has always been squeezed out of place by being related to the breathlessness of what went before, or the rush of what is yet to come.

Arrived at rehearsal in the neighbouring village church, Yehudi is immediately assailed as he walks up the path by a motley collection of eager souls speaking a minimum of three languages, which makes one feel the Tower of Babel has risen from among the tombstones and that Judgment Day has at last arrived. Each is hell-bent on making his particular tongue the most audible, but Yehudi, blithely oblivious of it all, metaphorically or literally, bestowing on all and sundry the delicious and uncommitted smile of a windy baby, passes through them into the church, takes out his violin, cocks an ear and discovers that the orchestra is not playing the work he expected.

Undisturbed, he finds someone who has the right music and plunging joyfully into the Brahms that he had intended to be Mozart, is lost to all else. At every pause in the music as the morning progresses I, sitting half-way up the aisle, scribbling endless letters in the manner of a desperate sailor baling a dinghy in mid-Atlantic, am attacked by the Tower of Babel flapping irrefutable affidavits of appointments with the *Herr Professor*, or *Monsieur le Maître*, or *Il Professore Maestro*, or plain Mr YM. I counter these, fending deftly with a few words reinforced by an illustrative gesture of my ball–point, hoping that for once, and in this instance, the pen will indeed prove mightier than the sword.

By one p.m. famished, exasperated, spattered with ink and the saliva of a dozen importunings, I dive down the aisle bent on collecting Yehudi and eating. Hope dies for the thousandth time in my all–too–human breast. Already surrounded, he turns to me as he closes his violin case and announces deprecatingly, but with the firmness of purpose of a bee going to the heart of the flower, that he has: *primo* an interview for French–Swiss Radio: '*La Musique, est-elle captive ou dominante, est-ce le caprice ou la logique?*' which, he hastens to add, will only last fifteen minutes; *secondo* an interview for German–Swiss Radio entitled '*Die Politische und Gesellschaftliche Rolle der Musik im Rahmen der Musikfeste*'; and finally, '*La Musica, la gioia, e l'amore*' for Swiss–Italian Radio. ('I promised only five minutes each, darling.') At the sight of darling's starved and uncooperative face he asks whether it was not clever of him to put them all together at one fell swoop? Feeling too hollow to respond with any degree of generosity, I subside upon a nearby tombstone and eat my nails.

At long last, on returning to the house I espy two extra places laid amongst the family eight and discover the owners to be an Arab gentleman come to discuss the distribution of funds raised for a concert hall in the Sahara and a promising Israeli violinist . . . The stickiness of the ensuing lunch is not solely due to the juiciness of the fruit served at the bitter end.

The guests having been speeded on their disparate ways by a beaming host, I suggest he have a good sleep and duly draw the curtains. It is three p.m., the children are invisible, the house is still: the acrid breath of argument has died upon the quiet air. Peace. At three-ten p.m. precisely the first cello case comes bumping up the steps, and within a few minutes a fair-sized chamber orchestra has materialised from nowhere. I go resignedly to rouse Yehudi, only to find him blinking like a new-born bird at the head of the stairs and declaring that he has slept four and a half minutes and feels marvellous. There follow four hours' rehearsal broken only by the intake of some thirty cups of tea, served by Madame Samovar Menuhin. At seven-thirty p.m. from my desk window I see the musicians gliding away; sighing voluptuously at the thought of a pleasant *détente*, dinner and chat by the fire, I descend to check up on the young and the meal. And my hopes are stillborn. The players have indeed left, but there, all over the music room, lies the testament of their return: cellos on their sides, violin cases strewn on the sofa, chairs and piano lid. I turn with goodness knows what expression of exhaustion and frustrated hope in my eyes, to meet those of Yehudi, focused upon some distant diminished seventh. 'When', say I dully, 'do you start again?' Flickers of something alien to the harmony appear in the eyes. 'Oh darling, here you are! Let's have dinner.'

'When', I repeat, 'do they return?' The alien thought is taking a grip and the blue eye seems to be struggling with a mote. 'Darling, did you hear the Corelli (or the Britten, or the Bartók)?' By this time we are all seated and he is serving the soup at the head of the table. 'When?' say I. 'Ah!' says he. 'Well?' says I. 'Darling!' says he, 'after dinner.' And he glows at the sophistry. I put down my spoon. 'When will that be?' The next course appears and Yehudi greets it like an old friend saving him from acute embarrassment. I wait till the effusion has evaporated and everyone is served, open my mouth to repeat my question and am answered with brutal finality by the doorbell and the sounds of Midianites prowling around in the hall outside.

I look at Yehudi. To do him justice, the mote has become a beam. 'Darling, it was a lovely dinner,' he says, embracing me and thus depositing a large part of the praiseworthy meal upon my hair, and is gone. 'You *will* be listening, won't you?'

At eleven-thirty p.m., having pushed in a trolley of refreshments, I retire to bed. Yehudi enters at midnight, gay as a cricket. 'I have only that piece on organic tomatoes to go over for tomorrow's early post, darling.' 'I've done it,' say I. 'Whenever?' says he, 'During the interval.'

After eighteen months or so spent in Gstaad we had two lovely years living in the great art critic Bernard Berenson's little farmhouse (opposite his villa 'I Tatti'), a few miles out of Florence. He and I had exchanged letters regularly since his ninetieth birthday. 'Gather ye BB while ye may,' he begged. So I hauled up our roots and planted them happily there in the pine-scented woods of Settignano, put Jeremy in an English primary school in Florence, while Gerard was in Salem,

Kurt Hahn's famous school and prototype for Gordonstoun, and Zamira, who to my delight had come to live with her father and me since she was twelve, went to the Tochterinstitut, a girls' school set in the beautiful mountains of the Engadin in Switzerland. Thus the cat's cradle grew – weaving warp and woof between all the elements: the children, the concerts, the school visits, the holidays. If they were all in school I would travel with Yehudi, Schwester Marie (my utterly dependable Swiss nurse) looking after Jeremy; the Gstaadfest summoning us back for every August. Despite the walks together, with the aged BB springing over the stony paths and patches of scrub like any small mountain goat, I knew that this lovely spell for us with the company and conversation of I Tatti replacing the mooing of cows (whose buttocks even were scrubbed in the hygienic propriety of the Berner Oberland) could be but a heavenly hiatus and I pressed upon Yehudi the need for a real home for the children. The Shangri-la of Alma, seen as though down the wrong end of a telescope, now seemed even less feasible as headquarters. 'Anywhere,' I said, 'anywhere in Europe,' sensing that men are organic and need to be where their heads and hearts and feet are comfortable, whereas women, the ever-adaptable, will find their balance like a gyro-compass.

'London,' Yehudi declared. 'My father, ever prey to self-torture of nervous suspicion, was always at his best and happiest in England.' Delighted that however little time the SS *Menuhin* might spend in that harbour we would at least drop anchor in the city of my birth and upbringing, we looked for and found a delightful house in Highgate (a seventeenth-eighteenth-century village in the north of that sprawling city), built around 1680 with a garden that offered a stupendous view.

It was a lovely, welcoming house we settled into by the autumn of 1959, wise too, after the manner of most beautiful old things whether they be furniture, gardens or buildings. It seemed to have grown out of its foundations like a plant in favourable soil, well-rooted and secure. Its worn red brick responded to all lights, all weather, as did its pitched roof of red Kelts tiles while the large-paned windows were so harmoniously set they looked out at one like so many benevolent eyes.

Inside it was mostly panelled which added to the sense of tranquillity and warmth and the long four-windowed drawing-room, stretching the whole width of the house, gave on to a pretty garden complete with an ancient oleander, a bay tree and, glorious in the spring, a whole *corps de ballet* of white cherry trees spanning the long wall adjoining the neighbouring house. From the upper floors at the back the view was pure benison. Hampstead Heath and Kenwood unfurled their great green tapestries to the Surrey hills and beyond. It was difficult to realise that one was in London and indeed in those early days before the traffic pouring through to the North used the village as a corridor to the heart of town, ideal for both Yehudi, who had never lived in a town centre, and the small boys who could benefit from the garden.

The house was alleged to belong to the very first 'semi-detached' terrace ever to be built in London. Numbers one and two, three and four, five and six were amicably joined together, forming an elegant row, in front of which lay a capacious flagged courtyard contained behind a low wall and wrought-iron fence, pierced by gateways before each house. Between that and the avenue of lime trees that comprised the main road lay yet another pleasant privilege, a private way paved with 'noggin', that is a mixture of earth, sand a largish pebbled gravel serving as a car-park for all the owners. Thus the houses were well set back from the road which in itself was not actually a main road, only a two-lane leading to the main road at the far end.

All this served to underline the feeling of a country house, further enhanced by the triangular patches of grass beautifully preserved that lay on the far side of the avenue like so many carpets, planted with may and hawthorn trees and yellow with daffodils in the spring. An early eighteenth-century pub completed the rural picture, still maintaining its air of an inn, a perfect watering hole for those who'd managed the steep climb up the vertiginous Highgate Hill. Lulled by the loveliness of this our first home-to-be since we left the far-off Californian one (albeit our constant touring was to take us away like a frolic wind more often than we would have liked), life there would be the epitome of Baudelaire's words: '*Là, tout n'est que beauté, luxe, calme et volupté.*' For once I would be settled, less tense, able at last to function from a real, a solid base. Our bedroom, just above the long drawing-room, was of the same length, with its four large windows letting in the light and colours of the garden.

For the next few months I shuttled between the Californian home, London and Gstaad (Yehudi decided to build his own chalet there), dividing the furniture, linen, glass, china, pictures, clothes, until the London house was ready, and the Californian one still equipped sufficiently to allow a period there to see the grandparents nearby. The nomads suddenly were to have two havens. I had at the same time been accompanying Yehudi on most of his tours, especially grateful for concerts in England that gave me the opportunity to dive into all the shops, from the big emporiums to my favourite flea markets in search of those oddments that give a room the touch of the individual taste and the symbol of a certain coherence that owes nothing to the interior decorator.

I had at long last been able to drag out of storage my share of the Mulberry House furniture and when the house was finally ready it was with a deep feeling of pleasure that I sat in the lovely Carolean drawing-room looking out at the autumnal garden full of chrystanthemums and dahlias and gold-leaved trees, enjoying the subtle home-coming my long-dead father's taste afforded me. My back ached, my nails were broken, I had not had more than a handful of hours' sleep in the week I'd dug out of the schedule to get all the furniture in. My ragged red exercise book in which I kept my sketches and lists lay dangling from my fingers. There were flowers in the vases and everything around me was familiar and my own. Twelve years of hotels and other people's taste. I shut my eyes blissfully and awaited Yehudi's return from Florence, too happy to be tired.

His arrival an hour later, complete with two Italian maids, Schwester Marie, two small boys and two cars full of luggage, shook me from my idyllic reverie; their joy in their first and new home swept away any tinge of nostalgia. Scampering up and down the stairs and out into the garden, hauling up the dozens of cases, delighting in their allotted rooms, filling the house with clamour, adding their child's magic to the objects of my child's past, was like a want at whose touch all my efforts sprang to life and into place.

But this was only a baptism after the Menuhin fashion, a taste of comforts to come. Yehudi and I were due to go for a long tour of America within ten days; Gerard went back to Salem, Jeremy and Schwester Marie to I Tatti to comfort Nicky Mariano over dear BB's recent death, Zamira to look for a job in London; No. 1 The Grove was to be caretaken till we could all settle in genuinely in the coming spring of 1960, and for the next twenty-five years or so.

Now, despite the gypsy-like tenor of our lives, the very fact that we would be returning to somewhere definitely and explicitly our own, where our personal belongings from a family chair to an old teddy bear would be awaiting us – grown-ups and children alike – created a fixed basis as steadying as putting one's foot on a quayside on leaving a heaving boat. There were occasional lurches, of course, such as occur in every household and even in this lovely happy house one such hiccup was to happen some time later.

It was eight o'clock in the morning and Millie, our housekeeper, knocked at the door to come in and draw the curtains. I was alone, Yehudi having gone abroad for a short tour and I, for once, remaining with the children. Only Millie didn't draw the curtains, instead she approached my bed and with blanched lips said, 'Burglars got in last night, they've cut out one of the big panes of the drawing-room leading to the garden and taken all the valuables from there!' Poor Millie. I leapt up, put on my dressing-gown and went down. Indeed all the silver ornaments, the jade figures, the ivory and china and glass, together with two lovely silk Persian prayer rugs, had gone, leaving the room raped and bare and sad.

I felt miserable – paranoid as I am, I also felt sure that I must in some way have been responsible, guilty. I dressed, soothed Millie as best I could and awaited the CID, the Criminal Investigation Department. Two extremely elegant men appeared. I told them my wretched tale. They were polite, offered no hope of recovery of anything, were obviously grateful that I was neither screaming nor ranting and we parted company. Whether their intentions contained anything that might lead to tracing my thieves they were far too aloof to suggest, and I too subservient to insist upon.

With a feeling of infinite sadness tinged with disgust at the utter meanness of human nature I went through the usual day's business of letters, telephone calls, 'alterations to the schedule' (those damnable things occurring every two or three days) and all the minutiae that keeps the SS *Menuhin* afloat. Yehudi rang, I decided not to worry him with miserable news. Bed, book and out with candle at one a.m.

At about three a.m. I woke, thinking I heard a noise. Waited. Tiptoed to the bedroom door while flinging on my gown. Listened. Nothing. Tiptoed down the stairs to the hall. Listened again. Nothing. Decided to go right down to the basement. Entered basement and standing on bottom step reached my hand round corner to doorway and flicked on switch and waited. Still nothing. Proceeded into basement. All seemed clear, so went up back to bed suddenly realising I had not even furnished myself with so much as a chair-leg had I met with an intruder. I was too angry to think clearly I suppose. Slept.

At eight-thirty the following morning. Millie entered again, with blanched lips. Failed yet again to draw curtains. Clutched foot of bed and stammered, 'There's a big brown plastic parcel on the front doorstep.' As there had been any number of such delightful objects containing bombs left of recent weeks in shops and offices by the delectable IRA, I again leapt out of bed, rang the police and begged the local constable to come at once. By the time I'd dressed, two very chic young lady policewomen had arrived and were in the kitchen. They apologised that the bomb disposal squad were so busy that we might have to wait up to half an hour. Millie went green. I suggested cups of tea all round (the classic British panacea). The lady police primly announced they were on duty. 'Nonsense,' I said, 'one of you can stay outside and be blown up first, if you choose, while the other has her cuppa, then you can change places if you both survive – anyway it's perishing cold.'

So we all resorted to the Great British Cure-All. At long last we heard a roar of engines and I dashed out. A big truck had braked violently on the gravel drive beyond the grille and two huge men jumped out as though from ejector-seats. They yelled at us to get back into the kitchen and brandishing a length of heavy metal piping attached to some unfathomable apparatus rather like an elongated elephant's trunk fashioned in iron, they tentatively and at a safe distance of some four yards, swung the contraption backwards and forwards in a curiously sensuous movement across the plastic parcel sitting malevolently on the worn step. We all held our breath, wondering what came next in this crazy scenario, looking like so many bad actors who have forgotten their lines. After a hiatus of about five agonising minutes the men shouted: 'All clear, Mum! It's not a bomb,' jumped into their truck, retracted their infernal machine and roared off to yet another delightful assignment no doubt.

By this time the local constable had arrived. Blond and pink-cheeked and about sixteen years old by the look of him, he whipped out his notebook. I said farewell to our two guardian police-angels and even while he was licking his pencil to begin his questions, pleaded: 'Officer [always safe when one is not sure of rank] as the parcel is not dangerous and I can now approach it, would you allow me to examine it?'

'Ow. Now,' he said firmly.

'But look, Officer, there is a message on that big strip of cardboard attached to it – can I at least read that?' As he hesitated, I leant over. It said in large illiterate print: 'SORRY, REST COMING LATTER.' Before the poor young constable could prevent me, with thumping heart, I had pulled open one end of the big baggy thing. There, jostling with a Chinese ivory carved figure, a jade phoenix poked out its beautiful head and below lay of small silver cigarette box inscribed 'To Yehudi Menuhin in gratitude for his generosity towards the Children of Athens'. The rest was a jumble sticking through the plastic sack at all angles in points and bumps and disjointed lumps, as though some rich child's nurse had thrown out an assortment of building bricks to be carried away to the junk heap.

'Officer,' I said, 'they've brought it *all* back during the night.' (Thereby confirming the odd noises that had engendered my nocturnal prowl.)

There can only be one explanation: on taking their spoils to the fence, he, seeing several signs of tributes to Yehudi stamped on silver tray, inside alabaster box or on the pedestal of a jade piece, must have said: 'Look 'ere, you've bashed Yehudi – that's not fair – take it all back!' We longed to thank them – but there was no means.

As we rattled and bumped from town to town in the States, swallowing three or four a week, strewing recitals with Hephzibah or concerts with orchestras from New York to San Franciso through East Overshoe to Vinegar Bend, I would marvel at Yehudi's freshness of spirit, at his never-waning appetite, at the eagerness with which he met each audience, whether in the sophisticated big cities or the simpler towns. The idea was born in me then and grew with the decades ahead that Yehudi's had never been a career but more explicitly a mission and that like some scientist, he was ever searching for solutions, experimenting towards a perfection in life as much as in music, never satisified with the static, ever journeying to more and more elusive horizons. I realised I could never contain him, only try to clear the way before him, and above all not weary in the enormous task. Obviously, it would be necessary to protect him from focusing too far and wide; from succumbing to the lure of projects presented him by crafty people anxious to apply his reputation to their own ends, who ending his innocence and his essential modesty would use his open-mindedness to their advantage. It has not been an easy task for he hates condemnation and shies away from the very idea of such a factor as evil.

Amongst the problems that faced me were not the psychological ones alone; those were elusive, mutable, needing a subtle surveillance as constant as that required by any captain on the bridge of a ship steering through unpredictable seas. There were also the mundane and wearying hazards of travel: the endless waiting in snowbound airports; the heart-stopping moments when, well over the Atlantic, a green-faced co-pilot would perambulate the cabin announcing that the bang we had just heard (accompanied by the sickening drop that had sent the tray upwards to descend upon the wretched stewardess's head baptising her with soup) was merely an indication that we had lost one propeller engine but (not to worry) we would easily make it to New York, albeit not as planned onwards to London. Or upon any of those pre-jet flights with a baby in Schwester Marie's arms and another awaiting emergence in a few months from my body – when the plane would catch fire and I, with the nose of a tapir, would be the only one to detect the acrid smell and insist the steward examine the lining where the scorched wires were creeping across the ceiling ready to drop lumps of flaming cloth upon all and sundry at any moment. And how many other such precarious moments when white-knuckled and tight-lipped I would repeat the Twenty-third Psalm over and over again under my breath like a mantra, while Yehudi would remain calm and reassuring (were he indeed not blissfully asleep throughout the whole episode).

Burnt into my mind was one such desperate journey. Passive courage has never been my forte – it is the helplessness of such situations which gnaws into one's hardihood, the paralysis that offers one no way of ridding one's fear by helping. Nothing to do but pray through clenched teeth.

We had left New York in deep winter bound for St Louis, Missouri. The snow outside beat at the windows importunately as though demanding to be let in out of the icy black night, the aeroplane swooped and swung, even staggered in an alarming way, fighting the headwind. Over the intercom came the voice of the co-pilot – we would be turning back at Blankville, he apologised, we couldn't make St Louis after all because blah blah snow blah blah visibility blah . . . Wearily I looked at Yehudi fast asleep and envied him his God-given capacity to withdraw from the actual into some Nirvana I could never reach, huddled into my own refuge of hidden nerves and suppressed fear. He awoke as we landed with a bump, stretched, yawned and smiled. 'No,' I said, 'we haven't made it darling, we're back where we last stopped.'

I sometimes think that as his vast repertory of music grew so – in reverse ratio – his facial expressions shrank. 'Ah,' he said, a small line showing between his eyebrows, to which after a pause he added, 'Um,' got up, collected his violin from the overhead rack and we both shuffled in that dogged, dim-witted way peculiar to stranded plane passengers towards the doorway. The stewardess, intoning in plane-speak that we should 'proceed to the egress on the right and then avail ourselves of the requisite transfer-card nominating our sitting position in the event that there would be news forthcoming of our future mobility', turned off her throat-button and we draggled into the airport past huge pink nylon teddy bears, multi-coloured candy and every bottle on the market.

We found two seats and slumped. People of all ages, sizes and shapes somehow managing to look identical moved to and fro, up and down, sideways and backwards, fast and slow before one, like a strip cartoon electrically manipulated. I was too tired to read, too bored to bother, too inanimate to be irritated. After a decent pause Yehudi said: 'I wonder what happens now?' without much enthusiasm.

'There is a destiny in man, rough-hewn,' said I listlessly.

Yehudi looked vaguely disturbed. 'Have you got that quite right, darling?' he says.

'No,' I said drearily.

'You are all right, aren't you?'

'A drowsy numbness fills my veins,' I answered.

'Ah,' said Yehudi.

'For I on filthy food have fed and flunked the Gates of Paradise.'

Yehudi, looking desperate, said: 'Can't I fetch you something, darling?'

'Ah! For a beaker of the warm south!' I replied, looking at the snow battering the panes and hearing above the melancholy motets common to all airports, the nutmeg-grating voices in fugue and canon announcing news, order, teasing titbits of false hope to all eager ears stuck in the snowdrift somewhere. 'Where, Yehudi, is the St Bernard dog bringing succour and brandy ere we succumb?' Poor Yehudi looked more and more bamboozled. Taking mercy on him, I relapsed into silent recapitulation of some sonnets, missing every third line and returning to the first hoping to jump the mnemonic obstacle by sheer force of habit.

Suddenly our number was called and we were to re-board, or re-plane or re-mount our trusty steed. Zombie-like we gathered our clutter: one Strad, two portfolios of 'reading material' (books and magazine) and what is known to most airlines as 'Mrs Menuhin's corpse', e.g. my varying coats for temperatures below zero to over a hundred degrees Fahrenheit, hung in a long sack headless except for the hook. Shuffle, shuffle, time and trouble on to the same stale-smelling plane and back to the same crumpled seats. We were told that the pilot was about to take another bash at making St Louis. Hooray, bravo and pray to the Good Lord not to abandon us in this our hour of improvident courage.

Accelerated roar, uncertain swing, uneasy levitation and we were off into the snowstorm once again. The blindness of night flying when the white flurrying snow only impedes rather than soothes the view of black nothingness before one's anxious eyes peering through the window in search of something, anything recognisable as land, must create in the mind of the most practised flyer (and by now I must have flown some thousand or more times in these thirty-five or so years), a certain dread, a feeling that one is tempting Providence just that little bit too far. Yehudi dozed. I shut my eyes. Turning off one sense, only concentrates the mind most wonderfully on the others. The overpowering staleness of smell assails the nostrils, one's mouth is fur-lined, while the airplane noises, e.g. rumbling engines, mumbling voices, the thump and stir of tired bodies trying to find comfort in yet another position seems eternal. Suspended in time there is virtually nothing to be done but suffer an inertia shot through with sharp arrows of fear.

At last we were losing height, the snow hurried past as though running from us at top speed. I prayed. Yehudi slept. Bump and we'd landed, a roar fit to split the plane and we skidded to a halt. Yehudi woke and stretched, offering me his second-best benign smile.

'I think, I hope, we've made St Louis,' I ventured. The stewardess confirmed. As the plane taxied through the beating snow, we all got up – a sorry lot, looking like second-hand clothing invaded by bodies – reached to the overhead racks for violin and coats, stretched aching ankylosed limbs and puppeted towards the door with weary longing.

The airport was almost deserted, our pilot's determined skill not matched by others'. We stumbled towards the carousel, picked out seven pieces of luggage, found a trolley, piled them on precariously and pushed the horrible perambulator towards the exit. Outside it must have been ten degrees Fahrenheit below zero, thick snow covered the roads and sidewalks. There was no car, no 'stretch limousine' as those hideous funeral-parlour black Buicks and Cadillacs are named. I looked at Yehudi, he returned the look, swivelling a hopeful head as he searched from side to side for something, anything, on four wheels. Finally he went back inside, found the local agent's number, spoke for a minute and returned. 'Sorry, darling, they sent the car well over an hour ago – the driver just rang to say he is in a ditch. They might find another.'

'Just like that?' I said.

'Yes, I'm afraid so.'

We sat outside on our suitcases; quite alone in the icy penumbra, the inadequate overhang did not prevent the snow gathering on our coats and making snowballs of our hats. What shelter we could get was provided by our small mountain of luggage. Peering this way and that into the freezing dark I felt unhinged from life. I tried to identify myself with the political prisoners in deepest Siberia and only felt even more sorry for myself. Yehudi was as usual calm and uncomplaining. I wondered miserably when frostbite would get in and made him put his gloved hands in his pockets. We did not dare go outside for fear of losing the chance of finding some stray vehicle on this ghastly deserted night.

Half an hour must have passed and we were in danger of becoming snowmen, when suddenly we heard an engine and out of the snow-flurried dark a battered small motel bus appeared, sliding and skidding. A kindly black face emerged. 'Whatya know!' it explained. 'You stranded?' We admitted, through frozen lips, he was right in his conjecture. Opening the door further, we saw to our dismay that the bus was crammed. The driver jumped down, dragged our trolley to the backside of the bus and managed by squeezing and bullying to get most of our cases in. 'Come on in, folks,' he cried, and as we clambered up clutching extraneous bags, the inmates dragged us in and somehow made room. I sat on an old man's lap. Yehudi spilled over between two friendly women.

And we slid off into the dark, white-spotted night, skidding and shuddering or pirouetting on the black ice. I was way beyond fear, revelling in a mixture of half-baked relief and heady vagueness, where life is reduced to the minute after next and one reins in the imagination. About half an hour or more of this weird contrivance and suddenly a light loomed as we made an accomplished glissade to the front entrance of a small motel. We all tumbled out into the blizzard and rushed through the door; the hall was a small lake where melting snow was blown in every time it opened. We went out again to help that dear black St Christopher with multiple bags, dumping them in the puddled hall, found the cafeteria and ordered sandwiches, tea and coffee. Dear Yehudi went again to the telephone. No, they hadn't yet traced the original car nor found another willing to come out in the blizzard. Yehudi gave them our present number and begged them to ring should they succeed.

We fell on the dreadful sandwiches and worse tea and coffee, relishing the warmth, the enclosing wall, the comfort of food however bad. My thoughts went back to the war and my youth when life was reduced to basics and the sheer fact of survival was the only thing that mattered. 'Why are you smiling?' asked Yehudi. 'Simply thinking of relative values,' I answered. 'Of ships and sealing-wax, of cabbages and kings.'

An hour passed, then the girl at the desk came in. The car was on its way and should be with us within the hour, should not the same fate befall it as with the first one. Yehudi fell asleep contentedly. I made myself as comfortable as possible on a slung steel-and-canvas chair, the aerodynamics of my behind not being in any way sympathetic to it, folded my arms and gazed at the plastic fern, my world narrowing to the immediate view.

Even I was dozing when the taxi finally arrived. Stiff and rusty we unbent our crooked limbs, collected our baggage, helped the bold driver get them into the boot without too much wildly flying snow getting there first, slammed down the lid, climbed into our seats as though we were attempting Everest and at long last took off into the icy dark, again slipping, sliding, jerking to a horrid stop just on the lip of the road, reversing, churning up small avalanches, pushing ahead yet again. Slow agonised hours, where time dissolved into the blizzard and was swept away by the scurrying snow. At last houses began to appear, surrounded by frozen shrubs looking like obscene meringues followed by whole deserted streets cloaked with snow and – oh dear Lord! lights and the hotel. Yes, the hotel, but in a state of siege evidently. No one to be seen. We dragged in our luggage and after calling as loudly as a couple of foghorns, kindled a draggled, sullen-looking night porter who took an age finding some keys and, reluctantly helping to shove our seven pieces into the elevator, led us to a room at the furthermost corner of the building. When he got the door open, a blast of air so icy that I was convinced he'd led us on to the fire escape, blew us back. He muttered something, shut the open window, stamped like a cross pony on the snow heaped inside it, threw us the key and made to take off. Yehudi stopped him. 'This is impossible – have you nothing else?' He shook his head and bolted. I sat down on the bed and at last burst into tears. Yehudi tried to comfort me. I blew my frozen nose, took off my fur cap and shoes and climbed between the ice-cold sheets. As dawn came, watery pale, I fell asleep to dear Yuhudi's contented, quiet snoring. He must have withdrawn to his spiritual isolation, his life-

leased Cloud Number Nine, where obviously there were constant central heating and warm dry blankets.

Poring through the palimpsest that is his schedule, I plotted out two periods of ten days each in the New Year during which on our return to Europe I could work on the chalet. It was with great excitement that I reached Gstaad, raring to start furnishing the rooms, anticipating that the large hole in the ground we had last seen in September would by now have grown in the intervening five months to at least a building from which I could fairly judge the size and shape of the rooms. My fury knew no bounds when I saw the identical hole now full of snow. The ensuing row rattled round the village like grapeshot as I summoned the builder, told him there would be no Festival unless we occupied the chalet by July and that – ten degrees Fahrenheit degrees below zero or not – he must get a double team of workmen to raise at least the outside walls before I left in ten days. Meanwhile, every other day or so I would attack the journey to Zürich, sliding down the ice-packed road from my hill-top hotel at seven in the morning and catching three different trains with changing gauges and five minutes between each from Gstaad to Zweisimmen to Spies to Berne to Zürich. Arriving just as the shops closed with a deliberate snap for their midday lunch, I would roam around the antique shops of the old city, pressing my nose against the windows and noting likeable pieces of furniture, record them in my exercise book, hare back to the Mowenpick Café, have a delicious sandwich and coffee, waiting impatiently for the awakening of the somnolent stores and retrace my steps, finally able to enter, appraise, judge and choose what tables and chairs and bookshelves I had noted. All at a cracking pace, for my last hope back to Gstaad left at three p.m. where I repeated my crazy daisy-chain of trains, drawing fresh sketches in my exercise book, listing prices and sizes alongside, diving under the platform tunnels to reach the next connection with seconds to spare and finally climbing the long snow-banked road in Gstaad to my small hotel, famished, frozen and passionately engaged in my task. Having picked up the rest of my furniture during convenient concerts in Vienna, where the Catholic taste is so much more exuberant in its painting of cupboards and closets and chests, I was ready for my second allowance of ten days due to fall in July.

Five months of concerts intervened before I reached Gstaad again. The chalet was all but finished except for the presence of a charming carpenter working late into the night on the attics and a divine gentleman of indeterminate sex giving the final touch with a gay flourish to the paint in the basement. It was everything we had hoped for while we had worked together in somewhat dislocated harmony with the architects over the past year, exchanging ideas from all over the world in cables and letters, discussing details from wrought-iron hinges to door handles and the exact colour of stone floors.

I set to with our dear bijou housekeeper Marisa and her willing husband and a couple of hefty youths to unpack crates from California, Zürich, Berne, Vienna and Lausanne from early morning till late at night for the rest of the week. To my relief and delight only one beautiful painted Bavarian armoire failed to fit into its allotted place and is now gracing the basement. Feeling like the Creator himself on the prescribed day (the tenth, not the seventh) I drove down to the international station at Spiez early in the morning and waited impatiently for the overnight train to draw into that most windswept and characterless of places, a sort of Pinter-cum-Beckett-like no man's land, cheerless and desolate. As the great train drew in, I could have wished for a hiss and a puff of steam, anything to add a dimension to all this blankness, to fill the hiatus before the carriage door of the wagon-lit opened and a whole cataract of Menuhins tumbled out. Yehudi, Gerard, Jeremy, Zamira, Schwester Marie and bags galore. The cold, grey, unsheltered platform seemed to melt under their warmth, the cries, greetings, general hubbub of our tribe. Packed into the big car we drove up the summer valley to a Gstaad where every chalet was decked with geraniums and the sun obligingly shone. For the second time within twelve months I was to welcome them to a real home and again they repaid me with hugs and shrieks of joy.

For me this twelve-month of creating two houses had signified a return to my old life in the theatre; it had been a symbol of all the décor and costumes, the different stages of planning that had gone into every production I had experienced, so that the two inaugurations in London and Gstaad had been for me like two premières with their accompanying hazards and hopefulness, nervous anticipation and ardent apprehensions. That my family would be a far more generous band of critics than any of those arrogant arbiters whose judgments had always been offered as gospel in the next day's newspapers and from whom all artists, performers and creators alike suffered, I could be confident.

So 1960 represented a harmonising of the family – at least a groundbase above which the varying melodic appoggiatura would sound more lyrical and less discordant: the hundred and fifty-odd concerts a year would be easier to contemplate, the children's returnings from school – whether day- or boarding-school – would offer them a permanent place for books and toys and treasures and that private nest that is so important for them all.

What I had failed to perceive was the reverse side of the medal; that from now on Yehudi would be a sitting target, attainable to every mendicant, malefactor or malcontent wanting to pick his brains, his goodwill, his pocket, so that the sieve through which I had hoped would pass only the worthiest of claimants would now have to assume vast proportions and a finer web of holes, else he would be buried and bankrupt. Yehudi's artlessness, his chronic optimism, his searching mind ever on the ramble was wonderful to behold, dangerous to handle. Schemes, requests, projects, plans good, bad, indifferent and plain dotty, would descend upon him in shoals. Manna to eager Yehudi, hailstones to battered Diana. Demands to become chairman, president, founder-member, onlie begetter, to music societies, orchestras, organic foodshops, to subscribe to a factory for canning ozone or a home for old tired bicycles, no suggestion was too bizarre for him to scan dutifully, take seriously and sometimes – oh! dear heaven – adopt.

In vain I would plead that both his money and his time were limited, that he was the busiest musician alive, that we travelled between eight and nine months out of the twelve; nothing stems Yehudi's appetite nor fatigues his wide-open mind. 'Dear God,' I would pray. 'Please make Yehudi bored' . . . All to no avail.

The Aldeburgh Festival came and went, a wonderfully gainful and valuable episode with Ben Britten and Peter Pears. At the end of a few days Peter brought me the hundredth letter to answer on my two-fingered typewriter or with my aching hand. I burst into tears all down his pullover. 'Diana, darling,' he said, giving me a hug. 'We all owe you an apology – we thought you with your energy and vitality were the one driving Yehudi to undertake all he does – now at close quarters we see it is his insatiable appetite for life that is the force behind his calm appearance. Blow your nose. Yehudi must find a secretary and you shall have a masseuse for that aching fibrositis.' So by the time we settled in London we had a whole series of lady secretaries whom Yehudi determinedly wore out and replaced and I only had to deal with the social and private mail.

In that first decade we had two memorable visits to India, invited by Pandit Nehru, lived in his house and got to love, admire and know him at close quarters for the remarkable man he was. Indira, his brilliant daughter, organised the concerts in the major cities. Yehudi left all the $80,000 he earned to help the Famine Fund and we got to know an India free of the British Raj, to share their pride in their classical music, their dance, to establish a lasting friendship with their great sitar player, Ravi Shankar, and to add a very valuable strand to our lives. We returned many times until Nehru's death and continued during Indira's presidency. Later, knowing how highly her father thought of Yehudi, she presented him with the Nehru Peace Prize. While always awake to India's beauty and culture it was impossible not to be painfully aware of the insuperable problems that existed in its struggle against poverty and uncontrollable growth of the population nor, becoming ever closer to both 'Panditji' and Indira, to watch their untiring efforts to bring their beloved country into the fulfilment of his vision: that India become the bastion between East and West.

A little time after those first two visits, the Museum of Modern Art in New York organised a big Indian Exposition and asked our advice over music and dancing. We happened fortunately to be in New York around the final stages before the opening and were dining with members of the Museum when the then director, Monroe Wheeler, whom we were meeting for the first time, turned to me saying he wanted to tell me of an extraordinary incident that had happened when he was recently in Madras. He had gone to meet one of those rare Indians who was both a great professor and an ascetic living in a spare two rooms on the outskirts of the city. He had been received by the man who served as attendant and companion and begged to wait as his master was in meditation but would soon join him. Wheeler said he looked round the small room and saw on the wall what appeared to be some kind of religious offering. On approaching it, it proved to be the figure of a god lighted by an oil lamp and beside it a photograph likewise illuminated. As he examined the votive objects his host entered, apologising for the delay. Wheeler, excusing his curiosity, asked the Guru whether he were mistaken but did he not recognise the photograph as that of the great violinist Yehudi Menuhin? 'Indeed it is,' he replied, 'that is how we consider him in India.' The little story moved me, but almost as much did the look of incredulity on Wheeler's face. Yehudi in his usual manner had never talked about his recent visits to India, his close friendship with Nehru, nor anything he had done. It had only been through mutual friends and Yehudi arranging for Ravi Shankar's first visit to the States that the Museum of Modern Art, learning of Yehudi's close links with Nehru and Indira, considered we were likely to be of service to them.

I can only give thumb-nail sketches of all that transpired in these four decades, to dwell at length on any one of them would overload this tale. Amongst Yehudi's many enterprises one of the most important was the music school he had founded (on a penny and a prayer as with all his projects). 'Not all musical children have the good fortune to have devoted Jewish parents as I have had,' he said and proceeded to organise a boarding-school on the lines of the famous Central School in

Moscow where, as in the Maryinsky Ballet School, children received scholastic and musical or ballet training under the same roof, sparing them the struggle between day-school, music or ballet lessons and all the travel and conflict this presented. After a few years (during which I developed calluses on my knees begging for funds), Mrs Thatcher in her then rôle as Minister of Education and Science under the Heath government, visited the school, by now in a big house in the country, pronounced it a 'splendid idea' and promptly put all the English pupils on the government payroll. The many foreigners who comprise a large part of the pupils are funded partly by their own countries and partly by private money raised by individuals. Now in its thirtieth year, it has linked itself definitively with its original model the Russian Central School, exchanging pupils and teachers and proving by its many young artists already launched on successful careers the worth of its existence.

One day I was walking through the tunnel-crossing beneath Baker Street when I heard the strains of a Bach solo sonata being very well played. I waited till the young man had finished, dropped some money in his upturned cap and asked him whether he came from up the road (the Royal Academy of Music in the Marylebone Road). He grinned and admitted that he had indeed. Sickened by the thought of him – and how many others? – having to beg for a livelihood, I told Yehudi about him and the next day we went together, finding him still working away in the tunnel. Yehudi talked with him, got his name and address and there and then conceived the idea of a non-profit-making organisation that would create a network of appearances all over the country in hospitals, schools, prisons, at banquets, soirées and town halls offering work to all these hopeful young musicians unwanted by the concert agencies, while at the same time bringing pleasure and entertainment to many facets of society. He entitled it 'Live Music Now' in contrast to the plethora of canned and taped music which had long since usurped the place of the actual performer; auditions would be held to weed out the really talented who would get a small fee, have all expenses paid, and be put up by local people willing to look after them for a couple of

357

days. Thus the young musicians would not only be heard but have a chance to connect themselves into the concert world. A painter can express himself on a piece of paper, a writer too, but the frustrations of a performer are multiple and agonising. 'LMN' has now been flourishing for fifteen years and is established in England, the USA, Holland, Belgium, France and Spain where the Queen is patroness.

During this time Yehudi had taken over the directorship of the Bath Festival at the invitation of his manager, Ian Hunter, filling the ten days or so in that lovely city with music of all kinds, lectures, discussions, jazz sessions, marshalling many of his friends, those great musicians with whom he's worked spreading himself across chamber music, concertos, joining forces with Johnny Dankworth for jazz, or Ravi Shankar in Indian ragas and founding his own Bath Festival Orchestra (later to become the Menuhin Festival Orchestra with which he travelled the world).

For myself it was a delight to be able not only to break the monotonous routine of travel-cum-rehearsal-cum-concert from Manchester to Minsk at his usual breath-taking pace, but to share the music-making with so many of Yehudi's cherished colleagues in the one city, the travel within it simplified to one vintage car driven by a devoted driver who ferried us from the magnificent Abbey to the eighteenth-century Assembly Rooms, the Guildhall, the Pump Room (the sober entrance to the primordial Roman Baths) and various other small churches usually at top speed. Furthermore, we would often end the evenings in a superb restaurant, the 'Hole in the Wall', run by a genius called Perry Smith, constructed out of the basement of an old crypt, there to round off the pleasure of a good concert together with the artists and delicious food.

Yehudi and dearest Hephzibah and I would take the London–Bath train a day or so before the opening performance. Here I offer you a description I wrote in a Festival programme of that time, describing the classical Menuhin-style of that annual journey. It should perhaps, for the enlightenment of the reader, be explained that Yehudi is, was and always will be an Organic Food Crank and that Hephzibah was a devoted sociologist.

A Thursday in June: Paddington Station, greasy, gritty, coughing up grey smoke into its verandah roof like some great consumptive gasping his last on a slag-heap. Faces pursued by time, preceding hurrying bodies, doors slamming, whistles shrieking reproval. Through the crowd a porter using a small mountain of luggage as a battering ram charges at the double, decants same into a carriage, piling the strange objects on to the racks, under seats and finally abandoning the overflow to the corridor.

Anxious wife trying to count it on the inadequate fingers of two hands suddenly discovers husband and sister-in-law missing amongst objects, traces them to a fruit stall half a league up the platform. Yells. Yell is drowned by guard's whistle. Train slides out leaving wife in lonely rage amidst plethora of useless baggage. Is much relieved when sudden appearance of two beaming guileless faces proves that the pair must have hopped on the rear end. In lieu of apology they are brandishing their bag: she apples, he a packet of biscuits which he triumphantly declares to be made solely of bone-meal and seaweed thereby comprising thirty-three and a half vitamins.

Wife declines latter on grounds that she is neither shrub nor mermaid and is treated to a look of mute reproach. Immediately moved to eat four biscuits, she condemns herself to acute indigestion for the rest of the journey.

YM is now seen to remove his shoes and settle in the lotus position on the seat. Buddha-wise he opens his music and, waving a pencil vaguely in the air, enters Nirvana. Sister-in-law attacks a huge grey cotton bundle looking like a cross between a coalsack and a Tartar saddlebag and produces therefrom large quantities of folders, dogeared pamphlets and about half a quire of foolscap.

Silence reigns. Train streaks past a countryside sugared with flowering elder and slinks into the hopeless sadness of Swindon. A head pokes itself in the doorway, contemplates the odd scene, squares its British shoulders, attempts to wedge a modest case amongst the crates, bundles, regimental hat boxes and wicker holdalls on the rack, fails, gives the occupants a withering First-Class look and sinks into the fourth corner. YM finishes marking his music, remarks upon the felicities of the D-major violin concerto. Wife, agreeing, asks whether opinion purely rhetorical as Bath Festival expecting A-major Mozart. YM swallows once and mildly asks when, as he does not remember playing it since he was seven in San Francisco? Wife says day after tomorrow. YM beams with relief . . . Wife suggests that as next two days contain four rehearsals and two performances she imagines joy is due to contemplation of learning A-major Mozart in the bathtub . . . Another look of mute reproach sends her scurrying back to the deciphering of a rough draft by husband on 'Batguana as a Basic Food'. YM, finding it impossible to open window upon howling English summer day, unlovely and intemperate, proceeds to compensate for lack of air by launching into Yoga breathing exercises; as this entails clasping the nose between thumb and forefinger, resulting in a roar like that of an object hurtling through a wind-funnel, First-Class passenger in fourth corner not unexpectedly glares from over his fluttering newspaper. Meeting angelic gaze of wind-god opposite, he subsides defeated. HM raises her bright head from the paper jungle: 'Do you know that since R and I started our work in W11 there has been an increase of five per cent in the murder of landlords? Such a healthy sign we feel.' YM returns from the Himalayas and grunts vague approval: 'Very nice. You'd get even better results if you fed them compulsorily on Swiss husk-porridge.' Wife in corner desperate for a release from her decoding, suggests the Government might be reluctant to issue sufficient Hessian nosebags for such an equine diet. Receives combined stare of limpid wonder from both the Ms. Decides to mention lunch as diversion. Greatly to relief of Stranger, YM replaces shoes. HM stuffs back statistics on state of plumbing in mental homes into the grey affair and all three repair to the restaurant car.

Here they are seen to peruse the menu with great solemnity. Along comes obliging waiter. Greets all three Ms with joy. Wishes them best of luck for Festival. Exchange pleasantries. All *couleur de rose*. YM asks whether fish caught that morning; shows hurt surprise when answered in negative and resigns himself to an apple and a chunk of mousetrap. *Couleur de rose* shows slight grisaille at edges. HM plunges sportingly into a plate of Something-or-other *à la*

British Railways; wife, struggling with the later digestive phase of the seaweed biscuits, confines herself to Brown Windsor soup, which she had always thought to be toilet soap of the same name. On sampling same, finds she hadn't been entirely mistaken.

YM launches into an explanation of the Discussion to be held as usual during the Festival. It appears it is entitled 'Health and Longevity among the Hunzas', and he is having half the tribe flown over by special plane from Kashmiri Valley. He suggests the Bath City Councillors will be delighted to push the rates up a penny to support this fascinating and far-seeing enterprise. Wife proposes idea might just possibly not meet with wild enthusiasm. HM observes that if title were changed to 'Social and Sexual Mores of the Hunzas' it would be more likely to attract both public and financial backing. YM, understand, proceeds to expound on the delights of starving for four months of every year, which is apparently what makes the Hunzas practically eternal. Wife admits to preferring short, gay life to hanging on full of internal wind for one third of eternity. HM laughs, whereupon both she and wife are banished from Paradise, kindly but firmly, by an Archangelic look.

To work their passage back into the Garden, HM asks how many concerts she is playing. YM looks faintly distressed, definitions being his bugbear. Wife says four. Five if you can play the organ. HM asks why? Because organist ill. When is particular concert? Day after tomorrow – that being the average span of time needed by an M to learn anything. HM says 'Delighted'. . . By the way may she have thirty-five tickets for each concert? She has a particularly fascinating group of psychopaths and wants to see therapeutic effect of beautiful city cum beautiful music upon them. Yes, they have all committed *one* murder, this is what makes the experiment so interesting and important. *No* trouble with regard to transportation. They can all come down in a number fifty-two bus two of them stole the preceding week and sleep in it outside the Guildhall.

While brother and sister discourse on relative healing properties of classical, romantic and modern music, YM announces that Alban Berg for breakfast is the only really nourishing one. Why? Because it is serial. Gales of laughter at pun.

But the pastoral beauty outside has given way to the first terraces of golden stone and dear Bath is approaching. The waiter asks gently to be paid. Wiping his eyes, YM produces from multiple pockets a quantity of crumpled bills which he presses into waiter's hand, murmuring, 'No change.' Race back to the carriage. Submergence of First-Class passenger under avalanche of baggage wrenched off racks and tumbled into corridor. A hiss and the train draws into the station. Ms tumble out, followed by a warehouse of luggage of ancient vintage and older origin. Relying on Somerset courtesy they abandon it all to the Stationmaster whom they greet with cries of joy, escaping down the stairs two at a time, blissfully oblivious of the waiter gesticulating furiously from the train carrying him to Bristol, his waving hand full of Greek drachmas, Hungarian pengoes and tattered Tunisian francs.

The Bath Festival proved to be one of the most enjoyable of all Yehudi's enterprises and was followed after a decade, when he retired from it, by the Windsor Festival in 1968, another conception of Ian Hunter's and a lovely venue with concerts in Windsor Castle and the beautiful Chapel, conducting military bands in the Castle courtyard and performances in the neighbouring Eton College (familiar territory to me whose father and brother were educated there and which Gerard and Jeremy had just left).

Thus the fugitive summer holiday was pushed even further away, for the Bath and Gstaad Festivals swallowed June and August, while Windsor followed Gstaad and digested September, so that after four years Yehudi decided to hand over Windsor as he had Bath, and both are still in successful existence.

Meanwhile the children were growing up fast, Gerard, who before he went to Eton had made a great success as the doctor in *Emil and the Detectives* at the Mermaid Theatre (however, when asked if he intended to become an actor, had replied loftily, aged twelve: 'No, I think it would mean a very shallow life!'), eventually went to Stanford University in California. Jeremy, whose profound musical talent had been clear from the very beginning when he refused to read or write anything but music as a tiny child, had made steady progress with his piano and went, after only one and a half years at Eton, to study theory and composition with Nadia Boulanger in Paris and from there conducting with Hans Swarowsky in Vienna and finally to start performing regularly. Zamira, by now a lovely young woman, was to pass successfully through several courses and got a job on *Studio* magazine. All three children had flown the nest as I always felt they should, so long as they are profitably and happily engaged in some kind of work, and so long as, by letters and telephone calls, I could keep in touch. Every so often we would join again for holidays or meet when Yehudi and I would be nearby with concerts. It was affecting to see them thus at intervals against another background, to watch them growing their own limbs and branches like young saplings, to try not to advise or interfere, only hopefully to drop in a word of counsel, never sure that it would be heard but trusting it would be taken as concern and not as meddling. Occasionally we would go back to Alma to visit Aba and Mammina, two very strong characters, deeply rooted in their own lives, in their comfortable, sunny house, not even growing perceptibly older, enjoying their hand-picked friends, Aba ever concerned with some human or political situation, Mammina always surrounded by the young who respected and admired her.

And we? Yehudi and I? We whirled across the world, tens of thousands of miles a year, every now and then landing in the London house for a week or a handful of days, according to the number of concerts to be given; Yehudi ever expanding his daily output.

Earlier, in 1962, we had bought and resuscitated a tiny peasant house on a Greek island where we took the boys in their school holidays in April and September, to swim, lie in the sun and glory in the Greek light for a precious ten days ripped out of the inflexible schedule.

In those five paradisiacal years, and ten heavenly visits, we had claimed for ourselves the perfect holiday. Alas! this idyll had been broken when in 1967 the *putsch* had brought about the flight of the young King Constantine and his family, replacing in their stead the fascist regime of the infamous colonels. Caught in Athens at this very moment, Yehudi and I (fortunately without the boys) had been trapped, only managing to get out after forty-eight hours when the airport finally reopened and we were all shovelled on to various planes, glad to leave for any destination whatsoever. From then until 1974 and the final overthrow of the fascist regime we refused to return, lending the little house to anyone needful of a holiday they could otherwise ill afford. At last a letter arrived from the office of Karamanlis, the new President, begging Yehudi to return and extolling him for his stout refusal to play in Athens or to return to a haven they knew we cherished.

So in 1975 we cleared a couple of weeks and flew to Athens, our hearts full of anticipation and excitement, discovering meanwhile that the ghastly little tubs that had taken eleven long and unsteady hours to reach the islands were no longer the sole means of transport but that an air-strip had been laid on the island. That hideous pilgrimage had been enough to dissuade the hardiest holiday-maker; but, by that very token, had been a wonderful protection. My relief, therefore, was alas short-lived, for the very comfort of that aeroplane journey, the very ease, had enabled 20,000 others to make that erstwhile unencouraging journey and we landed on our beloved island amidst a cacophony of motor cycles, vehicles of every description and a babble of noisy languages that would have made the Tower of Babel appear a building for mutes.

I burst into tears. The glorious panoply of stars now obscured by the lamp standards strung like false pearls along the roads, struggled feebly in the black sky, meaningless to the hordes dragging their baggage on to the multiple buses intent on gaining one of the dozens of hotels, a bed and an ouzo. The six ancient Buick taxis – the only vehicles once permitted – are now engulfed by dozens of Mercedes, while a horde of noisy motor cycles have turned the young tourists into aggressive hunters as they roar, Attila-like, up and down the two main roads. Discos blare from open doorways and every little house in the town has become a place of commerce, a lure for the pockets of the crowds ambling aimlessly up and down the narrow streets, gaping at dresses, jerseys, jackets hung in festoons from hooks driven into the walls, dodging racks of sandals, crates of fruit and vegetables, gazing into overstocked bottle shops and terrible displays of miniature gods, goddesses and temples. A kind of second-rate bazaar has engulfed the handful of early shops with their hand-loomed scarves and coverlets, a burlesque souk has taken over from the elegant simplicity of those stone-flagged alleys fringed with a slightly disorderly jumble of houses stretching in corridors down to the harbour or winding in and out of a mischievous tangle.

Now Yehudi and I sadly forged our way through the jostling crowd of fried, roasted and grilled humans, finding refuge in one of the few advantages brought about by the popularisation – the restaurants, where a large choice of food has replaced the old taverna offerings of spaghetti, various Greek salads, tinned octopus, lamb plus beans or *barbounia* – a fish resembling a starved red mullet composed entirely of bones of all sizes from a hair to a giant toothpick held together by a few unenthusiastic flakes of flesh.

I pondered all this as the following day I sat on our whitewashed terrace looking out over the silken evening sea at the other islands floating dark in the indeterminate light, watching a glory of a Greek sunset defying all taste in a bravura of great banners of bright-pink cloud thrown across an unlikely pale-green sky hanging over a now-magenta sea. The whole picture seemed to hold its breath while exacting the same of the beholder – it is a splendour of all that is ephemeral, the supreme philosophical statement. As the last flamboyance was sucked under the horizon and only variations of grisaille remained to taunt one, I thought over the quarter of a century when first we bought this ruin of a small peasant house set on its acre or two of dry, terraced earth just below the top of the cliff, looking for all the world as though it had slipped down and remained huddled against the rocky wall, its one tall cypress standing sentinel; an untidy casual collection of almond trees in various stages of decrepitude sheltering it on the west while the roofless kitchen, boasting half a southern wall and fragments of the remaining two like broken lower teeth, was host to a fine crop of grasses, weeds and thorny thistles. One room, up an outside flight of steps and along a groggy balcony, remained intact, however further steps leading up to the erstwhile bedroom only offered the dubious comfort of a night on nettles beneath the stars. In compensation the surrounding terraces held quinces and pomegranates while a mass, a positive defiance, of prickly pears guarded the entrance. But the view was paramount. A horseshoe bay lay below, its dark-blue waters ruffled by the melteme, the capricious local wind that blew asthmatically on and off all summer filling every orifice with dust while taming the burning sun to a tactful temperature. Between the sand and the horizon the sea was dotted with islands lending the vast expanse a friendly and inhabited air, as it were. A mere handful of small whitewashed houses were scattered in the folds of the hills opposite, dice amongst the bare bones of an autumn Greek landscape; the deep gash of a ravine choked with the only green to be seen lay long the base of a great outcropping of rock composed entirely of vast boulders, strewn like a sun-baked moraine tumbling down to the little coastal road skirting the beach and trailing off round the curve out of sight to the promontory beyond.

The chief weaver of the island and Queen of the town was Vienoula Kousathana who, together with her entire clan, took us under her wing, a woman of fine mind, sharp wit, endless humour, of that philosophical nature that comes of a long line of farmers full of common sense and percipience. Her weaver parents, when she was twelve, had travelled to Manchester to work for the great CPA (the Cotton Printers Association) for two years and it was comic to listen to dear Vienoula in her fluent broken English keening for the wet streets and gloomy clouds of that most inclement of English climates against the background of azure skies, crystal-clear light and the all-consoling sun of her own lovely island. No amount of teasing would deflect her from her passion for England and all things English, and in those blissful early days only scholars from professors to students of all nationalities studying Greek came to Mykonos which had provided a launching-pad for the Holy Island of Delos a spare hour away by the local fishermen's boats. The little town had been the centre for smuggling since Phoenician days to which the tortuously narrow streets bore witness as did the bafflement of the foreigners lost sometimes for an hour while they tried to distinguish a maze that would have made Hampton Court look like a Roman road in comparison.

Those were the days of Travellers, not Tourists, the very last days, in fact, when visitors offered something in terms of respect and admiration and learning, rather than the uncalculating appetites of tourists coming like locusts to swoop down, gobble up and eventually leave a lovely place destitute of its original and subtle significance.

The few shops provided crockery and hardware, and whatever vegetables and fruit were grown locally or brought in by caique or occasionally on the larger boats from Athens. Every day at noon we would plunge off one of the narrow streets down into the ancient vaulted cellar of the 'best' baker where he would be already drawing out of the archaic stone oven, fired by bundles of brushwood, the first loaves on his long-handled spade. We always bought two because we had demolished at least half of one as we walked back up out of the town and on to a path across the cliff-top edged with high dry-stone walls that led to our gate. If anyone knows a more wonderfully sensual taste than that of bread freshly baked I am ready to contest it. The gate opened on to a flight of stone steps leading perilously downwards and before one the sea stood on end like the hem of a backdrop. The large crop of prickly pears added to the challenge of the descent and as the years went by, our small enclave lovingly tended became full of oleander and hibiscus, jasmine and bougainvillaea, while purple and royal-blue morning-glories entwined the bamboo fences, the vestigious almond trees awoke, the pomegranates pregnant with fruit and the white and purple figs became once more heavy.

Poor Yehudi, assaulted while sunbathing on the roof by passionate German melomanes (female) intent upon autographs, decided to buy himself protection by acquiring the neighbouring land, so now we added the adjoining vineyard to our 'supermarket', as the boys called it and Apostolis Kousathana, our caretaker and gardener, planted pear, plum and lemon in the farther fields.

We looked after ourselves in our four-roomed house, Yehudi taking to house-keeping with a touching zest. He insisted that his duties should be marketing and making the breakfast – mine cleaning and cooking and laundry, although there was no definite drawing-up of Plans for Living which neither of us care for, a ghastly theoretical approach which owes everything to the abstract and nothing to the human and fluent. He loved running down to the little town in his shorts and summer shirts, getting to know the shopkeepers, enjoying at its very pleasantest an occupation he'd never known, and being Yehudi he would characteristically return with aubergines, courgettes, strings of garlic, ditto of onions, wilting lettuces, huge cucumbers, twisting tomatoes, oozing figs (if our own weren't ripe), great rounds of rather noisy cheese while a delighted vassal (Yehudi's genius for summoning confidantes in white linen is never-failing), sweating in rivulets, would stagger in counterpoint heaving a vast watermelon, eight kilos of potatoes, gangling bottles of olive oil, vinegar, mineral water, and the new frying pan I'd begged Yehudi to get, as the sea air had rusted the present one. Yehudi, looking like Radames returned from a successful campaign loaded with booty, would dump the lot on the marble kitchen table, panting with triumph. As this joyous shopping would repeat itself nearly every time he went down, I would have surreptitiously to toss rotting vegetables and fruit over the terrace wall, there to be absorbed, I fondly hoped, by the cactus roots or to fertilise the fig trees; it was with real anguish I had to curb his fervour, telling him that no frigidaire (we had one) nor my advance cooking of perishable food could possibly keep pace with his mercurial marketing. There was then little electricity in the bay, so at night no competition for the moon nor for the stars which covered the velvet blue sky in such sharp profusion they seemed to pierce through the fabric like myriad strands of broken glass. Alone the sounds of the sea licking the shore, the braying of a donkey, the eccentric roosters crowing anarchically in true Greek fashion at all hours, disturbed the peace of the island gone to rest. 'Sleep drifting sleep/Deep drifting sleep . . .'

Now, after eight years of attrition, back in our longed-for little house with the crescent bay lying below, my mind crawled back over those years since last we had left it, a refuge so perfect, so fitting our peripatetic lives as to be almost too sublime to last. Was it simply that with the encroaching years I had lost the capacity to adapt, to be tolerant and generous towards all those with whom I would now have to share this exquisite place?

I slept little that night, turning over and over in my saddened mind the inevitable and possibly insoluble problem of adjustment to mutation and not to mutation alone but to an acceptance of a loss of rhythm between oneself and the surrounding world.

Ageing, I came to the conclusion, is not simply a case of stiffening of joints and mutinous muscles, of the cruel calligraphy of time written in wrinkles as an affidavit of spent years; it lies also in the subtler and irreversible effect of unwelcome changes wrought by others whose habits and behaviour gradually alter a beloved space, a special haven, out of all recognition, so that one begins to wonder whether one's own mind is, in its rustiness, guilty of condemning what should be acknowledged as normal evolution. Perhaps the coarsening of life is inevitable and should be accepted philosophically, not rejected with sadness and revulsion?

Is it that one's own rhythm slowing down is unable to adjust to the pace in which values long-established and once basic are discarded to be replaced by others, in time alike to be jettisoned and replaced by standards evidently so shallow that they carry the shadow of adolescence almost as soon as they are created? Is one culpable of lagging because the moral climate has become alien, of being reactionary and costive?

The yachts lay like huge porpoises in the harbour, spewing forth hundreds of tourists to clog the streets. At night they were lighted up like Lunar Park afloat. One by one they belched a warning farewell, muffled like a dowager with a gloved hand to her mouth, and took to the open sea, there to strew their goggling cargo on to yet another island to roam naked and for the most part thoroughly anaphrodisiac on the beaches, slump around the discos, enervated and bemused, exhausted by their Valkyrie-rides astride their Japanese steeds from bay to bay, baying. I sound horribly contumacious, I fear, and yet I might plead forgiveness for a lost heaven, once shared by like lovers.

Back in Gstaad each August I had managed to organise visits from all the children. Krov, Yehudi's son by his first marriage, had married a lovely American girl, Ann, who was his partner in the beautiful nature films he was starting to make and which he has continued to do with great success to this day, even taking their baby son Aaron to the Galapagos Islands soon after his birth. Zamira had married Fou Ts'ong, the Chinese pianist, and was living in London with Lin, their small boy. So the family was expanding and time had to be allotted to give all of them a chance to see their itinerant father, who even then was busy from dawn to dusk with the Gstaad Festival. He, the Great Expander, had added an 'Akademie' there, a school for more advanced young musicians from all over the world, the director of which is the Argentinian violinist Alberto Lysy, Yehudi's first pupil who conducts his Camerata orchestra composed of the best of the students that passed through his hands, touring with them all over Europe, Canada and America. Here was yet another undertaking to add to the multiple enterprises. Yehudi played with them several times a year and gave them master classes.

That he has also taken on the Presidency of ESTA (which acronym reads 'European and English String Teachers Association'), an excellent proposition bringing together all the string teachers at meetings several times a year in whatever country happens to be host; that he was President of the Unesco Music Council for three terms of three years each, expanding its membership enormously which entailed going to Paris several times a year (no hardship and for me one of the pleasantest aspects of our over-charged life) is relating only the more important of his undertaking. Amongst others were his membership from early on of Amnesty International and his interests in Music Therapy. All this precluded any kind of social life other than that interwoven into the career itself and mainly official: memorably, there was the splendid and moving service in Edinburgh Cathedral where, from the pulpit,

Yehudi gave an address followed by the Usher Hall ceremony when he was given the Freedom of Edinburgh. Yet another honour was in Bath where again he was awarded the Freedom of the City; the thirty or more honorary doctorates from Oxford to Cambridge to St Andrews and Belfast or at the Sorbonne where he was the first musician ever to be so honoured.

Yehudi had been the first musician to be invited to Japan in 1951. As I was within a month of the birth of Jeremy, for once I did not join him. That it must have been sad to miss the fête with which they greeted him was proven by his return, with no less than eight crates of presents, ranging from ceremonial kimonos, through metres of brocade, of silks, of cases full of lacquered boxes, trays, bowls; of porcelain and pictures. There was just time to open all this booty before I went in to San Francisco for the birth of Jeremy. Yehudi seems able to control genetic timing to his wishes. . . . Jeremy was born three days later.

It was 1982 and time for China. Yehudi had been invited by the Chinese Section of the International Music Council as well as the Ministry of Culture in Beijing. It was a period of growing freedom. What struck us immediately was the warm and easy friendship of the people in the streets and shops, contrasting utterly with the fear and aloofness of their Russian counterparts. When I went to an ordinary store to buy stout black canvas shoes to clamber up the Great Wall, the people crowded round me laughing at my two words of Mandarin, encouraging me to search for other objects, interested in my clothes, at the English I spoke with our interpreter, unafraid and kindly. Our hotel waiter asked us whether we would like English or Chinese breakfast in our room. He grinned widely across his half-dozen teeth when we asked for Chinese and wheeled in an enormous table full of rice and spiced dishes, steamed dumplings and tea, which doubtless he finished off himself.

The orchestra was led by a charming man of about forty, recently released from prison where he had been incarcerated for fifteen years for the crime of playing Bach, Beethoven and Brahms. He apologised for the shortcomings in his technique, bringing home forcibly the placidity with which we accept our own freedoms. The audience were rapt and appreciative. The conductor was a fine fellow with the mien of a warrior, who spoke little English and took us round the 'Forbidden City' with its beautiful buildings and museums full of artefacts which despite one's familiarity with them in the houses of the West, none the less took on an added loveliness in the country of their origin. We were passing by a fairly large and attractive house set in a pretty courtyard when the conductor pointing at it said: 'That is the kind of house my parents owned before the Revolution.' He smiled. 'First is Sun Yat Sen. He say now everything really better. No change. Then come Mao Tse Tung. He say all will be very good. It is the same. What is that English saying about hay?' I said, 'You mean "make hay while the sun shines"?' He roared with laughter. 'Yes, that is the only thing to do.'

Two years later Yehudi, at the request of the Ministry of Culture in Beijing, brought over a section from both his English school and the Akademie in Gstaad – over fifty young musicians. The Chinese were splendidly pragmatic. They stamped a universal visa for all the pupils even though amongst them were citizens from countries such as Israel which they formally refused to recognise. The children had a wonderful time playing and being entertained; while we travelled from Beijing to Xian to Guilin, we saw some of that mysteriously beautiful countryside one had thought to be in the imagination of the painters alone and now beheld in all its stunning reality. A lovely film was made of the whole tour by a French cineaste, Bruno Monsaingeon, and had a great reception.

Nor can I, in this foreshortened log-book of four decades, omit the many and worthwhile trips we made to Israel, that fascinating country that we watched grow from a mainly stony land to one where forests covered the rocky landscapes and where indeed the desert was made to blossom as the rose. In our first visit, in 1950, the pioneering spirit still ruled; there was only ersatz tea and coffee and severely rationed food, Yehudi and Hephzibah played in the Kibbutzim, from En Gev in the north (with Syrian soldiers sniping from the Golan Heights down to the valley where they played) to the tiny concert hall in Tel-Aviv where the subscription to the concerts represented seventy-five per cent of the population and therefore the programme had to be repeated some ten times to accommodate them all. There reigned a spirit that reminded me, in its wonderful determination and common purpose, of the London Blitz.

Chaim and Vera Weizmann, the first President and his very Russian wife, living in the White House, an elegant villa built by the Jewish architect Mendelsohn, often invited us there and we would meet those extraordinary generals – Dayan and Yadin, both archaeologists as well as brilliant soldiers, bearing odd traces of British Palestine in their uniforms and their demeanour and whose vision and enthusiasm for their new country bore in those days little of the zealot. There was an extraordinary communal spirit within the Kibbutzim: architects, professors of all sciences, surgeons, doctors, every kind of erstwhile administrator, sank their one-time eminence in the common good, dug, built, laboured and shared in the making of these communities that were really inspiring to visit.

So much has happened within forty-five years: Gerard married a highly intelligent and attractive girl, Eva, who has given him his baby son Maxwell; Jeremy, whose career is now well-founded, married a Highland girl, a brilliant artist and has a daughter, Nadia, and a son, Petroc. Krov and Ann have Aaron. Zamira, now happily married to Jonathan Bentall, Director of the Royal Anthropological Institute, now has three sons; Lin, her eldest, by the pianist Fou Ts'ong, and Dominic and William. At the time of writing that makes so far altogether seven grandchildren ranging from two to twenty-seven, from tiny Max to handsome Lin.

Yehudi still tours eight or nine months out of the year, playing when it pleases him, but mostly conducting; interwoven are the eternal causes, exploits, enterprises which comprise the underpinning of his life.

The doyen of English critics, Neville Cardus, said of him: 'It is pure chance that Yehudi was born of Russian-Jewish parents and therefore became the great musician and violinist he is. Whomever he might have had as parents his genius would have brought him to the same eminence whether as philosopher, writer or statesman . . .' Again and again, he has flowed against prejudiced opinions, fighting lone battles, risking his career, suffering calumny and danger; he never flinches in his purpose to fulfil what he once said as a small boy discovering his voice in music: 'I would like to make people feel better when I play, if I could.'

However demanding and exhausting the life, however overburdened and weary I may sometimes feel at the end of a long day, at the finish of a crowded month, at the conclusion of each inevitable year of travel, I recall the words of that boy and realise my fortune in being allowed to share his life.

Spirit of place

To Diana Menuhin

(Written on menu: >Diner D'Adieu du Commandant<.
                    Menu dated 24 September 1962)

Dear Diana,

I believe our paths crossed by a few hours recently – a near graze!
What bad luck. I have been sent on a journalistic assignment for a
brief tour of Israel and Greece. As you can imagine the Greek visit
was most exciting though Israel was interesting and rather moving
and I hope to write something about it. But Athens gave me back at a
blow all my old friends whose touching warmth was really like a
home-coming; made it like one I mean. We did a swift autumn tour
of the Peloponnesus – deserted bare and blue! Dug out old taverns,
discovered new. Above all had Katsimbalis and Seferis to ourselves
for *days* on end. Such stunts, such gaales of laughter, such memories
exchanged! It was like a gasp of rare air and I felt twenty years
younger. >Fifty years seemed but a day<! And now we are back to
the problem of country-folk, leaking roofs and cisterns, damp wood
etc., etc. I won't bore you with them. I'm glad you've found
Mykonos. I first went there in 1936 and stayed with an old lady called
Poppeia – there were no hotels and no tourists. I shared a lavatory seat
with a hen and a bed with 1000 fleas . . .

                                        Larry D (Lawrence Durrell)

Delos

For Diana Gould

On charts they fall like lace,
Islands consuming in a sea
Born dense with its own blue:
And like repairing mirrors holding up
Small towns and trees and rivers
To the still air, the lovely air;
From the clear side of springing Time,
In clement places where the windmills ride,
Turning over grey springs in Mykonos,
In shadows with a gesture of content.

The statues of the dead here
Embark on sunlight, sealed
Each in her model with the sightless eyes;
The modest stones of Greeks
Who gravely interrupted death by pleasure.
And in harbours softly fallen
The liver-coloured sails —
Sharp-featured brigantines with eyes —
Ride in reception so like women;
The pathetic faculty of girls
To register and utter a desire

Delos

In the arms of men upon the new-mown waters,
Follow the wind, with their long shining keels.
Aimed across Delos at a star.

Lawrence Durrell (1946)

Mareotis

For Diana Gould

Now everywhere Spring opens
Like an eyelid still unfocused,
Unsharpened in expression yet or depth,
But smiling and entire, stirring from sleep.

Birds begin, swindlers of the morning.
Flowers and the wild ways begin;
And the body's navigation in its love
Through wings, messages, telegrams
Loose and unbodied roam the world.

Only we are held here on the
Rationed love – a landscape like an eye,
Where the wind gnashes by Mareotis,
Stiffens the reeds and glistening salt,
And in the ancient roads the wind,
Not subtle, not confiding, touches once again
The melancholy elbow cheek and paper.

Lawrence Durrell

The white country

Time, like snow, blurs the clear shapes of things;
And drifting even on our hands
Obscures the gesture and intent.
We do not know the landmarks any more,
Cannot tell what people we once were.
Like ghosts we wander in our tracks
Carrying dimmed intentions
Through the still white country.
If it were possible
To take a bearing and be gone
We should have found a way to go;
We should have left long since.
But Time, like snow, drifts everywhere,
Mantles the beating heart:
You see there's nothing here,
Nothing but the white fields;
And we can never leave.

Robin Fedden (Cairo 1944)

Index

Allen, Maud 54
Ashcroft, Peggy 152, 155
Ashton, Frederick 13, 16, 37, 38, 40, 45, 69, 71, 92, 142
Asquith, Anthony (Puffin) 51, 202, 254, 270, 275, 280, 282
Asquith, Cyril 208, 276
Asquith, Henry Herbert 208
Asquith, Margot 208, 209, 270
Astafieva, Serafina 13, 64
Astley, Edward 237, 238

Balanchine, George 18, 62, 75, 76, 77, 78, 79, 80, 81, 82, 83, 84, 89, 107, 111
Baker, Josephine 80
Barcynsky, Barry 172
Baronova, Irina 65, 76, 78, 101, 106, 156
de Basil, Colonel 65, 75, 76, 104, 106, 111, 141, 157
    company 77, 82, 89, 95, 102, 104, 156, 160, 173, 289
Bal 19
Bate, Philip 148

Bath Festival Orchestra 358
Bati, Mademoiselle 69
Beaumont, Binkie 218
Beaton, Cecil 138, 196, 208
Beethoven, Ludwig van 317, 322, 323
Benois, Alexander 40, 49, 99, 156
Berlin Philharmonic Orchestra 322
Bertaux, Pierre 312
Les Biches 19
Blum, Leon 275
Boulanger, Nadia 362
Brahms, Johannes 316
Britten, Benjamin 274, 334, 355
Busch, Adolf 158

Cardus, Neville 373
Carpenter, Freddie 251, 253
Carter, Howard 25
Casals, Pablo 278
Cavendish, Adele (Astaire) 171
Cazalet, Victor 214
Cecchetti, Enrico 15, 16, 19, 59, 61, 63, 64, 96, 147
Celibidache, Sergiu 322

Chamie, Tatiana 56
Chandos-Pole, Wakey 236, 238
Chappell, William 71
Chase, Lucia 289
Chevalier, Maurice 262
Churchill, Winston 203, 278, 284
Cochran, Charles B. 51, 52, 54, 57, 69, 79
Cooper, Lady Diana 51, 53, 143, 278
Cooper, Duff 143
Croom-Johnson, Henry 236, 238, 278
Cuff, Betty 75, 77

Danilova, Alexandra 18, 41, 62, 76, 105, 141
Daubeny, Peter 272
St Denis, Michel 152
Dennison, George 291
Dérain, André 81, 84
Devlin, William 152, 154, 243
Diaghilev, Sergei 13, 14, 15, 47, 49, 54, 55, 59, 64, 66, 75, 76, 105, 107, 111, 123, 128, 142
company 15, 17, 40, 41, 57, 65, 82, 131, 192
Dolin, Anton (Patrick Healey-Kay) 18, 59, 70, 107, 108, 109, 110, 112, 115, 117, 122, 123, 132, 133, 139, 156, 157, 159, 161, 165, 289
Doktor, Karl 158
Donat, Robert 161, 163, 199, 210
Doráti, Toni 289
Doráti, Klari 289
Doubrovska, Felia 18, 62, 76, 82, 84

Douglas, Lord Alfred 202, 203, 204, 269
Dowson, Ernest 232
Draper, Ruth 74
Dukes, Ashley 91
Dukes, Renée 47
Durrell, Lawrence 229, 230, 231, 232, 243, 246, 251, 264, 375, 377, 378

Egorova, Lyuba 57, 58, 60, 61, 62, 63, 65, 69, 95, 113, 147
Elliot, Madge 217, 225, 238, 239, 240, 243, 244, 247, 253, 256, 258, 260, 265, 267, 296
Epstein, Jacob 274
Evans, Clifford 209
Evans, Maurice 91
Evans, Nancy 221, 222

Fedden, Robin 379
Femmes de bonne Humeur 19
Fevrier, Jacques 301
Fistoulari, Anatole 193
Fokine, Mikhail Mikhailovitch 48, 76, 208
Fontaine, Joan 294
Fournet, John 299
Fou Ts'ong 370
Fox, William 152
Foxie 128, 129
Furtwängler, Elisabeth 300
Furtwängler, Wilhelm 135, 138, 143, 146, 190, 284, 287, 300, 316, 317, 322, 323, 324

Galitzine, Prince Vladimir 163

Galitzine, George 170, 171, 205, 206

Gandhi, Indira 355

Gazelle, Marcel 326

Gielgud, John 213

Godefroy, Jocelyn 118

Gore, Freddie 163

Gore, Walter 16

Gould, Constance (née Rawson Reed), 'Guggan', 25, 28, 33, 35, 58, 60, 61, 66, 67, 77, 95, 101, 104, 112, 116, 123, 188, 195, 252

Gould, Gerard (father) 5, 6, 123

Gould, Gerard (brother) 6, 7, 12, 20, 23, 24, 29, 30, 36, 62, 138, 139, 186

Gould, Gerard Louis Eugene (grandfather) 28

Gould, Griselda 6, 8, 11, 20, 22, 24, 25, 50, 57, 62, 68, 72, 88, 94, 120, 121, 125, 126, 135, 136, 138, 139, 145, 146, 157, 159, 160, 168, 177, 178, 186, 187, 190, 195, 196, 198, 200, 203–4, 209, 211, 213, 228, 229, 250, 254, 269, 272, 274, 275, 276, 277, 279, 281, 282, 283, 284, 285, 287, 288, 297, 299, 327, 330, 331

Granger, Stewart 161, 273

Grenfell, Joyce 237

Grunwald, Anatole de 208

Haggard, Stephen 152, 155

Hahn, Kurt 339

Hambourg, Mark 5

Hannen, Nicholas 152, 153, 207, 210

Harbord, Carl 51

Harcourt, Cecil (stepfather) 24, 26, 31, 32, 136, 142, 155, 177, 201, 204, 214, 219, 221, 255, 266, 275, 281, 328

Harcourt, Evelyn *see* Suart

Harriman, Averill 279

Haskell, Arnold 95

de Havilland, Olivia 14, 294

Heckroth, Hein 197

Helpmann, Robert 47

Henderson, Laura 160

Henley, David 202

Hess, Myra 166

Hitchins, Aubrey 44

Howard, Andrée 16, 89

Holst, Gustav 72

Hulton, Edward 180

Hurok, Sol 289

Hyman, Prudence 75, 77, 81, 85, 108, 115, 152, 153, 166, 176, 178, 181, 182, 184, 185, 189

Ingerson, Frank 291

James, Edward 77, 78, 79, 82, 85, 86, 142

Jasinski, Roman 78, 81

Jonnaiux, Alfred 68

Karinska 80

Karsavina, Tamara (Madame Ta-Ta) 16, 17, 48, 73, 74, 75, 91, 99, 270

Kempson, Rachel 254, 288

Kentner, Louis 135, 148, 155, 199,

276, 277, 280, 281, 286, 287, 331

Kerr, Deborah 210, 214
Kirsta, George 192
Kirstein, Lincoln 85
Kochno, Boris 81
Korda, Alexander 92, 93, 141
Kschessinskaya, Mathilda 58, 65, 95, 96, 97, 99, 103, 104, 107, 113, 116, 143, 147, 260, 261, 278
Kubelik, Ludmila 301
Kubelik, Rafael 301, 305

Laing, Hugh 91
Laughton, Charles 91
Lawford, Nicholas (Valentine) 146
Lehman, Beatrix 254
Leider, Frida 119
Leschetizky, Theodor 5
Lester, Keith 166, 167
Lichine, David 196
Lifar, Serge 41, 42, 76, 82, 101, 107, 141, 143
Lillie, Beatrice 117, 122, 139
Lion, Leon M. 94
Lloyd, Maude 166
Lopokova, Lydia 70, 169
Losch, Tilly 51, 54, 77, 78, 79, 81, 142
Lympany, Moura 190
Lynch, Charles 47
Lysystrata 71
Lysy, Alberto 370

McBean, Angus 138
Maclean, Donald 146
Mariano, Nicky 342

Markevitch, Igor 65
Markova, Alicia (Alice Marks) 13, 47, 59, 70, 92, 106, 110, 116, 132, 141, 156, 289
Markova-Dolin Company 110, 111, 122, 123, 126, 127, 141, 153, 157, 160, 166, 171, 192
Marvell, Josiah 328 9
Masaryk, Jan 305
Massine, Léonide 18, 52, 53, 54, 55, 57, 59, 60, 63, 64, 76, 77, 82, 89, 105, 106, 107, 111
Menuhin, Aba 292, 363
Menuhin, Ann 373
Menuhin, Aaron 373
Menuhin, Diana (née Gould)
At Rambert school 19–22, 29, 37–43
Ballet Club 46, 47, 69
Chosen by Diaghilev 40, 43
Classes with Egorova 58–66
Early meetings with Yehudi 139, 140, 254
in Egypt 223–233
Family 4–6
First performance in public 12
Subsequent performances:
in *L'apres-midi d'une faune* 49, 50
in *Beau Brummel* 90, 92
in *Les Biches* 128, 131, 132
in *La Bien-Aimée* 132
in *Carnaval* 110, 115, 133
in *Casse-Noisette* 108, 109, 112
in *Errante* 80, 83
in *Fastes* 80, 82
in *Faustus* 91–2
in *Fiddlers Three* 219

in *The Good-Humoured Ladies*
104, 105
in *Headlines*, 95
in *Jacobowsky and the Colonel*
270, 274
in *Lientenant Kijé* 201
in *The Merry Widow* 220, 230,
239, 251, 253
in *The Miracle* 51, 53, 89, 95
in *Mozartiana* 80, 83
in *Night on the Bare Mountain*
193–4
in *Russki Plasski* 150
in *Schéhérazade* 104, 105, 106
in *Les sept péches capitaux* 80
in *Songes* 80, 82, 84
in *Squaring the Circle* 91–2
in *Les Sylphides* 70, 109, 112
in *The Waltzes of Beethoven* 80,
83
in *What Every Woman Knows*
205, 207, 212
In Italy 234–250
Marriage 327–31
Presented at Court 118
Menuhin, Eva 373
Menuhin, Festival 34
Menuhin, Gerard 334, 338, 341,
342, 353, 362, 373
Menuhin, Hephzibah 139, 140,
293, 294, 295–7, 298, 303,
305, 306, 308, 345, 358, 359,
361, 372
Menuhin, Jeremy 334, 338, 341,
342, 353, 362, 371, 373
Menuhin, Krov 306, 308, 310, 315,
319, 370, 373
Menuhin, Yalta 293

Menuhin, Yehudi (Lord Menuhin)
1, 2, 7, 12, 29, 68, 94, 133,
134, 139, 140, 148, 190, 213,
254, 255, 270, 271, 274, 275,
276, 277, 278, 281, 282, 283,
285, 286, 289, 290, 292, 293,
294–7, 300, 301, 302, 303,
304, 305, 306, 307, 308, 309,
310, 311, 312, 314–5, 317,
318–9, 321, 322, 323, 324–6,
327, 328, 329, 330, 331, 334,
335, 336, 337, 339, 340, 341,
342, 345–351, 353, 354–5,
356, 358, 359, 360, 361, 362,
363, 364, 365, 367, 368, 371,
372, 374
Menuhin, Zamira 306, 308, 310,
315, 317, 319, 339, 353, 363,
370, 373
Messel, Oliver 53, 95, 191
de Mille, Agnes 64, 74, 94, 141, 143
Moltke, Adam, 327–8
Monsaingeon, Bruno 372
Moore, Grace 146
Morrison, Angus 47
Mullen, Barbara 207
Murphy, Robert 322
Mussolini, Benito 215

Nabokov, Nika 81
Nehru, Pandit 355
Nemtchinova, Vera 18, 19, 143
Nicolson, Harold 170
Nicholas, Nola 139, 286–7, 294,
298
Nicholas, Lindsay 293, 295, 297,
304
Nijinska, Bronislava 18, 107, 123,

126, 127, 128, 129, 130, 132, 133, 134, 156, 157, 160, 161
Nijinska, Kyra 65
Nikisch, Artur 5
Nikitina, Alice 76, 82
Nin, Joaquin 99, 100
Novello, Ivor 213

Oberon, Merle 93
Oistrakh, David 301, 302, 304, 305
Oistrakh, Tamara 304
Olivier, Laurence 213

Paderewski, Ignacy 5
Paganini, Niccolò 273
Parkinson, Norman 138
Pavane pour une Infante defunte 69
Pavlova, Anna 16, 44, 45, 55, 142
Pears, Peter 334, 355
Peel, Bobby 117, 122
Petipa, Marius 208
Playfair, Sir Nigel 48, 89, 90
Pomeroy, Jay 19, 202, 204, 209, 210, 214, 215
van Praagh, Peggy 72, 166
Preobrajenska, Olga 58, 78
Prokoviev, Sergey 201
Proudfoot, James 148

Rambert, Marie 16, 20, 21, 22, 29, 30, 37, 38, 41, 43, 49, 50, 60, 75, 89, 90, 92, 96, 111, 140, 142, 179
    Company 39, 45, 95, 166
Rattigan, Terence 208
Reboux, Caroline 156
Redgrave, Corin 255
Redgrave, Michael 210, 213, 254, 255, 256, 257, 264, 269, 272, 288
Redgrave, Vanessa 255
Reinhardt, Max 51, 53, 54, 55
Riabouchinska, Tania 65, 76, 102
Ricarda, Ana 289
Richter, Hans 5
Rispoli, Giulio 247
Ritchard, Cyril 217, 225, 229, 238, 239, 240, 242, 243, 244, 245, 246, 247, 248, 251, 253, 256, 258, 260, 263, 265, 267, 282, 296
Romanov, Grand Duke André 96, 97, 98, 107, 116, 260, 261, 278
Rothschild, Addie 101
Rothschild, Miriam 143, 261
de Rothschild, Robert 68
Rubin, Harold 166, 227

Sauguet, Henri 81
Schnabel, Artur 5, 72, 148
Schooling, Betty 75, 77
Schwester Marie 353
Shankar, Ravi 356, 358
Shostakovich, Dimitri 304
Schwarz, Solange 62
Sebastianoff, Gerry 156
Selznik, Myron 141
Sergeyev, Konstantin Mikhailovitch 108
Seyler, Athene 152
Sikorski, General 214
Sidorenko, Tamara 79, 81, 85
Simpson, Ann 289
Slavinsky, 82

Slobodskaya, Oda 193
Smith, Perry 358
Sokolova, Lydia (Hilda Munnings)
    18, 45, 59, 131, 132, 147, 148
Sorel, Cecil 36
Spessivtseva, Olga 18
Stanislavsky, 17
Stewart, John 207
Strakhova, Kira (Patik Thal) 173
Strnad, Oskar 55
Suart, Evelyn (later Gould) 3, 6, 7,
    8, 25, 26, 32, 34, 88, 94, 121,
    125, 126, 136, 138, 139, 157,
    177, 178, 190, 198, 254, 255,
    288, 296, 299, 305, 330
Suart, Katherine (née Lester),
    'Goggo' 22, 27, 50, 57, 58,
    112, 120, 123, 125, 195
Suart, William Henry Hodson 4,
    22, 26
Susskind, Walter 193
Sylvain 36

Tanqueray, Paul 138
Tchaikovsky, Peter Ilyich 111
Tchelitchev, Pavel 79, 81
Tchernicheva, Lubov 18, 41, 105
Toscanini, Arturo 140, 148, 158,
    190
Toumanova, Tamara 65, 76, 78,
    106, 141

Toye, Wendy 52, 108, 152, 197
Tudor, Anthony 16, 71, 91, 142,
    166, 179
Turner, Harold 40, 43, 64, 166, 167

Ustinov, Peter 163

de Valois, Dame Ninette 70, 71, 72,
    92, 142
Vanbrugh, Irene 207
de Villiers, Catherine 192, 193, 194,
    195, 197, 200, 201
Vansittart, Sir Robert 135, 159
Volkova, Vera 201

Walton, William 304
Walter, Bruno 148, 190
Walter, John 14
Weingartner, Felix 148
Weldon, George 193
Wheeler, Charles 167
Wheeler, Monroe 356
Wilde, Oscar 203
Williams, Gwyn 232, 243
Wimborne, Alice 304
Woizikovsky, Leon 18, 49, 62, 82,
    106
Wolf, Hugo 167

Ysaÿe, Eugene 4